Graduate Writing Across the Disciplines
Identifying, Teaching, and Supporting

Across the Disciplines Books

Series Editor: Michael A. Pemberton
Series Associate Editors: Michelle LaFrance and Christopher Basgier

The Across the Disciplines Books series is closely tied to published themed issues of the online, open-access, peer-reviewed journal *Across the Disciplines*. In keeping with the editorial mission of *Across the Disciplines*, books in the series are devoted to language, learning, academic writing, and writing pedagogy in all their intellectual, political, social, and technological complexity.

The WAC Clearinghouse, Colorado State University Open Press, and University Press of Colorado are collaborating so that these books will be widely available through free digital distribution and low-cost print editions. The publishers and the series editors are committed to the principle that knowledge should freely circulate. We see the opportunities that new technologies have for further democratizing knowledge. And we see that to share the power of writing is to share the means for all to articulate their needs, interest, and learning into the great experiment of literacy.

Other Books in This Series

Steven J. Corbett, Jennifer Lin LeMesurier, Teagan E. Decker, and Betsy Cooper (Eds.). *Writing In and About the Performing and Visual Arts: Creating, Performing, and Teaching* (2019).

Alice S. Horning, Deborah-Lee Gollnitz, and Cynthia R. Haller (Eds.). *What is College Reading?* (2017)

Frankie Condon and Vershawn Ashanti Young (Eds.), *Performing Antiracist Pedagogy in Rhetoric, Writing, and Communication* (2017)

Graduate Writing Across the Disciplines
Identifying, Teaching, and Supporting

Edited by Marilee Brooks-Gillies, Elena G. Garcia,
Soo Hyon Kim, Katie Manthey, and Trixie G. Smith

The WAC Clearinghouse
wac.colostate.edu
Fort Collins, Colorado

University Press of Colorado
upcolorado.com
Louisville, Colorado

The WAC Clearinghouse, Fort Collins, Colorado 80523

University Press of Colorado, Louisville, Colorado 80027

© 2020 by Marilee Brooks-Gillies, Elena G. Garcia, Soo Hyon Kim, Katie Manthey, and Trixie G. Smith. This work is licensed under a Creative Commons Attribution-NonCommercial-NoDerivatives 4.0 International License.

ISBN: 978-1-64215-040-7 (PDF) | 978-1-64215-041-4 (ePub) | 978-1-64642-022-3 (pbk.)

DOI: 10.37514/ATD-B.2020.0407

Library of Congress Cataloging-in-Publication Data

Names: Brooks-Gillies, Marilee, editor. | Garcia, Elena (Elena Adkins), editor. | Kim, Soo Hyon, 1982– editor. | Manthey, Katie, editor. | Smith, Trixie G., editor.

Title: Graduate writing across the disciplines : identifying, teaching, and supporting / edited by Marilee Brooks-Gillies, Elena G. Garcia, Soo Hyon Kim, Katie Manthey, and Trixie G. Smith.

Description: Fort Collins, Colorado : The WAC Clearinghouse ; Louisville, Colorado : University Press of Colorado, [2020] | Series: Across the disciplines books | Includes bibliographical references.

Identifiers: LCCN 2020016441 (print) | LCCN 2020016442 (ebook) | ISBN 9781646420223 (paperback) | ISBN 9781642150407 (pdf) | ISBN 9781642150414 (epub)

Subjects: LCSH: Academic writing—Study and teaching (Graduate) | English language—Rhetoric—Study and teaching (Graduate) | Communication in learning and scholarship.

Classification: LCC LB2369 .G885 2020 (print) | LCC LB2369 (ebook) | DDC 808.06/6378—dc23

LC record available at https://lccn.loc.gov/2020016441

LC ebook record available at https://lccn.loc.gov/2020016442

Copyeditor: Meg Vezzu
Book Design: Mike Palmquist
Cover Art and Design: Malcolm Childers
Series Design: Tara Reeser
Series Editor: Michael A. Pemberton
Series Associate Editors: Michelle LaFrance and Christopher Basgier

The WAC Clearinghouse supports teachers of writing across the disciplines. Hosted by Colorado State University, and supported by the Colorado State University Open Press, it brings together scholarly journals and book series as well as resources for teachers who use writing in their courses. This book is available in digital formats for free download at wac.colostate.edu.

Founded in 1965, the University Press of Colorado is a nonprofit cooperative publishing enterprise supported, in part, by Adams State University, Colorado State University, Fort Lewis College, Metropolitan State University of Denver, University of Colorado, University of Northern Colorado, University of Wyoming, Utah State University, and Western Colorado University. For more information, visit upcolorado.com.

Contents

3	Introduction: Graduate Writing Across the Disciplines *Marilee Brooks-Gillies, Elena G. Garcia, and Soo Hyon Kim*
21	PART 1: "Read and write like a grad student" OR 'Inside' the Institution: Graduate Writing Courses and Programs *Elena G. Garcia*
23	Snapshots, Surveys, and Infrastructures: An Institutional Case Study of Graduate Writing Courses *Laurie A. Pinkert*
49	Voicing Graduate Student Writing Experiences: A Study of Cross-Level Courses at Two Master's-Level, Regional Institutions *Brian R. Henderson and Paul G. Cook*
71	Developing an English for Academic Purposes Course for L2 Graduate Students in the Sciences *Jennifer Douglas*
93	PART 2: "If you really want to know something, teach it" OR Learning to Write by Teaching Writing: Professionalization through Instruction *Katie Manthey*
95	Graduate Student Perspectives: Career Development Through Serving as Writing-Intensive GTAs *Amy A. Lannin and Martha A. Townsend*
121	Towards an Integrated Graduate Student (Training Program) *Elliot Shapiro*
143	The Space Between: MA Students Enculturate to Graduate Reading and Writing *Terri Fredrick, Kaylin Stravalli, Scott May, and Jami Brookman-Smith*

167   Creating a Culture of Communication: A Graduate-Level STEM Communication Fellows Program at a Science and Engineering University
Steve Simpson, Rebecca Clemens, Drea Rae Killingsworth, Jesse Priest, and Julie Dyke Ford

189   PART 3: "Help each other. Find a writing group!" OR Collaborations and Programs 'Alongside' Curriculum
Marilee Brooks-Gillies

191   Making Do by Making Space: Multidisciplinary Graduate Writing Groups as Spaces Alongside Programmatic and Institutional Places
Marilee Brooks-Gillies, Elena G. Garcia, and Katie Manthey

211   Graduate Writing Groups: Helping L2 Writers Navigate the Murky Waters of Academic Writing
Soo Hyon Kim and Shari Wolke

243   Camping in the Disciplines: Assessing the Effect of Writing Camps on Graduate Student Writers
Gretchen Busl, Kara Lee Donnelly, and Matthew Capdevielle

269   Crossing Divides: Engaging Extracurricular Writing Practices in Graduate Education and Professionalization
Laural L. Adams, Megan Adams, Pauline Baird, Estee Beck, Kristine L. Blair, April Conway, Lee Nickoson, and Martha Schaffer

291   PART 4: "Stop reading. Start writing. The best dissertation is a done dissertation." OR Examining Discourse Communities and Genres
Soo Hyon Kim

295   Discourse Community Fail! Negotiating Choices in Success/Failure and Graduate-Level Writing Development
Michelle LaFrance and Steven J. Corbett

315   Disciplinary Corpus Research for Situated Literacy Instruction
Sarah Blazer and Sarah E. DeCapua

337   Genres and Conflicts in MBA Writing Assignments
Nigel A. Caplan

359   Contributors

Graduate Writing Across the Disciplines
Identifying, Teaching, and Supporting

Introduction: Graduate Writing Across the Disciplines

Marilee Brooks-Gillies
INDIANA UNIVERSITY–PURDUE UNIVERSITY INDIANAPOLIS

Elena G. Garcia
UTAH VALLEY UNIVERSITY

Soo Hyon Kim
UNIVERSITY OF NEW HAMPSHIRE

Our Story

This project has been part of our lives for a long time. It began in 2011 when all the editors were working at the Michigan State University (MSU) Writing Center, Trixie Smith as the director and the rest of us as graduate students. Every day we found ourselves grappling with issues and ideas connected to graduate writers through our work at the writing center: working one-to-one with graduate writers, facilitating graduate writing groups, and offering workshops for graduate students, such as our Navigating the Ph.D. workshop series. The work was also personally relevant to most of us since we were graduate students at the time, frequently finding ourselves experiencing imposter syndrome and letting our identities as graduate students consume our lives. Little did we—excepting Trixie, perhaps—know then that our interest in graduate writing would intensify when we became junior faculty and found that we still faced many of the same writing-related concerns that we did as graduate students.

Our motivations for developing this edited collection on graduate writing across the disciplines began when we turned from interacting with graduate writers to researching graduate writers and graduate writing. When the Writing, Rhetoric, and American Cultures department at MSU began an initiative to create research clusters that bring faculty, staff, and students together to engage in conducting academic research and developing publications, we decided that a research cluster focusing on graduate writing would be ideal. We participated in this Graduate Writing Research Cluster for the two years that we were all still at MSU and continued to collaborate when we began moving into faculty positions outside of MSU. Our collaboration culminated in a special issue of *Across the Disciplines* and

DOI: https://doi.org/10.37514/ATD-B.2020.0407.1.3

this edited collection. What started as a local interest in how graduate writers were supported in various settings across MSU became a larger interest in ways graduate writing is supported across the country.

In *Writing in the Academic Disciplines*, David Russell (2002) discusses how writing instruction has historically been pushed to the margins, especially for graduate students who are often expected to be expert academic writers of a variety of specialized genres—such as academic articles, conference proposals and papers, and grant applications. In many cases, expertise in these academic and professional genres is gradually acquired through implicit and embedded models of teaching and learning. As Simpson (2016) has pointed out, "graduate education has long relied on one-on-one mentoring between an advisor and a student as the primary mechanism of instruction in graduate school" (p. 5). While this type of mentoring has its benefits, both a more diverse and systematic approach to graduate writing education is needed to provide opportunities for graduate students to learn outside the typical advisor-advisee apprenticeship. Yet, disciplinary communities "have rarely integrated systematic writing instruction into their curricula to initiate the neophytes consciously into the written conventions of a particular field" (Russell, 2002, p. 17), which has prompted graduate students to seek out additional university resources, activities, or other third spaces (Grego & Thompson, 2008; Soja, 1996) offered outside their departments such as writing center consultations, writing groups, and writing workshops, and often leads them to develop their own "underground" support systems.

Since we began this project several years ago, we see the wealth of recent scholarship focused on graduate writing (see for instance, Aitchison & Guerin, 2014; Badenhorst & Guerin, 2016; Eriksson & Makitalo, 2015; Lawrence & Zawacki, 2016; Madden & Eodice, 2016; McAlpine & Amundsen, 2011; Olinger, 2014; Simpson, Caplan, Cox & Phillips, 2016), as well as the founding of the Consortium on Graduate Communication, as both encouraging and indicative of the need for ongoing conversations in this area. In our special issue of *Across the Disciplines*, we worked to bring together articles focused on discussions, strategies, programs, and courses that all address different ways of meeting the diverse writing needs of graduate students. This collection, *Graduate Writing Across the Disciplines: Identifying, Teaching, and Supporting*, also attends to that premise (and includes brief extensions/reprints of four of the articles from the special issue) and emphasizes that addressing diverse writing needs requires multiple forms of writing support.

Graduate Writers Need Multiple Forms of Support

Our experiences as graduate writers and as writing consultants who worked with graduate writers emphasized the reality that, "Writers embody not only desires for the production of certain kinds of texts, but also carry with them the weight of expectations of other structural and human networks" (Aitchison & Guerin, 2014, p. 11). That is, writing is an inherently social process and one that is embedded in the working lives of graduate students. We have seen first-hand again and again how the practice of writing gets reduced to sentence-level considerations. A simplistic notion of writing reinforces beliefs that the nature of writing is arhetorical, which has produced a decidedly consequential paradox for doctoral student writers.

> On the one hand, the demands placed on doctoral students [are], of course, deeply rhetorical: students [are] expected to perform in the highly contextualized and historically evolved discursive practices of their research cultures. On the other hand, given the non-research-based assumptions about writing as a universal skill, these discursive practices [remain] shrouded in silence and therefore difficult to access for doctoral scholars. (Starke-Meyerring, 2014, p. 68)

At the graduate level, writing is the dominant way in which knowledge is presented and assessed. For graduate students, this happens through coursework, comprehensive exams, theses and dissertations, conference presentations, and—increasingly—publications. Graduate students write frequently, though the actual requirements vary across departments and disciplines. However, as Margaret Salee, Ronald Hallett, and William Tierney (2011) state, "the expectation is that students already know how to write before they begin grad school. Instructors of graduate students may assume that students learned basic writing skills during their high school and undergraduate years" (p. 66). Given this assumption, it is no surprise that many graduate faculty express "exasperation about the quality of student writing" (Rose & McClafferty, 2001, p. 28). Yet, as Mike Rose and Karen McClafferty (2001) also state, "We seem to do little to address the quality of writing in a systematic way at the very point where scholarly style and identity is being shaped" (p. 27), that is, at the graduate level. There is a disconnect between what graduate students are expected to know and the ways they approach and practice writing as they begin their graduate work. In this collection, we emphasize that "writing and knowledge-making are intertwined" (Aitchison & Guerin, 2014, p. 9) and, therefore, both are important to explicitly teach at the graduate level.

Another important consideration that influences the fast-changing landscape of graduate writing education is the increasing diversity of graduate students, including an increase in underrepresented minority and international student enrollments (Kent, 2016). Findings from the 2015 International Graduate Admissions Survey by the Council of Graduate Studies (Okahana & Allum, 2015) indicated that international students had a strong presence (24%) in master's and doctoral programs in the U.S. According to this report, the rate of growth in first-time enrollment for international students (5%) also outpaced that of domestic students (2%). Among domestic students, graduate enrollment of Hispanic/Latino students showed strong and steady growth (6.8%), and to a lesser extent, other underrepresented minority students (Allum & Okahana, 2015) also increased.

Attention to access and equity in graduate education, then, is more important than ever, and we recommend the recent special issue of *Praxis* on this topic edited by Shannon Madden and Michele Eodice (2016). Madden writes, "When graduate programs fail to offer writing instruction of any kind or when they offer graduate-level writing classes for international students only, they position writing as equivalent to language learning, as a remedial skill that is separate from—rather than constitutive of—disciplinary content knowledge" (para. 3).

Typically, advisors have been responsible for working with graduate student writers, but this can be insufficient for several reasons: "Not all graduate students have the language and other interpersonal skills to activate advice from their supervisors. In addition, not all supervisors have the knowledge and skills to identify exactly what it is that needs to be done in order to improve the comprehensibility of a given piece of writing" (Allison, Cooley, Lewkowicz & Nunan, 1998, p. 199–200). We would add that advisors often do not have enough dedicated time to work with individual writers consistently over several months or years, meaning writers need both direct curricular instruction as well as various forms of writing support and mentoring.

Unfortunately, the "absence of direct writing instruction for graduate students reinforces misperceptions that writing competency amounts to a set of static skills learned once and for all" (Micciche & Carr, 2011, p. 494). These kinds of "misperceptions" are then transferred to students who seek to learn these static skills, believing that writing is a transparent "vehicle or a conduit for delivering one's findings" (Rose & McClafferty, 2001, p. 29) and nothing more. Additionally, assumptions that writing is a static skill dismiss the nuances of academic writing as they vary by discipline and sub-discipline. We've all seen these beliefs in action while working with graduate students at the MSU Writing Center. Students are often surprised at some of the questions they are asked that basically boil down to: "Why did you make this choice?" Their responses are frequently: "Because that's the way we do it in *x* discipline." The invisibility of genre, voice, style, data presentation, active versus passive writing, structure, and epistemology in writing instruction often allow students to refrain from critically examining their presentation of information and recognizing that the way something is written is just as important as the content being written about (and that the two are inescapably intertwined).

Graduate students need "structured writing support in order to succeed" (Phillips, 2012, para. 1) rather than being expected to "learn how to write critically through repeated exposure and an osmosis-like process" (Micciche & Carr, 2011, p. 485). However, the needs of graduate student writers extend beyond the scope of being explicitly taught to write. Graduate education is fraught with identity struggles and self-doubt, much of which centers around the ability to write effectively to meet the expectations of faculty mentors and the field at large. Thus, professionalization and support in graduate writing education needs to include emotional support. As Micciche and Carr (2011) write: "the pain so many of us experience [while graduate students] need not be private, shameful, or an indicator of unfitness for graduate school," and they go on to argue that "a curricular space devoted to critical writing represents one effective counter-narrative to such ideas while also serving intellectual and professional goals" (p. 479; see also Thesen, 2014). Whether that curricular space is part of coursework or mentoring outside of classes, faculty need to help graduate students understand the demands facing them, and they need to demonstrate how such demands can be met successfully.

One of the primary goals of graduate education is to provide graduate students training for careers in academic disciplines. Despite this purpose, some graduate students are not mentored into the professional writing norms of their disciplines nor do they engage in the process of writing for professional scholarship until they face their thesis or dissertation writing task (Cafferella & Barnett, 2000). The need for attending to professionalization within graduate programs has intensified as the expectations of professionalization change. There is a greater range in expectations and increased demands on scholarly productivity. Claire Aitchison and Cally Guerin (2014) argue this point:

> For both doctoral students and academics, a strong publication record is indispensable for securing certification, establishing an academic career, promotion, grants, awards and privileges. Despite rhetoric to the contrary, higher education institutions continue to reward academics who publish over those whose contribution may be in teaching, administration, or service to the community. So, at all stages, the ability to write well and develop and maintain a strong publication output is a fundamental literacy for academic success. (p. 3)

Having a scholarly identity before entering the job market feels essential and may be a great source of stress and anxiety. Anyone involved with the academic job market knows that the expectations placed on newly graduated masters and Ph.D. students are intense, particularly for those seeking tenure-track positions. With the numbers of graduating students far surpassing the number of jobs available each year (more so in some disciplines than in others), students clamor to produce publications while completing coursework, exams, and theses/dissertations.

The need for strong writing skills becomes even more important once graduate students complete their degrees and move into faculty positions since expectations for promotion and tenure often hinge on the number and quality of publications. In fact, despite the evident importance of writing and publishing to faculty life, "much research shows that it continues to be marginalized and squeezed out of the everyday practices of researchers and academics" (Aitchison & Guerin, 2014, p. 4).

Supporting graduate writers early—before they move on to faculty positions—can have a significantly positive impact on their ability to persist in their graduate programs and become productive faculty members. As Deborah Page-Adams, Li-Chen Cheng, Aruna Gogineni, and Ching-Ying Shen (1995) found in their study, "New faculty members who learned to balance writing, teaching, and collegiality early in their academic careers had relatively high levels of publication productivity" (p. 406).

In addition to faculty who help graduate students navigate their way through the struggles of academic text production, peer support is also important. Damien Maher, Leonie Seaton, Cathi McMullen, Terry Fitzgerald, Emi Otsuji, and Alison Lee (2008) discuss their experiences working within writing groups: "when the writing became difficult and an end was difficult to imagine, sharing our frustrations and concerns gave us momentum that we perhaps would not have had if we were working in isolation" (p. 273). Encouraging graduate students to discard the image of the struggling lone scholar and to take up practices that provide support and commiseration regarding the emotional struggles of graduate work are just as important as direct writing instruction.

Graduate Writing Across the Disciplines: Identifying, Teaching, and Supporting

Although we knew there was room for more conversations on graduate writing, we were surprised to receive 62 initial proposals for the special issue of *Across the Disciplines*. The enthusiasm of potential contributors seemed to reflect the newly invigorated interest we saw across disciplines in supporting graduate writing, and it also renewed our own commitments to promoting scholarship about graduate writing. This brought about the possibility of not just a special issue but an extended conversation through this collection as well. In this collection, we foregrounded graduate student work, whether pieces were authored by individuals while they were graduate students or dedicated to highlighting graduate voices and stories.

There are many scholars actively researching graduate writing education. In particular, a wealth of literature exists in the field of second language writing spanning various aspects of graduate writing and support. In addition to shedding light on the complexities of navigating scholarly publication (e.g., Aitchison, 2009; Aitchison, Kamler & Lee, 2010; Curry & Lillis, 2004; Flowerdew, 1999; Flowerdew & Li, 2009; Lillis & Curry, 2010), this body of research has contributed to better understanding how graduate students learn to write in their disciplinary genres (e.g., Castello & Donahue, 2012; Cuthbert, Spark & Burke,

2009; Dressen-Hammouda, 2008; Simpson, 2013a; Simpson, 2013b; Tardy 2005, 2009). For instance, through her longitudinal study of multilingual graduate students in the STEM fields, Christine Tardy (2009) theorized how graduate students gradually learn how to write in their discipline's specific genres, and how the literacy practices they engage in across various contexts affect this development. Her framework for building genre knowledge—for both monolingual and multilingual writers—has been valuable in understanding how writers acquire expertise in genre knowledge and how we can facilitate this process.

The mentoring and apprenticeship of graduate advisees has also been a fruitful area of research in second language writing with implications for graduate writing education across the disciplines (e.g., Belcher, 1994; Casanave & Li, 2008; McIntosh, Pelaez-Morales & Silva, 2016). Many of the chapters on mentors and mentees in Christine Casanave and Xiaoming Li's edited collection (2008), *Learning the Literacy Practices of Graduate School*, share the stories, conversations, and interactions between graduate writers and their academic mentors, and the process through which graduate students become familiar with the ways of thinking and writing within their disciplines.

In addition to scholarship on the mentoring of multilingual graduate student writers, there is much insight we can gain from previous research on the development and implementation of English for Academic Purposes (EAP) courses as well as other initiatives designed for graduate writing support such as dissertation boot camps, writing groups, workshops, and writing center programs (e.g., Fredericksen & Mangelsdorf, 2014; Lawrence & Zawacki, 2016; Phillips, 2013, 2016; Simpson, 2012; Starfield, 2003). These programs, coupled with pedagogical texts designed for multilingual graduate students and/or their academic advisors (e.g., Paltridge & Starfield, 2007; Swales & Feak, 2012), have been instrumental in helping disciplinary newcomers become familiar with the expectations of academic and professional writing. They also point to future directions and possibilities for graduate writing support across the disciplines.

It seems, then, that the central complication is not so much the lack of scholarly work on graduate writing education and support, but that much of this work is carried out in disparate disciplines that do not always speak directly to each other, including but not limited to Rhetoric and Writing, Writing Centers, TESOL, Education, Communication, Speech Pathology, Linguistics, Second Language Acquisition, Writing Across the Curriculum, Writing in the Disciplines, Technical Communication, Professional Writing, and Curriculum and Instruction. We've attempted to work across these disciplines by organizing the collection into four sections that emphasize sites where graduate writers receive writing support: in the classroom through their coursework; in the classroom as teachers and writing fellows; from programs and facilities that exist alongside the curriculum; and from the various discourse communities they engage in and the genres produced in those communities. We've given each section a title that echoes advice we were given as graduate students; the advice might sound familiar to you. There is overlap across these sites, but we hope the organization shows a need for support in direct and structured ways that are both disciplinary and institutional and for support that is informal and peer-focused that might be less structured.

PART 1: "Read and write like a grad student" OR 'Inside' the Institution: Graduate Writing Courses and Programs

In our first section, we focus on the ways graduate curricula are structured to push graduate students toward a disciplinary identity. Reading and then creating academic writing like a graduate student involves learning the practices they will be expected to enact as professionals in their discipline. However, being told to "read like a graduate student" then "write like a graduate student" is usually unclear advice while that initial disciplining is occurring. It is also difficult for faculty to explain— what exactly does reading like a graduate student look like? What does this practice entail? While it is clear when it is, and is not, being done, explaining the process itself is complex. After all, most of us learn how to engage in these activities through trial and error, through years of experience receiving feedback about what is and is not working, so breaking down these practices requires careful examination and self-reflection. The four chapters in this section speak directly to the disciplining process, explaining some ways that existing programs have approached this task.

We begin broadly with Laurie Pinkert's "Snapshots, Surveys, and Infrastructures: An Institutional Case Study of Graduate Writing Courses." Although scholars have often studied the development of undergraduate writing courses, evidence of curricular support for writing at the graduate level is not as well-documented. Addressing this need, Pinkert adapts questions from Golding and Mascaro's (1987) survey of writing courses; however, unlike Golding and Mascaro's study, her project includes graduate students as participants alongside their faculty and administrative counterparts, offering a more contextualized understanding of how courses are perceived by various stakeholders as an infrastructure for engaging writing.

We then move to a focus on specific courses and graduate student populations. Brian R. Henderson and Paul G. Cook look to specific classroom environments in "Voicing Graduate Student Writing Experiences: A Study of Cross-Level Courses at Two Master's-Level, Regional Institutions." They note that while much scholarly attention has been given to undergraduate writing pedagogy, relatively few research studies have explored the writing experiences—pedagogical, curricular, institutional, and otherwise—of graduate students, particularly graduate students pursuing master's degrees at regional, branch, or satellite campuses. This qualitative study makes a step toward filling the gap by addressing so-called "hybrid" courses (i.e., courses with both undergraduate and graduate enrollments), which are fast becoming a fixture at many regional colleges and universities.

An emphasis on support for the growing L2 populations in American graduate programs is featured by Jennifer Douglas in "Developing an English for Academic Purposes Course for L2 Graduate Students in the Sciences." She describes strategies for teaching an interdisciplinary, graduate-level scientific writing course for non-native English speakers. Teaching strategies emphasize the students' transitioning from the role of consumer to the role of producer of knowledge. English for Academic Purposes (EAP) courses like the one outlined by Douglas are important to graduate education both for and beyond the population of non-native speakers of English because they can address needs that are difficult to meet through campus-wide programming, such as writing centers staffed primarily by undergraduate writing tutors less familiar with writing at the graduate level.

PART 2: "If you really want to know something, teach it" OR Learning to Write by Teaching Writing: Professionalization through Instruction

Graduate students exist in liminal spaces: between being students and faculty. As graduate instructors, there is an added layer of complexity to their professional identities. In our second section, we look to ways that graduate student experiences as teachers provide a clearer and deeper understanding of writing pedagogy that can provide them with important teaching tools and influence their writing in positive ways. Teaching writing comes with the assumption that the person teaching is an expert; in this section, we look at the ways that graduate students are both writing experts and learners. In "Graduate Student Perspectives: Career Development Through Serving as Writing-Intensive GTAs," Amy Lannin and Martha A. Townsend examine the ways Graduate Teaching Assistants in writing-intensive (WI) courses that sponsor writing across the curriculum (WAC) and writing in the disciplines (WID) programs acquire experience with discipline-based writing. This chapter reports on one such well-established program in which over 100 GTAs each semester serve in a variety of capacities for WI courses in their own disciplines.

The next chapter presents an important, additional consideration to the way teaching writing and being trained to teach writing can impact graduate students as writers. In "Towards an Integrated Graduate Student (Training Program)," a reprint from *Across the Disciplines*, Elliot Shapiro describes how being teachers of writing can help graduate students become better writers. He focuses on the two training courses for graduate writing TAs that are offered through Cornell's Knight Institute for Writing in the Disciplines: a course that prepares graduate students to teach first year writing courses and a course that prepares graduate students to teach writing within specific majors. These classes also include particular features of the training curricula that help graduate students learn to write as academic professionals through their practice of teaching discipline-based writing. Shapiro discusses "the idea that teaching can be research into how students learn—in this case, how graduate students learn." Graduate students in this teaching program create a community of shared knowledge which helps them develop discipline-appropriate reflective writing practices as they learn how to be disciplinary teachers.

Terri Fredrick, Kaylin Stravalli, Scott May, and Jami Brookman-Smith provide personal narratives of the enculturation experience of students transitioning into graduate school and moving from the role of student to teacher in "The Space Between: MA Students Enculturate to Graduate Reading and Writing." The chapter concludes with brief suggestions for how faculty might support students during this transitional period.

In "Creating a Culture of Communication: A Graduate-Level STEM Communication Fellows Program at a Science and Engineering University," Steve Simpson, Rebecca Clemens, Drea Rae Killingsworth, and Julie Dyke Ford report on a graduate-level Communication Fellows Program developed in cooperation with three science and engineering disciplines along with their Center for Graduate Studies. In this reprint from *Across the Disciplines* with an epilogue by Jesse Priest, the new writing center director at New Mexico Tech, the authors focus on the specific environment of New Mexico Tech (where this research was conducted) and how the voices of graduate student Fellows has led to adapting programs to local conditions.

PART 3: "Help each other. Find a writing group!" OR Collaborations and Programs 'Alongside' Curriculum

In our third section, we look to programming and collaborations outside of classroom experience. Graduate students are often asked to consider their support networks inside and outside the institution and are encouraged to participate in campus-sponsored co-curricular activities such as writing center visits, writing camps, and writing workshops. Graduate students are sometimes directed by faculty members to "find a writing group" and "help one another," but it can be a nerve-racking task to ask colleagues to participate in a writing group. Even when students are successful in forming a writing group, the group may not be sustainable because members want different types of support. For instance, some members may want to use the time to write, while others want to use the time to discuss works in progress, and another member sees the meeting time primarily as a way to be social with other graduate students. It is easier to "help one another" if students have some structured advice and programming to guide the ways that they provide and receive support. The four chapters in this section speak to the benefits of structured support "alongside" the curriculum.

First, we look to programming that is multidisciplinary in nature and accessible to graduate students across the disciplines. In "Making Do by Making Space: Multidisciplinary Graduate Writing Groups as Spaces Alongside Programmatic and Institutional Places," Marilee Brooks-Gillies, Elena G. Garcia, and Katie Manthey present the perspectives of four graduate students who participated in graduate writing groups through the Writing Center at Michigan State University. They find that because of the multidimensional roles graduate students have to play there is a great need for spaces that are free from the judgment of institutional assessment—outside but alongside department and curricular spaces—while still meeting the institutional writing needs of graduate students.

Soo Hyon Kim and Shari Wolke also look to the potential of writing groups in "Graduate Writing Groups: Helping L2 Writers Navigate the Murky Waters of Academic Writing." Their chapter examines the discourse practices at a U.S. graduate school via Graduate Writing Groups (GWGs) sponsored by the University's Writing Center. Unlike the simple portrayal of all L2 graduate student writers as novices and their enculturation into academia as linear and unidirectional, L2 graduate students have multi-faceted identities as writers depending on academic task, context, and previous academic literacy experiences. Their work suggests that the complexity inherent in multidisciplinary GWGs can create a favorable environment for socialization into graduate writing discourse communities.

In "Camping in the Disciplines: Assessing the Effect of Writing Camps on Graduate Student Writers," Gretchen Busl, Kara Lee Donnelly, and Matthew Capdevielle look to another co-curricular program. Their chapter, an extended reprint from *Across the Disciplines*, advances a research-based set of best practices for the design and implementation of writing camps to support advanced graduate student writers across the disciplines. By tracing the trends they saw emerging in data collected from twelve graduate writing camps occurring over the span of three years, they suggest that writing camps that teach students strategies for managing their writing processes result in small but meaningful improvements in student attitudes and behaviors.

We complete this section with "Crossing Divides: Engaging Extracurricular Writing Practices in Graduate Education and Professionalization," by Laural Adams, Megan Adams, Estee Beck, Kristine Blair, April Conway, Martha Schaffer, and Lee Nickoson. This chapter features six graduate student voices and two faculty voices and explores the potential for multimodal and collaborative writing to disrupt the hierarchy among participants. The constellation of these eight voices can be seen as an investigation into how writing currently figures in these particular students' professionalization in rhetoric and composition.

PART 4: "Stop reading. Start writing. The best dissertation is a *done* dissertation." OR Examining Discourse Communities and Genres

In our fourth section, we look to specific disciplinary expectations in terms of discourse community and genre norms. Graduate students are exposed to a range of new discipline-specific genres as they move through their graduate school career. They may need to become familiar with writing response papers and seminar papers while completing their coursework, comprehensive exams, dissertation prospectus, and dissertation. Outside of the course environment, they are asked to learn how to write for publication in their fields: conference papers, book reviews, book chapters, and journal articles. What often goes unnoticed, however, is that becoming familiar with these disciplinary genres goes beyond simply learning the specific textual features of each genre. Learning how to read and write in disciplinary genres requires graduate students to learn how to *be* a graduate student writer: how to be conversant with literature in the field, how to make meaning from the texts they read, and developing and performing their scholarly identities through intertextuality. For students in interdisciplinary fields, it also means learning how to navigate and move between different fields by connecting and synthesizing ideas from different disciplines. In this sense, faculty advice such as "Stop reading; start writing," "The best dissertation is a *done* dissertation," and "Go deeper" can often come across as cryptic to graduate students who have yet to fully experience participating in their discourse communities. The following three chapters address how graduate student writers gradually develop their scholarly identities and become familiar with their disciplinary genres in the academy.

We begin with Michelle LaFrance and Steve Corbett's discussion of identities threaded through the collection indicating that our scholarly identities are shaped not only by meeting and exceeding the expectations of graduate school but also by our failures in graduate school. In "Discourse Community Fail! Negotiating Choices in Success/Failure and Graduate-Level Writing Development," an autoethnographic essay, they explore the implicit assumptions about the productivity of failure, as it discusses the difficulties of learning to write as a graduate student. They draw on Halberstam's notion of queering the institution and recent transfer theory to argue that failing is a crucial part of learning to be academic authors.

Sarah Blazer and Sarah DeCapua attend to the ways corpus research can be helpful to support structures advising students on various disciplinary-specific genres. In "Disciplinary Corpus Research: A Data-Driven Approach to Developing Situated Literacy Instruction," they use a sociocultural framework to demonstrate how corpus research can help writing center, composition, and WAC/WID disciplinary outsiders prepare to support graduate students who are newly engaged in reading and writing the genres of their discipline.

We finish our collection with Nigel Caplan's work, which focuses on results from a needs analysis conducted by one pre-matriculation program that teaches international MBA students speaking English as Second Language (ESL) in "Genres and Conflicts in MBA Writing Assignments." He notes that in addition to online surveys and focus groups, a verbal protocol analysis was conducted with four MBA professors to better understand one key written genre that emerged from the analysis as both important for and challenging to ESL students: the case study write-up. His work can inform other programs on designing needs analysis that can promote helpful classroom approaches to disciplinary-specific genre expectations.

Conclusion

Research into the practices of graduate writing and the experiences of enculturating into graduate school and academic life abounds. Such research can be found in many disparate disciplines, and we are eager to share a publication that directly addresses multiple disciplines. We argue, like Starke-Meyerring (2014), that

> Approaches to research writing in doctoral education must be research-led to help students understand why they find themselves in the situations they do; how research writing works to produce particular kinds of knowledge; what politics are involved; and how writing groups might work to push that knowledge work as well as the sedimented knowledge systems doctoral scholars are entering. (p. 78)

Graduate education must include various forms of writing support that seek to identify writers' needs, teach writers through direct instruction, and support writers through various programs such as writing centers, writing camps, and writing groups. We are looking forward to how conversations in this area of research continue to develop.

Of course, publications like this are only one way to increase awareness and access. Campus-wide initiatives that link writing programs in all their forms—including but not limited to EAP, WAC, WID, Writing Centers, and First-Year Writing (FYW) programs—could be productive local ways to address graduate writing education and support. Additionally, national and international initiatives are important to improving graduate education and support in writing. To this end, organizations such as the Consortium on Graduate Communication (CGC), "an independent community of educators who provide professional development in academic written and oral communication to (post-)graduate students before and during their master's and doctoral degrees" (Consortium on Graduate Communication, n.d.) created in April 2014, can provide momentum for the movement and important resources for educators and students. The CGC creates "online and face-to-face opportunities to discuss and share resources, ideas, research, and program models for this vital segment of international higher education" (Consortium on Graduate Communication, 2015, para. 1). As the articles showcased here demonstrate, attending to the needs of graduate writers requires various approaches and attention to the unique circumstances and available resources of individual universities while being mindful of research on and across similar programs at other universities.

References

Aitchison, C. (2009). Writing groups for doctoral education. *Studies in Higher Education, 34*(8), 905–916.

Aitchison, C. & Guerin, C. (2014). Writing groups, pedagogy, theory and practice. In C. Aitchison & C. Guerin (Eds.), *Writing groups for doctoral education and beyond: Innovations in practice and theory* (pp. 3–17). Routledge.

Aitchison, C., Kamler, B. & Lee, A. (Eds.). (2010). *Publishing pedagogies for the doctorate and beyond*. Routledge.

Allison, D., Cooley, L., Lewkowicz, J. & Nunan, D. (1998). Dissertation writing in action: The development of a dissertation writing support program for ESL graduate research students. *English for Specific Purposes, 17*(2), 199–217.

Allum, J. & Okahana, H. (2015). *Graduate enrollment and degrees: 2004 to 2014*. Council of Graduate Schools.

Badenhorst, C. & Guerin, C. (Eds.). (2016). *Research literacies and writing pedagogies for masters and doctoral writers*. Brill.

Belcher, D. (1994). The apprenticeship approach to advanced academic literacy: Graduate students and their mentors. *English for Specific Purposes, 13*, 23–34.

Cafferella, R. S. & Barnett, B. G. (2000). Teaching doctoral students to become scholarly writers: The importance of giving and receiving critiques. *Studies in Higher Education, 25*(1), 39–52.

Casanave, C. & Li, X. (Eds.). (2008). *Learning the literacy practices of graduate school*. University of Michigan Press.

Castello, M. & Donahue, C. (2012). *University writing: Selves and texts in academic societies*. Brill.

Consortium on Graduate Communication. (n.d.). *About the consortium*. Retrieved October 17, 2019, from https://www.gradconsortium.org/

Curry, M. J. & Lillis, T. (2004). Multilingual scholars and the imperative to publish in English: Negotiating interests, demands, and rewards. *TESOL Quarterly, 38*(4), 663–688.

Cuthbert, D., Spark, C. & Burke, E. (2009). Disciplining writing: The case for multidisciplinary writing groups to support writing for publication by higher degree

by research candidates in the humanities, arts, and social sciences. *Higher Education Research and Development, 28*(2), 137–149.
Dressen-Hammouda, D. (2008). From novice to disciplinary expert: Disciplinary identity and genre mastery. *English for Specific Purposes, 27*(2), 233–252.
Eriksson, A. & Makitalo, A. (2015). Supervision at the outline stage: Introducing and encountering issues of sustainable development through academic writing assignments. *Text & Talk, 35*(2), 123–153.
Flowerdew, J. (1999). Writing for scholarly publication in English: The case of Hong Kong. *Journal of Second Language Writing, 8*(2), 123–145.
Flowerdew, J. & Li, Y. (2009). English or Chinese? The trade-off between local and international publication among Chinese academics in the humanities and social sciences. *Journal of Second Language Writing, 18*, 1–16.
Fredericksen, E. & Mangelsdorf, K. (2014). Graduate writing workshops: Crossing languages and disciplines. In M. Cox & T. Zawacki (Eds.), *WAC and second language writers: Research towards linguistically and culturally inclusive programs and practices* (pp. 347–367). The WAC Clearinghouse; Parlor Press. https://wac.colostate.edu/books/perspectives/l2/.
Golding, A. & Mascaro, J. (1987). A survey of graduate writing courses. *Journal of Advanced Composition, 6*(1–2), 167–179.
Grego, R. C. & Thompson, N. S. (2008). *Teaching/Writing in thirdspaces: The studio approach*. Southern Illinois University Press.
Kent, J. (2016.). *Graduate schools report strong growth in first-time enrollment of underrepresented minorities.* Council of Graduate Schools. http://cgsnet.org/graduate-schools-report-strong-growth-first-time-enrollment-underrepresented-minorities.
Lawrence, S. & Zawacki, T. (Eds.). (2016). Writing center support for graduate thesis and dissertation writers. *Writing lab newsletter: A journal of writing center scholarship, 40*. https://wlnjournal.org/archives/v40/40.5-6.pdf.
Lillis, T. & Curry, M. J. (2010). *Academic writing in a global context: The politics and practices of publishing in English*. Routledge.
Madden, S. & Eodice, M. (Eds.). (2016). Access and equity in graduate writing support. *Praxis: A writing center journal, 14*(1). http://www.praxisuwc.com/141-final.
Maher, D., Seaton, L., McMullen, C., Fitzgerald, T., Otsuji, E. & Lee, A. (2008). "Becoming and being writers": The experiences of doctoral students in writing groups. *Studies in Continuing Education, 30*(3), 263–275.
McAlpine, L. & Amundsen, C. (Eds.). (2011). *Doctoral education: Research-based strategies for doctoral students, supervisors, and administrators*. Springer.
McIntosh, K., Pelaez-Morales, C. & Silva, T. (2016). *Graduate studies in second language writing*. Anderson, SC: Parlor Press.
Micciche, L. R. & Carr., A. D. (2011). Toward graduate-level writing instruction. *College Composition and Communication, 62*(3), 477–501.
Okahana, H. & Allum, J. (2015). *International graduate applications and enrollment: Fall 2015*. Council of Graduate Schools.
Olinger, A. R. (2014). On the instability of disciplinary style: Common and conflicting metaphors and practices in text, talk, and gesture. *Research in the Teaching of English, 48*(4), 453–478.

Page-Adams, D., Cheng, L., Gogineni, A. & Shen, C. (1995). Establishing a group to encourage writing for publication among doctoral students. *Journal of Social Work Education, 31*(3), 402–407.

Paltridge, B. & Starfield, S. (2007). *Thesis and dissertation writing in a second language: A handbook for supervisors*. Routledge.

Phillips, T. (2012). Graduate writing groups: Shaping writing and writers from student to scholar. *Praxis: A Writing Center Journal, 10*(1). http://praxis.uwc.utexas.edu/index.php/praxis/article/view/81.

Phillips, T. (2013). Tutor training and services for multilingual graduate writers: A reconsideration. *Praxis: A Writing Center Journal, 10*(2). http://www.praxisuwc.com/phillips-102.

Phillips, T. (2016). Writing center support for graduate students: An integrated model. In S. Simpson, N. A. Caplan, M. Cox & T. Phillips (Eds.), *Supporting graduate student writers: research, curriculum, and program design* (pp. 159–170). University of Michigan Press.

Rose, M. & McClafferty, K. A. (2001). A call for the teaching of writing in graduate education. *Educational Researcher, 30*(2), 27–33.

Russell, D. R. (2002). *Writing in the academic disciplines: A curricular history* (2nd ed.). Southern Illinois University Press.

Salee, M., Hallett, R. & Tierney, W. (2011). Teaching writing in graduate school. *College Teaching, 59*, 66–72.

Simpson, S. (2012). The problem of graduate-level writing support: Building a cross-campus graduate writing initiative. *WPA: Writing Program Administration, 36*(1), 95–118.

Simpson, S. (2013a). Systems of writing response: A Brazilian student's experiences writing for publication in an environmental sciences doctoral program. *Research in the Teaching of English, 48*(2), 228–249.

Simpson, S. (2013b). Building for sustainability: Dissertation boot camp as a nexus of graduate writing support. *Praxis: A Writing Center Journal, 10*(2). http://www.praxisuwc.com/simpson-102.

Simpson, S. (2016). Essential questions for program and pedagogical development. In S. Simpson, N. Caplan, M. Cox & T. Phillips (Eds.), Supporting graduate student writers: Research, curriculum, and program design (pp. 286–298). University of Michigan Press.

Simpson, S., Caplan, N. A., Cox, M. & Phillips, T. (Eds.). (2016). *Supporting graduate student writers: Research, curriculum, and program design*. University of Michigan Press.

Soja, E. W. (1996). *Thirdspace: Journeys to Los Angeles and other real-and-imagined places*. Wiley-Blackwell.

Starfield, S. (2003). The evolution of a thesis-writing course for Arts and Social Sciences students: What can Applied Linguistics offer? *Hong Kong Journal of Applied Linguistics, 8*(2), 137–154.

Starke-Meyerring, D. (2014). Writing groups as critical spaces for engaging normalized institutional cultures of writing in doctoral education. In C. Aitchison & C. Guerin (Eds.), *Writing groups for doctoral education and beyond: Innovations in practice and theory* (pp. 65–81). Routledge.

Swales, J. & Feak, C. (2012). *Academic writing for graduate students: Essential tasks and skills* (3rd ed.). University of Michigan Press.

Tardy, C. (2005). "It's like a story": Rhetorical knowledge development in advanced academic literacy. *Journal of English for Academic Purposes, 4*(4), 325–338.

Tardy, C. (2009). *Building genre knowledge*. Parlor Press.

Thesen, L. (2014). "If they're not laughing, watch out": Emotion and risk in postgraduate writers' circles. In C. Aitchison & C. Guerin (Eds.), *Writing groups for doctoral education and beyond: Innovations in practice and theory* (pp. 162–176). Routledge.

PART 1: "Read and write like a grad student" OR 'Inside' the Institution: Graduate Writing Courses and Programs

Elena G. Garcia
Utah Valley University

I entered my Ph.D. program in Rhetoric and Writing at Michigan State University with a BA and MA in English Language Arts for Secondary Education. While I certainly had some experience with grad school expectations, my education had been largely practical. So my first semester at MSU felt a bit like a punch in the gut. My very first class was History of Rhetoric, a traditionally brutal course, heavy with theory, reading, and writing. We were intensely challenged in new and uncomfortable ways. Yet I didn't feel that I had much guidance for how to face the challenges set before me. I was being asked to do "Ph.D. grad student" work without knowing what that even meant.

That same semester I was required to take a Research Colloquium course, which had the fairly broad aim to introduce us to the program and the discipline. The course met its aim, I suppose, but it felt like the right information at the wrong time. I couldn't think about comp exam procedures or how the different narratives of our discipline overlapped while I was struggling to get through each week. I wanted more guidance, but I didn't know how to, or even if I should, ask for it. My classmates and I were encouraged to seek peer support, to work together, to struggle together. For History of Rhetoric, a few of us did that for a few weeks. The lack of structure led the group to, basically, fade away.

I eventually learned how to read and write like a graduate student, but I'm not sure I could explain what that entails: How well-equipped am I, even now in my fifth year as faculty, to teach someone what it means? What, exactly, does "graduate-level reading and writing" look like? Clear, structured, focused instruction on the ways I needed to examine and develop texts might have helped me answer these questions—and might have prevented a lot of stress and struggle.

Because in-class, curricular instruction is the first and most powerful aspect of a graduate student's education, that is where we start our collection. The following three chapters all describe institutional programming, beginning with a survey of graduate writing courses, moving into descriptions of specific graduate writing courses at two different institutions, and ending with a multivocal discussion of structured academic professionalization.

Snapshots, Surveys, and Infrastructures: An Institutional Case Study of Graduate Writing Courses

Laurie A. Pinkert
University of Central Florida

> **Abstract:** This chapter increases our understanding of graduate-level writing engagement by exploring survey responses across more than 48 departments at one large Midwestern research university. The survey methodology adapts questions from Golding and Mascaro's 1987 survey of graduate courses; however, it revises their methodology to include graduate students as participants and to allow multiple respondents from each graduate program at the selected institution. By allowing for this variation, the study offers a contextualized, institutional case study that highlights the ways that writing courses may be simultaneously visible and invisible to a range of stakeholders and points to the need to more fully explore rather than erase contradictions in the perspectives of stakeholders.
>
> **Keywords:** Graduate Writing Survey, Writing Across the Curriculum, Writing Courses, Survey Methods, Infrastructure

Introduction: Snapshots of Graduate Writing

When researchers attempt to characterize trends or practices in writing pedagogy or programs, they often turn to surveys to create a "snapshot" that can momentarily stabilize the landscape, making it easier to analyze. In the case of graduate writing, two surveys provide notable snapshots from which we can draw characterizations of the role that graduate courses play within the landscape of graduate writing engagement.[1] Golding and Mascaro's (1987) survey of deans and faculty at over 200 universities across the U.S. remained, until recently, one of the most comprehensive surveys of graduate writing. Golding and Mascaro sought to understand "the extent and range of graduate writing courses nationwide and the rationale

---

1   To acknowledge the complex relationship between teaching and learning without emphasizing one over another, I employ the term "writing engagement." Although the term "engagement" is often used to discuss the relationship of universities to public initiatives (e.g., civic engagement), my use of this term does not imply an extra-university commitment. Instead, it highlights the activities, both teacher-, student-, and peer-initiated, that span or move between the narrower categories of teaching or learning.

DOI: https://doi.org/10.37514/ATD-B.2020.0407.2.01

for offering them" (p. 167). Of the 144 schools that responded to their survey, 51 schools reported 78 writing courses. Their survey of deans and faculty reported important information on writing courses in different kinds of graduate programs. But that survey grew outdated as years passed and the landscape of graduate education continued to evolve. More recently, Caplan and Cox's (2016) survey, which reports 270 responses from 22 different countries, provided a new starting point from which to identify possible trends in "systematic graduate communication support, support that moves beyond the individual initiative to the program level" (p. 23). Caplan and Cox surveyed members of the Consortium on Graduate Communication (CGC), who reported that "more than three-quarters of the universities in the survey (81.2 percent) offer some kind of writing course focused on graduate communication" (p. 28).

These surveys represent an important step in grounding the discussions of graduate writing courses in survey data on such courses. However, they also face challenges in representing graduate writing. First, these studies report data that are often offered by a single individual who is taken to be representative of an institution. Given the prevalence of program-specific requirements and resources at the graduate level, individuals may be able to represent their department or program but may have a difficult time representing the entirety of an institution. As Caplan and Cox (2016) note, participants often work in isolation, mistakenly believing they are the only ones on their campuses working on graduate writing. Second, these studies surveyed primarily administrators and faculty without engaging the graduate students for whom courses and other resources are designed. As such, they may describe a faculty perspective on existing infrastructures for graduate writing development, but they fall short in helping us better understand how the students, the users of such resources, identify and characterize them. Third, in the case of Caplan and Cox's survey, which aimed to report on resources available, the research design combined contradictory responses from participants at the same institution. They note: "Considerable confusion often existed about the services available"; therefore, "responses were combined" when it seemed two or more respondents knew of different services available on campus (p. 26). By combining responses, the results may offer an account that is accurate at an institutional level but may not accurately represent the access that all graduate students have or perceive to those reported resources.

This chapter reports on an institutional case study that responds to such limitations by providing survey data that can account for variance across an institution and can represent student experiences with writing courses in graduate programs. The case study was developed from 324 survey responses at Midwestern Research University (MRU).[2] The results highlight the kinds of infrastructure that make

---

2   Midwestern Research University is a pseudonym.

graduate writing courses most visible and the activities that support writers when courses are not available to them. Arguing for the importance of including student experience alongside faculty perception, this study takes contradictions in participant responses as an important site to be explored more fully rather than combined. In doing so, this chapter highlights the ways that our snapshots of graduate writing must be supported by a rich framework for understanding relevant infrastructures.

Method of Inquiry: Survey as Institutional Case Study

The IRB-approved survey designed for this study takes seriously Sullivan and Porter's (1997) notion that ethical research activities and methodologies must remain responsive to the rhetorical situatedness of the participants and, therefore, must also remain open to the possibility of messiness. The purpose of this case study was not to pin down an exact number of writing resources provided at the selected institution but rather to bring into focus participant-generated descriptions of the ways that graduate students developed their writing abilities and to allow for the possibility of contrast in various participants' experiences of their graduate program. Accordingly, the survey design was not intended to define specific writing infrastructures and ask participants to confirm their existence; rather, the design was intended to highlight the frameworks participants themselves used to describe writing activities, writing support, and writing courses. By foregrounding participants' own descriptions of writing development, the methodology is positioned as a set of "heuristic guidelines" rather than "a set of immutable principles" (Sullivan & Porter, 1997, p. 66).

This approach results in complex and sometimes contradictory data (i.e., multiple respondents from the same program might respond differently to the same question) that represent the often-overlooked variance in the perceptions of and access to writing resources at the graduate level. Additionally, this approach provided an important opportunity for writing across the curriculum specialists and writing program administrators to listen to and learn from the descriptions and vocabulary provided by students, faculty, and staff within graduate programs, aligning with Segal, Pare, Brent, and Vipond's (1998) argument that if writing researchers seek to contribute to the practices surrounding writing across the disciplines, they must first understand the discourse practices and rhetorical knowledge that may otherwise remain tacit: "Part of our ideology as rhetoricians and part of the rhetoric of our rhetoric is the assumption that language ought to be treated as opaque: something to look at. We pay attention to language qua language in order to amass information on how it works in context" (p. 76). Inviting participant-provided language is, by design, messier than providing a list of multiple-choice options, but understanding the language used in the context of different graduate programs offers an integral foundation for further work within the disciplines being examined.

Motivation and Literature Review

By 2012, when this survey was developed and distributed, numerous scholars had issued calls for the development of graduate writing courses, but very rarely did these calls rely on research about course availability and configuration. These calls for courses have persisted as writing specialists see courses as a promising and institutionally visible means of engagement for graduate writers. For example, Micciche and Carr (2011) argued "for an explicit commitment to graduate-level writing instruction in English studies that goes beyond incorporating drafts, peer reviews, and workshops into seminars and entails more than extracurricular writing workshops to supplement course work" (p. 478). Micciche and Carr argued that a "critical writing course," should fill the "glaringly empty spot" in English graduate programs (p. 480). Drawing from their experiences in a College of Education, Rose and McClafferty (2001) advocated for a course that allows students to "slow down a bit, reflect on what they're doing and why, and think about the language they are using to represent it" (p. 32). Dobrin (1993) described graduate writing courses that were developed in response to conversations with faculty who claimed that "graduate students were not producing writing that met professional standards" (p. 65). Delyser (2003) argued for the role that courses can play in dissertation writing, and several scholars suggested that courses can play a crucial role in the development of writing abilities for non-native English speakers or international students (Aranha, 2009; Fredericksen & Mangelsdorf, 2014; Frodesen, 1995; Norris & Tardy, 2006). These scholars and others (Fairbanks & Dias, 2016; Fredrick, Stravalli, May & Brookman-Smith, this collection; Mallett, Haan & Habib, 2016; Nolan & Rocco, 2009; Street & Stang, 2008) most often argue for the relevance of courses by describing writing courses at their own institutions, distinguishing such courses from extracurricular models,[3] and arguing that graduate writing courses should be developed because they are beneficial in ways that other models are not.

Research Questions

In response to the need for deeper, more contextualized research on the existence and role of graduate writing courses, the survey responses discussed here provide an institutional case study that aims to answer the following questions:

1. Does a respondent's position within a program affect their perception of the existence and availability of writing courses?

---

3   For further discussions of extra-curricular models see, for example, Gere (1987), Brooks-Gillies, Garcia & Manthey (this collection), and Kim & Wolke (this collection) on writing groups; Gillespie (2007) and Phillips (2016) on graduate writing center consultations; and Adams et al. (this collection) on collaborative writing with faculty and graduate editorial positions with journals.

2. What are the characteristics of courses that are highly visible as a means of writing engagement in graduate programs?
3. When courses are not taken by students in a program, do respondents see a need for courses?
4. Do respondents within a program agree on whether or not students take courses?

Research Site

Midwestern Research University[4] was selected as an ideal site to study graduate writing due to its size and diversity of graduate programs. At the time the survey was conducted, MRU reported over 7,000 graduate students in 75 graduate programs that represent a variety of disciplines and was classified by the Carnegie Foundation as RU/VH (Research Universities-very high research activity) with a CompDoc/MedVet (comprehensive doctoral with medical/veterinary) graduate instructional profile. As a large institution with a variety of graduate programs at the master's and doctoral levels, MRU provided a relevant site to examine potential complexity and variance in the perceptions of graduate writing courses.

Participants

In order to recruit participants from various positions in graduate programs, the survey invitation was distributed via email to program representatives as well as sent to existing listservs. Snowball sampling was used to recruit additional participants from the programs. The initial recipients for the survey invitation were generated from the university website's list of 81 graduate programs, each with a program code and corresponding list of "Graduate Program Heads, Chairs, Directors, and Contacts." One survey invitation email was sent per program code, copying all contacts associated with that code and requesting that the survey invitation be forwarded to all faculty, staff, and students within their specific graduate program.

Program contacts who worked with multiple programs (i.e., who were listed under multiple program codes) received multiple emails, each listing a particular program in the request to forward the survey link. For example, the Graduate Contact for American Studies was also the Graduate Contact for Comparative Literature and for Linguistics, each of which have their own program code. Therefore, this person was a recipient of three different emails, each one listing one of these programs and asking them to forward the survey invitation to graduate faculty, staff, and students in that program. In addition to the initial invitations, which were sent to program contacts

---

4   The survey was also distributed nationally within selected disciplines; however, this chapter focuses only on the institutional data collected at MRU.

with a request to forward to members of their respective programs, a secondary invitation was sent to students through the university's graduate student government listserv.

By snowball sampling a range of stakeholders involved in graduate programs, I employed non-probability sampling techniques. This design contrasts many surveys that follow probability sampling protocols similar to Golding and Mascaro's (1987), recruiting specific administrators and faculty. While the benefits outweighed the drawbacks in this case, this choice to solicit responses from a wide range of stakeholders within graduate programs through snowball sampling complicates the typical discussion of response rates since it becomes difficult to effectively quantify the number of faculty, staff, students, postdocs, etc. involved in a graduate program. A narrower participant pool of only graduate deans, for example, makes a discussion of sample size much easier to quantify.

Accordingly, my investigation, concentrated at a single institution with its population crossing typical faculty/student/staff boundaries, was less focused on counting an exact number of courses offered and more interested in understanding when and how courses are visible for different participants in different programs. This method allowed for multiple respondents to discuss the same course and for multiple respondents to suggest opposing views about whether graduate students take writing courses. Alternate approaches that invite only a single representative from a program (often someone with authority over that program) can shed light on what we might consider to be institutional responses, giving an element of certainty to the results reported—if the Dean says there's a course, there must be a course. However, such an administrator- or faculty-focused investigation is unable to account for students' experience and perception of such courses and resources. While a student-inclusive approach cannot simply report the number of courses that are offered at MRU because stakeholders in the same department might contradict each other, it offers an important case study that exposes the ways various members of graduate programs take similar or opposing views of courses and their relevance to graduate study.

Data Collection and Analysis

To collect data for this case study, I adapted Golding and Mascaro's (1987) survey questions[5] and distributed the revised survey instrument to faculty, staff, and students across disciplines. The survey (See Appendix A for print version) was admin-

---

5   The graduate writing survey instrument was adapted from Golding and Mascaro's (1987) survey, a copy of which I received from Alan Golding in Fall of 2012. I adapted the survey questions through changes in wording that would accommodate a more diverse respondent population that included students and staff as well as the graduate deans and faculty who were the invited respondents to Golding and Mascaro's original survey. As noted above, this survey was developed and distributed before Caplan and Cox's 2016 survey had been published; therefore, it relied primarily on Golding and Mascaro as a point of comparison.

istered online through Qualtrics, which allowed for skip logic that tailored the questions based on the respondents' previous answers. All participants received the initial questions requesting information about their graduate program, the common ways that students within the program develop their writing abilities, and whether students take any writing courses. For those who indicated that students in their program take writing courses, the survey asked additional questions about the course format and rationale. It also provided an option for participants to attach a syllabus or course description or to include a link to an online version of these documents. For those who indicated that students in their program did not take writing courses, the survey asked whether they thought such courses were needed.

Narrative responses were coded using grounded theory to develop an open coding schema (Miles, Huberman & Saldana, 2013). An open coding schema allowed for the analysis to follow the participant-generated data in this study. The specific coding schemes, which varied according to question, are described in the corresponding sections that follow.

Overview of Responses: Breadth of Representation

Three hundred and twenty-four participants responded to the survey distributed at MRU.[6] Since this study aimed to explore various perspectives within graduate programs at MRU, two elements of representation were crucial to the cases examined in this exploration. First, the study must have a wide range of participants across the institution. That is, to explore the potential variance in experience, participants must come from different programs, different departments, and different colleges. The respondents came from 48 different departments across nine colleges.[7] In most cases, someone responded to the survey from a majority of the departments within each college.

The second necessity for exploring variance and perspective was that respondents must occupy different positions within graduate programs. If only faculty

---

6   This number excludes 54 responses. Of these excluded responses, 51 contained no input data, which may indicate that someone read the consent form and elected not to participate or opened the survey but did not enter any responses; 3 contained only data for the respondents' positions in their program but did not provide additional responses to other survey questions. All other responses were included in the data described in the following sections.

7   Although the term "program" was used by the graduate school to describe its graduate offerings (as in "more than 70 graduate programs at the [MRU] campus"), program turned out to be a less useful category than "department" since program titles provided by the respondents often differed from those that The Graduate School described. Thus, to use a category that was more consistently employed across responses, I grouped responses based on department. "No Department Listed" was used for any responses that were included in the survey results but did not have a department affiliation entered.

responded or if only students responded, there would be no way to compare their perceptions and experience. Of the 324 survey respondents, 108 indicated that they were faculty; 11 indicated that they were staff; 54 that they were master's students; 162 that they were doctoral students; and 8 that they held other positions. The other positions were described as one program head, one department head, three postdocs, two teaching assistants, and one former graduate student. The total number of responses (324) and the total number of position descriptions (343) differ due to a survey design that did not limit respondents to using only one designation to describe their position. For example, of the 108 respondents who indicated that they were faculty, six selected additional designations to describe their positions: one staff, one master's student, two doctoral students, and two other. Of the 11 respondents who indicated that they were staff, six selected additional designations: one faculty, three master's students, two doctoral students, and one other. Most importantly, in 34 of the 48 departments, the respondents came from multiple positions within the graduate program. (See Appendix B for the full distribution of positions within each set of departmental responses.) This allows for comparison of stakeholder perspectives in many programs.

Findings: Course Visibility and Corresponding Infrastructures

This section explores three relevant cases of graduate writing drawn primarily from participants' responses to the multiple choice question about whether or not students take writing courses in order to develop their writing abilities and the corresponding open-ended responses that ask participants to discuss the courses they identified or to discuss the reasons that students do not take courses. Before discussing these cases, which center on responses at the department/program level, I provide a brief analysis of the variation in overall responses as related to the participants' positions within the department/program.

Finding 1: Participants' Positions May Affect Perception of Course Infrastructures

When I began to develop this study of graduate writing courses, I talked with graduate students from a composition and rhetoric graduate program who noted that they didn't feel like they had courses that focused on writing. Even though they were taking composition/rhetorical theory courses and composition pedagogy courses, they didn't feel their writing was well-supported through meaningful instruction. However, when I talked to the faculty in this same program, they assured me that they were teaching writing in their courses. Here, I saw variation in perspective: The faculty believed that they were teaching writing, but the students didn't believe that they were being taught to write. This experience left me wondering whether similar variance would exist in other programs: Would faculty believe that their courses were writing courses even though students could not identify them as such?

Table 1.1. Responses to the question of whether graduate students in their program take writing courses

	Yes	No	No Reply	Total	% Yes	% No	% No Reply
Faculty	34	62	12	108	31.5%	57.4%	11.1%
Staff	2	6	3	11	18.2%	54.5%	27.3%
Master's Student	7	38	9	54	13.0%	70.4%	16.7%
Doctoral Student	44	97	21	162	27.2%	59.9%	13.0%
Other (Program Head, Postdoc, Etc.)	2	4	2	8	25.0%	50.0%	25.0%

Note. This table compares responses to the question of whether or not graduate students take writing courses based on respondent's self-identified positions. Since respondents could select multiple position types, the number of position types reported here is larger than the number of overall respondents in each Yes/No/No Reply. For example, in the Yes column, the 89 position types shown represent 83 respondents who reported that their students take writing courses.

When asked if students in their graduate program take writing courses, 83 respondents said yes and 197 said no, which means that 30 percent of the total respondents stated that the graduate students in their department take writing courses. For this question about whether students take writing courses, the survey invited participants to use their own definitions of "writing course" rather than being offered a definition that might include or exclude activities they would associate with this term.[8] This participant-driven defining activity follows Jeffrey Bowker and Susan Leigh Star's (1999) pragmatic turn in their discussion of classification systems:

> We take a broad enough definition so that anything consistently called a classification system and treated as such can be included in the term . . . With a broad pragmatic definition we can look at the work that is involved in building and maintaining a family of entities that people call classification systems rather than attempt the Herculean, Sisyphian task of purifying the (un)stable systems in place. (p. 13)

---

8   This contrasts Golding and Mascaro's (1987) survey, which defined "graduate-level writing course" as "a course that focuses primarily on writing for an academic or professional field" (p. 170).

In the same way that Bowker and Star privilege an understanding of "the work that is involved in building and maintaining" over the need to pin those systems in place, this question design emphasizes the work that courses do conceptually and physically in engaging graduate writing over the need to pin the definition of writing course in place. In doing so, the survey focuses on the infrastructures that participants identified as courses and the ways that such configurations build and maintain writing engagement.

Doctoral students were slightly more likely than their faculty counterparts to report that students did not take graduate writing courses (see Table 1.1); however, the minor difference in percentages suggests that, contrary to my hypothesis about courses being more readily visible as writing courses to faculty than to graduate students, the identification of writing courses was not necessarily linked to faculty positioning within departments. Rather, the responses suggest that faculty and doctoral students at the institution were not significantly more or less likely to respond a certain way to the question of whether graduate students in their program take writing courses. That is, their responses seem more significantly influenced by their department/program than by their position.

As Table 1.1 indicates, however, master's students were much less likely to identify a writing course as an existing infrastructure for developing graduate writing abilities. Within this group, 16 percent responded yes to the question of courses and a corresponding 84 percent responded no. This difference in percentage may indicate that master's students, having been in a graduate program for less time than their doctoral student counterparts, are less likely to know about courses that do exist or less likely to know if students take writing courses that are offered. Or it may suggest that although we might expect master's-level programs to introduce new graduate students to writing conventions in their fields, these courses seem to be less visible, if they are offered at all at MRU.

Finding 2: Visible Writing Courses Were Disciplinarily-Specific

In 11 departments, respondents unanimously reported that their graduate students took writing courses (see Table 1.2). While most of these departments were represented by only one or two respondents, which does not provide the level of depth needed to examine the consistency of the responses, Botany and Plant Pathology and Nuclear Engineering, which had a total of five and seven responses, respectively, provide a generative site for examining the courses that were visible to a range of stakeholders. In both programs, all respondents agreed that students in these graduate programs take writing courses, indicating that the writing course(s) in these departments are highly visible to members within the graduate program.

In the case of Botany and Plant Pathology, all respondents (four faculty, one doctoral student) mentioned a writing course when initially asked the open-ended question, "How do students in your graduate program develop their writing abilities?" This question was the very first non-demographic question in the survey, and the consistency of responses that included a course suggests that the writing course is an infrastructure that is highly visible in the department and program—so visible that participants did not need to be further prompted to consider courses in order to name them. When later asked whether students take writing courses, all respondents said yes and all respondents named and described "Scientific Writing" as the course that their students take. Additionally, all respondents noted faculty support as another way that graduate students develop their writing abilities. These faculty support responses included discussion of meetings with faculty, writing with faculty, and working with a major professor. In this program, faculty support was described as working alongside the structured course model.

Table 1.2. Departments unanimously reporting that students take writing courses

Department	Total Number of Responses
Agronomy	1
Biochemistry	2
Botany and Plant Pathology	5
Computer and Information Technology	1
Food Science	2
History	1
Hospitality and Tourism Management	2
Industrial Technology	2
Nuclear Engineering	8
Pharmacy Practice	2
Youth Development and Agricultural Education	1

Note. This table provides responses for each department in which all respondents reported that students within their graduate program take writing courses.

In the case of Nuclear Engineering, eight members of the department (one faculty, two master's students, five doctoral students) responded to the survey. Of those eight, seven responded to the open-ended question, "How do students in your graduate program develop their writing abilities?" and six of these respondents mentioned a writing course that students take. They mentioned the course in the following ways:

- "Writing course"
- "We have a specific writing class for Nuclear Engineers, it is very helpful."
- "NUCL 597"
- "We have a mandatory writing class."
- "All incoming graduate students are required to take a writing course."
- "For graduate students in our department, a writing and communication class is required to take in the first semester"

For most respondents, the course was mentioned as the first comment in the response, and subsequent resources and infrastructures were listed "in addition" to the writing course, suggesting that the course was visible as the primary infrastructure for supporting graduate writers and that other infrastructures were less central to that support. The "Essential Communication Skills for Nuclear Engineers" course was later described in detail by several participants. The course entails instruction in technical and non-technical communication: from how to make an effective phone call to how to write the literature assessment that is part of the qualifying exams.

In both Botany and Plant Pathology and Nuclear Engineering, the respondents identified writing courses as an infrastructure for developing graduate writing abilities regardless of their position as faculty or student. The Botany and Plant Pathology respondents noted that the Scientific Writing course was taught by a different department, while the Nuclear Engineering respondents described a required, departmentally-taught course. This variation suggests that, at MRU, having a departmentally-offered writing course was not essential to its visibility.

In both cases, the course titles offer disciplinary connection—to "Science" for Botany and Plant Pathology and to "Nuclear Engineering" explicitly for that graduate program. They also offer a connection to writing/communication that is highly visible in the course title. These courses contrast models that, for example, embed writing in a disciplinary seminar course. Respondents from departments in which the participants did not agree that students take courses sometimes mentioned courses such as "Seminar in Global History" and "Insect Biology" as writing courses. These seminars, which may involve substantial writing engagement, may not be as visible as the courses in which writing/communication was featured more prominently in the course title.

Finding 3: When Courses Aren't Taken, Examining Existing Infrastructures Can Enhance Frameworks for Alternate Writing Support

In 18 departments, respondents unanimously reported that students did not take graduate writing courses. Mechanical Engineering had the highest number of respondents (18) who agreed that writing courses are not taken by their students. In

Mechanical Engineering, the 18 respondents identified themselves by the following positions: four faculty, seven master's students, and 10 doctoral students, with three of those respondents selecting both master's student and doctoral student.

Mechanical Engineering responses to the question of how students develop their writing abilities were coded first based on common models of writing engagement discussed in the literature including faculty/mentor, peers, and writing center. The literature suggests that curricular models may include activities such as a series of writing courses such as Radner's (1961) "Communications Sequence," a single writing course such as Rose and McClafferty's (2001) professional writing course for students across the disciplines in a Graduate School of Education and Information Technology, and even a writing process pedagogy such as Mullen's (2001) Writing Process and Feedback (WPF) model that can be integrated into existing courses. Commonly discussed extra-curricular models include the mentor model in which students are mentored by a faculty member (Mullen, 2003), the writing center model in which students receive feedback from writing consultants (Gillespie, 2007), the writing camp model in which students participate in intensive, often-daily programming (Busl, Donnelly & Capdevielle, this collection), and the writing group model in which groups of students meet with or without faculty member supervision (Gere, 1987).

Then a second round of codes was generated from participant responses: Additional codes for practice, workshops, and reading were added. *Practice* was used to code responses that explicitly included the word "practice" or that mentioned "writing journal papers and theses" without a reference to a mentor with whom students might work. Responses that discussed "working with faculty" or writing papers under faculty guidance were coded as the *Faculty/Mentor*, and those that discussed working with fellow graduate students or peers were coded as *Peer*. *Workshops* was a term not only used in Mechanical Engineering responses but also in other programs. Most often it was used to describe events that took place in a single session rather than in a series of sessions across a semester. For example, the Graduate School at MRU offered workshops on "How to Write a Thesis" or "How to Conduct a Literature Review" and one program offered an annual weekend-long writing workshop. Occasionally, it was used in contrast to the idea of a course as in "I'm not sure if a course would be the best setting for that. A workshop might be fine." Additionally, one response that included "reading papers" as a way to develop writing abilities (and perhaps, using papers as models for writing manuscripts) was coded as "*Reading*." The prevalence of the codes was as follows:

Faculty/Mentor 14
Practice 3
Peers 2
Workshops 2
Reading 1
Writing Center 1

The open-ended comments make clear that the faculty/mentor model is most visible for the respondents and provides an important site for writing specialists and program administrators to conduct further research regarding the faculty and student satisfaction with this model. In this survey, the respondents were merely asked to explain how students develop their abilities but were not asked to rate the efficacy of the existing infrastructures.

Table 1.3. Mechanical Engineering responses to the question of how students develop their writing abilities

Response	Position
Individual mentoring with faculty members.	Faculty
Individually with faculty by practice.	Faculty
Thesis students work closely with their advisors. Non-thesis MS students do not take writing courses.	Faculty
Working on conference and journal papers closely with faculty advisors.	Faculty
Working with faculty if they have time and are willing to give feedback. Some get help from fellow students.	Master's
Use the [writing center].	Master's
Meet with faculty members on an individual basis; discuss with peers.	Master's
Writing workshops, meeting with faculty members, writing courses.	Master's
Meet individually with faculty.	Master's & Doctoral
Usually students improve their writing by working with their advisers on publications.	Master's & Doctoral
Baptism by fire, merciless revisions, and practice.	Master's & Doctoral
Meet individually with faculty member, read papers.	Doctoral
We write reports over projects we do in class. We also write journal papers and theses. I have not taken a writing class or workshop since I was an undergrad.	Doctoral
Meet with faculty members / advisor.	Doctoral
The students that I'm familiar with developed their writing skills prior to joining the graduate program at [MRU]. Except for those for whom English is a second language, I don't think any of them do anything to develop their writing skills any further.	Doctoral
There are workshops available. I develop my writing by working on papers, reports, and proposals with input from my advisors.	Doctoral
In my research group, we meet individually with our adviser for editing and suggestions. Practice and experience are a good way to develop writing abilities too.	Doctoral
Working directly with their own adviser.	Doctoral

Note. This table provides the full responses of Mechanical Engineering respondents who replied to the question of how graduate students develop their writing abilities. To allow for comparison across respondent positions, the respondent's position (as identified by the respondent) is provided in the second column.

Not all respondents' open-ended replies elicited codes for developing writing abilities in graduate school because, as one respondent explained, students already had abilities prior to graduate school: "The students that I'm familiar with developed their writing skills prior to joining the graduate program at [MRU]. Except for those for whom English is a second language, I don't think any of them do anything to develop their writing skills any further." The respondent notes their belief that multilingual writers may continue to develop their writing abilities but does not offer any explanation of the strategies for such writers or the resources available to them.

In their subsequent responses to the question about why students did not take courses and whether they see a need for such courses, nine responses were coded as seeing a need for graduate writing courses. These responses included explicit positive comments about the use or helpfulness of such courses. For example, one respondent explained: "I think such writing courses could be very useful in that a more integrated and intense way of developing writing skills could save graduate students more time and efforts than learning those skills by oneself."

Four Mechanical Engineering respondents saw no need for graduate writing courses. These respondents noted, for example, that the program was already full and courses had not proven useful to them in the past. An additional four respondents offered a reply to the open-ended question but could not be coded as affirming or denying the need for courses. Responses such as, "There are no graduate level writing courses. Personally, I took a technical writing course as an undergraduate that was very useful," sometimes made declarative statements about the existence of courses and about past experience but did not relate that experience to the current program under discussion.

Many of the Mechanical Engineering respondents addressed the constraint of time, whether they foresaw a need for courses or not. One respondent stated:

> So many other courses are needed to graduate, there usually isn't time for a writing course. Also, professors do not tend to suggest taking a writing course as a part of a plan of study. I think that a writing course would be good since there are usually seminars on how to write a thesis, but none that discuss writing for journal articles (that I am aware of).

They also suggested that courses were not likely to be taken or could not fit into the existing curriculum unless they were credit-bearing with credit counting toward the degree earned:

> While a formal writing course would certainly be useful, there is generally insufficient time to complete a course. Making such a course count for graduate credit would likely increase enrollment significantly.

This connection between writing courses and program requirements was highlighted by respondents from programs beyond Mechanical Engineering. Some students noted the struggle to balance their desire to develop writing abilities and their advisor's admonitions about how their time and energy ought to be spent. One student respondent explained, "In my personal case I wanted to take a technical writing c[o]urse at the beginning of my second year but my advisor oppose to it saying that it won't help me and it will be time consuming." Several respondents framed this lack of time for courses in comments about the ways that courses don't count toward a degree. This particular framework indicates that writing courses are not seen as curricular in relationship to a student's stated degree program. One student wrote, "I do not take writing courses because they do not count toward my degree"; another explained, ["Courses are] not required. It would probably benefit all graduate students to take such a course."

Finding 4: Variance in Visibility Highlights Relationships Among Infrastructures

In an additional 18 departments, participant responses conflicted with each other, indicating that some members of the department thought that graduate students in their program took writing courses while others did not. Responses from Veterinary and Clinical Sciences (VCS) provide a generative site for examining the infrastructures recognized by respondents and the potential reasons for contradictory responses at MRU. In the case of VCS, responses to the question of how students develop their writing abilities were coded first based on common models of writing engagement discussed in the literature, with a second round of codes generated from participant responses. The responses were coded in the following frequency:

Workshop 7
Faculty/Mentor 6
Coursework 2
Reading 1
Publishing 1
Writing Course 1

In addition to the codes discussed in the Mechanical Engineering case, we see an additional *"Publishing"* code, which was used to code responses that mentioned students being encouraged to publish as a way to develop their writing abilities, and a *"Coursework"* code, which is used when respondents noted that core courses contained writing instruction on specific techniques or strategies or that assignments in courses helped develop writing abilities. Additionally, in this program, the code *"Reading"* was used to refer to a "Journal Club" in which members of the program read and discussed journal articles.

Responses demonstrate that the workshop was a visible model of writing engagement. In this case, the respondents discussed an annual event in which graduate students and residents were invited to attend a weekend session on scientific writing. Additionally, the faculty/mentor model was a highly visible means of support articulated by graduate students and faculty.

Table 1.4. Departments represented by conflicting responses to the question of whether graduate students take writing courses to develop their writing abilities

Department	Yes	No	Total	% Yes	% No
Animal Sciences	3	1	4	75.00%	25.00%
Anthropology	1	5	6	16.67%	83.33%
Civil Engineering	1	14	15	6.67%	93.33%
Communication	1	14	15	6.67%	93.33%
Computer Graphics Technology	1	4	5	20.00%	80.00%
Consumer Sciences and Retailing	1	1	2	50.00%	50.00%
Curriculum & Instruction	1	13	14	7.14%	92.86%
Engineering Education	3	8	11	27.27%	72.73%
English	14	22	36	38.89%	61.11%
Entomology	2	2	4	50.00%	50.00%
Forestry and Natural Resources	1	6	7	14.29%	85.71%
Interdisciplinary Comparative Literature	2	2	4	50.00%	50.00%
Nutrition Science	4	3	7	57.14%	42.86%
Psychological Sciences	13	3	16	81.25%	18.75%
Speech Language and Hearing Sciences	3	3	6	50.00%	50.00%
Technology Leadership & Innovation	2	5	7	28.57%	71.43%
Veterinary Clinical Sciences	3	4	7	42.86%	57.14%
Visual and Performing Arts	1	1	2	50.00%	50.00%

Note. This table reports all departments in which participants gave contradictory responses to the question of whether graduate students in their program take writing courses. The replies (yes or no) are reported along with the total number of respondents. The last two columns offer percentages for yes and no replies

While only one respondent mentioned a writing course in their initial discussion of the ways that graduate students develop their writing abilities, three respondents later indicated that graduate students in their program take writing courses; these respondents listed a required grant writing course alongside the previously-discussed scientific writing workshop. This participant-generated discussion of both credit-bearing courses and workshops as meaningful writing courses breaks typical curricular and extra-curricular boundaries, suggesting that in Veterinary and Clinical Sciences, writing might be scaffolded throughout a student's curricular and extra-curricular experience. Lee Nickoson (this collection) notes that the extra-curricular moves beyond "coursework and visible, required/expected sites of academic performance" (in Adams et al., "Crossing Divides").

Yet, as graduate education is often understood not only as a credentialing process that grants degrees but also a process that professionalizes or "disciplines" future colleagues, the required curriculum can be blurry at best. Some requirements, such as numbers of courses, may be very explicit while others, such as publication or participation expectations, can be felt as part of the hidden curriculum composed of the "messages that students read 'between the lines'" even when they are not stated (Strong, 2003). Carr, Rule, and Taylor (2013) reiterate the challenges graduate students face in navigating such hidden curriculum, noting that graduate students are often "piecing together through time a sense of how to 'do' reading, writing, collaborating, and professionalizing." Blurring these traditional curricular/extracurricular boundaries, Boquet et al. (2015) articulate a nascent programmatic approach in their concluding discussions of the ways that [extra-curricular] orientation workshops might introduce concepts to be reinforced in required [curricular] coursework.

Future Directions: Inclusive Frameworks for Understanding Engagement

While this case study uses courses as a lens, it serves to shed light on the relationships among various participants in the infrastructures for graduate writing engagement. In doing so, the responses to the survey of graduate writing demonstrate the complex curricular space in which courses operate. While calls for courses (Micciche & Carr, 2011; Rose & McClafferty, 2001; etc.) suggest, based on faculty or student experience, that courses will be a uniquely effective model of engagement for graduate writers, these calls often argue for the benefits of courses without acknowledging the constraints of time and credit that the respondents to this survey highlight. This time constraint, as described by respondents in this study, may lead to a consistent emphasis on the mentor/advisor as instructor model in departments that don't have identifiable writing courses. Such interplay between these various models suggests that the graduate education landscape is particularly ripe for innovative models that occupy spaces within and between the commonly adopted mentor/advisor model and the course model.

An important element of this data that might be further explored is the way that attitudes and perceptions also serve as part of an infrastructure for writing. In particular, further analysis of the narrative survey responses could not only describe how and where courses emerge in particular departments and disciplines, but also which configurations of activities emerge as a course for the program participants. Such data pertaining to a particular institution could be used to connect those on the same campus who are interested in further developing writing initiatives within their programs. Further, similar data would allow for future research on how effective different types of engagement are in supporting graduate writers. This might be paired with interviews such as those conducted by Henderson and Cook (this collection) to further explore students' experiences with the available models. Additionally, this method of investigation opens discussions of writing across the curriculum to find out what students and faculty believe to be the common ways that writing abilities are developed within their program or within their institution and where these perceptions align and diverge.

While similarities are important to note and explore, the contradictions and complexities of the data reported here suggest that to develop a comprehensive understanding of writing engagement, we need not just more survey data but also richer frameworks for understanding the infrastructures of graduate writing engagement. Such frameworks can help us include students as participants in our surveys in order to, for example, understand whether the configurations deemed by faculty or administrators to be explicit writing courses are experienced as such for students. Additionally, a more comprehensive framework will recognize that survey methods that don't account for the variation of experience at the graduate level may mask the everyday realities for many graduate students who may not have particular kinds of access to the courses that faculty and administrators designate as explicitly dedicated to writing development. Thus, we need a commitment to developing analytical frameworks for understanding ever-developing instructional models at the graduate level and for contextualizing our research about them.

References

Adams, L., Adams, M., Baird, P. F., Beck, E., Blair, K., Conway, A., Nickoson, L. & Schaffer, M. (2020). Crossing divides: Engaging extracurricular writing practices in graduate education and professionalization. In M. Brooks-Gillies, E. G. Garcia, S. H. Kim, K. Manthey & T. G. Smith (Eds.), *Graduate writing across the disciplines: Identifying, teaching, and supporting*. The WAC Clearinghouse; University Press of Colorado. https://wac.colostate.edu/books/atd/graduate.

Aranha, S. (2009). The development of a genre-based writing course for graduate students in two fields. In C. Bazerman, A., Bonini & D. Figueiredo (Eds.), *Genre in a changing world* (pp. 465–482). The WAC Clearinghouse; Parlor Press. https://wac.colostate.edu/books/perspectives/genre/.

Boquet, E., Kazer, M., Manister, N., Lucas, O., Shaw, M., Madaffari, V. & Gannett, C. (2015). Just care: Learning from and with graduate students in a Doctor of Nursing practice program. *Across the Disciplines, 12*. https://wac.colostate.edu/atd/special/graduate.

Bowker, G. C. & Star, S. L. (1999). *Sorting things out: Classification and its consequences.* Massachusetts Institute of Technology Press.

Brooks-Gillies, M., Garcia, E. G. & Manthey, K. (2020). Making do by making space: Graduate writing groups as spaces alongside programmatic and institutional places. In M. Brooks-Gillies, E. G. Garcia, S. H. Kim, K. Manthey & T. G. Smith (Eds.), *Graduate writing across the disciplines: Identifying, teaching, and supporting.* The WAC Clearinghouse; University Press of Colorado. https://wac.colostate.edu/books/atd/graduate.

Busl, G., Donnelly, K. L. & Capdevielle, M. (2020). Camping in the disciplines: Assessing the effect of writing camps on graduate student writers. In M. Brooks-Gillies, E. G. Garcia, S. H. Kim, K. Manthey & T. G. Smith (Eds.), *Graduate writing across the disciplines: Identifying, teaching, and supporting.* The WAC Clearinghouse; University Press of Colorado. https://wac.colostate.edu/books/atd/graduate.

Caplan, N. A. & Cox, M. (2016). The state of graduate communication support: Results of an international survey. In S. Simpson, N. A. Caplan, M. Cox & T. Phillips (Eds.), *Supporting graduate student writers: Research, curriculum, and program design* (pp. 22–51). University of Michigan Press.

Carr, A. D., Rule, H. J. & Taylor, K. T. (2013). Literacy in the raw: Collecting, sharing, and circulating graduate literacy narratives. *Computers and Composition Online.* http://cconlinejournal.org/winter2013/literacy_raw/index.html.

Delyser, D. (2003). Teaching graduate students to write: A seminar for thesis and dissertation writers. *Journal of Geography in Higher Education, 27*, 169–181.

Dobrin, S. I. (1993). Writing across the graduate curriculum. *Dialogue: A Journal for Writing Specialists, 1*(1), 65–77.

Fairbanks, K. & Dias, S. (2016). Going beyond L2 graduate writing: Redesigning an ESL program to meet the needs of both L2 and L1. In S. Simpson, N. A. Caplan, M. Cox & T. Phillips (Eds.), *Supporting graduate student writers: Research, curriculum, and program design* (pp. 22–51). University of Michigan Press.

Fredrick, T., Stravalli, K., May, S. & Brookman-Smith, J. (2020). The space between: MA students enculturate to graduate reading and writing. In M. Brooks-Gillies, E. G. Garcia, S. H. Kim, K. Manthey & T. G. Smith (Eds.), *Graduate writing across the disciplines: Identifying, teaching, and supporting.* The WAC Clearinghouse; University Press of Colorado. https://wac.colostate.edu/books/atd/graduate.

Fredericksen, E. & Mangelsdorf, K. (2014). Graduate writing workshops: Crossing languages and disciplines. In T. M. Zawacki & M. Cox (Eds.), *Writing across the curriculum and second language writers: Research toward linguistically and culturally inclusive programs and practices* (pp. 347–367). The WAC Clearinghouse; Parlor Press. https://wac.colostate.edu/books/perspectives/l2.

Frodesen, J. (1995). Negotiating the syllabus: A learning-centered, interactive approach to ESL graduate writing course design. In D. Belcher & G. Braine (Eds.), *Academic writing in a second language: Essays on research and pedagogy* (pp. 331–350), Ablex.

Gere, A. R. (1987). *Writing groups: History, theory, and implications.* Southern Illinois University Press.
Gillespie, P. (2007). Graduate writing consultants for Ph.D. programs. *Writing Lab Newsletter, 32*(2), 1–6.
Golding, A. & Mascaro, J. (1987). A survey of graduate writing courses. *Journal of Advanced Composition, 6*(1–2), 167–179.
Henderson, B. R. & Cook, P. G. (2020). Voicing graduate student writing experiences: A study of cross-level courses at two master's-level, regional institutions. In M. Brooks-Gillies, E. G. Garcia, S. H. Kim, K. Manthey & T. G. Smith (Eds.), *Graduate writing across the disciplines: Identifying, teaching, and supporting.* The WAC Clearinghouse; University Press of Colorado. https://wac.colostate.edu/books/atd/graduate.
Kim, S. & Wolke, S. (2020). Graduate writing groups: Helping L2 writers navigate the murky waters of academic writing. In M. Brooks-Gillies, E. G. Garcia, S. H. Kim, K. Manthey & T. G. Smith (Eds.), *Graduate writing across the disciplines: Identifying, teaching, and supporting.* The WAC Clearinghouse; University Press of Colorado. https://wac.colostate.edu/books/atd/graduate.
Mallett, K. E., Haan, J. & Habib, A. S. (2016). Graduate pathway programs as sites for strategic language-supported internationalization: Four pedagogical innovations. In S. Simpson, N.A. Caplan, M. Cox & T. Phillips (Eds.), *Supporting graduate student writers: Research, curriculum, and program design* (pp. 118–138). University of Michigan Press.
Micciche, L. & Carr, A. (2011). Toward graduate-level writing instruction. *College Composition and Communication, 62*(3), 477–501.
Miles, M., Huberman, M. & Saldana, J. (2013). *Qualitative data analysis: A methods sourcebook* (3rd ed.). Sage.
Mullen, C. A. (2001). The need for a curricular writing model for graduate students. *Journal of Further and Higher Education, 25*(2), 117–126.
Mullen, C. A. (2003). The WIT cohort: A case study of informal doctoral mentoring. *Journal of Further and Higher Education, 27*(4), 411–426.
Nolan, R. & Rocco, T. (2009). Teaching graduate students in the social sciences writing for publication. *Journal of Teaching and Learning in Higher Education, 20*(2), 267–273.
Norris, C. & Tardy, C. (2006). Institutional politics in the teaching of advanced academic writing: A teacher-research dialogue. In P. K. Matsuda, C. Ortmeier-Hooper & X. You (Eds.), *The politics of second language writing: In search of the promised land* (pp. 262–279). Parlor Press.
Phillips, T. (2016). Writing center support for graduate students: An integrated model. In S. Simpson, N. A. Caplan, M. Cox, and T. Phillips (Eds.), *Supporting graduate student writers: Research, curriculum, and program design* (pp. 159–170). University of Michigan Press.
Radner, S. (1961). Communications sequence on the graduate level. *College Composition and Communication, 12*(4), 225.
Rose, M. & McClafferty, K. A. (2001). A call for the teaching of writing in graduate education. *Educational Researcher, 30*(2), 27–33.
Segal, J., Pare, A., Brent, D. & Vipond, D. (1998). The researcher as missionary: Problems with rhetoric and reform in the disciplines. *College Composition and Communication 50(1)*, 71–90.

Street, C. & Stang, K. (2008). Improving the teaching of writing across the curriculum: A model for teaching in-service secondary education teachers to write. *Action in Teacher Education, 30*(1), 37–49.

Strong, W. (2003). Writing across the hidden curriculum. *The Quarterly, 25*(1). http://www.nwp.org/cs/public/print/resource/525.

Sullivan, P. & Porter, J. (1997). *Opening spaces: Writing technologies and critical research practices*. Ablex.

Appendix A: Survey Instrument

The following is a 15-minute survey intended to gather information on the existence of graduate-level writing courses and their role in graduate programs. Please respond to the questions below as they pertain to your current graduate program.

Your university:_____

Your department: _____

Your graduate program: _____

Your position in the program: (Check all that apply)
_____ Faculty _____ Staff _____ Master's student _____ Doctoral student
_____ Other (Please specify: _____)

1. What are the common ways that graduate students in your program develop their writing abilities?

2. Do students in your graduate program take any writing courses?

    _____ Yes (If yes, survey proceeds to #2) No (If, no or no reply, survey skips to #7.)

3. Please list the titles of any writing courses that graduate students in your program take.

4. Have you taught or taken any of the above listed courses?
    _____ Yes _____ No

5. Based on your knowledge or experience, what role do writing courses play in your program?

6. Questions A-M (below) populated the online survey in response to each course that was named by participants in Question #2. For example, if a participant listed "Science Writing" in response to Question #2, that participant would have received course-specific instructions: "Please answer the following questions in relationship to the 'Science Writing' course." If the participant did not list any course titles in response to Question #2, questions A-M would not have populated their survey.

A. What type of students is the course designed for?
   _____ master's _____ doctoral _____ postdoctoral _____ combination

B. Is the course required, recommended, or optional?
   _____ required _____ recommended _____ optional

C. What type of writing is emphasized? (Check all that apply.)
   _____ Writing for Publication
   _____ Writing Theses or Dissertations
   _____ Writing Grants or other Proposals
   _____ Other (Please describe:_____)

D. What is the primary course format?
   _____ Lectures/Discussion of Writing
   _____ Peer Reviews of Document Drafts
   _____ Both Reviews and Lectures/Discussion Equally
   _____ Other (Please describe: _____)

E. Do students receive feedback on their writing?
   _____ Y _____ N

If yes, what type(s) of feedback do students receive? (Check all that apply)
   _____ Instructor Comments Verbal
   _____ Instructor Comments Written
   _____ Peer Comments Verbal
   _____ Peer Comments Written
   _____ Other (Please describe: _____)

F. Who offers the course?
   _____ A university-wide writing program
   _____ Your home department
   _____ Another department (Please indicate, which one: _____)
   _____ A Professional Development Program
   _____ Other (Please describe: _____)

G. Who teaches the course?
   _____ Instructor from your home department
   _____ Instructor from another department
   _____ Other (Please describe:_____)

H. Number of students per course _____

I. Number of hours per session _____

J. Number of sessions per week _____

K. Number of weeks per course _____

L. Number of times the course is offered per year _____

M. Number of years the course has been offered _____

Please attach or provide a link for a sample syllabus or course description.

7. If students in your program do **not** participate in writing courses, please indicate the reasons they don't and whether you foresee a need for such courses. (This question was only given to those who responded to question #2 with "no" or no reply.)
8. If you would like to provide any additional information about writing in your graduate program, please do so here:

Appendix B: Departmental Responses by Respondent Position

	Faculty	Staff	Master's	Doctoral	Other	Total
Agronomy		1	1	1	1	4
Animal Sciences	2		1	1		4
Anthropology	6			3	1	10
Aviation Technology	1			1		2
Biochemistry	2					2
Biomedical Engineering				1		1
Botany and Plant Pathology	4			1		5
Chemical Engineering	2			11	1	14
Chemistry	7	1		7		15
Civil Engineering	4	1	8	5		18
Communication	3		3	11		17
Computer and Information Technology	1					1
Computer Graphics Technology	2		3			5
Computer Science	1					1
Consumer Sciences and Retailing	3			1		4
Curriculum & Instruction	3		1	10		14
Educational Studies	1		1	6		8
Engineering Education	3		1	9		13
English	17	5	20	3		45
Entomology	3		1	1		5
Food Science				3		3

	Faculty	Staff	Master's	Doctoral	Other	Total
Forestry and Natural Resources	1	4	3	5	1	14
History	1					1
Hospitality and Tourism Management			1	1		2
Human Development and Family Studies	4			4		8
Industrial Engineering	3			1		4
Industrial Technology	1	1		1		3
Interdisciplinary American Studies				2		2
Interdisciplinary Comparative Literature	1			3		4
Interdisciplinary Life Science				1		1
Interdisciplinary Linguistics				3		3
Interdisciplinary Philosophy and Literature		1		2		3
Materials Engineering				3		3
Mechanical Engineering	4	1	8	10		23
No Department Listed				1		1
Nuclear Engineering	1		2	5		8
Nutrition Science	1		1	7		9
Pharmacy Practice	1			1		2
Philosophy			1	3		4
Physics	1					1
Psychological Sciences	5			13		18
Sociology	2					2
Speech Language and Hearing Sciences	3		2	1		6
Statistics	2		7	2		11
Sustainability, Technology, and Innovation			1			1
Technology Leadership & Innovation	5	1	2			8
Veterinary Clinical Sciences	4	1	1	2		8
Visual and Performing Arts	1		1		1	3
Youth Development and Agricultural Education	1					1
						345

Voicing Graduate Student Writing Experiences: A Study of Cross-Level Courses at Two Master's-Level, Regional Institutions

Brian R. Henderson
SOUTHERN ILLINOIS UNIVERSITY EDWARDSVILLE

Paul G. Cook
INDIANA UNIVERSITY KOKOMO

Abstract: Much scholarly attention has been devoted to the study of writing, writing pedagogy, and writing curricula at the undergraduate level, but relatively few studies have taken into account the graduate student writing experience, particularly at the master's level. This is especially evident in the case of so-called "cross-level" courses—that is, courses with both undergraduate and graduate enrollments, which have become a fixture at many colleges and universities in the last decade. By means of recorded interviews with nine current or recent graduate students from Southern Illinois University Edwardsville and Indiana University Kokomo, this study seeks to add valuable data about (1) graduate student writing expectations in cross-level courses, (2) available institutional and pedagogical supports for graduate student writing, and (3) graduate students' experiences with writing pedagogy and training more broadly. Given the breadth and diversity of graduate student responses represented in this study, results emphasize themes that (1) involved the greatest number of graduate student voices and (2) offered the most provocative questions for scholars and teachers of graduate student writers. The study concludes with a call for a reconsideration of how we teach graduate writing and the role of cross-level courses in the master's curriculum.

Keywords: Writing Pedagogy, Graduate Writing Pedagogy, Regional Campuses, Branch Campuses, Cross-Level Courses, Dual-Listed Courses, Concurrent Courses, Qualitative Study

This qualitative study is underwritten by a simple premise: namely, that a significant gap exists between what graduate students know and what they are expected to know, particularly at regional, master's-granting institutions. Our goal in this project is to explore this premise as it relates to something we regard as vital—graduate writing pedagogy and, specifically, the preparedness of graduate students as *writers*.

DOI: https://doi.org/10.37514/ATD-B.2020.0407.2.02

We think this situation can be particularly problematic in regional, master's-granting institutions like Southern Illinois University Edwardsville (SIUE) and Indiana University Kokomo (IU Kokomo), where there may be a greater degree of isolation between students than occurs in traditional doctoral programs where students are more likely to work with each other and with faculty more extensively.

Despite the convenience of cross-level courses with both undergraduate- and masters-level students, particularly when it comes to staffing and other administrative expediencies, research in this area should not ignore the fact that the goals and needs of graduate students differ significantly from those of undergraduates. In short, we argue that although administrative convenience and efficiency should never take the place of pedagogical concerns—for example, we maintain that graduate student writers must be conceived of as pedagogically distinct from their undergraduate colleagues—the fact is that it often does. This chapter details these challenges and creates a space for graduate students' voices to be heard and analyzed.

Our particular focus involves an institutional innovation often called "cross-level" courses. Cross-level courses are ones that enroll undergraduate and graduate students simultaneously. As a point of reference, we examined the graduate policies and curricula of all eight of Southern Illinois University Edwardsville's (SIUE) peer institutions as determined by the Illinois Board of Higher Education and found that, though specific details varied, seven of them offer cross-level courses.[1] While this arrangement can be pedagogically productive and may help decrease time-to-graduation, it also poses unique challenges; this is especially true in the context of teaching and mentoring graduate student writers.

In our view, teaching writing at the graduate level should entail a complex, thoughtful negotiation between the mastery of disciplinary ways of knowing, on the one hand, and writing-focused pedagogical approaches tailored specifically for graduate students writing in their disciplines, on the other. A growing body of research calls attention to some of these challenges in connection to Ph.D.-level students (Bryant, 2009; Hoborek, 2002), the writing challenges of master's students more broadly (Casanave & Li, 2008), and the institutional infrastructures that can best engage graduate writers (Pinkert, this collection), but no one has focused exclusively on students in cross-level courses at the master's level.

Imagine a senior-level Advanced Composition course in creative nonfiction, for instance, that also offers graduate credit. This single class might enroll senior English majors for whom this course represents the culmination of their undergraduate writing experience, while simultaneously enrolling first-semester graduate students and students finishing thesis projects. Similarly, some students might be secondary teachers

---

1   These universities include East Tennessee State University, Grand Valley State University, Marshall University, Oakland University, University of Missouri-Kansas City, University of North Carolina at Greensboro, and University of South Alabama. Only Western Carolina University did not appear to offer such courses.

who want to teach dual-enrollment writing courses, while others might be graduate students on their way to Ph.D. programs. And while many cross-level courses are discipline-specific, we must not forget that quite a number of writing courses at this level are designed as interdisciplinary introductions to (or "refresher courses" for) scientific, technical, or some other non-discipline-specific writing conventions, strategies, and so forth. Given the unique ecology of the typical cross-level course, the clash between theoretical and pragmatic questions is a constant source of tension in the curriculum, course design, and assessment of graduate student writing. Add to that the way that different institutions historically carry contrasting assumptions regarding the goals of undergraduate versus graduate education—to take one example, that undergraduates should be trained more broadly while graduate students must learn how to specialize in and explore a topic or problem—and the difficult, often ill-fitting, role that such courses bear in the graduate curriculum becomes clearer.

Considering the broad array of purposes, histories, and unique institutional configurations of cross-level courses, we do not claim that our findings regarding graduate student writing experiences are representative of all cross-level courses or even of all regional institutions. Rather, our goal is to turn the focus from the economic and institutional needs that seem to drive the creation of such courses to a reflection on student-driven pedagogical needs. Specifically, our interview-based study calls attention to the challenges and assumptions that are inherent even in the most well-designed cross-level courses. By creating a space where graduate student writers can offer their own perspectives, this project highlights some of the most common themes that emerged among the fairly diverse population we interviewed. Ultimately, in this chapter, we are more interested in starting conversations about the pedagogical and curricular disconnects that we observed rather than in arguing for any particular solution—whether ours or theirs.

Cross-Level Courses or Cross Purposes?

Known variously as "dual-listed," "cross-level," or "concurrent" courses, a number of institutions of higher education have come to recognize the pedagogical and curricular challenges cross-level courses pose. For example, Pennsylvania State University, the University of Michigan, California State University at San Marcos (another regional campus), Marquette University, and Brandeis University have each developed specific policies and guidelines for creating, proposing, and evaluating cross-level courses, which includes any courses that concurrently offer credit to both graduate and undergraduate students. The guidelines vary, but they tend to coalesce around three main concerns: (1) that finding and maintaining the right balance is difficult in cross-level courses—that cross-levels have a tendency to become either de facto undergraduate- or graduate-level courses; (2) that rigor and an appropriate level of sophistication must be maintained simultaneously for both sets of students; and (3) that concerns over enrollment and resource allocation should not become an overriding factor in the development and approval of cross-level courses. At our own institutions, both of which are regional campuses with primarily master's-level graduate programs, cross-level courses have become a strategy for ensuring that courses "make" or meet enrollment requirements, on the one hand, and that graduate students have enough courses available to graduate in a timely manner, on the other. At SIUE, only specially-designated 400-level courses may be taken for graduate credit, and those courses are expected to include additional assignments and/or more rigorous evaluation of the students taking them for graduate credit. And for a course to be so designated, it must go through a review by both the Curriculum Council of the Faculty Senate and the Graduate Course Review Committee.

Similarly, at Indiana University (IU) Kokomo, instructors in the Master of Arts in Liberal Studies (MALS) program are directed to provide graduate students in cross-level courses with a separate syllabus that addresses multidisciplinary learning outcomes specific to the MALS program, and instructors are further required to give assignments that reflect these outcomes ("Constructing," n.d.). However, the abundance of such cross-level courses and the relative lack of research on graduate student writing relating to these types of courses suggest that, at least on an institutional level, graduate student writing is thought of more as a baseline standard that entering students are expected to meet rather than a process or a practice to which students are habituated as they learn how to write and think in their various disciplines. One way this plays out is in the familiar command to "write a paper" without always providing pedagogical attentiveness to what that might mean for master's students in particular disciplines (Hedgcock, 2008) or for how such expectations and processes might differ between graduate and undergraduate students in the same course.

So the guiding questions of this project are simple: How do we teach our graduate students to be graduate student *writers*, whatever that might mean or might come to mean in any given context, in the increasingly-common circumstance of the cross-level course framework? And how does this differ from the ways we teach undergraduate or graduate writing in traditional courses? To begin to address these questions, we will first examine the cross-level courses as they are currently configured in two representative institutions.

Rise of the Regionals: Southern Illinois University Edwardsville (SIUE) and Indiana University Kokomo (IU Kokomo)

Together, we represent two regional campuses. Brian teaches at SIUE, a regional comprehensive campus in the Southern Illinois University (SIU) system. Paul teaches at IU Kokomo, a regional campus of Indiana University (IU). These campuses share a few interesting similarities. First, both schools emerged as regional campuses of large, flagship Midwestern state schools; second, each institution offers a range of master's and professional degrees in everything from nursing, education, and business administration to liberal studies and English; and third, both universities regularly rely on cross-level courses.

A relatively young university, SIUE opened its doors in 1957 in order to fulfill the increased need for college-educated employees in Illinois' second most populated region. Over the decades, SIUE has grown to become a premier Metropolitan University (currently with an M1 Carnegie classification) serving the Metro-East area of greater St. Louis and offering a variety of undergraduate, graduate, and professional degrees to roughly 14,000 students. Economically, it is one of the largest employers in the region, and over the last decade, it has transformed itself into a traditional residential campus while continuing to serve a large number of commuter and transfer students.

With just over 3,000 students, IU Kokomo is significantly smaller than SIUE, though as a regional commuter campus it serves a similar function ("IU Kokomo," 2013). IU Kokomo opened its doors in 1932 as "Kokomo Junior College." Today, it serves a fourteen-county area in north central Indiana, a region whose economy has historically depended almost exclusively on agriculture and automobile manufacturing. Within the last decade or so, as the automotive industry has gradually lost its sacrosanct status as the region's primary economic driver, residents have turned to higher education; as a result of these and other factors, IU Kokomo has seen an unprecedented enrollment boom in recent years (Rush, 2009).

In general, master's-granting institutions are enjoying something of an enrollment renaissance across the United States, with an increase of 6.1% in graduate applications between Fall 2006 and Fall 2011, according to the Council of Graduate Schools (Allum, Bell & Sowell, 2012). According to the National Center for Education Statistics (n.d.), the total number of master's degrees conferred yearly has increased from 463,185 in 1999 to 693,025 in 2009. As students have acclimated their educational priorities to the new economic realities of the decade, studying closer to home; saving on gas, food, and rent; and earning a degree from a nationally-recognized, accredited university have made regionals an attractive option for both undergraduates and graduate students. The increased number of accelerated master's degrees and graduate certificate options has played an important role in this trend as well.

In the last fifteen years, the branch campuses of Purdue University and Indiana University (of which IU Kokomo is a part) have benefited significantly from the establishment of Ivy Tech, a statewide community college system in which students can earn inexpensive associate degrees and then transfer to any four-year institution in the state ("Enrollment Soars," 2001). This growth in higher education in Indiana has fueled enrollments at both the undergraduate and graduate levels.

Similarly, SIUE has seen record numbers of undergraduates in recent years, even as other universities in the state are suffering from decreased enrollments at the undergraduate level. And SIUE continues to position itself as a regional source for a wide variety of graduate and professional degrees. In terms of the larger landscape of higher education in Illinois, public universities continue to make a strong showing in master's programs even in the face of budgetary challenges at the state level. According to the Databook on Illinois Higher Education (http://www.ibhe.org/), for example, in fiscal year 2016–17, public universities in Illinois granted a total of 14,081 master's degrees, an increase of 11.5% from fiscal year 2012–13, even with the two-year budget stalemate, which ended in 2017.

For these and other reasons, regional campuses are ripe for scholarly exploration, and our decision to interview master's-level graduate students at these institutions stems from our observation of a trend towards using cross-level courses as an administrative "shortcut." For instance, if a given graduate program is thought to have too few students to justify a full slate of graduate-only course offerings, cross-level courses are a convenient cost-saving measure: Rather than fill a graduate-only course with three or four students, a cross-level course with six or seven undergraduates and the same three or four graduate students seems much more palatable to administrators for purely economic reasons. Since master's-level programs at regional institutions like SIUE and IU Kokomo are more likely than flagship research universities to have fewer graduate students, cross-leveling graduate course offerings has become a pervasive practice, and, in some instances, as much as half of all coursework may consist of such cross-level classes.

Second, we were intrigued by the lack of available literature that specifically examines master's-level students in higher education. In rhetoric and composition studies, for example, there is no shortage of literature geared towards helping students write theses, dissertations, article manuscripts, application letters, etc. (Aitchison, Kamler & Lee, 2010; Clark, 2006; González, 2007; Nielsen & Rocco, 2002; Rudestam & Newton, 2007; Swales & Feak, 2012), but very little of this material has examined the cross-level phenomenon we propose to study in this chapter, particularly as it relates to students who do not plan to pursue a Ph.D.

Methods

After receiving approval for the study by the Institutional Review Boards at both SIUE and IU Kokomo, we began collecting data during the summer of 2013. Participants were recruited in two ways: (1) through a formal "call for participants" sent out via email to students in SIUE's and IU Kokomo's MALS, MBA, MA, and other graduate programs and (2) through more informal channels, such as contacts with alumni who expressed interest in participating in the interview process. Of the nine study participants, seven were female and two were male, and all were assigned gender-specific pseudonyms. All interviews were recorded using a digital audio recording device; they were then uploaded to password-protected cloud data storage to ensure privacy. To qualify for the study, participants had to be current or former graduate students at SIUE or IU Kokomo, and they had to have taken one or more cross-level courses before the summer of 2013. Four participants were current or former students at SIUE; five were current or former students at IU Kokomo.

Other than two interviews conducted by phone, all interviews took place either on the campus of SIUE or IU Kokomo. Each participant took part in a single open-ended interview that lasted on average between 20 and 35 minutes, and all were provided with a copy of the planned interview questions in advance to help them prepare, as some participants drew on cross-level course experiences that were several years old. Once all interviews were completed and transcribed, we analyzed the data qualitatively, focusing on patterns of response that could offer unique pedagogical, disciplinary, or institutional insights about the teaching and learning of writing from the graduate student perspective. In total, we interviewed nine participants from seven different degree programs: MALS, Master of Public Management, and Master of Science in Nursing Administration from IU Kokomo, and Master of Arts in English, specializing in either Teaching of Writing or Teaching English as a Second Language, Master of Science in Civil Engineering, and Post-Baccalaureate Certificate in English, specializing in Teaching of Writing from SIUE.

We consider our study to be both descriptive and exploratory. It is descriptive in the sense that one of our primary methodological goals is to provide a sample of student descriptions *in their own words* of their experiences with writing and writing instruction, primarily in terms of specific pedagogical practices and implications. The questions were open-ended and emphasized cross-level coursework experiences, although they allowed room for students to discuss other graduate (and even undergraduate) experiences. (See Appendix A for our list of questions.)

We also consider our methodology to be exploratory: Besides our initial questions, we did not attempt to impose artificial parameters on our participants' responses. Rather, we decided to allow them to follow out their own narrative itineraries more or less at will. So if a response meandered over to another topic or blurred into another line of questioning, we did not attempt to stop or limit the response. Although we certainly framed the initial questions, we wanted our findings to emerge from the graduate student experiences and perspectives to the fullest extent possible. (See Appendix B for a detailed breakdown of study participants in terms of institution, participant's pseudonym, and specific degree program.)

Discussion

The results of this study suggest that our two initial premises were correct. First, respondents persistently noted gaps between what they knew and what they felt they were expected to know as graduate student writers. Second, respondents described various ways in which the goals and needs of graduate students conflicted with the goals and needs of undergraduate writers in the cross-level course format. As to the latter, we wish to make it clear that respondents tended to see value in such courses—however, that value was seen primarily as one that benefited undergraduates, pedagogically speaking. (As a credentialing practice, it may well have been appreciated by graduate students seeking timely graduation.) One finding we did not expect was the perceived lack of mentoring or sufficient feedback on writing reported by respondents. In order to better explore the pedagogical and curricular implications, we framed our discussion around two key themes relevant to graduate education more broadly but seemingly intensified in the context of cross-level courses: (1) the ambiguous nature of graduate student writing expectations and (2) the performance of graduate student identity.

Ambiguities and Contradictions: What "Counts" as Graduate Student Writing?

Across disciplines, all interviewees agreed that graduate student writing should be different from that of undergraduates. But when it came to the site of the cross-level course itself, a host of vagaries, miscues, and contradictions emerged. The most fruitful comments in this regard appeared in answer to the question of whether they were ever explicitly told what to expect or what "counts" as graduate student writing. Students who answered this question in the affirmative inevitably linked their answer to a particular (non-cross-level) course that operated along the lines of an introduction to graduate studies, and, in fact, those students were notably silent about such explicit discussion when it came to other courses. On the other hand, other students offered comments to the effect that in some important ways, they never felt they adequately understood what it meant to be a graduate student writer, even after they had successfully completed their degrees. Of course, even the students with less confidence in themselves as graduate student writers had to develop strategies that they used to navigate their various courses. Student self-expectations, and even self-doubt, seemed to play a primary role in their perception of themselves as writers, suggesting that the pedagogical and curricular disconnects noted across the interviews have much to do with the unarticulated expectations from graduate faculty in both cross-level and graduate-only courses.

When we asked participants to what extent they were explicitly told what counts as graduate student writing, the majority of responses we received included answers like Angela's "probably never" or Neal's "it's not really talked about—it's understood." Amy said, "I would honestly say not at all. I think it has been assumed that we applied [to the graduate program] and therefore we can do it." Later, Amy reiterated the point, "There was no higher instruction—'this is what you'll do the whole time you are a graduate student,' 'this is what is expected.' You start with the class and then you do each assignment." Similarly, Angela stated, "I don't recall that any of the . . . instructors in the graduate courses said as an example, 'here's what one looks like, here's what a scholarly paper looks like and should be.'" In Tracy's experience, "Only one professor took the time to share that with us." Interestingly, Cynthia, who said she was told "very clearly" that graduate work carried high expectations, had great difficulty articulating any specific expectations and ended up focusing on APA style and the length of the assigned papers (rather than any kind of disciplinary knowledge, methodological approach, scholarly tone, etc.). She went on to say that the "largest stumbling block" for new master's students in her field (Nursing) was APA and she thought all such students should take "an APA class," which suggests that, for her, APA style is an external set of stylistic markers one "adds" to a paper rather than an academic style imbricated within certain kinds of disciplinary thinking.

Debbie stated that she was not told what counts as graduate student writing "overall," but that the instructor of her cross-level course "was very helpful to tell us what she expected for this graduate paper for this particular class." Danny offered an answer that pointed to a common strategy for figuring out what graduate student writing should do:

> There was a set of requirements that you'd have to have this, this, this, and this, had to be a certain style, had to have all the proper citations. . . . But it was mostly, in my experience, . . . write the paper, get the feedback from the instructor, and correct that the next time around—you know, iteratively getting better each time you did it.

On the other hand, those who were given explicit expectations for their graduate work seemed to have taken either a specific graduate-level writing class, as Beth did, or an introduction to graduate studies course, like Nancy. Nancy probably gave the clearest example of what graduate student writers should be able to do when she said, "The expectation of graduate-level writing was that it could be presented at a conference." Then she elaborated as follows in her attempt to distinguish graduate from undergraduate writing expectations:

> There was a higher expectation for grad students, but these were not as clearly outlined, but professors expected higher caliber

> [work]. . . . I thought they did a good job in communicating to us the expectations for the program, the caliber of work that we would be doing, and those sorts of things. I would say that as a teacher of undergraduates, we do a better job providing written material to undergraduates about what is expected in terms of outcomes. . . . When I was there, it seemed like there was a greater expectation that we learn about the discourse community, but there was not explicit instruction beyond MLA style.

Beth also described a particular course that helped prepare her for graduate writing, but she described it more as a course designed to "weed out" un(der)prepared students rather than teach them to be effective graduate student writers as such:

> Coming into the graduate program, we had the introductory writing class . . . or the introductory class to the Master's in Liberal Studies class, and in that class we were given a lot of . . . specific instructions about what our writing was supposed to be, and we were pushed to the max on that as well, that was hardcore, it was make it or break it moment, so, it was definitely "this is what you should be doing at the graduate level."

Neal had a different experience in that he was not told explicit expectations for graduate writing, which he suggested might account for the inconsistent understanding that graduate students seemed to have about writing expectations. However, rather than pointing to a gap in disciplinary or genre knowledge or to confusion regarding MLA or APA style, Neal locates the problem in terms of what might be called an unsuccessful "professional" ethos. Specifically, he points to a lack of appropriate editorial care:

> It seems to me like some students don't realize the level of professionalism that is expected. With the team project I worked on, it didn't seem that some of the other students took notice of the high standards that were expected. Some of them didn't go back and make sure that every "i" was dotted and every "t" was crossed per se. I guess part of it might be, like what I said before, [faculty] don't really come out and say [what the expectations are]. They just expect you to know that, hey, you are a graduate student now and a lot more will be expected of you.

Indeed, few of us receive much explicit guidance on what it means to "be" a graduate student professional. Rather, we tend to pick up on these cues to varying degrees as part of our graduate training. In the next section, we explore the connections between graduate writing pedagogy, curricular expectations, and our students' burgeoning identities as graduate-level scholars and learners.

Shoring up Identities: Struggling to Distinguish Graduate Expectations

Throughout the interviews, participants provided responses that suggest the importance of developing and maintaining their identities as "authentic" or fully-professionalized graduate students, an emergent theme in the research that has been noted in two recent studies (Phillips, Shovlin & Titus, 2016).[2] This theme was most noticeable in our research when students provided responses in three broad, interrelated areas: (1) when detailing their expectations of how their graduate coursework would be more professionalized and their matter-of-fact assumptions about the increased rigor of graduate-level coursework; (2) when expressing the need for a greater emphasis on drafting and revising practical documents related to the job search (CVs, cover letters, course syllabi, and even emails); and (3) when hoping for (and at times even longing for) a course that focuses on the specifics of developing a scholarly writing style and demystifies documentation formats (APA, MLA, Chicago, and so forth).

Angela, a master's student whose program was Teaching English as a Second Language (TESL) at SIUE, compares her expectations of graduate-level coursework to her undergraduate experiences: "I would say that there is more of an applied expectation . . . that you are able to read this . . . article from a journal and extract some information and kind of analyze it or criticize it or use it, try to interpret it and how it would be used in particular contexts, specifically since my classes were teaching classes." She then links her discussion almost immediately back to her *personal* perception of "standards." Discussing her "Senior Assignment" experience, she distinguishes her project regarding "religious syncretism in a particular group of indigenous people from Mexico" from the projects of fellow students who wrote on topics like Salsa dancing.

Her point wasn't to critique her classmates so much as to demonstrate the way that personal expectations significantly affected the kind of writing that was produced. She then moves back to a discussion of graduate student writing: "You can start with a question and . . . come to a new idea as long as you [support] it with other people's ideas, you can make connections. And I think that does happen on some level in undergraduate work, but I think it's more supported and desired . . . in graduate work."

---

2   For more on the unique challenges facing L2 graduate students in adapting the identity of graduate writers, see Jennifer Douglas (this collection).

Here, Angela struggles to come up with concrete examples of precisely how her graduate-level work compares to her undergraduate projects; it's almost as if she knows there is a difference, and certainly she implicitly recognizes that there is *supposed* to be a significant difference, but she has difficulty articulating what some of these differences might be.

Compare Angela's passage above to Tracy's response to a similar question about her expectations of graduate-level coursework before beginning her Master of Public Management (MPM) degree at IU Kokomo:

> So my expectation of grad school was that things were going to be higher and harder than undergrad. . . . I had a lot of reticence about my abilities. Okay. So, when I got there, I discovered there is a higher expectation, the material is deeper, in that there's a lot more material to cover in such a short time, and the critical reviews and analysis, and instruction is just deeper, okay, than undergrad. . . . So the rigor of grad school is so much higher than undergrad. Unless you have done your research or been told about it, then you may be in for a little shock. . . . I read a few things . . . and noticed the fine difference between the works, you know, and I'm quite sure . . . well, I can't assume, I don't want to assume that doctoral-level work is that much different from grad school-level because I don't want it to be that much harder if I decided to go!

She then attempts to concretize her perceived expectations about graduate writing. In the process she says graduate writing must be succinct, must "connect the dots," and must be "cogent and coherent." But she moves back to more ambiguous language by asserting that "your whole structure has to be, just simply, a higher level." She then states that her key term for this kind of writing is "analysis." Ultimately, she claims that the ability to analyze means "the difference between an 'A' and a 'C'" in graduate classes. But, as she continues her line of thought, the difference between students and professors is knowledge of "their material." And writing plays a key role in that because it is through assessing graduate student writing that professors use their knowledge of "material" to distinguish students who are "parroting something" from those who demonstrate "real creative thought on a subject . . . not *repeating* something verbatim, but you know, really putting some thought into it."

Danny's response to the same question indicates a similar dynamic at work in terms of how graduate students perceive the professionalization process vis-à-vis writing projects and curricular rigor, as well as how they feel about their preparedness and their general resolve to embark on a graduate program:

> Upon entering the graduate program that I am pursuing [the Master of Arts in Liberal Studies program at IU Kokomo], I had no idea of what a scholarly paper was. Now I had seen papers in journals and stuff like that before, but I had not linked the term to that. So I had had some experience of what a journal article would look like, but I had no idea what was expected [of] me. You know, I was walking into this blind and I had made up my mind that, hey, I'm going to tackle this all the way through.

Even when one recent graduate of the Master of Arts in Liberal Studies (MALS) program at IU Kokomo admitted that she felt the coursework lacked rigor overall, she was careful to note that she *expected* that the program would be more challenging than her undergraduate coursework: "If I'm being honest, I really thought [the program and "the writing portion"] was going to be a bit more rigorous. . . . In addition to my bachelor's in English I have a writing minor, so maybe it wasn't a challenge for me because I do have that . . . experience in writing. . . . I never stopped writing after I was teaching." The one exception to her critique of writing in her coursework was her introduction to graduate studies class, which she said "kicked my butt." Other than that, her courses generally and writing assignments in particular were "like smooth sailing." She wasn't simply commenting that the writing was not difficult, but that it *should* have been and the lack of rigor was "very frustrating" to her. She attributes this in large part to the cross-level courses she took. She says, "I wish the content courses, the cross-level courses that we're talking about here specifically, I wish that it had been less teaching the undergrads and more learning myself. Um, and through the writing I wanted to do that." But her comments were more ambivalent when she began discussing her thesis:

> I'm [teaching full-time] at a community college now, so I'm not expected to do the, the research element that you would at a university, but that's something that I still am very interested in. Um, when it came to write my thesis, that's when I got that rigor back again, that's when I got that hardcore, but it was a topic that . . . my committee didn't really know about. So, it was new, it was something that they hadn't really heard about, so it was teaching them at the same time I was writing. So it wasn't as rigorous as I expected it to be in that aspect of the thesis writing, but um that was okay, that was okay, because . . . it was a learning process, and it was time-consuming, and it was crazy and chaotic.

Shoring up Identities: Graduate Students as Professionals

Since it is reasonable to assume that students who pursue advanced higher education do tend to be more ambitious on the whole, it's not exactly surprising that these students seemed to approach their graduate studies with an attitude similar to Danny's: "I'm going to tackle this all the way through." This attitude is also evident in some of the students' remarks concerning their drive and ambition, as well as their general readiness to downplay challenges or setbacks. For example, Tracy remarks at one point that she "might cheat a little bit" in answering a question about a time that she felt unprepared to successfully complete a writing project, because she has "too much experience in making something out of nothing." She later draws upon her career experiences in non-profit radio broadcasting to indicate how that experience had prepared her for certain kinds of writing at the graduate level. Neal makes a similar move when he comments on the way his professional experience made him aware of two distinct audiences that engineers typically need to learn how to address in their academic programs. Danny remarks that he was never assigned something that he didn't feel prepared to do, because "having chosen to do this program, you know, I'm going to do whatever I'm asked to do, because it's a learning experience." We think it significant that their confidence in their abilities doesn't seem to translate into a laissez-faire attitude regarding professionalization in their graduate curriculum, particularly professionalization as achieved through improved writing abilities. In other words, graduate students on the whole may be a confident and ambitious lot, but for all that, they have a keen appreciation for being shown the ropes, for learning the "basics" of writing for graduate studies. They sense that it is different—that it is supposed to be different—and this seems to leave them with a craving for a more explicit articulation of these differences in order to shore up their identities as graduate students and as burgeoning professionals.

Almost across the board, students wanted more explicit instruction in writing professional documents for graduate studies, whether these were job search-related or research/publication-related. Beth, for instance, concluded her interview with a sort of plea for more graduate courses with an explicit focus on writing:

> We did call for more writing classes. We did want more writing courses. Um, I had to take one course that I had taken as an undergrad, and it was really bad as an undergrad and it was really bad as a graduate. And it was really frustrating for me . . . um, I wish there were more options [for writing courses]. . . . And it was very frustrating because I had to take it again as a graduate student, and . . . it was really bad the second time around. Every

aspect of it was really bad; we had several graduate students who dropped from that course.

Even so, she wished "there had been more options for graduate students that were writing focused." So the prevalence of cross-level courses and the role that graduate students were expected to take in such courses as "teachers" was seen as a significant barrier in her attempt to "master" graduate writing. And we see this as implicitly related to the prevalence of cross-level courses in her program of study. Interestingly, this respondent expressed a desire for any non-cross-level graduate-level writing courses, covering anything from rhetoric to creative writing. Her strongest interest was in what she called graduate "research writing courses." She says that not only were graduate students "expected to do that" but also, she wanted to publish. And while she identified herself as "an English person" with a love of literature, she wanted graduate courses that helped her focus more on writing. In part this had to do with her profession as a community college teacher of writing. For example, she says, "I am confident in my teaching, I do teach the entry-level classes [in writing], but I would've liked to have more experience with [writing] in my graduate-level courses."

Professionalization matters for Nancy, too. She articulates the importance to her career as a community college teacher of being shown how to draft a conference proposal. She gives the example of colleagues "who have gone on to do Ph.D. work [and] brought back information about how to write proposals—for CCCC [Conference on College Composition and Communication] and that sort of thing." Then she says, "If it is the goal of graduate school to do research and writing and presentations and published papers then we can do like we do with our undergraduates and explain our expectations." She then suggests a graduate course or workshop that orients students to professional organizations like CCCC and MLA (Modern Language Association) as well as their expectations regarding conference proposals.

For Neal, who is pursuing a Master of Science degree in Engineering at SIUE, "sound[ing] professional" is key, but developing this professionalization remains largely implicit: "As far as the engineering classes go, it's not really talked about. It's understood." Neal thinks that "more could be expected of [graduate students]" in terms of writing, and he explicitly notes a desire for more instruction in writing his thesis, although he describes himself as a "pretty decent" writer. Through his example of email, he suggests the broader importance of rhetorical training for graduate students and professionals:

> I guess a good example is email etiquette. I didn't really use email in my undergraduate career because I lived on campus and I would usually just go talk to [my instructors]. But in my career, obviously email is a big part of our business and therefore I was

> able to learn a lot from the professional engineers I work under about what you are supposed to say in an email and what you are not. For example, if we are trying to sell a product or trying to give some information, we may not want to give all of our information at one time because we may not want the person [to whom] we are giving the information to share it with our competitors with whom they might have a relationship. [I also learned] email etiquette, knowing how to express yourself in an email so that you do not come across as brash or aggressive.

Amy also highlights the need for explicit instruction in some rather specific genres and styles. Like other respondents she wants more explicit focus on scholarly writing; she wanted to know: "not just the form but how to write a research project, not that it has to have an abstract or annotated bibliography or whatever it may be, *but actually how to write for a research project*. That was far more technical than anything I had ever written before" (emphasis added). But she adds another genre to the mix. She specifically mentions the importance of learning "how to design a syllabus" and says, "I think . . . more time [should be] spent on the language of writing these documents."

Cynthia and Debbie, both second-year students in the Master of Nursing Administration program at IU Kokomo, expressed a similar need for explicit instruction in specific genres and documentation and style guides that they feel their program has lacked. Interestingly, whereas this instruction was lacking in their coursework, both students found the Writing Center tutors to be a significant help. Cynthia describes a recent paper "where the APA [was] really stressed and really counted" and her feeling that she was unprepared "to just sit down and be able put it all in the computer and get it to come out right. So I spent three days in the Writing Lab," which she described as a "wonderful" resource. Debbie, though, offers a somewhat more candid assessment:

> I really felt lost when I started at IUPUI [Indiana University–Purdue University Indianapolis], it was like, "well I'll turn this in and see how it works." And you know, I don't like feeling that way. . . . There's this one gal that I did this paper with, she said, "here, I don't know how to do APA format, here you take this to [the Writing Center] and make sure it's okay." But . . . if I'm going to write something, then I want to know why I'm doing what I'm doing. To me [using APA] seems like an exercise in stupidity. And I know that you have to reference stuff, but gosh, you know, and there's so many different formats out there to reference things in. . . . I want things, when I look at them, or when somebody explains them, . . . to make sense, in order for

it to not be a barrier. And I think that's part of the problem, no matter what I look at—no matter what I purchase or what I look at—it's still confusing to me. . . . And until I have a better understanding, it's going to be a barrier to writing papers.

Taken together, these passages suggest that graduate students in these programs are receiving messages—from professors, other students, even perhaps the larger culture—that the expectations for writing in graduate studies will be higher, more intense, and more challenging and "professional." But these messages tend to be blurry and vague. When it comes to explicit instruction in writing, whether specific genres or even scholarly research papers, students feel that they should receive more explicit instruction—through a required course or in their subject-matter coursework—in how to write at the graduate level. The process that emerges from these interviews is one of continuously groping towards an unclear target: Students implicitly know that "something else" will be expected of them as graduate student writers; what that is, however, too often remains unclear.

Conclusion

A crucial assumption we bring to this study, and one generally responsible for all the institutional policies that have emerged regarding cross-level courses, is that undergraduate pedagogy is and should be different in some fundamental ways from graduate pedagogy. The first and most far-reaching implication of this study is that cross-level courses writ large should be given careful reconsideration at both the pedagogical and institutional level. In a variety of ways, respondents indicated that cross-level courses are not always effective environments for graduate student pedagogy. For example, even in cases where there was undoubtedly more work required of graduate students, which was not always the interviewee experience, it was unclear the degree to which such assignments typically differed from undergraduate assignments in purpose or in evaluative criteria. For example, does adding ten pages inherently transform an undergraduate assignment into graduate-level work? Does the addition of "research" to a reflection automatically constitute a scholarly genre? Similarly, interview subjects often commented on the limitations that undergraduates inherently brought into both the scope and style of class discussion, even more so when students from different fields were taking the course as an elective. In fact, it was notable that while some interview subjects spoke extremely favorably of various cross-level courses, the majority of positive comments regarding cross-level courses were framed around the benefits of such courses for undergraduates.

So at the level of class discussion and in terms of writing assignments, respondents offered comments that suggested cross-level courses as they are commonly conceived may not adequately respond to graduate student pedagogical needs. In fact, this perceived conflict in pedagogical goals may be impossible to avoid in the confines of the traditional course. If this is the case, then institutions interested in building or maintaining effective master's-level programs should consider ways to frame cross-level courses that include assignment sequences and readings typical of other graduate course offerings, but they should also be aware that due to their pedagogically-conflicted design, cross-level courses may not be as amenable to graduate pedagogy as their prevalence suggests, such as when the only tangible distinction from an undergraduate course is an additional assignment or an individual's (or an institutional policy's) often vague notion of rigor. More explicitly, faculty (and programs) should carefully consider the ways that writing gets taught (not merely assigned) in cross-level courses. It leaves us with a provocative question: Are cross-level courses primarily the result of, and hence driven by, economic/logistical factors or disciplinary/pedagogical ones?

The second implication suggested by our study is that graduate students across disciplines would like more explicit discussion about the process of becoming a scholar/professional writer in their different fields. Some reported anxieties at the point of coursework in terms of specific academic genres or conventions; others commented on the gap they saw in their graduate studies in terms of preparing them to publish or present at academic conferences. Of course, not everyone reported this experience. The primary difference between students who expressed anxiety about their writing and those who did not seemed to center on the degree to which students perceived they had been told explicitly what was expected of their writing. Further, the students who knew what was expected also had something else in common—a graduate writing course or an introduction to graduate studies seminar. As potentially useful as such a course might be, such arrangements do carry the potential to lead graduate students (and others) to the conclusion that writing can be taught and "inoculated" in a single course. Anyone familiar with WAC/WID research or writing studies in general will readily recognize the dubiousness of this claim.

But the other component of the discussion about how students learn to become scholars and professionals centers on the role of feedback and mentorship.[3] We were surprised in particular at how often subjects noted a lack of feedback from faculty on major writing projects. And one respondent stands out for his comment that no writing was required in one of his cross-level courses. This is doubly troublesome because students across the board implicitly described how they became successful graduate student writers in terms of a process. It is encouraging to note that some researchers have begun to investigate ways that faculty can productively mentor

---

3 For an interesting take on the role of mentoring in extracurricular writing, see Adams et al.'s chapter in this collection.

graduate students in discipline-specific genres (Eriksson & Makitalo, 2015). In our study, more than one participant discussed the role of instructor feedback, both written and spoken, as a key means for calibrating themselves to what was expected of them as writers and presenters. If it is indeed the case that successful scholarship and professional writing emerge via an iterative process rather than from, say, an attribute students supposedly already possess upon acceptance to a program, then faculty feedback is a crucial part of the graduate student socializing process. Taken together, these implications both point to the need for more focused institutional and pedagogical reflection about (1) how we teach writing at the master's level and (2) how and why we offer cross-level courses in our various programs.

References

Adams, L., Adams, M., Beck, E., Blair, K., Conway, A., Schaffer, M. & Nickoson, L. (2020). Crossing divides: Engaging extracurricular writing practices in graduate education and professionalization. In M. Brooks-Gillies, E. G. Garcia, S. H. Kim, K. Manthey & T. G. Smith (Eds.), *Graduate writing across the disciplines: Identifying, teaching, and supporting*. The WAC Clearinghouse; University Press of Colorado. https://wac.colostate.edu/books/atd/graduate.

Aitchison, C., Kamler, B. & Lee, A. (Eds.). (2010). *Publishing pedagogies for the doctorate and beyond*. Routledge.

Allum, J., Bell, N. & Sowell, R. (2012). *Graduate enrollment and degrees: 2001–2011*. https://cgsnet.org/graduate-enrollment-and-degrees-2001-2011.

Bryant, M. (2009). Graduate mentoring: A poetics. In M. Rothberg & P. K. Garrett (Eds.), *Cary Nelson and the struggle for the university: Poetry, politics, and the profession* (pp. 187–192). State University of New York Press.

Casanave, C. P. & Li, X. (Eds.). (2008). *Learning the literacy practices of graduate school: Insider's reflections on academic enculturation*. University of Michigan Press.

Clark, I. L. (2006). *Writing the successful thesis and dissertation: Entering the conversation*. Upper Saddle River, NJ: Prentice Hall.

Constructing a graduate course. (n.d.). *Indiana University Kokomo*. Retrieved October 17, 2018 from http://www.IUKokomo.edu/academics/majors/liberal-studies/graduate-program/.

Databook on Illinois Higher Education. (n.d.). Retrieved October 17, 2018 from http://www.ibhe.org/.

Douglas, J. (2020). Developing an English for Academic Purposes course for L2 graduate students in the sciences. In M. Brooks-Gillies, E. G. Garcia, S. H. Kim, K. Manthey & T. G. Smith (Eds.), *Graduate writing across the disciplines: Identifying, teaching, and supporting*. The WAC Clearinghouse; University Press of Colorado. https://wac.colostate.edu/books/atd/graduate.

Enrollment soars at Indiana's new community college campuses. (2001, October 15). *Community college week*. http://www.thefreelibrary.com/Enrollment+Soars+at+Indiana%27s+New+Community+College+Campuses.-a079514214.

Eriksson, A. & Makitalo, A. (2015). Supervision at the outline stage: Introducing and encountering issues of sustainable development through academic writing assignments. *Text & Talk, 35*(2), 123–153. https://doi.org/10.1515/text-2014-0032.

González, A. M. (2007). *Shaping the thesis and dissertation: Case studies of writers across the curriculum* [Doctoral dissertation, Texas Christian University]. ProQuest Dissertations & Theses Global (3278278).

Hedgcock, J. S. (2008). Lessons I must have missed: Implicit literacy practices in graduate education. In C. P. Casanave & X. Li (Eds.), *Learning the literacy practices of graduate school: Insider's reflections on academic enculturation* (pp. 32–45). University of Michigan Press.

Hoborek, A. (2002). Professionalism: What graduate students need. *Symploke, 10,* 52–70.

IU Kokomo enrollment hits highest numbers in 68-year history. (2013, August 16). *Indiana University Kokomo.* http://newsroom.IUKokomo.edu/campus/17-campus-news/578-iu-Kokomo-enrollment-hits-highest-numbers-in-68-year-history.html.

National Center for Education Statistics. (n.d.). Retrieved January 21, 2020 from https://nces.ed.gov.

Nielsen, S. M. & Rocco, T. S. (2002, May). *Joining the conversation: Graduate students' perceptions of writing for publication.* Paper presented at the annual meeting of the Adult Education Research Conference, Raleigh, NC.

Phillips, T., Shovlin, P. & Titus, M. L. (2016). (Re)Identifying the WPA experience. *Journal of the Council of Writing Program Administrators, 40*(1), 67–89.

Pinkert, L. A. (2020). Snapshots, frameworks, and infrastructures: A Survey of graduate writing. In M. Brooks-Gillies, E. G. Garcia, S. H. Kim, K. Manthey & T. G. Smith (Eds.), *Graduate writing across the disciplines: Identifying, teaching, and supporting.* The WAC Clearinghouse; University Press of Colorado. https://wac.colostate.edu/books/atd/graduate.

Rudestam, K. E. & Newton, R. E. (2007). *Surviving your dissertation: A comprehensive guide to content and process.* Sage.

Rush, D. (2009, September 20). IU Kokomo sets record for undergrad enrollment. *Kokomo Tribune.* https://www.kokomotribune.com/news/local_news/iuk-sets-record-for-undergrad-enrollment/article_8de15ea1-3a95-514e-b33d-072ef46dcc81.html.

Swales, J. & Feak, C. (2012). *Academic writing for graduate students: Essential tasks and skills* (3rd ed.). University of Michigan Press.

Appendix A: Interview Questions

1. What kinds of writing projects were assigned in your "cross-level" graduate-level coursework? How do these projects compare to the types of writing projects you've been assigned in your undergraduate coursework in terms of length, complexity, sophistication of research, etc.?
2. To what extent have you been explicitly shown or told what "counts" as graduate-level writing?

3. When it comes to writing projects in your graduate coursework, can you describe what is expected of you as a graduate student? How do these compare to what was expected of you when you were an undergraduate student?
4. To what extent would you say you were aware of these expectations of your writing before coming into the program? How were these expectations communicated to you once you began completing coursework in your program?
5. What kinds of comments, margin notes, edits, or emendations do instructors or advisors make on your writing projects?
6. Have you ever been assigned a writing project that you felt unprepared to complete successfully? What are some specific challenges that you have faced as a writer in your graduate coursework?
7. Are there any types or genres of writing projects that you wish would be covered in your graduate coursework?
8. How have your experiences with cross-level coursework compared to other graduate-level courses? Is there anything else you would like to add about cross-level coursework?

Appendix B: Participant Overview

Southern Illinois University Edwardsville (SIUE)		Indiana University Kokomo (IUK)	
Participant's Pseudonym	Degree Program	Participant's Pseudonym	Degree Program
Angela	Master of Arts in English, specializing in Teaching English as a Second Language (MAE—TESL)	Danny	Master of Arts in Liberal Studies (MALS)
Nancy	Post-Baccalaureate Certificate in English, specializing in Teaching of Writing (PB—TOW)	Beth	Master of Arts in Liberal Studies (MALS)
Neal	Master of Science in Civil Engineering (MSCE)	Tracy	Master of Public Management (MPM)
Amy	Master of Arts in English, specializing in Teaching of Writing (MAE—TOW)	Cynthia	Master of Science in Nursing Administration (MSN)
		Debbie	Master of Science in Nursing Administration (MSN)

Developing an English for Academic Purposes Course for L2 Graduate Students in the Sciences

Jennifer Douglas
AMERICAN PUBLIC UNIVERSITY SYSTEM

> **Abstract**: Graduate students face a fundamental change in identity when transitioning from undergraduate writers to graduate writers. In their new role as graduate writers and researchers, they must move from consuming knowledge to producing knowledge through their writing. Often, they must learn new genres of writing, new disciplinary conventions, and new rhetorical models. For non-native English speakers, these tasks are even more complex because of the advanced language skills required and the cultural differences in rhetorical models. This article explains teaching strategies for an interdisciplinary, graduate-level scientific writing course for non-native English speakers. For Teaching English to Speakers of Other Languages (TESOL) instructors who are accustomed to general undergraduate writing, this article will offer suggestions for scientific writing at the graduate level. For composition instructors who do not specialize in TESOL, this article provides ways of adapting graduate-level scientific writing conventions to an audience of international students.
>
> **Keywords**: Scientific Writing, English for Academic Purposes, Graduate Students, L2 Students, Interdisciplinary, STEM Disciplines, Disciplinary Conventions, Rhetorical Models, Courses

Graduate students form a distinct group of nascent scholars—neither established faculty nor novice undergraduates—who are becoming acculturated into their disciplines through the process of writing about their research. These students occupy a unique place in the academic community: They are transforming from students learning about a discipline to bona fide members contributing knowledge to that discipline (Abasi, Akbari & Graves, 2006). Expectations for graduate student writing are different and more rigorous than undergraduate writing, including more emphasis on synthesizing literature, constructing original arguments based on their own data, and integrating data from other research into a cohesive argument (Moore, Tatum & Sebetan, 2011; Ondrusek, 2012; Sallee, Hallett & Tierney, 2011). Through their writing, graduate students are shifting their identity from learner to producer of research in order to make new knowledge claims in their field and to join the research community for that discipline. Making new

DOI: https://doi.org/10.37514/ATD-B.2020.0407.2.03

knowledge claims involves an identity change in academic status as well as an epistemological change in relation to the field; graduate students must learn how to critique previous knowledge claims, articulate a gap or niche in the field, and argue that their research addresses this area by contributing new knowledge. From the sociocultural perspective, research writing for graduate students is not simply "writing up" results; rather, the writing process socializes these students into the norms of the discipline and begins to offer them legitimacy as scholars in that discipline. Making new knowledge claims requires a sophisticated conceptual framework as well as an authoritative voice, both of which are challenging for emerging members of the discipline.

A growing body of literature articulates the need for specific graduate writing support to aid in such development, including courses, writing groups, tutoring, and mentoring (Delyser, 2003; Harris, 2005; Kamler & Thomson, 2004; Polio & Shi, 2012; Rose & McClafferty, 2001). Previous studies highlight the benefits of these endeavors: Writing groups, for instance, help writers to navigate between the macro-level conceptual framework of the dissertation and micro-level revisions, develop peer review strategies, and articulate connections between different parts of the dissertation (Maher et al., 2008). Similarly, group peer critique has been identified as the central pedagogy for improving writing because groups provide a demonstration of the dialogic nature of writing and "a heightened sense of the processes and craft of writing when readers were not content specialists, [and] access to alternative non-discipline-specific perspectives" (Aitchison, 2009, p. 909). Simply remaining accountable to a group or course, practicing writing on a regular basis, and having a support system in place contributes to productivity and confidence throughout the process (Belcher, 2009; Brooks-Gillies, Garcia & Manthey, this collection; Ferguson, 2009; Kim & Wolke, this collection; Maher et al., 2008). As seen in the literature, graduate writing courses have been developed by faculty teaching in various disciplines as an attempt at scaffolding and direct integration of writing skills into the curriculum (Delyser, 2003; Harris, 2005; Sallee, Hallett & Tierney, 2011). Many graduate students have not taken a writing course since early in their undergraduate career, if ever, and the transition to graduate writing places a host of new demands on these students. Their undergraduate writing assignments may not have required the same skill sets as graduate writing in terms of engaging in academic discourse, and this skills gap leads to considerable frustration and anxiety by both students and faculty (Belcher, 2009).

Beyond the challenges faced by graduate writers in general, multilingual writers must overcome cultural differences in writing style; for instance, in American academic writing, the argumentative style emphasizes stating the main point first and then supporting it rather than inductively circling the main point and leaving the conclusion until the end (cf. Lakoff & Johnson, 1980). Compounding the difficulties of mastering argumentative frameworks, students also encounter new rhetorical/linguistic conventions for academic writing and disciplinary conventions for research writing in their area. Recent research has noted multilingual writers' difficulties in establishing new knowledge claims because these writers are doubly removed from the linguistic and social context in which authorial identity, voice, and academic discourse are established (Abasi et al., 2006; Polio & Shi, 2012). Abasi and Graves (2008) note that second language (L2) students need extra development in order to implement writing conventions for making new knowledge claims, critiquing previous knowledge, and establishing an authoritative research identity because they are seeking to acquire the norms of American academia, the writing conventions of their field, and the general language ability to write original research articles.

English for Academic Purposes (EAP) courses provide one way to focus on rhetorical conventions for research writing by analyzing experts' examples, offering rhetorical strategies, and providing extensive feedback on students' drafts (Fenton-Smith et al., 2017). EAP courses can provide a safe space for fledgling scholars to receive developmental feedback on writing and to explore conventions in their discipline. As universities develop curricula to support multilingual writers, these courses offer a productive way of equipping students with writing skills that promote academic success throughout their college careers (Crosthwaite, 2016; Fenton-Smith, Humphreys & Walkinshaw, 2018). EAP courses allow for linguistic experimentation and growth with coaching from composition experts who can model rhetorical conventions and help students gain writing confidence through course activities.

In this chapter, I describe a pilot writing course for multilingual graduate students in the sciences, Science Writing for Non-Native English Speakers. I approach the development of a graduate writing course for L2 students as an action research endeavor that brings together the iterative processes of action research and the writing process itself. As described in the *SAGE Handbook of Action Research* (Bradbury, 2015), this type of research is grounded in practice and is fundamentally collaborative in "researching with" stakeholders rather than researching *about* a phenomenon. Action research, similar to academic writing, relies on a dialogic and iterative process that continues to evolve through ongoing inquiry, as noted by Carter (2012). The emergent nature of this research means that it includes ongoing learning, adaptation, and action through cycles of dialogue. Developing, teaching, and revising this course brings together the key tenets of the action research process in collaborating with stakeholders in the class—students and a writing consultant—as well as adapting to the conventions of the disciplines represented. Much like academic writing consists of argument, evidence, dialogue, and iterative revisions, the course likewise evolved through ongoing evaluation and response. This course arose from a specific need at the university, and the process of responding to that need provided the foundation for this action research endeavor.

The development of this course arose because of my unique role at West Virginia University. Beginning in 2009, I created and directed professional development programs for graduate students across the university. Many of these programs were based on core competencies for career success, as defined by the Council of Graduate Schools, Science Careers, the Versatile Ph.D., and other disciplinary societies. Writing, one of these core competencies, became a concern because specific writing support at the graduate level is often scarce or lacking. Although the university's Writing Center offered tutoring to both undergraduate and graduate students, no graduate courses focusing on research writing existed at the university level. Interest in this type of course had been expressed by students and faculty during events and individual meetings. Many of the graduate professional development programs attracted a large number of international students, who often commented on the difficulty of improving their writing and completing drafts of their research papers. Based on this feedback and my background working in composition and ESL programs, I was motivated to develop more writing resources for graduate students, and especially multilingual writers. This course was first conducted in Fall 2012 at West Virginia University, a Carnegie classification high-research university with approximately 5,100 master's and doctoral students. The course was available to all students in the science disciplines, broadly defined. Scientific writing was chosen because the format for research papers usually follows consistent sections (introduction, methods, results, discussion), and the conventions of scientific writing are more uniform than for humanities writing. Fourteen students and a visiting scholar enrolled in the course, from the disciplines of geology, geography, forestry, wood science, physics, psychology, chemical engineering, human and community development, biology, and public health. Students ranged from first-year master's students to third-year doctoral students. The course met twice per week for fifty minutes each session.

In keeping with research on the primary skills needed for graduate writing, this course focused on both higher-order and sentence-level skills needed to compose academic writing at the advanced level required for graduate school. Graduate writing courses, as described in the literature, recognize the importance of scaffolding in order to break the complex task of writing a research paper into more discrete tasks, such as writing a literature review, writing article critiques, and presenting data (Delyser, 2003; Harris, 2005; Sallee, Hallett & Tierney, 2011). In keeping with this strategy of breaking down the academic writing enterprise into more manageable chunks, I focused on the idea of rhetorical moves as a way to frame academic writing discourse and associated tasks (Thonney, 2011). This concept of "rhetorical moves" has been examined in order to analyze commonalities and differences across a corpus of academic writing (for instance, Chang & Schleppegrell, 2011; Petrić, 2007; Tankó, 2017). For that reason, my course structure drew on *Academic Writing for Graduate Students* (Swales & Feak, 2012) because it provided a welcome blend of global and sentence-level strategies that could be analyzed and practiced across an array of disciplines. Organizing the course around rhetorical patterns provided a way to examine aspects of academic writing that remain fairly similar across disciplines as well as conventions that change depending on discipline or sub-discipline (Fenton-Smith et al., 2017).

The course outline focused on major skill sets in research writing, such as general-specific texts, data commentary, processes, problem-solution texts, and critiques in the context of research paper sections, such as introductions, methodology, results, and discussion areas. By the end of the semester, students practiced all the major components of creating an original research paper or dissertation chapter. During the course, many of the writing assignments were based on practicing the specific skillset at hand, such as writing an introduction that establishes the research gap and the contribution of that paper; writing a literature review to synthesize rather than simply summarize sources; and writing about data from students' disciplines. Assignments, then, were tailored and adapted to the specific students in the course based on their disciplines and their goals at that point in their program. The following sections will outline teaching strategies employed in the class, challenges associated with each strategy, and future directions for revising the course design.

Teaching Strategies

Strategy 1: Consultations

In order to make the course's writing assistance more personalized, I partnered with an ESL specialist, Iwona, to provide individual writing consultations with the students on a biweekly basis. This specialist had a wealth of experience teaching multilingual writers on the secondary school level and was eager to return to the university setting, where she had taught earlier in her career. She attended each class session, circulated among groups to offer feedback and suggestions, and addressed specific grammatical or rhetorical questions that had arisen during individual consultations in order to help the whole class think about a particular point. Iwona's own status as a multilingual writer also helped her to have affinity with the students as she could relate their process of language learning with her own. Her perspective also enriched the course because of her exposure to different areas of research writing through her partner in the forestry department. During twenty-to-thirty-minute individual consultations, students often talked about drafts of work they had produced for class, and on which Iwona or I had already commented. In meetings, then, Iwona could further interpret and expand on comments while helping students find solutions to their language questions. Some students also brought external work to appointments if they had other pieces of research papers or assignments due. Iwona was able to talk about general language conventions and often answered questions that the students were reluctant to pose at first to their advisors; in this way, her consultations created a safe place for students to articulate questions or ideas before meeting with their advisors. She noted differences in students' questions based on their level of experience. She states:

> In general, the more advanced students (the majority of them already at the end of their Ph.D. process) were actually coming with specific questions and passages that they wanted to work on from the grammar and style standpoint. They would actually point to the specific sentence, phrase, or paragraph and ask my opinion on how it worked in the whole of the paper. . . . The beginner Ph.D. and master's students were lost and overwhelmed with the format of the work and they were trying to figure out what they needed to do in what order. Working with them and following our textbook outline of how to build a research paper was a good exercise for them. (I. Cynk-Dahle, personal communication, March 20, 2013)

These comments align with the research on academic discourse communities in noting that students begin without a conceptual framework for developing a research paper and need to learn the large conventions of framing research questions before focusing on specific sentence-level revisions (Abasi et al., 2006). More advanced students seemed to have internalized the overall structure of research writing and sought more help on specific passages. Iwona and I met regularly to discuss the interactions in these individual meetings and to adapt class activities according to student needs. For instance, if many students struggled with switching between active and passive voice in their introduction sections, I developed a class activity examining published samples and providing guidance on this point. In this way, the class curriculum was responsive and adaptive to the writing needs articulated by the students, and evaluation of the curriculum was an ongoing activity.

She also noted that her position as a tutor rather than a teacher allowed students to be more open with her about their questions. She observes:

> I think I was able not only to help with the writing process but I also in a few cases answered some interesting cultural questions concerning interacting with teachers in other classes. Many of the students we had last semester were new here. They do not feel comfortable asking questions and do not know the convention of interacting with the teachers. Since I was not a de facto teacher, I made the point to speak to them about some of the issues openly. Some of the students needed to go back to the lead

teacher [in their department] and ask some specific questions to help them with their writing. (I. Cynk-Dahle, personal communication, March 20, 2013)

These comments reveal the difficulty of negotiating cultural expectations in a new academic system while simultaneously negotiating scholarly identity within the discipline. Multilingual students encounter the challenges of entering the American educational system, working with new professors, and completing complex writing assignments in a different language (Gilmore, Strickland, Timmerman, Maher & Feldon, 2010). Although the course did not specifically collaborate with content-area experts, Iwona and I were sometimes asked by students to interpret comments that faculty advisors had written on students' work. This role of interpreter carried both advantages and disadvantages for instructors and students: While students benefited from having another source to triangulate information they were receiving, we instructors were wary of making definitive judgments that might not align with the faculty member's opinion. One benefit we could provide was a way for students to ask more productive questions of their faculty advisor after their individual writing sessions in this course. Having a preliminary discussion in the context of the course provided students a framework to make a revision and ask their advisor a focused question for additional feedback.

These interactions with students highlight the pros and cons of teaching writing as a set of advanced skills versus teaching writing *through and within* disciplinary content (Fenton-Smith et al., 2017). Examples of interdisciplinary writing courses as well as discipline-based writing courses show that both models provide value, but their emphases may be different. One argument in favor of an interdisciplinary writing course is that students of different disciplines provide a broader perspective on genre and rhetorical expectations, both outside of disciplinary silos and outside of a particular faculty advisor's writing style. However, a discipline-based course would provide more critique of the research content and integrate content with discourse in a different way.

Strategy 2: Templates

Activities in the course provided different forms of language scaffolding, both at the level of rhetorical moves and specific grammatical points. Since students often articulated their writing weaknesses in terms of grammar, it was important to acknowledge and spend time on grammar practice, as I will discuss in Strategy 5. However, for the purposes of understanding the dialogic nature of academic writing and the idea that research must enter into a conversation within the field, it was equally important to establish frameworks for students to position their work. This process of positioning is an integral part of the shifting identity from learner to producer of knowledge; students in essence must begin to view themselves as peers with other researchers in their discipline and enter into the scholarly dialogue around a particular research area. Even more important, students need to articulate why their own research is unique or significant in relation to other work. This type of declaration requires several rhetorical moves in order to establish the claims of previous work, show a gap or unanswered question, and explain how their research addresses this gap.

Textbooks used in the class aimed to help students negotiate the rhetorical conventions necessary to join the academic dialogue. The primary text, *Academic Writing for Graduate Students* (Swales & Feak, 2012), operates on the valuable "Creating a Research Space" (CaRS) model of framing research projects while offering specific rhetorical and grammatical solutions for writing tasks, including writing definitions, identifying a research problem, commenting on data, describing methods, and discussing results (Swales & Feak, 2012, p. 331). A secondary resource, *They Say/I Say: The Moves that Matter in Academic Writing*, 2nd edition (Graff & Birkenstein, 2010), was used in a limited way for the idea of identifying writing patterns in texts. This book is aimed primarily at undergraduates, but it is valuable for multilingual writers because it provides templates for agreeing, disagreeing, commenting on sources, and articulating an argument. Narrow portions of this text were used as a resource for the purpose of constructing a sentence and paragraph structure based on templates, as adapted to research writing in different disciplines. Both texts offered a wealth of specific language strategies for framing a research argument and composing segments of that argument. The accessible tone and reading level of *They Say* made it an effective entry point for students to grasp the dialogic nature of academic writing even as they delved into more sophisticated explanations in the *Academic Writing* text.

During the course, I often employed templates from the texts or created my own templates in order to help the students practice rhetorical moves in class. For instance, based on a problem/solution paragraph the students had revised, we used various templates to practice different patterns for linking past research with present research. Each of the templates below uses a different approach to reference past research and create a transition to the present topic.

- Experiments showing _____ and _____ have led scientists to propose _____.
- Because _____ does not account for _____, we instead chose _____ method.
- Our data support/challenge the work of Zhang by showing that _____. (adapted from Graff & Birkenstein, 2010)

Working with templates provides students with tangible, practical structures that help them overcome initial language barriers when expressing research ideas.

The templates can be easily adapted to different disciplines and allow students to insert ideas from their own research area. Templates help to break down the complexities of research writing into manageable chunks of argument while also reducing some of the writing fatigue that occurs when writing in another language. To encourage students to write drafts in English rather than writing in their first language and translating, templates provide an avenue for creating effective, grammatically-acceptable sentences.

The generalizability of templates is also their weakness; any one template may not match the typical disciplinary vocabulary or sentence structures employed in a particular journal. For this reason, templates are a good building block for exploratory writing but may not always contribute to final drafts. Templates may also appear disconnected from the larger argument structure unless deliberate connections are made between the specific template and its place within the CaRS model, for instance.

Students in the course often used templates when constructing their homework drafts; learning to manipulate these templates to match their writing needs was itself a valuable exercise in understanding rhetorical strategies and sentence forms. This technique could be extended by asking students to create their own templates based on analysis of journal articles in their disciplines, similar to the corpus research of Blazer and DeCapua (this collection). Identifying common sentence structures across several articles would help solidify disciplinary writing conventions while building a foundation of rhetorical moves that introduce specific research components.

Strategy 3: Textual Analysis of Research Writing

In order to help students understand the conventions of research writing in their disciplines, we spent extensive time analyzing excerpts of articles in class. Adapting to the group of students in the course, I selected articles that aligned with one of the disciplines represented in the class: for instance, a public health article on the effects of coal mining in Appalachia or a geology article on mine runoff into watersheds. Students were also assigned to find articles in their own disciplines, preferably related to their research areas. Some homework assignments required them to analyze a specific aspect of the text and share their findings in a small group during the following class. During class, our group composition varied, but most often students worked in interdisciplinary groups, which proved to be a great advantage for students explaining or commenting on disciplinary conventions in the chosen writing sample and from their own discipline. Explaining both the general content of a research article and the mode in which that research is presented provided the students an opportunity to step back from their own fields and speak about the norms that they had perceived in the writing. An added benefit of the course was this blend of formal and informal academic dialogue that encouraged both oral and written communication adapted to a broad audience. For instance, the psychology students were accustomed to working with qualitative research, in which the writers often have to describe their instrument and coding scheme in detail, while the biologists were accustomed to genomics-based research that emphasized the equipment and specific procedures that were conducted in the experiment.

Based on our topic at a given point, we would analyze the excerpts for specific rhetorical functions, such as how the writers identified their research problem, how they described figures, how they presented results, or how they cited previous research.

Example 1: Presenting limitations in previous research

Students analyzed the transitions (underlined), "limitations" language (*italicized*), and "future directions" language (**bolded**) in a short passage to determine how the author critiqued previous research (as in the following example). We could then discuss how to introduce gaps in the field and ideas for future projects.

> Although long fire history data sets will be required to validate models and determine whether fire regimes have experienced a change of state, these data are difficult to collect, are limited in occurrence, and inferences are restricted by the spatial and temporal resolution of the data. As previously noted, few regions of the world maintain long observational records of past fire activity, and satellite records are currently too short to detect change. Climatic variability and human activities are also strong drivers of fire activity, therefore studies of anthropogenic climate change and fire must take these variables into account. While fire history data have the potential to address some of these challenges, inferences remain somewhat limited. (Hessl, 2011, p. 399)

Example 2: Reading abstracts

Students read the following "Editor's Choice" abstract from *Science* and answered these questions:

- What is the major research question or problem?
- What is the gap that this study fills?
- What is the novel finding in this study?

This exercise helped to present the CaRS model in a condensed space and helped students to understand the importance of writing for different audiences; in this case, the abstract uses a football analogy to make the study relatable to a lay audience.

Abstract excerpt from "A Strategic Defense":

> Just as in American football, during the immune response, the location of your defenders is key. One player out of line can make the difference between a sack or a touchdown, or in the case of the immune system, a localized versus systemic infection. How the immune system orchestrates this careful defense, however, is not well understood. (Mueller, 2012, p. 17)

This introduction helped the students understand the use of an analogy for a complex scientific topic and the differences in writing for a specialized audience in the discipline versus a layperson. The abstract continues:

> Kasternmuller et al. now demonstrate that the organization of cells within the lymph nodes of mice is critical for preventing pathogen spread during the first few hours of an infection. Infecting bacteria drain to nearby lymph nodes, where they are immediately collected by a specially localized population of macrophages. (Mueller, 2012, p. 17)

Reading abstracts demonstrates that a significant scientific contribution can be condensed into a brief explanation if skillfully constructed. This brief genre essentially supplies students with a thumbnail sketch of an entire research dialogue in which new research fills a need or a gap within the discipline. By seeing the research space represented in such a brief format, students then could find these moves in longer research articles.

These exercises helped students understand rhetorical conventions in the Creating a Research Space model, and they gained strategies for positioning their own work. Textual analysis also helped to reveal differences in research writing between disciplines. For instance, some engineering papers do not follow the introduction-methods-results-discussion format if they are proposing an algorithm, system, protocol, or other model. In these types of papers, the sections generally follow a progression of explaining variables or aspects of the model in detail before presenting the results of running that model in a test or simulation. Explaining the model often appears similar to a mathematical proof in which variables and assumptions are systematically defined using present tense verbs. Contrasting this genre, research papers in many basic and social sciences rely on procedural methods sections, using past tense verbs, that are often quite short in relation to the results or discussion. When students encountered these sub-genres of research writing, they then considered the specific norms within their discipline as they related to the larger enterprise of academic writing. Seeing differences helped to solidify their understanding of conventions within their own discipline.

Strategy 4: Peer Review

Students frequently came to class with short pieces of writing, making peer review a key component of class time. The process of peer review—learning to critique others' writing and provide constructive comments—is a central part of acquiring scholarly identity and becoming a competent academic writer (Aitchison, 2009, p. 906). Consistent peer review also reinforces the iterative and dialogic nature of the writing process. For students who felt insecure about their writing, having a supportive community created a "no-failure" type of environment in which questions and suggestions were encouraged and accepted. Based on the *Academic Writing for Graduate Students* text, many of our writing assignments dealt with specific tasks in academic writing, such as creating definitions, forming problem/solution pairs, commenting on data, or describing a process. During peer review, then, we used the core components of that task in order to decide the elements of the critique.

Example: Peer review of definition paragraph

Look at your partner's draft and answer the following questions:

- What term is the writer defining, and what are the key traits of that term?
- How is the definition organized? Does it have a logical order? How could the organization be improved?
- As a reader, do you have questions about this definition or notice any information that's missing? What information would make the definition easier to understand?
- Look at the structure of the sentences. Do you notice any grammatical errors that could be changed?

Peer review in our interdisciplinary setting offered students fresh perspectives on their own research projects because they needed to explain the project, as well as their own writing conventions, to others who were not in the field. The most productive discussions in the course occurred as students summarized their research questions or processes to others who were unfamiliar with the area. Peer reviews offered a layer of comments, different from instructors' comments, to augment the writer's perspective. Peer reviews often led to issues we could discuss as a whole group, such as what common terms from the field could be used without citations, or what an acceptable paraphrase would look like.

Strategy 5: Grammar Warm-Ups

Students appreciated the opportunity to review thorny grammatical issues, such as pronoun agreement, compound/complex sentences, run-on sentences, and verb tenses. I incorporated grammar warm-ups using common resources such as online grammar worksheets and Dave's ESL Café. Including grammar exercises at the beginning of class helped the students transition into language-thinking mode, in which they were attuned to common language issues. Many grammatical constructs, such as prepositions and articles, require years of practice and "ear training" to implement because rules are often inadequate to explain their usage. When practicing specific elements, such as the construction of compound sentences with semicolons versus coordinating conjunctions, students developed a large base knowledge that we instructors could use in future paper comments. Rather than trying to write out the grammatical rule, we could refer students back to the exercise as a reference for improving the sentence in question. The *Academic Writing* book incorporates grammar exercises as they apply to different rhetorical tasks, such as using linked passives to describe a process in the methods section of a paper. Students reviewed these grammatical structures and then look for them in research articles or individual writing for that day. I sometimes followed up on a grammar warm-up by asking students to rewrite one of their own sentences using a point we had just practiced, such as including a semicolon correctly.

Strategy 6: Dialogue

Although this was a writing course, students benefited from *speaking* about their research to other graduate students across different disciplines. Throughout group exercises and whole-class discussions, they explained their research projects and responded to others' writing. The physical and mental work of public speaking reinforces language learning in a different way than the act of writing. Both are valuable for encouraging clear explanations of difficult research topics and contextualizing their research within the larger field. Even the act of asking questions during class and engaging in dialogue about writing conventions prompted students to create more complex language frameworks. In other words, dialogue promoted building connections and deepened understanding through extended explanation and elaboration.

Near the end of the semester, students were also asked to give a two-minute elevator speech about their research projects. They delivered these elevator speeches as a dialogue, in which another graduate student asked them follow-up questions about their projects. Coming at a point when students had great rapport with each other, this exercise showcased their increased ability to articulate their research niche. The exercise helped to confirm their changing identity from learner to producer of new knowledge. In a larger sense, this exercise was also in keeping with the transferable skill of scientific communication, as evidenced in burgeoning activities such as the 3Minute Thesis competition and the American Academy for the

Advancement of Science's initiative on communicating science. Since these students would later have to present their work in formal defenses or conferences, this exercise also helped to provide a friendly foundation for other public speaking. Interestingly, the low stakes nature of these presentations seemed beneficial to this group, while other research on integrating oral presentations into an EAP writing course found that students regarded the presentations as an extra high-stakes assessment (Salter-Dvorak, 2016). Creating a classroom culture and building the presentations in at the right time appear to be key in their benefit to students.

Discussion and Future Directions

In general, this course was successful in providing students with necessary feedback to make progress and continue their academic journeys. One student commented:

> Thank you so much for this email and also for great experiences that we shared in class. I made great (HUGE) progress in my "writing process" development, although it's not looking like that. Before this semester, every time when I have to write something, and it is more then [sic] 5 sentences long I had headaches. Now it's much better situation. Probably, the reason for that is that you gave me confidence and also I know that there are lot of other people with same problems as mine. I just needed to "start", and this class literarlly push [sic] me into that. Now everything is much better. (Personal Communication, December 7, 2012)

Following the first iteration of the course, the writing consultant, Iwona, and I evaluated the class format, content, and activities based on student performance and feedback throughout the course. We also considered the aspects of the students' writing that would benefit from more attention, and we adapted the curriculum accordingly in the second iteration. This dialogic adaptation and action based on a variety of inputs allowed this course to proceed as its own form of action research responding to the needs of a diverse and decentralized graduate culture at the university.

To revise the course, I implemented several specific changes in Fall 2013: First, the course moved from two credits to three credits, which allowed a change from 50-minute class periods to 75-minute class periods. This significant increase in class time provided more opportunity for in-class writing, student interaction, and writing exercises. Second, I introduced the Creating a Research Space model (Swales & Feak, 2012) immediately as a way to frame the writing tasks in the semester. Some students commented verbally that they did not grasp the big picture until the latter stages of the semester when this model is introduced in the *Academic Writing* textbook. By introducing the model early, we framed specific writing tasks throughout the course within the larger goals of the research paper.

For in-class activities, I revised my lesson plans with several considerations: Although we sometimes included self-assessments on writing assignments, I ensured that we always completed this step so that students could direct their readers to focus their critique. Students also tended to form consistent groups for peer review. This continuity created rapport and a high comfort level for the students, but the contents of critiques were limited by the perspective of those group members. I then ensured that peer review groups rotate on a regular basis in order to provide different perspectives for the writers. Further, we incorporated more writing time to revise work in class based on peer reviewers' comments. Making immediate changes helped to consolidate the learning and improve the draft quickly, thus allowing the student to turn in a revised draft at the end of class.

In addition to changing the logistics of writing exercises, increasing the frequency of short, verbal presentations based on homework assignments ensured that every student contributed to discussion. The students made more frequent, informal class presentations on articles in their own disciplines in order to target the writing conventions of their field. Having one or two students present to the entire class during each session increased their accountability to examine articles closely and ensured that they were articulating trends from the literature in their discipline. Likewise, asking the students to produce an introductory elevator speech in the first week, a mid-semester speech about their research progress, and a final speech about the significance of their research helped to reinforce the CaRS model and prepare them to attend conferences or job interviews. In addition to spoken dialogue, students completed more in-class writing based on the samples we examined. For instance, when we analyzed an abstract, students then composed a three to four sentence abstract of their current research and shared it with peers during the class. To integrate rhetorical analysis with grammar instruction, isolated grammatical structures need to be consistently applied to the students' own writing through follow-up exercises and peer review checks.

In order to foster long-term writing progress, students developed a writing plan at the beginning of the semester to indicate their goals and the major project they would complete. Since students in the class were at different stages of their graduate work, having one static research paper assignment was not feasible. Rather, students worked on projects appropriate to their stage: literature reviews, review articles, thesis prospectuses, and portions of their dissertations. Students charted their writing goals so that more assignments throughout the semester could be targeted toward their own projects. Many of their short writing tasks then contributed to the larger project in a more meaningful way. In addition to considering a full-semester plan, including self-assessment on a daily basis would help to chart students' progress. During individual consultations, we followed a standard writing center practice in which students articulate their concerns at the beginning of a session and their action plan at the end of the session to encourage continued work.

Challenges arose in all aspects of the course in working with the various disciplines represented, yet the variety of disciplines also enriched the course greatly by offering a range of research projects and writing patterns to study. To work with this group of students, both Iwona and I analyzed journal articles in the students' disciplines in order to understand the conventions at a reasonable level. Placing more responsibility on students to regularly analyze and report on these conventions in journal articles from their own disciplines provided one avenue to deepen their learning experience (Fenton-Smith et al., 2017). Asking students to analyze examples of academic writing in their research areas helped them to differentiate methods of interpreting previous research, identifying a research niche, and creating an argument for new knowledge. Students need to be coached to find these conventions and practice them in a structured environment (Abasi et al., 2006, p. 114). Asking the students to analyze articles in their field more regularly also helped them to develop templates and recognize common rhetorical moves in their discipline.

Research on rhetorical moves in academic writing helps to suggest norms that students might examine throughout the course. For instance, students should analyze the citation practices and the functions of citations in their disciplines in order to understand how new knowledge claims are constructed (Dong, 1996). Research on L2 writers provides the groundwork for these activities. In one study, Chang and Schleppegrell (2011) explore the CaRS model to identify "expansive and contractive" rhetorical devices for identifying a research area and narrowing the niche. As they note, the social sciences place more importance on explicit interpretation of sources compared to the hard sciences (Chang & Schleppegrell, 2011). Perhaps these differences in interpretation arise from the nature of the data; more qualitative data may call for more interpretation of results in order to relate them to the student's current study. By asking students to identify and practice these expansive and contractive rhetorical devices, they can see the specific means of narrowing the research niche within their target journals.

Lim (2012) also employs a cross-disciplinary comparison of specific language for indicating a research gap. Sharing his findings and figures on linguistic mechanisms—essentially, groups of templates—for indicating a gap would allow students to seek the most common mechanisms in their discipline and emulate those mechanisms. Further, techniques for incorporating citations in order to make new knowledge claims need to be further explored. Mansourizadeh and Ahmad (2011) have examined citation practices of novice and expert writers and have found that novice writers use citations in less complex ways (i.e., attributing previous knowledge) than expert writers (i.e., justifying findings or supporting methodology). These practices are complicated by the fact that hard and soft disciplines rely differently on integral vs. non-integral citations (whether the researcher is named in the text) (Mansourizadeh & Ahmad, 2011). Since literature reviews are a foundational component of most graduate programs, asking students to analyze the purpose and method of citing sources would make these practices more apparent in defining their own research projects.

If this course were adapted for specific departments in the future, I would advise a co-teaching model in which a content specialist from the discipline teamteaches with a writing specialist who can elucidate the rhetorical conventions. Since content specialists have already been socialized into disciplinary norms, often without formal instruction, their ability to articulate or explain these norms may be limited (Abasi & Graves, 2008). A co-teaching model provides the advantage of a professor with content knowledge and discipline-focused writing projects alongside a professor specializing in writing instruction targeted to that discipline's norms.

Although courses focused on English for Academic Purposes are one way to offer writing support to multilingual graduate students, other resources at the university also help to provide this scaffolding for graduate students in general. To increase attention to writing as a core competency for graduate students, I partnered with the Writing Center to offer week-long dissertation boot camps open to any graduate student in the dissertation stage, and a faculty member taught a cross-disciplinary grant writing course as an introduction to that genre of writing. My office offered financial support for two graduate assistants from the Department of English to offer graduate writing consultations through the Writing Center for the first time. These graduate assistants were already experienced instructors with prior tutoring experience, enabling them to work with graduate writers producing dissertations or other high-level research writing across disciplines. All of these efforts increased the attention to graduate writing instruction as a whole and provided additional scaffolding for graduate writers' advancement. Initiatives such as the graduate writing tutors provided enhanced opportunities for multilingual writers to receive more intensive instruction, aside from taking the course.

As emerging members of their disciplines, graduate students need specific writing instruction in how to articulate their research contribution to their field, and multilingual students benefit from additional training that combines the rhetoric of academic writing with specific language concerns. Students are transitioning from the role of learner to that of scholar, from internalizing previous work in the discipline to creating new knowledge claims in the discipline; these tasks require scaffolding to recognize and apply writing conventions. This science writing course for multilingual writers provides one model that relies heavily on responsive instruction, developing rhetorical templates, analyzing articles from students' fields, and writing frequently about students' own research. At the same time, the collaborative and dialogic nature of this course provided fertile ground to implement action research on graduate writing in the L2 context. The project of creating, teaching, and revising the course revealed that this type of course could be beneficial for graduate students across disciplines and stages of their program. Beginning from composition strategies vetted in the literature, my colleague and I were able to assess and critique these strategies through two iterations of the course to offer a productive learning environment that supported student growth in their writing skills. As an ongoing contribution to graduate student success, I hope to refine this model in order to provide even better assistance to aspiring researchers.

Epilogue

Since 2015, I have held a leadership position in graduate studies at an institution serving adult learners in online programs, many of whom are in the military or public service professions. In my graduate studies role at American Public University System, I support curricular quality as well as initiatives to increase student persistence and retention in our thirty-five master's programs. These degrees are intended for working professionals and frequently integrate application into the research because of the practitioner emphasis. For our adult learners, whose average age is 37 at the master's level, academic writing for graduate courses continues to be one of the greatest challenges students face in acclimating to graduate school and succeeding in their programs. Many students also rely on Veteran's benefits or military tuition assistance to complete their education, and taking extra courses for credit is prohibitive to completing the degree. Given the unique circumstances of these working adults completing their master's degrees online, I have employed techniques from the scientific writing course in new ways to offer academic support without the cost of additional courses. Specifically, I have developed seven self-paced, ungraded online modules that students can opt to complete through our virtual campus platform. These self-paced modules are organized according to typical sections of a research article, beginning with two introductory modules that establish expectations for the scholarly dialogue in graduate writing, followed by additional modules that focus on writing introductions, literature reviews, methods sections, results sections, and discussion sections.

Each self-paced module incorporates a short video to explain the central purpose of that research paper section, and the majority of the module provides examples of rhetorical moves drawn from published articles that mirror the predominantly social science disciplines at the institution. To illustrate a rhetorical move within an article, I developed infographics that pair a brief excerpt from an article with a commentary about the rhetorical move taking place in order to mirror some of the exercises used in the writing course. Students can then apply the same technique to analyze a segment of an article they are reading for a class or research project.

Throughout the modules, students have the opportunity to submit brief, formative assessments in which they analyze articles from their own discipline to trace the rhetorical moves and assess their effectiveness. These modules are advertised in our graduate student orientation as a writing resource, through course announcements embedded in the curriculum, and in the *End of Program Assessment Manual* that guides students toward their capstone experience. Students who are entering academic probation are instructed to complete these modules as a way of strengthening their writing skills and promoting better performance in the program. To date, over 3,600 students have self-enrolled in these modules. Examining the data on module completion versus graduation rates and academic standing will be the basis of a future project.

Reflecting on the complexities of teaching and learning academic writing skills, I am encouraged by the fact that these rhetorical models continue to be relevant despite differences in learning modality, student demographic, and type of degree program. As adult learners increasingly return to school seeking graduate degrees for promotion or career change, these models can be applied and transformed to serve different purposes and support learning across higher education institutions.

References

Abasi, A. R., Akbari, N. & Graves, B. (2006). Discourse appropriation, construction of identities, and the complex issue of plagiarism: ESL students writing in graduate school. *Journal of Second Language Writing, 15,* 102–117. https://doi.org/10.1016/j.jslw.2006.05.001.

Abasi, A. R. & Graves, B. (2008). Academic literacy and plagiarism: Conversations with international graduate students and disciplinary professors. *Journal of English for Academic Purposes, 7,* 221–233.

Aitchison, C. (2009). Writing groups for doctoral education. *Studies in Higher Education, 34,* 905–916. https://doi.org/10.1080/03075070902785580.

American Association for the Advancement of Science. (2018). Communicating to engage. https://www.aaas.org/comm-toolkit.

Belcher, W. L. (2009). *Writing your journal article in 12 weeks.* Sage.

Blazer, S. & DeCapua, S. E. (2020). Disciplinary corpus research for situated literacy instruction. In M. Brooks-Gillies, E. G. Garcia, S. H. Kim, K. Manthey & T. G. Smith (Eds.), *Graduate writing across the disciplines: Identifying, teaching, and supporting.* The WAC Clearinghouse; University Press of Colorado. https://wac.colostate.edu/books/atd/graduate.

Bradbury, H. (2015). *The SAGE handbook of action research.* Sage. https://doi.org/10.4135/9781473921290.

Brooks-Gillies, M., Garcia, E. G. & Manthey, K. (2020). Making do by making space: Graduate writing groups as spaces alongside programmatic and institutional places. In M. Brooks-Gillies, E. G. Garcia, S. H. Kim, K. Manthey & T. G. Smith (Eds.),

Graduate writing across the disciplines: Identifying, teaching, and supporting. The WAC Clearinghouse; University Press of Colorado. https://wac.colostate.edu/books/atd/graduate.

Carter, N. (2012). Action research: Improving graduate-level writing. *Educational Action Research, 20*(3), 407–421. https://doi.org/10.1080/09650792.2012.697403.

Chang, P. & Schleppegrel, M. (2011). Taking an effective authorial stance in academic writing: Making the linguistic resources explicit for L2 writers in the social sciences. *Journal of English for Academic Purposes, 10,* 140–141. https://doi.org/10.1016/j.jeap.2011.05.005.

Crossthwaite, P. (2016). A longitudinal multidimensional analysis of EAP writing: Determining EAP course effectiveness. *Journal of English for Academic Purposes, 22,* 166–178.

Council of Graduate Schools. (2017). https://cgsnet.org.

Dave's ESL Cafe. (2017). http://www.eslcafe.com.

DeLyser, D. (2003). Teaching graduate students to write: A seminar for thesis and dissertation writers. *Journal of Geography in Higher Education, 27*(2), 169–181.

Dong, Y. R. (1996). Learning how to use citations for knowledge transformation: Non-native doctoral students' dissertation writing in science. *Research in the Teaching of English, 30,* 428–457. https://www.jstor.org/stable/40171551.

Fenton-Smith, B., Humphreys, P. & Walkinshaw, I. (2018). On evaluating the effectiveness of university-wide credit-bearing English language enhancement courses. *Journal of English for Academic Purposes, 31,* 72–83.

Fenton-Smith, B., Humphreys, P., Walkinshaw, I., Michael, R. & Lobo, A. (2017). Implementing a university-wide credit-bearing English language enhancement programme: Issues emerging from practice. *Studies in Higher Education, 42*(3), 463–479. https://doi.org/10.1080/03075079.2015.1052736.

Ferguson, T. (2009). The 'Write' skills and more: A thesis writing group for doctoral students. *Journal of Geography in Higher Education, 33,* 285–297. https://doi.org/10.1080/03098260902734968.

Gilmore, J., Strickland, D., Timmerman, B., Maher, M. & Feldon, D. (2010). Weeds in the flower garden: An exploration of plagiarism in graduate students' research proposals and its connection to enculturation, ESL, and contextual factors. *International Journal for Educational Integrity, 6*(1), 13–28.

Graff, G. & Birkenstein, C. (2010). *They say/I say: The moves that matter in academic writing* (2nd ed.). W. W. Norton.

Harris, M. J. (2005). Three steps to teaching abstract and critique writing. *International Journal of Teaching and Learning in Higher Education, 17*(2), 136–146.

Hessl, A. E. (2011). Pathways for climate change effects on fire: Models, data, and uncertainties. *Progress in Physical Geography, 35,* 393–407. https://doi.org/10.1177/0309133311407654.

Kamler, B. & Thomson, P. (2004). Driven to abstraction: Doctoral supervision and writing pedagogies. *Teaching in Higher Education, 9,* 195–209. https://doi.org/10.1080/1356251042000195358.

Kim, S. & Wolke, S. (2020). Graduate writing groups: Helping L2 writers navigate the murky waters of academic writing. In M. Brooks-Gillies, E. G. Garcia, S. H. Kim,

K. Manthey & T. G. Smith (Eds.), *Graduate writing across the disciplines: Identifying, teaching, and supporting*. The WAC Clearinghouse; University Press of Colorado. https://wac.colostate.edu/books/atd/graduate.

Lakoff, G. & Johnson, M. (1980). *Metaphors we live by*. University of Chicago Press.

Lim, J. M. (2012). How do writers establish research niches? A genre-based investigation into management researchers' rhetorical steps and linguistic mechanisms. *Journal of English for Academic Purposes, 11*, 229–245. https://doi.org/10.1016/j.jeap.2012.05.002.

Maher, D., Seaton, L., McMullen, C., Fitzgerald, T., Otsuji, E. & Lee, A. (2008). 'Becoming and being writers': The experiences of doctoral students in writing groups. *Studies in Continuing Education, 30*, 263–275. https://doi.org/10.1080/01580370802439870.

Mansourizadeh, K. & Ahmad, U. K. (2011). Citation practices among non-native expert and novice scientific writers. *Journal of English for Academic Purposes, 10*, 152–161. https://doi.org/10.1016/j.jeap.2011.03.004.

Moore, M., Tatum, B. C. & Sebetan, I. (2011). Graduate education: What matters most? *Journal of Research in Innovative Teaching, 4*(1), 65–77.

Mueller, K. L. (2012, October 5). A strategic defense. *Science, 338*(6103), 19. http://science.sciencemag.org/content/338/6103/19.3.

Ondrusek, A. L. (2012). What the research reveals about graduate students' writing skills: A literature review. *Journal of Education for Library and Information Science, 53*(3), 176–188.

Petrić, B. (2007). Rhetorical functions of citations in high- and low-rated master's theses. *Journal of English for Academic Purposes, 6*, 238–253. https://doi.org/10.1016/j.jeap.2007.09.002.

Polio, C. & Shi, L. (2012). Perceptions and beliefs about textual appropriation and source use in second language writing. *Journal of Second Language Writing, 21*, 95–101. https://doi.org/10.1016/j.jslw.2012.03.001.

Rose, M. & McClafferty, K. A. (2001). A call for the teaching of writing in graduate education. *Educational Researcher, 30*, 27–33.

Sallee, M., Hallett, R. & Tierney, W. (2011). Teaching writing in graduate school. *College Teaching, 59*(2), 66–72.

Salter-Dvorak, H. (2016). Learning to argue in EAP: Evaluating a curriculum innovation from the inside. *Journal of English for Academic Purposes, 22*, 19–31.

Science Careers. (2017). American Association for the Advancement of Science. https://www.sciencemag.org/careers.

Swales, J. M. & Feak, C. B. (2012). *Academic writing for graduate students* (3rd ed.). University of Michigan Press.

Tankó, G. (2017). Literary research article abstracts: An analysis of rhetorical moves and their linguistic realizations. *Journal of English for Academic Purposes, 27*, 42–55. https://doi.org/10.1016/j.jeap.2017.04.003.

Thonney, T. (2011). Teaching the conventions of academic discourse. *Teaching English in the Two Year College, 38*(4), 347–362.

University of Queensland. (2018). Three minute thesis. https://threeminutethesis.uq.edu.au/Versatile Ph.D. (2017). https://versatilePhD.com.

PART 2: "If you really want to know something, teach it" OR Learning to Write by Teaching Writing: Professionalization through Instruction

Katie Manthey

SALEM COLLEGE

There are many lessons in life I keep relearning. One of these lessons is to honor the writing process. I have been teaching writing since 2009, and since that time I have told my students countless times smart adages like, "Don't wait until the last minute to start writing," and "a shitty draft is better than no draft."

I never seem to be able to take my own advice.

Sure, over the years I've gotten better. Graduate school forced me to readjust my yardstick for measuring "the last minute"—if something is due next month, chances are you're already behind. This is just the graduate/faculty version of waiting until the last minute. As the writing projects get larger and larger, my capacity for procrastination grows. It should be no surprise, then, that I write this introduction in the hour before a group meeting about this project. I can hear my own voice in my head, as though I were my own student, "You know you won't have the best product if you wait until the last minute and don't give yourself time to revise."

Oops.

The thing about being a writing instructor is that I am both a teacher and practitioner. Just this last summer—my second summer as a faculty member—I finally started to feel like I had a handle on *how* to write. During graduate school, learning to write happened mostly by trial and error—with an emphasis on "error." As a graduate instructor and a graduate writing consultant, though, I learned to slow down and put myself in the shoes of the student. Being on the "other" side of academic writing allowed me a chance to try to see where my professors were coming from. It also helped me realize that maybe I should start taking the advice I kept giving the students I worked with. I find that having learned to write through teaching others has made me not only aware of my own process, but has given me a lot more empathy for my students as they struggle to find their own processes and to find how these dynamic processes fit in the ever-changing contexts of their college lives.

As a professor, I find that I cut student writers slack more often than not. I try to do this for myself as well. So does this make me a terrible writer? A terrible teacher? Both?

It definitely makes me human, which is at the crux of the multiple identities of graduate student writers/instructors. This section of the book shares experiences and ideas from a variety of disciplinary perspectives about graduate instructors who teach and learn writing. Specifically, this section starts with a discussion of graduate students teaching discipline-specific writing, moves on to address the importance of graduate training courses, showcases graduate student voices telling their own stories of enculturation, and ends with an example of how graduate students can influence programming.

Graduate Student Perspectives: Career Development Through Serving as Writing-Intensive GTAs

Amy A. Lannin and Martha A. Townsend[1]
UNIVERSITY OF MISSOURI

> **Abstract**: One potentially significant but little-examined opportunity for graduate students to acquire experience with discipline-based writing is to serve as a Graduate Teaching Assistant (GTA) for Writing-Intensive (WI) courses at universities that sponsor writing-across-the-curriculum and writing-in-the-disciplines programs. This chapter reports on one such well-established program in which over 100 GTAs each semester serve in a variety of capacities for WI courses in their own disciplines. The chapter features both qualitative and quantitative data demonstrating the success of the program. Voices of representative GTAs, combined with independently obtained survey data, show that multiple outcomes are achieved: Graduate students are engaged with discipline-based writing, graduate students are prepared for their future careers, graduate students' discipline-based teaching ability is improved, and mentorships between graduate students and their supervising faculty develop—all of which add up to being much more than just a "grader" for a professor in a WI class.
>
> **Keywords**: Graduate Education, Graduate Writing, Writing Across the Curriculum (WAC), Writing in the Disciplines (WID), Career Development, Career Preparation, Teaching Assistant (TA), Graduate Teaching Assistant (GTA), Qualitative Research on Writing, Quantitative Research on Writing, Survey Research, Survey Protocol, Graduate Satisfaction with Career Preparation, Mentoring, Professional Acculturation, Writing-Intensive Courses, Tutoring, Writing Program Administration, Writing Program Development, Public University, Discipline-Based Writing, Graduate Student Professionalization, Undergraduate Education, General Education

We are struck by the similarities between Cornell University's John S. Knight Institute for Writing in the Disciplines, which Elliot Shapiro writes about in Chapter 5, and ours at the University of Missouri, which we write about here. Indeed, we

---

1 The authors acknowledge with gratitude the work of Dr. Joe Green, former CWP Graduate Research Assistant and chief liaison between CWP and the RJI Center for the project. He is now Associate Dean for Undergraduate Studies at the University of Dubuque. Townsend served as CWP director from 1991 to 2006. Lannin became CWP director in 2011.

DOI: https://doi.org/10.37514/ATD-B.2020.0407.2.04

find our chapters remarkably complementary. Like Shapiro, we argue that teaching writing can help graduate students become better writers. The two programs are alike in that they are stand-alone writing programs situated within large, land grant research universities; they are responsible for training graduate students from diverse disciplines who in turn contribute significantly to the education of undergraduate students; and they hold similar principles about how writing is learned and should be taught. The Cornell and Missouri programs are similar in scale and complexity, both programs exist in an educational milieu that values research over teaching, thus creating specific challenges we must address, and both programs play significant roles in the careers of the graduate students who are affiliated with them. In the comments of the graduate students quoted from each program, readers will hear similar refrains, both positive and problematic. Although similar in many respects, the two universities (as is to be expected) have developed very different systems for delivering their undergraduate writing curricula as well as for involving and training the graduate students they employ. We begin our chapter with thoughts expressed by a former graduate student who has worked with Missouri's program for a number of semesters.

A Poster Graduate Student for Interdisciplinarity

> I started my professional life as an independent, private (and relatively untrained) writing tutor for students age six to fifty-six, where I operated from a practical standpoint of knowing what worked and didn't work. In grad school, becoming a WI [Writing Intensive] TA helped me plug into the university system. My life's goal is to spread knowledge in an atmosphere of comfort and trust; tutoring and TAing have given me the opportunity to do that. It is safe to say that I would not be where I am today without having been a WI TA and tutor. (personal interview)

With a B.S. in Business Administration and Marketing, an M.S. in Political Science, and a Ph.D. in Literacy Education, Jonathan Cisco is a poster student for interdisciplinarity. (All names are real and used with permission.) Jonathan was one of two full-time professional coordinators and then assistant director for the University of Missouri's Campus Writing Program, working with faculty across the disciplines to plan and review Writing Intensive (WI) courses. His path included seven semesters as a tutor in the university's Writing Center and three semesters as a Writing Intensive (WI) graduate teaching assistant. In the Writing Center, he consulted with faculty and students for up to thirty different WI courses each semester. His own account of this work provides insight into the connection between his WI TA work, WI tutoring, and the writing he did as a doctoral student:

The effect of those experiences on my learning to think critically is phenomenal. To give you an example, as a WI tutor many of my repeat clients were political science students taking the Intro to Research Methods course. When we were talking about how to write a methods section we had to go into the statistics. I was teaching statistics through writing almost every day. Now, when I'm talking with faculty about statistics or reading quantitative papers, I feel far better prepared when it comes to understanding quantitative analysis, simply because of the hundreds of times I taught statistics as a tutor. (personal interview)

As Jonathan's example shows, tutoring and serving as a teaching assistant for an undergraduate writing-intensive (WI) class provides a deeper experience with discipline-based writing. At our university, graduate students have been serving as WI TAs for nearly three decades. Presently, as many as one hundred or more TAs each semester work with faculty members who teach WI courses. In this chapter, we report on a study in which we researched the question: "What are the perspectives of graduate students as teaching assistants in Writing Intensive courses?" We present their voices, stories, and experiences to understand how their work transcends being merely "graders" for WI faculty but instead provides valuable career preparation, especially when it comes to writing. We include data that spans more than 10 years of the program's history, including interviews, surveys, and previous program research. This compilation includes excerpts from interviews conducted with WI TAs who worked in our program. We cite former WI TAs (now full-time academicians) who studied professor/WI TA teams. We also report on an independent survey of 467 former WI TAs, alumnae of this program who served in this capacity during their graduate studies, who reflect on how their WI TA work helped prepare them for their careers and professional writing demands. Overall, we believe the findings offer compelling evidence for the efficacy of the WI TA model in achieving multiple aims: engaging graduate students with discipline-based writing, preparing graduate students for their future careers, improving graduate students' discipline-based teaching ability, creating mentorships between graduate students and their supervising faculty—and, of course, becoming better writers.

The Missouri Model

We are fortunate that University of Missouri administrators recognize that an important symbiosis exists between graduate education (an essential component of which is graduate student professionalization), undergraduate education (which, at our university, requires two WI courses for graduation), and faculty's need for support if WI courses are to be delivered at the 20:1 student-to-teacher ratio our WI guidelines call for. One of the motives for the initial survey we report on was to document for our administration, the value of the university's investment in this model. We believe the findings are convincing, and we hope other similar universities might consider such a model, in light of the professional benefits our former graduate students report. Though this survey was conducted for internal uses of program assessment, as we later reflected on this data, we found this to be useful information even now, and thus sought to study the TA landscape and build on this initial survey.

Program History

The University of Missouri's Campus Writing Program (CWP) came into being in 1984, to support delivery of the undergraduate WI course requirement that faculty had voted to enact. (See Townsend, Patton & Vogt, 2012, for a program history.) Like many writing-across-the-curriculum/writing-in-the-disciplines programs, CWP designates approved courses as "writing intensive," which undergraduate students are required to complete in order to graduate. A long-standing set of guidelines, developed by a faculty-driven Campus Writing Board, helps faculty interpret how to design and teach WI courses. Key among the requirement's underlying principles is the idea that writing is a vehicle for learning and that WI classes will require students to "express, reformulate, or apply the concepts of an academic discipline" (University of Missouri Campus Writing Board). Annually, some 400 WI courses are taught by faculty in 86 undergraduate degree-granting programs across the university. Thus, student writing is based on the specific conventions, expectations, and vocabularies of the disciplines in which those courses are taught. Additionally, the writing must be "complex enough to require substantive revision for most students" (University of Missouri Campus Writing Board). Such writing and revision, of course, require feedback from knowledgeable experts in each field.

The 20:1 student-to-faculty ratio for WI courses was established at the program's outset to ensure that students would receive constructive feedback on their writing. At the same time, program framers recognized the need to be sensitive to the research and publication demands on the professoriate at an Association of American Universities (AAU) institution. The provision for graduate teaching assistance is both an incentive for faculty to teach WI courses as well as a concession to the enrollment pressures of a large, public university. Early WI classes enrolled just 20 students with one professor so that faculty could experiment and become confident with the new pedagogies. It was clear from the beginning, though, that course enrollments would have to increase to accommodate the now 14,000 students who take WI courses each year in order to graduate on time. The adoption of new general education requirements increased the requirement from one to two WI courses per student, which also added increased enrollment pressure. Hiring graduate students to assist faculty offering the WI courses has been the practice, then, virtually since the program's origin. The involvement of TAs is vital to the sustained success of the CWP, and because of this, we need to understand and build on the research of the TA experience.

Involvement of Teaching Assistants: Some Background

Funds to help staff WI classes with GTAs are based on the total number of WI students enrolled. Departments are reimbursed $110 per student *beyond* the first 20 students in a WI class (for whom the professor is responsible). WI faculty, in consultation with their departmental Directors of Graduate Study, select the GTAs they want to work with from their department's pool of available graduate students. Faculty members and departments determine their own criteria for selecting GTAs, based on varying circumstances and needs, with CWP stepping in to consult on request. Occasionally, graduate students may cross over to another department if the pool is small; a doctoral student in Art History, for example, might TA for a course in the Art Department or vice versa.

Before the start of each semester, the Campus Writing Program offers a TA/Faculty workshop at which the TA and often the supervising faculty member practice reading and responding to student papers, consider assignment design, explore issues of plagiarism, and discuss other trouble-shooting topics for working as a TA in a WI course. CWP also works with faculty to hold department-specific "norming" sessions and TA workshops to look at papers and issues that arise in a particular course. These TA-focused development opportunities are one part of a fuller scope of workshops, seminars, and retreats offered by the Program to support the teaching of WI courses at MU. By far the biggest part of our budget funds the academic work these graduate students perform.

The Gap We Hope to Help Fill

As the editors of this collection note, the literature on the writing-related aspects of graduate education needs expansion. Among the resources we found are four we mention here. In "The Effects of Writing Pedagogy Education on Graduate Teaching Assistants' Approaches to Teaching Composition" (2012), Reid, Estrem, and Belcheir report on a three-year, two-site, multimodal study of the relationship between formal pedagogy education and teaching practice. Their analysis shows "uneven integration of key composition pedagogy principles into TAs' views of teaching writing" (p. 32). But their study focuses on TAs in first-year composition and does not address cross-disciplinary TAs in WAC settings. In "The GTA Mentoring Program: An Interdisciplinary Approach to Developing Future Faculty as Teacher-Scholars" (2003), Gaia, Corts, Tatum, and Allen describe a lack of professional development for graduate students and outline an interdisciplinary mentoring program for graduate teaching assistants. As their title suggests, however, their focus is on mentoring the future professoriate, and they do not address graduate student writing nor include reference to graduate students who go on to professional careers outside academe.

Rodrigue's "The (In)Visible World of Teaching Assistants in the Disciplines: Preparing TAs to Teach Writing" (2012) comes closest to addressing the cross-disciplinary graduate students we write about in this chapter. She notes that even though WAC *faculty* development has a strong presence in the literature, surprisingly little attention has been devoted to the training, teaching roles, and participation of TAs in WAC efforts. Her essay examines the history of TAs in WAC programs, shows why TAs have been excluded from the literature, and argues for more attention to the role and training of TAs in WAC settings. Although Rodrigue's conclusion briefly mentions the benefits to graduate students of receiving WAC TA training, the essay does not offer in-depth commentary on the benefits to their own writing experience. None of these sources, though, address the ways that GTAs' own writing practices benefit from involvement in WAC programs.

One recent source does begin to get at the matter of developing graduate student writing, albeit somewhat indirectly. Although Geller and Eodice's *Working with Faculty Writers* (2013) focuses primarily on the benefits of institutions' emphasizing faculty development activities related to writing, the authors also invoke benefits for "graduate writers—[those who are] on the cusp of becoming faculty writers" throughout the book (p. 16). We believe our chapter, and this collection, begin to address some of the missing links needed for writing programs that rely so heavily on graduate students by asking: What do graduate students find important and useful from their experiences as WI TAs?

A Study of TA Writing-Intensive Experiences: Genesis and Methodology

This study began when Marty Townsend, CWP director from 1991–2006, and Amy Lannin, current CWP director, met to discuss data from a previous study of TAs who had worked over a 10-year span. Though this survey was dated (completed in 2005), the findings were useful in understanding (and making visible) the perspectives of these hundreds of graduate students. It was a bit of a holy grail moment when we both realized the value of this data, and that due to the program's minimal changes over the years, the data provided a richer view of what constitutes a significant part of the CWP work. However, we still questioned what current TAs would say, and we wondered how other types of data could inform the survey data.

To help us answer the question, "What are the perspectives of graduate students as teaching assistants in Writing Intensive courses?," we planned a mixed methods exploratory study (Creswell & Clark, 2007). Data started with the collection of survey responses that included both Likert scale and open-ended responses. Quantitative data analysis was completed by an outside entity, the RJI (Reynolds Journalism Institute). With IRB approval and consent from interviewees, we then collected and analyzed interview transcripts and the surveys' open-ended responses. Qualitative analysis included exploring the data (reading and re-reading), coding the data, grouping codes into categories, forming categories into larger themes, comparing themes, and naming the over-arching findings.

In the sections below, we describe the survey and initial findings. We then present the mixed collection of data that led to our findings and discussion of those findings.

The RJI/CWP Survey

The survey we undertook was designed to inform us about WI TAs' perspectives as related to their career development, an essential component of which is discipline-based writing. Survey design was a joint endeavor between CWP and the University of Missouri's RJI Insight and Survey Center (formerly the Center for Advanced Social Research) housed in the Donald W. Reynolds Journalism Institute. Data collection was done by RJI. Operating under the guidelines of the American Association of Public Opinion Research in Ann Arbor, the RJI Insight and Survey Center was at the time one of the country's leading providers of survey research for the news media, government agencies, academic institutes, and private foundations. CWP had engaged the Center to help us with an earlier study, and we trusted them to help us with this one. Given the substantial monetary investment made by the university in WI TAs, we wanted to ensure objective data obtained by an independent organization of the highest reputation. And, frankly, we knew the research we had in mind was beyond our scope and ability.

In consultation with RJI Center experts, we arrived at a 25-question telephone survey that examines the usefulness of WI TAs' experiences for their career development. (See Appendix A for the survey protocol.) CWP provided the names of former WI TAs, some of whom had finished their graduate work as much as 12 years earlier; the university's alumni association provided telephone numbers. The Center's trained interviewers and supervisory staff conducted 228 interviews over a 35-day period in the spring of 2005, with a response rate of 82.3 percent. Cost per survey was $18.

Quantitative Findings

The survey findings, which were used internally but never published, offer strong support for the WI TA model as we practice it. (The final report is available at http://cwp.missouri.edu.) Although the survey was conducted a while back, the findings and implications are no less relevant today. Indeed, recent WI TA interviews Lannin has conducted corroborate the survey data and reinforce what we learned from it. (See Appendix B for interview protocol.) During 2013–2014, three 60-minute interviews were conducted and transcribed. The interview questions were based on the original survey questions and allowed us to go more deeply into the survey topics and to hear from current TAs how they were viewing the TA experience. We believe the survey findings and interviews studied together offer a fuller picture of the WI TA perspectives.

Among the survey's quantitative findings are these:

1. 70 percent of the graduate students who responded perceive their WI TA experience to be valuable to their career development;
2. 69 percent perceive that their WI TA work enhanced their communication skills;
3. 62 percent perceive their WI TA work helped them understand the content of the courses they were helping to teach;
4. 52 percent perceive their WI TA work helped them with writing in their careers;
5. 49 percent perceive they better understand their own writing;
6. and a surprising 96 percent report they would advise current graduate students in their respective fields to serve as WI TAs if given the opportunity.

Findings 2, 4, and 5 relate directly to the purpose of this book.

Qualitative Findings & Discussion

Perhaps more revealing than the numerical data are the WI TAs' responses to the survey's open-ended questions, reported in the RJI Center's transcript. These comments represent voices from disciplines across the entire spectrum of the university, a *partial* list of which includes: Agricultural Economics, Agricultural Engineering, Animal Science, Archeology, Art and Design, Art History, Biology, Business, Finance, Chemical Engineering, Classical Studies, Communication, Education, English, Entomology, Environmental Design, Fine Arts, Fisheries and Wildlife, Forestry, History, Human Development and Family Studies, Journalism, Law, Nursing, Sociology, Political Science, Sociology, and Theater. In the graduate students' own voices is evidence of the benefits the WI TA experience offers.

A number of themes emerged as we analyzed the open-ended survey responses and the transcripts of the more recent interviews. We begin with a broader focus of the GTAs' acculturation into the academy, those responses that describe how they made the transition into the world of higher education as a TA. Then we look more specifically at the preparation they found helpful in becoming TAs. We also find many of the responses address the educational benefits of being a TA, mainly for learning course content as well as for the development of their own writing. A final theme deals with life beyond the TAs' career at MU as many respondents describe how they were aided in getting and succeeding in their jobs because of their experiences as a TA.

Survey responses are short because interviewees were answering a series of twenty-some questions on the phone, in contrast to the longer in-person interviews that we also share. The themes are presented below with responses from the surveys (participants are anonymous) and interviews (participants are named).

Stepping into Unfamiliar Waters: Acculturation into Academe

Being a graduate student is daunting, yet the experiences of serving as a TA in a writing-intensive course provided our graduate students with a supportive environment to transition into the academy. Jennah Sontag is one of the rare TAs whose WI appointment was far afield from her own discipline. She was just beginning her graduate studies in Journalism when she agreed to step out of her comfort zone to work with Professor Mark Morgan in Parks, Recreation, and Tourism. The students in his course, titled "Social Aspects of Fishing," were about to undertake an innovative project, and Morgan was intentionally seeking someone who could contribute not only writing expertise, but also provide an outsider's perspective on their work. Sontag says:

> In preparation for the course, Dr. Morgan involved me in organizing materials, planning the syllabus, and gathering background information. I learned a lot about the field and his research. This experience exposed me to what kinds of research are done in the field of Parks, Recreation, and Tourism, what drives certain professors, what their interests are. I've always been a quantitative research person. Learning about Dr. Morgan's research exposed me to qualitative research in other areas. I struggle with that kind of research at times. Seeing how it is used in fields outside Journalism helped me understand it. (personal interview)

Throughout her WI TA assignment, then, Sontag received a "double dose" of acculturation—both into academe as well as into a new disciplinary setting. Although we don't recommend this double whammy, the exposure to a new discipline's research methods proved beneficial to Sontag, whose experience we recount in greater detail later in this essay.

Several respondents speak to the value of building closer relationships with the professors in their fields: "It is a really good learning experience working with professors who have had a lot of experience and can become mentors." The closer exposure to more professors' experiences (including perhaps even some who are not their immediate supervisors), the mentoring that develops, and the relative ease of getting to know them were valuable to this group—"priceless" in the words of one. Sontag describes this relationship with Professor Morgan, as he mentored her into a different discipline as well as into the work of a TA. Her experience corroborates this survey response from another TA:

> [TA work] helps you form a different relationship with the professor. You have the ability to work together as a team. I got to know all the professors in my department, and it was easier to work with them, rather than if they were professor and I [were just] a student.

With any course, the larger the enrollment, the more challenging course management becomes, especially when TAs are helping to deliver the curriculum—and even more so because the Campus Writing Board works hard to ensure that TAs are *not* relegated to the marginalized role of "grader" while faculty attend to "more important" issues. Our program has worked hard to balance faculty and TA experiences when they work together. We want faculty to retain responsibility for their classrooms and their teaching, while at the same time both receiving the TA help they need *and* mentoring their GTAs about the uses of writing in their discipline-based contexts. Thus, *WI Guideline* number eight, and its explanatory comment, read:

> **In classes employing graduate teaching assistants, professors should remain firmly in control not only of the writing assignments, but of the grading and marking of papers.**
>
> The most common practice in courses with enrollment below 50 is to have the professor read every major written assignment and either assign a grade or approve the GTA's grade. In such courses marking and commenting on papers is usually a responsibility shared by the graduate teaching assistant and the professor. As courses get larger, the professor's role becomes increasingly managerial: he or she may train GTAs in "standard-setting" sessions such as those featured in Campus Writing Program TA workshops and then entrust the actual grading to the graduate teaching assistants. In such circumstances,

the Board needs to be assured that the GTAs assign essentially the same grade the professor would, for essentially the same reasons. Professors are, therefore, encouraged to read a large enough sample of the GTAs' graded papers to verify the accuracy of their evaluations. This sampling will also help the professor assess the effectiveness of the assignment and the need the class may have for additional instruction. (University of Missouri Campus Writing Board)

Before they became full-time academicians, Lisa Higgins and Ginny Muller (1994), then WI TAs themselves, undertook an ethnographic study of professor/WI TA teams at the University of Missouri. Discovering that the specifics of the professor/WI TA relationship often remain unarticulated, and that the roles TAs fulfill vary widely, Higgins and Muller propose a set of generative questions to facilitate a dialogue between professors and TAs. These questions help clarify how the team will work together, thus determining the quality of experience the faculty, the TAs, and their students will have. Higgins, now director of the Missouri Folk Arts Program, and Muller, an award-winning associate teaching professor at MU, conclude:

> Working as WI TAs has richly benefited our student and professional careers through acculturation into the academic community, collegial relationships with students and faculty, introductions to teaching in our chosen disciplines, and opportunities to develop and practice our own pedagogical theories with the help of faculty mentors. (p. 2)

Although we can't say for sure that Higgins' and Muller's research led directly to the *WI Guideline* quoted above, or to the item we discuss below, we are sure there is a strong influence. CWP closely heeds the experiences reported to us by faculty and graduate students working together in WI classrooms; the program follows through with changes both subtle and substantive to its guiding documents.

For example, since Higgins' and Muller's article, the Board has developed a complementary set of guidelines to address the special challenges of large-enrollment WI courses. (See Appendix C.) We think it notable that the Board seeks to ensure not only that GTAs' grading across sections is consistent, but also—as indicated in item four—that they are offered professional acculturation into the discipline itself. In CWP's view, this acculturation is as important as grading consistency.

Preparing for the Professional Work of a Teaching Assistant

Part of the acculturation process includes the preparation that TAs should receive to make sure that expectations are clear for their work as a TA and for their working relationships with faculty. Higgins' and Muller's ethnographic study was born, in part, of their frustration over unspoken assumptions about how WI faculty and TAs would work together. Through comparing notes on their own TA experiences in separate WI classes, they realized that better communication between WI faculty and TAs was needed if TAs were to fulfill their responsibilities. Thus, their work warrants inclusion under this theme as well. Turning their desire for a better TA preparation system into a research project for the WAC/WID seminar they were then enrolled in, they interviewed WI faculty and TAs about their working relationships, ultimately developing a rubric for dialogue that improves professional preparation. Part of this preparation includes questions for the professor and TAs to discuss:

- What are the specific tasks of the professor and TA in this class?
- How would you describe your expectations for this particular TA/professor relationship?
- What kind of relationship does the professor have with the students in the class?
- What is the role of writing in this course?
- How does the professor facilitate writing?
- How does the TA facilitate writing?
- Would the TA benefit from more training? What sort would you recommend?

As we mentioned earlier, the Campus Writing Program offers workshops for TAs at the start of each semester. Sontag, the Journalism student who worked with Parks, Recreation, and Tourism Professor Mark Morgan, found the TA workshop helpful in preparing her for her assignment:

> The TA workshop was really great because we worked with people from other departments and I got to see what their expectations were. We first graded a paper individually and then as a team to see how differently we graded the same assignment. That put grading into perspective about the expectations of us and other teachers of writing and of professors. This helped me see the big picture of writing across all of the curricula. Writing isn't just in journalism but in every field.
>
> Dr. Morgan and I graded papers separately and then together. He involved me at every step: designing the syllabus and requirements, giving feedback. I was hired the semester before the course started. This was smart on his part. It gave me more of a sense of ownership in the course. I'm excited that our students' project, "Hook, Line, and Sinker: A Collection of Fish Tales from Missouri Anglers," is now published. (personal interview)

For Morgan's part, his acknowledgment for the book reads, "Writing, like fishing, is a process that requires careful attention to details. Successful authors and anglers learn to rely on feedback from various sources. I am indebted to . . . Jennah Sontag, our graduate teaching assistant for this project. Already a published author, Jennah provided some much-needed writing savvy. When I found out she enjoyed fishing, [working with her as a TA] was an easy decision—the best one I made."

Preparing to work with a TA, as well as serving as one, requires varied levels of support. From the individual consultation with the faculty, to attending a campus-wide workshop, we strive to ensure that the TAs in this program are well prepared for the demands of assisting in a writing-intensive course.

Learning through Teaching

Our third emergent theme harkens to Seneca's dictum *docendo discimus*: "By teaching, we learn." We turn now to the phone survey responses to hear the voices of these former TAs who make up the 62 percent who perceive their WI TA work as helping them understand course content. Some respondents specifically note that teaching the material helped them learn it, as demonstrated in this survey response:

> There's a saying that you never really learn to do something until you have to teach it. You have to understand it well in order to make an essay. I had some [students] writing articles about opera who had no prior writing experience . . . I found myself just pulling out basic structure on how to write an essay. When you are teaching that is very valuable.

Another survey respondent echoes the power of learning through teaching:

> I was studying some of the same material I was teaching as a TA. The material actually overlapped with the graduate program as far as the philosophy and some of the ethics [and] legal issues. So, in teaching that I was learning it as well.

One of the strengths of the Missouri model is that WI TAs are selected to work with WI courses in their own disciplines. (Sontag's case is a rare exception.) So, as graduate students help the WI professor prepare teaching materials, attend the WI classes, read and respond to student writing, and occasionally teach the WI class themselves, they are not only gaining extra exposure to content that may be quite close to their own area of interest, but also reinforcing it in their own minds. In Cisco's interview, he elaborated on his own learning through his work as a TA:

> Graduate work in quantitative methods is so complex and so swift that it's easy to forget why something works. The tutoring

and teaching of writing put me in an environment where I had to make sense of things to the undergraduate students who were terribly unprepared for advanced statistics. I had to find a way to teach multiple regression—and how to write about it—in a 50-minute tutorial session. I did this over and over and over again. Through that process, I learned how to explain regression simply and in such a way that the hows and whys made quick sense to the students. Transference was inevitable. I learned by doing. (personal interview)

Developing as a Writer

> The more I looked at others' writing styles, the more I focused on my own.
> —Survey Respondent

As shown in the quantitative results, 52 percent of the respondents perceived that their WI TA work helped them with writing in their careers, and 49 percent perceived that it helped them better understand their own writing. This finding was explained in the open-ended responses. Spending time reading and grading student papers helped respondents analyze their own writing: "[Working as a WI TA] made me critique my own writing much more. I had friends editing my own class papers and my dissertation and I got fewer red marks from my friends after I had been forced to see others' writing. It improved my critical eye." The "critical eye" seemed to result in TAs considering the development of ideas, the role of audience, and the stylistic moves in their writing.

Inasmuch as the ability "to think more clearly and express thoughts more precisely" (University of Missouri Campus Writing Board) is an integral part of WI courses and writing assignments, it's not surprising that logic is mentioned by several respondents. Examples include:

> It made me be more concise and use more logic in my own writing.
>
> I learned how to be more clear, concise, and logical; the more you see other people's writing, and the more you write, the better you get.

The importance of audience awareness—one of the hardest things for all writers, expert and novice, to nail down—appeared in a couple of responses, such as this one: "I learned about taking into consideration the audience that I'm writing to—developing a style that's having a conversation with the reader and having a discussion be logically consistent. And just nuances about the art of writing." The concept of audience connects, of course, to the academic reality of being in a conversation with those whose thoughts and research have preceded your own.

Whether the respondent is familiar with the Burkean parlor metaphor is unknown to us, but we suspect it would make complete sense to her.

The idea of concision in some of the responses suggests that in reading unfocused undergraduate writing, these graduate students have become more attuned to producing prose of their own that is as direct and succinct as they can make it—a trait that will no doubt cause their readers to value their work more highly.

From a reference to "nuance" and another respondent's comment that it "makes you think about how to put words together," we might deduce an increased awareness of how language works—and maybe even an increased appreciation for using words as effectively as possible. And even though only two respondents directly mention style, several responses could be seen to invoke it generally. Overall, we think this group of respondents would enjoy coming together for a seminar based on Joe Williams and Gregory Colomb's *Style: Ten Lessons in Clarity and Grace* (2010)—and might then teach it competently as well.

> I was reviewing technical science writing for the [WI] course and that's what I'm doing as I prepare my dissertation now.

Three of the survey respondents specifically refer to the effect of WI TA work on their own dissertations, while two other respondents allude to wanting their writing to be better for their professors as a result of WI TA work:

> After I started grading others' papers I understood what my professors had been telling me all those years. It was before me in black and white and it made me change what I was doing.

The ideas of critique, having a critical eye, and seeing something "in black and white," suggest the transfer that students found as they connected their TA experiences with writing to their own writing tasks.

Getting a Job and Succeeding in the Workforce

Based on the survey responses, 70 percent of these former graduate students believe that the WI TA experience helped with job acquisition, from high school, to college, to an extra job within the new place of employment. As one respondent remarks: "Monitoring the students helped me tighten up my own writing and went a long way toward getting me my present job at a university." This comment also fits into the group that responded about how the WI TA experience affected their own writing. Other responses indicate that what they gained from their TA work became necessary aspects of their jobs: "I'm a trial lawyer and my job is to speak for a living—and that's what I did every time I went to class to teach and help my students."

The WI TA experience was also significant in helping students acquire jobs: "My primary professor has asked me to come back and be an adjunct professor for a couple of classes. Last winter semester and this one, I was an adjunct professor on top of my [regular] job." Or in the next example, the former TA found a job that was directly connected to his university teaching: "I taught the German Civilization recitation sections and this was the most helpful to my professional development because I'm now teaching that class at a high school."

Another aspect of job success was in the people skills, as well as writing skills, that this respondent noted:

> Working with the students some interesting situations arose due to the controversial subject matter. Dealing with students' emotions tactfully while trying to get them to think analytically. It taught me how to deal with people's emotions when I went into sales. A lot of employers liked that I had taught writing and knew how to write. I was assigned to teach a professional writing class for a company I worked for.

Other responses represent benefits the former graduate students perceive as worthwhile to them in their careers, whether in academe or not. Knowing how much writing to assign in a class is key to a new faculty member's success: "The process helped me later as a professor to know how much writing is appropriate to assign." Throughout our years in WAC, we have observed several first-time faculty instructors assign far too much writing than is appropriate, as well as assignments beyond the level of ability of undergraduate students. We see value in the lessons learned about amount of writing and appropriateness of expectations for different levels of students.

The following respondent sees the benefit from a continued relationship with her supervising faculty mentors toward her professional success:

> I'm still in contact with the professors I worked with, and have presented on panels together with them since then. We continue having a professional collaboration. There were forty-some students in the class, and I was actually able to teach the class sometimes. That was great for my professional development and preparing me to teach college courses. The professors that I worked with treated me as a colleague. It was a very enriching experience.

Very likely, these faculty mentors might well be among the recommenders who helped this former WI TA get her job.

The autonomy that comes with these assistantships, whether the future includes teaching or not, was highly valued by some respondents: "Having to TA the class by myself gave me an idea of what teaching was like in case I go into the teaching field at some point. Having a little teaching background helps in working with others."

Finally, this next response demonstrates the many ways that serving as a TA can help students prepare for getting and succeeding in a job:

> WI courses teach you how to better express yourself in a professional environment no matter what further career steps you take. Consulting and learning and dealing with both students and professors at all these levels helps you see various sides of writing and compare and contrast your own skills to skills of other professionals in your area of expertise.

Overall Benefits of Working as a TA: Support and Preparation for the Future

An astonishing 96 percent of our respondents replied affirmatively that they would advise graduate students in their field to serve as WI TAs. Following are comments that address these overall benefits. Respondents 1–3, below, speak to some of the ways that WI TA appointments prepare graduate students for future careers: the ability to critique one's own work, the "well roundedness" that comes from seeing differences between disciplines, and the ability to tackle the range of writing tasks that lie ahead. Again, improving one's communication skills in both writing and speaking is invoked.

1. As a WI TA, one of your primary focuses is critiquing the writing and communication skills of others. As you critique others you begin to critique your own work simultaneously. That ultimately flows over into your professional life, too.
2. For the opportunity to sharpen their writing and communication skills: writing and speaking. My experience was in an economics course in agriculture before I was a law student. It was interesting to see the differences in the two disciplines, and it gave me a more well-rounded experience.
3. It's good experience for what lies ahead. I had no idea how much of my current professional life I would spend writing. I'd say about 70 or 80 percent of the time I'm writing reports, memos, or even emails that have to be written in a certain way.

Many responses constitute a sort of "catch all" category: "If nothing else, financially [being a TA] was great for me as a single mom. It was enjoyable and interesting work." Presumably, as a single mother, this graduate student was able to do much of her WI TA work at home, while still earning money to support her children. Some of the respondents felt that the work as a TA resulted in acquisition of knowledge that will be important to new graduate students just starting their studies: "It would strengthen their overall knowledge of our field." And our final comment in this theme provides a summary of all the advantages in one short reply: "The experience, the money, the practice, everything."

The Naysayers

So, what did the four percent who *wouldn't* recommend WI TA appointments for their peers say? And what were some of the other negative answers to survey questions? Although a clear minority, those voices are worth hearing as well.

Those who said the WI TA work didn't help them better understand their own graduate writing cited the difference between graduate and undergraduate writing or noted they were working in a discipline not their own. Response number 4 speaks to why CWP rarely assigns TAs cross-disciplinarily and only if there is a special need, such as the one Morgan presented us with for his students' unusual research project.

1. The WI class I was teaching was introductory level, and my own studies were more of a research angle.
2. The kind of writing was different: different goals, different audience.
3. The kinds [of tasks] that undergrads have to do are not tasks grad students have to do. It's apples and oranges.
4. What they were writing about didn't have anything to do with what I was studying. I was getting my degree in one discipline and being a TA in another one.

To our question about what aspects of their experience WI TAs wish could have been different, we received a wide variety of responses. Most center around interaction with their faculty supervisors—wanting more involvement with the curriculum, workload, training, and pay. (Recall Higgins' and Muller's study here.) Most aspects are outside of their control; many are outside of CWP's control as well. Some of these responses include:

1. I had a professor who was in her first year and wasn't prepared. Anytime you have a professor who is getting up in front of students as a professor for the first time, it creates chaos.
2. I wish I had more time to go over the course content with the students.
3. I didn't attend the [pre-semester training workshop] that WI TAs were supposed to go to. I think that would have helped me a lot.
4. I wish the students would actually come to my office hours; the bulk of the students did not.
5. I wish I had more control over the assignments.
6. I wish I could have had a better place to meet with students. My office was dark and small and not very inviting.

7. There was no reason I had to be hired as a TA when I already had a master's degree and was qualified to teach undergraduate courses. They should have hired me as interim faculty.

Those who wouldn't recommend that their fellow graduate students serve as WI TAs referred either to the time commitment or to the lack of fit with their discipline. They said things like:

1. It is very time consuming. It does help with networking but it significantly adds to the workload.
2. The photojournalism track is a very time-consuming travel-oriented course and the WI course requires an enormous amount of time. It is almost a full-time teaching position because you not only grade papers but you are working with the students to improve their work.
3. In my field, the reward for being a WI TA is strictly for personal development. My enhanced abilities to work with students one-on-one won't translate in political science. It won't help me get published, get tenure at a Research I facility. It won't help my personal advancement.
4. The degree that I am doing is so very narrowly focused you probably should be working in a library, not teaching a writing class.

We don't discount these negative responses. Discerned in some of the comments above can be signs of the tension that exists at a research university when teaching becomes the focus. This tension is echoed in the following chapter when Shapiro writes of the disparaging discourse that shapes some graduate students' perceptions of teaching as "a distraction from the real work of research."

WI TA assignments are not perfect for every graduate student, just as WI teaching isn't a comfortable fit for every faculty member. When talking with prospective WI teachers, CWP staff make a point of not dissembling about the effort required. As the WI guidelines read, "The success of a Writing Intensive course depends more on the teacher's commitment to this style of teaching than on adherence to any particular formula. Because of the importance of this commitment, the Campus Writing Board encourages courses from willing faculty participants" (University of Missouri Campus Writing Board). The same goes for graduate assistants, as well. If we were to become aware of a WI TA who is dissatisfied with his appointment, we would try to help that graduate student finish out the semester as comfortably as possible and suggest that the WI faculty instructor seek a replacement for the next term. Or, in a worst-case scenario, we would help find a mid-term replacement, although neither of us recalls this happening. As the WI guidelines suggest, the success of any WAC program depends on the instructors' willingness to commit to this style of teaching. The same goes for WI TAs, as well.

Conclusion

To our knowledge, no similar study of TA involvement in WI courses has been conducted—even though many institutions employ TAs in similar roles. Moreover, we believe the independent nature of the data collection lends credibility to the findings. In our university, where support for graduate student writing is limited, the WI TA model has developed as an essential aspect of graduate students' professional preparation. Earlier in this chapter, we list some of the fields in which these WI TAs were earning their graduate degrees. At the time of their RJI/CWP telephone interviews, they had moved on to more than 50 different colleges and universities (into more advanced graduate work, post-doctoral positions, or faculty appointments) or to a variety of professional jobs.

To illustrate the wide perspectives from which our WI TA alumnae speak, a sample of their titles includes: art director for an advertising firm, senior television producer, student services coordinator, research scientist, senior policy research analyst, alumni coordinator, editorial assistant, consultant, project coordinator, curator of visual art, speech language pathologist, national marketing director, director of human resources, child birth educator, account executive, trial lawyer, entomologist, attorney, and president of a self-owned company. Having this many voices from such a wide array of perspectives illustrates the interdisciplinarity of the WAC program and the caliber of people whose careers have been developed who have then taken on leadership roles in their professions.

This study has helped us answer our question of "What are the perspectives of graduate students as teaching assistants in writing-intensive courses?" Through the mixed qualitative and quantitative data, we have a better understanding of how graduate students at our university have perceived their work as TAs. As we noted earlier, we believe the findings offer compelling evidence for the efficacy of the WI TA model in achieving multiple aims: engaging graduate students with discipline-based writing, preparing graduate students for their future careers, improving graduate students' discipline-based teaching ability, and creating mentorships between graduate students and their supervising faculty. All of that adds up to being much more than just a "grader" for a professor in a class. It is the efficacy of meeting multiple institutional goals—the symbiosis we describe in our introduction—that explains and justifies our university's substantial commitment, fiscal and philosophical, to this model.

We don't claim that Missouri's model is the only—or even the best—way to structure a WAC/WID program. Nor do we claim that our model works perfectly every semester or for every course or for every student. But we do claim that the hundreds of TAs who have been involved with MU's writing mission over the years have made significant contributions to undergraduate education at MU. More relevant to our chapter in this collection, we also claim that the vast majority of these

GTAs have received significant professional benefits from their work—especially with regard to their own writing.

We believe these findings, and the corroborating WI TA interviews, are relevant to other WAC/WID programs because of the growing importance of TAs in universities such as ours. We encourage other institutions that use graduate students as part of their writing-based instruction to conduct similar studies, to add to the literature. And, we invite other programs to explore whether their institutions could benefit from the extraordinary symbiosis that we see between graduate education, undergraduate education, and WAC/WID curriculum delivery.

Even though CWP is a 35-year-old program, the writing-intensive course guidelines and variation in class sizes of WI courses have remained. CWP changes have been mostly in the growth over the years. At times of higher University enrollment, the program reviews and approves upwards of 400 courses during an academic year and up to 14,000 students enrolled. Because of this growth, the demand of TAs has increased. Another change is in the increases to minimum stipend for graduate students. This increase has created a burden on departments and CWP to provide funds to hire graduate students. Because of these pressures, this study is even more important for institutions such as ours to pay attention to the role that GTAs provide, the support and benefits they receive, and the challenges they face, which could be a future study.

We give the closing words in our chapter to Jonathan Cisco, the "poster graduate student for interdisciplinarity" who opened our discussion:

> I cringe at what I would have become without these experiences because I think so differently now than I did before. There is a critical thinking piece, and we use that term a lot. It was a semester into my graduate education when I think I started to really critically think about stuff. I'm defining critical thinking in all the ways: I am critical of sources; I also reflect on my own type of thinking; I am able to identify what is important and not important. As a WI TA and tutor, I was immersed in various levels of critical thinking on the part of the student. *Most important, the TA and tutoring experiences dramatically influenced my own writing*. (personal interview, emphasis added)

References

Creswell, J. W. & Plano Clark, V. L. (2007). *Designing and conducting mixed methods research*. Sage.

Gaia, A. C., Corts, D. P., Tatum, H. E. & Allen, J. (2003). The GTA mentoring program: An interdisciplinary approach to developing future faculty as teacher-scholars. *College Teaching, 51*(2), 61–65.

Geller, A. E. & Eodice, M. (2013). *Working with faculty writers*. Utah State University Press.

Higgins, L. & Muller, V. (1994). An other teacher's perspective: TAs in the WI classroom. *The Writery, 1*(2), 1–2. http://cwp.missouri.edu/publications/index.php/.

Morgan, M. (Ed.). (2013). *Hook, line, and sinker: A collection of fish tales from Missouri anglers*. University of Missouri.

Reid, E. S., Estrem, E. & Belcheir, M. (2012). The effects of writing pedagogy education on graduate teaching assistants' approaches to teaching composition. *Writing Program Administration, 36*(1), 32–73.

Rodrigue, T. K. (2012). The (in)visible world of teaching assistants in the disciplines: Preparing TAs to teach writing. *Across the Disciplines, 9*(1). https://wac.colostate.edu/docs/atd/articles/rodrigue2012.pdf.

Townsend, M., Patton, M. D. & Vogt, J. A. (2012). Uncommon conversations: How nearly three decades of paying attention allows one WAC/WID program to thrive. *WPA Writing Program Administration, 35*(2), 127–159.

University of Missouri Campus Writing Board. (n.d.). (1984, revised 2019). *Guidelines for writing intensive courses*. Retrieved March 17, 2019, from https://cwp.missouri.edu/wi/guidelines/.

Williams, J. & Colomb, G. (2010). *Style: Lessons in clarity and grace* (10th ed.). Pearson.

Appendix A: WI TA Survey Protocol

The following survey does not include demographic questions.

1. On a scale of 1 to 5, where 1 is not at all significant and 5 is very significant, how significant was each of the following to your professional development?

   - Attending the writing intensive classes themselves
   - Discussing the WI assignments with the professor
   - Discussing the WI assignments with other WI TAs
   - Discussing students' writing with the professor
   - Discussing students' writing with other WI TAs
   - Discussing course content with the professor
   - Discussing course content with other WI TAs
   - Conferencing with students during your office hours
   - Commenting on papers and helping students revise their work
   - Assigning grades to students' papers
   - The rapport that developed between you and the professor
   - The camaraderie that developed between you and other WI TAs

2. Are there any other aspects of your experience as a WI TA that have been significant to your professional development?

3. Of all the aspects mentioned, which one stands out the most? Why do you say so?

4. Using a scale of 1 to 5, where 1 is strongly disagree and 5 is strongly agree, please indicate how much you agree with each of the following statements:
   - My work as a WI TA was valuable to the students who were studying in the courses.
   - My work as a WI TA was valuable to my own studies at the University of Missouri.
   - My work as a WI TA is valuable to my own career development.
5. Using the 1 to 5 scale, how would you describe your level of agreement with each of the following statements:
   - Working as a WI TA helped me better understand the course content that students were studying. Why do you say so?
   - Working as a WI TA helped me better understand the writing I was doing in my graduate studies. Why do you say so?
   - Working as a WI TA helped me with communication skills I have now in my career. Why do you say so?
6. As you now think about it, what aspects of your experience as a WI TA at the University of Missouri were most beneficial to you?
7. What aspects of your experience as a WI TA at the University of Missouri do you wish could have been different?
8. Would you advise current graduate students in your field to serve as WI TAs? Why do you say so?
9. Is there anything else about your WI TA experience at MU you would like us to know?
10. Would you be willing to be interviewed by the researchers of the study in the future?

Appendix B: Guide for TA Interview

Questions
1. How do you perceive your WI TA experience in relation to your career development? Please explain.
2. How did your work as a TA influence or affect your communication skills? What examples can you provide?
3. How did your work as a TA affect your understanding of the content of the course you helped to teach? What examples can you provide?
4. How do you see your work as a TA influence your writing in your graduate studies and/or in your career? How do you see your work as a TA influencing your own writing?

5. In what ways were you mentored (or not) through this WI TA teaching experience?
6. Have you shared your own writing experiences with your WI students? (If so, give examples).
7. What resources, services did you receive as a TA? Did you see your WI TA work as a service to others? Did you bring writing to your CWP mentors? Did you receive help with your own writing from these services?
8. Do you have any stories or memorable moments from your WI TA experience that might help us flesh out our study (on your perspectives of the WI TA-ship as career prep)?

Appendix C: Guidelines for Large-Enrollment Writing-Intensive Courses

1. Before submitting an application for WI status for a large-enrollment course, the department chair and the prospective WI instructor should meet with Campus Writing Program staff and representatives of the appropriate Board subcommittee.

    The Campus Writing Board envisions these meetings as an opportunity to clarify the role of writing in the course and to anticipate logistical problems and possible solutions. In particular, these discussions should focus on the use of writing to further course goals, assignment design, the role of TAs, and methods for ensuring grading consistency.

2. An instructor who applies to teach a large-enrollment WI course is expected to attend a CWP workshop within the academic year prior to the scheduled beginning of the large course.

    CWP research shows that participation in a CWP workshop is essential to introducing prospective WI instructors to the philosophical principles and practical methods that underlie successful WI courses. Conversely, faculty who teach WI courses without having attended a workshop comprise the largest category of faculty who do not offer subsequent WI courses.

3. Before WI status is granted to a large-enrollment WI course, the instructor should expect to pilot a somewhat smaller version of the course.

    The complexities of teaching a large-enrollment WI course demand that an instructor have an opportunity to rehearse major components of the course—writing assignments, grading standards, training sessions with TAs—before being faced with the myriad logistical problems presented by large-enrollment WI courses.

4. Instructors of large-enrollment WI courses should not be assigned additional teaching responsibilities during the semester they are first teaching the course. In subsequent semesters, additional teaching assignments should be very carefully considered.

The Board understands that this guideline may be difficult for some departments to achieve. In stating this preference, the Board wishes to stress the dual teaching responsibility of large WI courses: teachers of such courses actually teach two classes—one for the undergraduate students and another for the graduate student TAs assigned to the course. The latter is as labor-intensive as the former in order not only to ensure grading consistency but also to achieve the professional acculturation of TAs into the teaching of their discipline that is also a purpose of the WI course. The Board encourages departments to consider offering a concurrent, credit-bearing graduate practicum in conjunction with the WI course for those TAs working with the course. In recognition of the work involved and of the service to the University as well as the department, departments might arrange to "count" a three-hour large-enrollment WI course as the equivalent of six credit hours of teaching or take into account the number of FTEs generated.

Towards an Integrated Graduate Student (Training Program)

Elliot Shapiro

CORNELL UNIVERSITY

> **Abstract**: This chapter argues that teaching writing helps graduate students become better writers. Every year, more than 100 graduate students from more than 30 departments participate in one of two required six-week training courses offered through Cornell's John S. Knight Institute for Writing in the Disciplines. This chapter describes specific features of the training curricula that help graduate students learn to write as academic professionals. Primary source material is drawn from graduate writing produced for course evaluations, assignments, or in response to surveys sent to current and former graduate students. Graduate student observations that figure prominently in this article include a focus on writing process, the connection between teaching writing and learning writing, the value of reflection, and the efficacy of building communities where writers read each other's work.
>
> **Keywords**: Teaching Writing, Enculturation, WAC/WID, Coursework, Writing Process

Reflection and Methods: Integration, Enculturation, and Genres of Data

The chapters that appear on either side of this one—"Graduate Student Perspectives: Career Development Through Serving as Writing-Intensive GTAs" and "The Space Between: MA Students Enculturate to Graduate Reading and Writing"—underline the importance of two areas of concern that were buried in the version of this chapter that appeared in *Across the Disciplines* (*ATD*). Reading the chapters that bracket mine has pushed me to address these two concerns directly.

This reflective introduction is followed by four sections and a postscript. The first section, "When Teaching 'Teaching Writing' means Teaching Writing," lays out the chapter's claims and methodology. "Writing and the Writing in the Disciplines Curriculum" describes foundational principles of the Knight Institute and features of the training programs that have had an impact on our graduate students' development as writers. Although the voices of graduate writers appear throughout the chapter, "Voices from the Field," is structured by observations about writing made by graduate student writers who have participated in one or more of the

DOI: https://doi.org/10.37514/ATD-B.2020.0407.2.05

Knight Institute's training programs. "Learning Something Practical" makes concluding observations about the critical importance of being a flexible and agile learner, one of the findings about graduate writing and graduate education that this material repeatedly reinforces.

One issue brought to light by my essay's placement within this collection concerns genres of data that deal with writing and writing programs. By definition and design, quantitative data is impersonal. Collecting data points that can be efficiently recorded, sorted, and reported on may involve suppressing individuals' voices. In suppressing voice, data collection can steamroll the very features of writing that make writing *writing*. Qualitative data can provide counterweight. The study designed by the University of Missouri (UM)'s writing program—discussed by Lannin and Townsend (this collection)—demonstrates how quantitative and qualitative data can work together to tell a compelling story. A key question in the UM study elicits quantitative *and* qualitative data by asking students to rate their agreement with the following statement: "Working as a WI [writing-intensive] TA helped me better understand the writing I was doing in my graduate studies. Why do you say so?" Tallying responses to the agree/disagree statement revealed an agreement rate of 49 percent. But, as Lannin and Townsend note, the qualitative data is ultimately "more revealing" because responses to follow-up questions, like the one quoted above, "represent voices" (this collection).

I have generally operated with a strong bias in favor of qualitative data, which includes graduate writing. However, my experience setting up, running, and reporting on a program largely independent of Cornell's writing program taught me how hard it can be to work with qualitative data on any scale. Voiced narratives do not translate easily into data points. A handful of compelling anecdotes represents a limited sample size. Just as important, narratives take longer to read and digest than a snappy chart: a key point when addressing audiences that include university administrators. More anecdotes increase sample size but also increase reading time. These inherent shortcomings reduce the persuasive power of qualitative data.

For this article, I relied heavily on qualitative data drawn from graduate students who have participated in one or more of my program's six-week training courses, required for First-Year Writing Seminar instructors or Writing in the Majors TAs. With IRB approval, I reviewed course evaluations and wrote to current and former graduate students—particularly those who had participated in more than one sub-program under the Knight Institute umbrella. (For example: some graduate students took both courses; some took one course and served as writing tutors. Every year we hire TAs as co-facilitators to co-teach our training courses.) I also asked graduate students for permission to quote from writing samples written for the classes I teach, notably informal responses written during each class session. Students in my courses have the option to sign release forms authorizing me to quote from writing assignments—including informal in-class writing—for teaching and research purposes. For this article, I sometimes asked for permission to quote from a specific piece of writing.[1]

My chapter, built around a relatively small sample of qualitative data, would be less compelling if I did not also have access to the self-study conducted by Cornell's Anthropology department, generously shared with me when I was working on this article. Anthropology's survey of alumni generated a combination of qualitative and quantitative data that (happily) reinforced much of what my smaller-scale operation had revealed.[2] In addition, Lannin and Townsend's substantial study—focused on graduate TAs in Writing-Intensive (WI) classes, taught in a broad range of disciplines—provides compelling evidence that the training and experience that come with working as a TA in a writing program can shape graduate careers in ways that go beyond the goals of a particular course. I hope (and believe) that the placement of these two chapters next to each other, with findings that reinforce each other, will serve to strengthen the arguments presented in each chapter, for audiences within our respective institutions and outside them.

The second buried concern deals with what Fredrick, Stravalli, May, and Brookman-Smith (this collection) call enculturation, a central concern of their chapter and of Fredrick's teaching. Enculturation is closely related to integration—a central concern of my chapter and my teaching. In this chapter, I describe certain features of an integrated graduate program. I also discuss the structural obstacles that make such a program difficult to imagine at the research university where I teach. I say little about social integration into a graduate program. "The Space Between" is more directly concerned with intellectual and disciplinary enculturation; I would consider social integration another element of graduate student enculturation.

The reflections of the graduate co-authors of "The Space Between" demonstrate how powerful personal narrative can be. The texture of these narratives could not be represented in quantitative terms. These reflections demonstrate the possibilities of qualitative data, of voice. Together, this bloc of chapters helps demonstrate how different genres of data reinforce one another. Neither qualitative nor quantitative data can do as much alone as they can do together.

---

1   All comments on teaching, training, and writing submitted by graduate students who took Writing 7100 or Writing 7101—whether from class-related assignments or in response to specific queries—are published with written permission from the student quoted. These and other data are part of the ongoing *"Study of the Impact of Knight Institute Training Programs on Participating Graduate Student Instructors and Teaching Assistants,"* IRB protocol #1307003989, for which I am the lead researcher.

2   *A Survey of Cornell Anthropology Majors and Cornell Ph.D.s After Graduation, 1990–2013* was shared by the study's lead researcher with permission of the department chair. Anonymous samples of raw data were shared by the lead researcher. The study was conducted with IRB approval.

This selection of chapters also engages with questions of professionalization and attrition. Not everyone who enters a graduate program will complete it. But greater attention to enculturation and professional development, along with increased institutional commitment to integrating both sets of concerns into the curriculum, can make the path smoother.

In my original chapter, I say little about the idea of an integrated graduate student. The narratives of Fredrick, Stravalli, May, and Brookman-Smith reminded me how painful graduate school can be, for reasons that may be hard to recognize (or remember), even for those of us who serve as teachers and/or mentors. I remember times when I felt as if I were being pulled apart or as if some parts of me were being pressed or squeezed. (Recognizing how many people around the world are subject to actual torture, I hasten to add that these feelings were psychological.) Michel Foucault (1975/1995) reminds us that the language of discipline is rooted in things done to the body. Graduate students are integrated into disciplines by being disciplined. Those who are not disciplined, for any reason, do not continue.

When Teaching "Teaching Writing" Means Teaching Writing

Every year, more than 100 graduate students from more than 30 departments participate in one of two six-week training courses offered through Cornell's John S. Knight Institute for Writing in the Disciplines. Writing 7100: Teaching Writing prepares Ph.D. students to teach in the First-Year Writing Seminar program (FWS). Writing 7101: Writing in the Majors Seminar prepares Ph.D. students to work as teaching assistants in Writing in the Majors (WIM) classes. The Knight Institute's funding structure ensures that all graduate students who teach first-year writing seminars or TA in Writing in the Majors classes are required to take the course aimed at these particular teaching responsibilities.

While these classes focus on teaching, our not-so-hidden curriculum supports professional development for TAs and graduate instructors, most of whom will (we hope) follow short teaching careers at Cornell with long, productive careers elsewhere.

This chapter describes some of what we have learned from these students about graduate student writing and some of the strategies we use (within institutional constraints) to address an often-neglected aspect of graduate education: learning to write as an academic professional. Teaching people about *teaching writing* means teaching people about *writing*. In both 7100 and 7101, we try to demystify the practices and processes by which writing is produced, not just for undergraduates, but for apprentice professionals who are in the process of defining themselves relative to a discipline, an identity shaped above all else by how and what they write.

Teaching as Research

Tenure expectations at the research universities that train graduate students promote a narrow vision of what it means to be an academic professional. At research universities, professors are hired and promoted based on research: everything else is secondary. This incentive system pushes people to focus their limited energy and time on developing one aspect of a professional persona while neglecting others. Ironically, even though the primacy of research overshadows other aspects of academic work, the medium through which research is produced, presented, and evaluated—writing—is often assumed to be something smart graduate students just learn to do. One graduate student notes: " . . . graduate school does not necessarily encourage students to devote much time to thinking about how we write." A recent Ph.D. writes, "I was one of those students in the sciences who must have been expected to learn to write by osmosis."[3]

A truly integrated graduate training program would prepare graduate students to become colleagues who could fully integrate into all aspects of academic life: writing, research, teaching, and service.[4] The department-centered character of graduate education at my university ensures that our stand-alone writing program cannot aspire to be part of a fully integrated program. However, as we help graduate students prepare for their immediate assignments as writing teachers and teaching assistants, we can also help them prepare for careers as professional academic writers.

This chapter takes as a central premise the idea that teaching can be research into how students learn (this includes graduate students).[5] The chapters on either side of this one provide evidence to support this claim. Two different approaches are represented in these chapters: the large-scale self-study undertaken by University of Missouri's writing program and the intimate conversation between faculty and graduate students from Eastern and Illinois University in "The Space Between."

Cornell's training programs provide self-refreshing sources of information about

---

3   With two exceptions, all quotations from current or former graduate students are anonymous.

4   I make this argument at greater length in "Survival and Failure, Adaptation and Acceptance" (2008). I use integration in two ways here: to describe a program's relationship with other institutions that shape graduate education and to describe the different aspects of professional life that graduate students aspire to learn. I do not explicitly refer to a third relevant meaning of the term. In her work on graduate student attrition, Barbara Lovitts writes about the importance of *social integration* for graduate students. She writes, "the better integrated students are into their programs, the better their cognitive maps will be because they are in closer and more frequent contact with people who can help them develop the understanding necessary for degree completion" (2004, p. 117–118).

5   I owe this insight to Katherine Gottschalk and Keith Hjortshoj's invaluable book, *The Elements of Teaching Writing* (2004). They write, "You can think of teaching as research into the ways in which students actually learn the material. You can think of your course, therefore, as an ongoing experiment" (p. 24).

how graduate students learn, think, and write. To call these sources of information repositories would be inaccurate. Repository suggests something static, an archive into which information is deposited. In fact, the process is dynamic: participating students learn from each other, even as we learn from them.[6] When graduate students teach us something, we don't have to wait until the next course or the next year to apply it: it can become part of the teaching and learning dialectic immediately.[7] The primary goal of this research into graduate student learning is not to pile up stuff in archives, or to pile up publications (although both are valuable), but to improve the support we provide to our students. Certain challenges and opportunities are unique to Cornell, but much of the information this process yields may be relevant to graduate students and graduate programs across the country and/or across the world.

This chapter draws substantially on locally-produced material on the teaching of writing, including work published by long-time teachers and administrators in our program, some of which has been integrated into the curriculum of our graduate training courses. Primary source material is drawn from writing produced by graduate students: some in course evaluations, some in assignments, and some in response to surveys sent to current and former graduate students.

This chapter is intended to reflect the dynamic, collaborative culture of teaching and learning we try to foster in the Knight Institute. We strive to help graduate students teach each other. This goal is front and center in the course rationale for Writing 7100: Teaching Writing, which (in a recent iteration) includes the following statement:

> Writing Seminars succeed when they help build communities of writers. We hope this course will help build communities of teachers. Sharing assignments with other teachers and, we hope, learning from the work colleagues produce will be among the central tasks of Writing 7100.

The importance of learning from one another is evident in the many comments graduate students make about the value of sharing their work. One recent graduate student, who took Writing 7100 and worked as a graduate student co-facilitator for the class, writes:

> 7100 emphasizes collaboration and sharing of teaching materials, and at a certain point I began to wonder why the graduate

---

6   For evidence of the ways that local knowledge travels from students to instructors and back, one need look no further than some of the publications that have emerged from these collaborations. Notable examples cited in this article include *The Elements of Teaching Writing*, *The Transition to College Writing*, and *Writing from A to B*.

7   For instance, after reading a draft of this article, my colleague, David Faulkner, said he would discuss some of the issues examined here in the section of Writing 7100 he was teaching at the time.

community doesn't practice this more often and more broadly. I think it's incredibly logical and so clearly beneficial, it's almost comical how we (grad students) never share our writing with each other. . . . So, I've been actively encouraging my peers to share their work with me, and bugging them to read my work.[8]

Having benefited deeply from these collaborations, I am committed to representing not only what my colleagues and I have taught to our graduate students, but what we have learned from them.

Writing and the Writing in the Disciplines Curriculum

The writing in the disciplines model enshrined in our program's full name, Cornell's John S. Knight Institute for Writing in the Disciplines, is founded on one central premise: writing expertise cannot be fully separated from disciplinary knowledge. When one writes in the university one writes for an audience, on an occasion, within a context. Whether a piece of writing is produced for a class or for presentation or publication, context, occasion, and audience are determined by the practices and conventions of an academic field.

The small staff of the Knight Institute teaches only a handful of courses. The vast majority of the more than 300 first-year writing seminars offered at Cornell every year are taught by faculty and graduate students in approximately 30 departments. All of the 40 Writing in the Majors (WIM) courses offered each year are taught by faculty in approximately 20 departments, with significant roles played by graduate TAs. The Knight Institute provides TA funding for graduate instructors of first-year writing and for WIM TAs, in addition to the 7100 and 7101 required training courses for graduate students.

The Institute's greatest impact on the teaching of writing is, therefore, indirect. While Knight Institute faculty teach a small percentage of Cornell's undergraduates, we train dozens of their teachers every year. Moreover, our training courses play significant roles in the careers of more than 100 graduate students each year, albeit a role that may not be widely acknowledged as a feature of graduate education at Cornell.

When these courses are recognized as a feature of graduate education, they are typically praised as teacher training. Two examples illustrate this. A music professor who has taught several Writing in the Majors courses says the following about the training course for WIM TAs: "I consider this a key component of grad students' training as they prepare for their academic careers. . . . grad students also value this

---

8   Each section of Writing 7100 is led by a member of the Knight Institute faculty and assisted by a graduate student who has taken 7100 and taught one or more first-year writing seminars. Graduate students apply for co-facilitator positions and receive a stipend for their six weeks of work.

training, even when their research topics are distantly- or unrelated to the . . . topic [of the course they TA]." A recent self-study conducted by the Department of Anthropology, which included surveys sent to the program's graduate alumni, included the following summary comments: "recent alumni uniformly praised as necessary, important and excellent the training received through the Knight Program for Freshman Writing Seminars. Often it was the only intense and focused training in pedagogy they ever received at Cornell, and was seen as still valuable years after leaving Cornell" (Greenwood, Carrico & White, 2013, p. 32).

The data generated by the anthropology study provides evidence for two unsurprising findings: First, many graduate students receive little, if any, formal training as teachers. Second, good teacher training can play a pivotal role in their careers. As this article argues, good training can also help prepare graduate students not just to teach writing, but to write.

Who We Teach

To understand the Knight Institute's training mission, it helps to know how many people take our courses each year and how many disciplines they represent. The combined enrollment for all sections of 7100: Teaching Writing and 7101: Writing in the Majors Seminar in 2013–14 amounted to 111 graduate students from 34 departments and programs. Tables 5.1 and 5.2 show the departments these graduate students represented during the 2013–14 academic year.

Table 5.1. Departments represented in Writing 7100: Teaching Writing, Summer 2013/Fall 2013 (25 total departments)

American Indian Studies	Anthropology
Art History	Asian Studies
Astronomy	City and Regional Planning
Classics	Comparative Literature
Development Sociology	English
French (Romance Studies)	German Studies
Government	History
Horticulture	Italian (Romance Studies)
Linguistics	Medieval Studies
Music	Neurobiology and Behavior
Performing and Media Arts	Philosophy
Psychology	Science and Technology Studies
Spanish (Romance Studies)	

Table 5.2. Departments represented in Writing 7101: Writing in the Majors Seminar, Fall 2013/Spring 2014 (21 total departments)

Anthropology	Applied Economics and Management
Asian Studies	Astronomy
Cognitive Studies	Communications
Development Sociology	Ecology and Evolutionary Biology
Entomology	Government
History	Human Development
Medieval Studies	Molecular Biology and Genetics
Music	Neurobiology and Behavior
Performing and Media Arts	Physics
Psychology	Science and Technology Studies
Sociology	

While these numbers vary from year to year, they are reasonable indicators of the number and range of departments whose graduate students participate in the FWS and WIM programs.

The Rhetoric of Teaching

During the years I've been positioned to shape the curricula of 7100: Teaching Writing and 7101: Teaching in the Major Seminar, I have learned to see these courses not just as modes of content delivery but also as laboratories for teachers, and as research in learning. More surprisingly, I've learned to see these courses as arguments. These courses argue for themselves as professional development. Explaining this rhetorical function requires discussing some features of research institutions that will likely be news to no one reading this article. I frame my remarks primarily with a discussion about Writing 7100.[9]

Cornell's first-year writing seminar instructors, whether graduate students or faculty, must follow certain guidelines.[10] Within these parameters, instructors have considerable freedom to design discipline-based courses on topics of their

---

9   I focus on 7100: Teaching Writing for four reasons. First, I began teaching 7100 nine years before I started teaching 7101. Second, I assumed administrative and curricular responsibilities for 7100 long before I assumed similar responsibilities for 7101. Third, my work with 7100, starting my first year at Cornell, has shaped everything I have done since. Finally, the FWS program, and the training program that supports it, is both larger and more visible than is Writing in the Majors.

10 The basic parameters of all Cornell first-year writing seminars are posted on the program's website and described in the "Indispensable Reference for Teachers of First-Year Writing Seminars," a pamphlet updated annually and distributed each year to FWS instructors.

choice. These parameters structure the Writing 7100 curriculum. The central task of 7100, and the task with the greatest immediate value, is described in the course rationale: " . . . we want you to leave the course with an advanced draft of a syllabus and a selection of assignments you can use in your First-Year Writing Seminar." This task is one of three course goals laid out in the rationale incorporated into the syllabus when I began administering the course. The other two goals are as follows: "we want to introduce you to the challenges of teaching Writing Seminars with a disciplinary focus" and "we hope this seminar will be a laboratory in learning and teaching."

In addition to explaining why we ask students to do certain kinds of work, this rationale is intended to defuse resistance to the course. The first few times I taught Writing 7100 it was impossible to miss the resentful attitudes many students brought to the class. True, many came to the course with an open mind. The course won over some skeptics. But, graduate student discourse in general circulation sometimes disparaged Teaching Writing as a waste of time; this discourse shaped student perceptions of the course before they ever enrolled.

Negative attitudes are to be expected whenever you impose a requirement on anyone, and 7100 and 7101 are taught as requirements for our TA positions. Add to that an attitude towards teaching, itself, that can border on disdain. The position of some research faculty—learned and imitated by some graduate students—can be summarized as follows: Teaching is a necessary and sometimes pleasurable part of our job, but it is a distraction from the real work of research. Time spent teaching is time taken away from higher priority activities. Teacher training is an even lower priority: first, because faculty and graduate students should be able to translate their own intelligence and experience into their teaching; second, because too much devotion to teaching can be interpreted as a lack of commitment to research. One respondent to the anthropology study wrote, "Let's be honest, too much time spent developing one's teaching can be detrimental to one's career in academe." [11]

When I began directing Writing 7100, I initiated curricular changes intended to foreground the value of the course to the people who were required to take it. I hope this value is now apparent—not when the course ends, or years later, after they have enough teaching experience to value the experience—but before students walk into the first session on the first day. One significant change involved making graduate student writing an explicit element of the course, particularly through the first writing assignment.[12] During the time I have taught 7100 and 7101, I have

---

11   Citation information for the complete report is included in the references page and cited within the text as necessary. Some quotations are taken from the raw data, which the department shared in a form that protected respondents' anonymity.

12   While this was not an explicit focus of Writing 7100 before I began directing the course, it has long been a significant element of Writing 7101.

learned that attention to graduate writing can help foreground the value of these courses. Since graduate students have to write their way *out* of graduate school, and (hopefully) into jobs, a course that helps them develop as writers, even if that is not its primary function, has real and lasting value.

After six weeks, students should leave each course with a toolkit they can use in their own classes. Students should also leave with a clearer sense of themselves as writers, and a clearer sense of their position as writers relative to the undergraduates they teach (who they once were) and the faculty who teach them (who they hope to become). By focusing attention on the immediate value of these required courses (the toolkit) and the long-term value (professional development as teachers and writers), I hope we are able to build a more receptive audience for these courses. A receptive audience makes for an improved learning environment.

Anatomy of the Writing Process

One of the first Writing 7100 assignments (due before the first class meeting) asks students to reflect on themselves as writers. To a significant degree, I can trace my interest in the subject matter of this chapter to the fascinating responses to this assignment I have read while teaching both Writing 7100 and Writing 7101. Called "Anatomy of the Writing Process," a recent version of the assignment includes the following guidelines:

> Choose a specific piece of academic writing you've produced during your time at Cornell. . . . Write a short essay in which you narrate the process of writing it . . .
>
> You may want to address some of the following questions: what sequence of steps did you follow as you produced this piece? Was this sequence typical for you? How many distinct drafts did you write? What made them different? What texts or data did you engage with as you wrote? How does this piece participate in the discourse of your discipline? What observations can you make about language and style in your writing? What did you learn in the course of writing this piece? As noted in the learning outcome above, writing about your own work should advance your capacity to participate in reflective discussions on theories and practices of teaching and writing.

Completing this assignment, reading the submissions of their classmates, and discussing them in class should make clear to our graduate students how important we think it is that *they* help *their* students become more aware and self-reflective as writers. When it works, the impact is substantial, as is clear from the comments made by a current graduate student who has taken both Writing 7101 and Writing 7100, and has worked as a co-facilitator for Writing 7100:

> Preparing for Knight Center courses, working with students as a co-facilitator, and preparing my own first year writing seminars have all made me much more cognizant of my own writing process.... Having to articulate the anatomy of my own writing method helped to formalize, in my mind, the steps I need to take with each piece of writing I commence.... In many ways, the classes I have taken with the Knight Center have offered the first serious critique of my writing technique, rather than the sole merits of my argument, since high school.

Both 7100 and 7101 offer participants focused discussions on teaching and writing among people working in a broad range of fields. For many graduate students, these cross-disciplinary conversations represent significant learning opportunities. Engagement with field-specific writing practices is of evident interest to those graduate students who take advantage of professional development opportunities beyond the required training courses. The observations below were written by a graduate student who has taken 7101 and 7100, worked as a co-facilitator in 7100, and (when this was written), was working as a writing tutor for undergraduate and graduate students.

> Working with other graduate students as a writing consultant has been, I believe, even more valuable to me as a writer because it let me see what graduate writing looks like across the disciplines and at different stages of the Ph.D.. Looking at writing in unfamiliar subjects made it easier for me to see the rhetorical moves that writers—and writing—at different stages of development looks like. As I learned to see the ways in which other writers introduced an argument, contextualized a citation, or summed up a point, I became more sensitive to when and how I did these things in my own writing.

For this student, engaging with the writing of others teaches her about her own writing practices; greater understanding of unfamiliar disciplinary practices helps her locate herself within her own discipline. In a different context, a current graduate student succinctly describes the impact of teaching writing on the teacher as a writer:

> I have become almost hyperaware of the skills I teach my students when editing my own writing. As my students learn about constructing arguments, my own arguments become more cohe-

sive. When I teach my students the merits of concise writing, my own sentences become clearer.

Voices from the Field

As previously stated, this section is structured around observations about writing from graduate student writers who have participated in one or more of the Knight Institute's training programs.

The Backbone: Writing Process

Describing the process through which he produces writing, a graduate student in the sciences describes a crucial phase of his writing process as follows:

> Before I even start writing the outline or even thinking about the paper, I just spend a few days going through my sources and notebooks and I write down anything that I feel should be a part of the paper, from numbers, to references, words, sentences, or just ideas. . . . When sorting my words and ideas into categories . . . I start recognizing the few that will eventually become the backbone of the paper. . . . Then, within each paragraph I condense every idea or group of ideas into one sentence. . . .

For this student, a significant portion of the work of writing a scientific paper involves turning groups of ideas into 10 or 12 tightly-packed sentences which contain "all the relevant information."

> . . . once this is achieved it really feels like the paper is written. After days of sorting and condensing and struggling to strip every sentence of all non-necessary words, the reverse process is easy enough! Turning sentences into paragraphs is much easier than turning paragraphs into sentences.

This student's sequence of writing activities—sort, compress, outline, expand—closely resembles an approach recommended by George Whitesides (2004), an extraordinarily prolific chemist whose essay on "Writing a Paper" provides guidelines for the collaborative production of scientific articles. Writing to the graduate students and post-docs in his lab, Whitesides emphasizes the critical importance of an outline as a way to organize a paper and as a way to organize the *production* of a paper. He writes:

> An outline is a written plan of the organization of a paper, including the data on which it rests. . . . think of an outline as

> a carefully organized and presented set of data, with attendant objectives, hypotheses, and conclusions, rather than an outline of text. (p. 1375) [italics in original]

According to Whitesides, successful researchers write and revise as they experiment, to understand the data they are collecting and why it matters. His definition of a paper makes it clear that writing is integral to planning and executing research: "A paper is not just an archival device for storing a completed research program; it is also a structure for *planning* your research in progress" (p. 1375; emphasis in original).

As a humanities-trained writing teacher, I have long been comfortable with the idea that the writing process is part of the thinking process. My own ideas come into focus as I write and change as I revise. Years of working closely with individual writers as a teacher and tutor have confirmed and reinforced this lesson. When I work with writers at any level, I feel comfortable telling them that writing is not about putting fully-formed ideas on paper. Learning happens through writing. (This should be a recipe for helping writers relax.)

As my work has increasingly brought me into contact with graduate students and faculty in the social, natural, and physical sciences, I have tried to learn more about writing practices characteristic of academic fields that are rhetorically and methodologically distant from my own. I first read the Whitesides article because a graduate student gave me a copy. (In this instance, as in many others, the teaching flows both ways.) When I meet a graduate student, like the one quoted above, who has already figured out that his job includes building a compressed outline of each paper, I feel confident that this student is establishing writing habits and practices that will serve him well.

Unnecessarily Raising the Stakes

> . . . As a graduate student I have learned to write in a way that assumes that someone is going to argue every point that I make — I am intentional in every word choice I make, anticipating potential areas where people will take issue. [written by a current Ph.D. student before a class on writing]

> This was one of the most useful classes I've taken since starting graduate school because we talked about issues I am currently facing in my own writing. . . . Because I write defensively, I often feel that I often have too many subsections, breaking down my rationale for using my particular analytical frameworks and in doing so, show my hand — aka my lack of confidence about

the subject I'm trying to engage. [written by the same student after class]¹³

Writing to new undergraduates about the writing they should be doing as college students, Keith Hjortshoj (2001) states: "Although there are many variations of form and style in academic writing, almost all of these variations occur within a consistent range of style and tone of voice: a tone of rational *explanation and discussion*" (p. 82). Though directed at undergraduate writers, this advice is far from irrelevant to graduate students. There may be many reasons why a piece of writing produced by a savvy, motivated graduate student may fail to exhibit a calm tone of rational explanation. As the comments quoted above suggest, confidence can play a significant factor. When I picture a writer who believes every sentence will be challenged, I picture someone in a defensive crouch. Defensive writing is likely to be what Hjortshoj calls "gripped."

This graduate student's defensiveness may be well-founded. Perhaps graduate classes have been contentious. Perhaps she has received negative feedback from professors. Perhaps this is just part of being a graduate student.¹⁴ Even if the student's advisors and colleagues have been supportive and the feedback has been helpful and encouraging, the graduate student is right to recognize the limits of what she can express in her own work. She writes elsewhere, "My writing is supposed to push on the boundaries of knowledge . . ." This is a tall order for someone who is learning where the boundaries are.

The official curriculum (should) help graduate students map the field and then help them identify questions which will "push the boundaries." The unofficial writing curriculum for WIM TAs and FWS instructors can help students build confidence, partly by stimulating greater awareness about what it takes to produce writing in a field. Our defensive writer has the following to say about the unofficial curriculum:

> . . . graduate school does not necessarily encourage students to devote much time to thinking about how we write. . . . In 7101 we broke down the different stages of writing, the things that make us comfortable when we write, and the things we want to change . . .
>
> One of the most meaningful experiences that impacted my development as a writer surrounded our discussion regarding the

---

13   The before and after comments quoted at the beginning of this section are excerpted from in-class reflective assignments, produced on the same day, and used by permission.

14   The conversations in "The Space Between," in which graduate students respond to the experiences of other graduate students, in addition to narrating their own, serve as reminders that almost any comment can feel like an attack. What looks like a supportive response to one person can feel, to another, like kneecapping.

> importance of having a separate set of eyes read over my writing. I have always worked very privately but I realized that for the past year and a half I had been unnecessarily raising the stakes on each paper by having the first pair of eyes besides mine to look at the paper be those of my evaluator. It sounds like a simple enough idea, but as a graduate student I had become used to operating solo and my sense is that this is the case for many of my peers.

I suggested above that this graduate student's defensiveness might have something to do with the challenges inherent in building what Lovitts (2004) calls a "cognitive map" of her program (p. 120–124). The student's follow-up comments suggest that the official curriculum may play a role, although not necessarily because her department has failed her in some way. Graduate students thrive when they develop writing practices that include drafting, revising, and informal peer review. Graduate students who write in public tend to complete their programs more quickly than do students who are isolated when they write, particularly during the long haul of dissertation writing.[15] Graduate students can, and do, build writing communities on their own. But graduate programs could do more to foster these communities, and to make them part of the curriculum, rather than an informal feature of graduate life.[16]

The graduate student quoted above wrote about how valuable it has been to share her work with peers. One striking fact about this observation—echoed in many other comments—is the path the realization travels. In 7100 and 7101, we discuss modes of informal peer review and their value in undergraduate writing classes. But the writing graduate students share with each other in class would not typically "count" as academic writing. Asked to name genres of academic writing, most people would probably include the following: articles, conference papers and posters, dissertations, books, book chapters. But few current or aspiring scholars would classify course materials—or a reflective essay about writing—as examples of academic writing.

Reading graduate student comments on Writing 7100 and 7101, I realized that graduate students discovered the value of sharing their work with others because of an essential feature of both courses: people read each other's work every

---

15   Hjortshoj (2010) notes that, "Research on doctoral programs indicates…that isolation is a fundamental cause of difficulty and delay in the completion of Ph.D.s" (p. 34). Lovitts (2004) has explored the issues of social integration that have an impact on degree completion. One striking finding from her research into graduate student attrition is the fact that, "completers were almost twice as likely as non-completers to have shared an office" with another graduate student (p. 125).

16   In "Demystifying the Dissertation" Karen Cardozo (2006) outlines strategies for building into graduate programs support for graduate student writers.

week. However, the work typically consists of things like assignment sequences and in-class writing exercises. In the introduction, I quoted one student on this topic: "7100 emphasizes collaboration and sharing of teaching materials, and at a certain point I began to wonder why the graduate community doesn't practice this more often and more broadly. I think it's incredibly logical and so clearly beneficial. . . ." What is significant, for this student and others, is that she made the connection between the value of sharing teaching materials—which figures prominently in our training courses—and the value of sharing her scholarly work.

Practicing peer review is practice for the profession. While collaborative authorship of scholarly material is routine in some fields (such as biology) and relatively rare in others (such as English), academic life is built on other forms of collaboration, including the systems of peer review that govern academic publication. Even in fields where scholarship is typically produced by individual authors, other kinds of professional writing are produced collaboratively: job descriptions, committee reports, departmental review documents. Gateway decisions such as hiring and promotion include review of candidates by peers, often working in teams. Informal peer review is routine for most scholars: few would send an article to a journal that has not been read by at least one colleague. While the sharing of work is deeply embedded in academic culture, even the savviest graduate students will not necessarily learn this from coursework or department colloquia. Some learn it in a seminar officially devoted to something else.

"Writing Is a Process Which at Times Will Be Messy."

This section quotes Lindsay Cummings and Sarah Senk, two tenure-track professors who earned Cornell Ph.D.s. They describe lessons they learned about writing as process through their multiple modes of participation with Knight Institute programs. Both took Writing 7100 early in their graduate careers and taught several first-year writing seminars. Both participated in the peer collaboration program; both won teaching prizes. Senk worked as a writing tutor and served several times as a graduate co-facilitator in Writing 7100. Cummings received a one-year teaching post-doc in the Writing Workshop and co-facilitated Writing 7101.

Writing about writing as process, Senk and Cummings describe issues ranging from the utilitarian (time management) to the epistemological. Their discussions of process move beyond the fact that writing proceeds through steps and stages, especially when the product under construction is a long-term project like a dissertation. Both attribute what they learned about writing process largely to their work with the Knight Institute. Cummings describes the ways teaching writing reinforces good writing practices:

> . . . the Knight Institute really reinforces the idea that writing is a process which at times will be messy. This keeps you writing. . . . When you keep the overall writing and thinking process in mind, there is less stress placed on a single day's output . . . it also keeps you from worrying too much about a single sentence. It's hard to be too much in love with your own language after you spend a half an hour in a conference with a student convincing them to cut through the meaningless rhetorical flourishes. . . . Teaching that lesson reinforces it for the teacher.

Senk writes about how thinking and writing are intertwined:

> I think that I never really internalized the idea that writing was an epistemic process. In college I always thought that one should formulate an idea and then transparently translate it into an essay; in grad school I learned (partly through course work but mostly through teaching and training) to think of thought as something that came into being through writing, and to think of thought itself as something mutable.

As contributions to the academic study of writing, Cummings' and Senk's insights into writing process are hardly earth-shaking. Indeed, much of what they say follows from texts we read in Writing 7100 and 7101. What is potentially earth-shaking *for these two writers,* is that—largely through their work as writing teachers—they were able to transition from successful careers as undergraduate writers to successful careers as graduate writers who produced dissertations and landed tenure-track jobs. Both describe the training they received and their experience as writing teachers as crucial to their ability to make these transitions.

In describing the survival skills mastered by these talented and accomplished scholars, I make no attempt to control for other features of training or temperament that made their interests compatible with the Knight Institute's philosophy. Before we met them, their talents were recognized by the small, highly selective graduate programs that admitted them: Comparative Literature for Senk, Performing and Media Arts for Cummings. They would probably have been successful without the training and support they received from the Knight Institute and the community of teachers they chose to join. I would argue, however, that their success can be attributed, in part, to their willingness to take advantage of the opportunities presented to them, and their ability to adapt to the new circumstances they have faced as students, instructors, and, now, professors. The practice of graduate education need not be premised on admitting talented students and seeing how much they can accomplish on their own. Programs could admit talented students and provide them with the tools they need to succeed.

Learning Something Practical

This section begins with stories from four Anthropology Ph.D.s who responded to their department's alumni survey and noted learning something they could take with them. The survey included questions about training they received as teachers and TAs while in graduate school. The quotations below are responses to questions about Writing 7100 and Writing 7101:

> Amazing! I cannot say enough about this course. . . . It made me prepared, and more confident, to teach on my own. Teaching a Writing Seminar meant that I had a course ready to go when I got a teaching postdoc and later an assistant professor position.
>
> Very important to me. Improved my teaching, and changed my scholarly orientation. Became more interested in helping others articulate their ideas.
>
> A wonderful class that I got a lot out of and still use in terms of how I teach composition courses in my current job. This was a fabulous class which I still draw on for inspiration in my teaching.
>
> I thought this class was very good, because it was the first time I really felt I was learning something PRACTICAL. . . . To this day, I still feel that, although I do not teach, the clear steps and structure associated with what I learned in that class continue to influence how I approach the actual work that I do.

I have written elsewhere about survival and adaptation in the academic world (Shapiro, 2008). In the comments above, I am reminded of the range of cognitive transitions graduate students must confront, the number of times they must adapt to new circumstances if they are to survive in their chosen fields. For the first student, teacher training was preparation for a teaching post-doc, then for a job. The training course shifted the scholarly interests of the second respondent. The third has a job which includes teaching composition. The fourth has found that teacher training informs professional experiences outside academia.

Although they are frequently taught separately (if at all), and valued along different matrices, teaching, writing, research, and service can be mutually reinforcing. Graduate education at my institution is likely to continue to be fragmentary: students who succeed will continue to make use of the tools they can find, sometimes in unexpected places. Until such time as truly integrated graduate programs take root, programs like ours are likely to continue providing graduate students with access to tools they may not find anywhere else.

Postscript

A version of this chapter originally appeared in an issue of *ATD* devoted to Graduate Writing (2015, August). While revising our contributions for this collection, we were asked to provide updates on the programs and studies discussed in our respective chapters. One striking feature of the programs described in my chapter is how little has changed.

For example, the tables included above in "Writing and the Writing in the Disciplines Curriculum" provide data from 2013–14: hardly cutting edge by the time this book goes to press. However, if I were to replace these tables with data from a more recent year, the numbers would be largely the same: a similar number of TAs trained, a similar number of departments represented, a similar range of departments represented in the FWS and WIM programs.

Our writing program's stability is one of our greatest assets. As priorities shift, both within the university and within the College of Arts and Sciences (which houses the Knight Institute), support for Cornell's writing in the disciplines program has remained widespread. Indeed, recent curricular reviews have, by some measures, reinforced the central place occupied by the writing program.

I do not consider it cynical to hypothesize that the investment many departments share in the program's continued strength is connected to our program's reach. The place of the writing program in the lives of our undergraduates is obvious: each of Cornell's seven undergraduate colleges mandates that their undergraduates take at least one first-year writing seminar (most require two). Faculty can (and do) complain that students don't come out of these classes knowing how to do everything they wish our students knew how to do. But these complaints often crumble in the face of evidence, or when alternatives are considered.

This chapter underlines the less obvious, but equally important impact of this program on the academic lives of graduate students from approximately 40 departments in five colleges. Major upheaval might result in painful consequences for the graduate programs with which we collaborate. Contractors who do business with the federal government figured out long ago that, when contracts are distributed across a range of states and congressional districts, legislators from many parts of the country have a stake in seeing projects funded. My program's commitment to working with a range of departments has less Machiavellian motives. Our commitment to breadth represents an essential component of our program's mission. If writing is embedded in the work of disciplines, this work should happen in as many departments as are willing to participate. In this case, utopian motives may have realpolitik consequences.

While no program is ever completely secure, we have, on the credit side, 50 years of history, a generous endowment, and strong relationships with faculty and departments across the university. Maintaining these interlocking relationships involves a healthy dose of mutual self-interest. Sometimes, maintenance includes advertising the value of our program's services for the departments we work with. Conducting the research embedded in this article, and sharing it with the wider world, may provide, when needed, evidence to support our continued value to the institution we are a part of.

Acknowledgments

My first thanks go to the many current and former graduate students with whom I have had the pleasure of working during my time at Cornell. Special thanks to those who contributed to the ongoing study of graduate student writing and teaching, which provided material for this article. Thanks to the editors of this collection, and the other contributors, for enriching this chapter over the course of its production. Thanks to Davydd Greenwood and Nerissa Russell for sharing results —both the summary report and some of the survey data—from the self-study conducted by Cornell's Department of Anthropology. Thanks to my colleagues at the Knight Institute for providing a supportive and engaging place to work, teach, and write. It's been a particular honor to collaborate with colleagues in our graduate training programs: this work has provided some of my greatest learning and teaching opportunities. Thanks to David Faulkner and Paul Sawyer who read portions of this essay in progress. Thanks, as always, to Deborah Starr, who is my closest colleague and friend, in addition to being my wife.

References

Cardozo, K. M. (2006). Demystifying the dissertation. *Profession, 17,* 138–154.
Foucault, M. (1995). *Discipline and punish: The birth of the prison.* Vintage books. (Original work published in 1975).
Fredrick, T., Stravalli, K., May, S. & Brookman-Smith, J. (2020). The space between: MA students enculturate to graduate reading and writing. In M. Brooks-Gillies, E. G. Garcia, S. H. Kim, K. Manthey & T. G. Smith (Eds.), *Graduate writing across the disciplines: Identifying, teaching, and supporting.* The WAC Clearinghouse; University Press of Colorado. https://wac.colostate.edu/books/atd/graduate.
Gottschalk, K. & Hjortshoj, K. (2004). *The elements of teaching writing: A resource for instructors in all disciplines.* Bedford/St. Martin's.
Greenwood, D. J., Carrico, K. J. & White, E. D. (2013). *A survey of Cornell anthropology majors and Cornell Ph.D.s after graduation, 1990–2013.* Cornell University.
Hjortshoj, K. (2001). *The transition to college writing* (1st ed.). Bedford/St. Martins.
Hjortshoj, K. (2010). *Writing from A to B: A guide to completing the dissertation phase of doctoral studies.* Cornell University.

Lannin, A. & Townsend, M. A. (2020). Graduate student perspectives: Career development through serving as writing-intensive GTAs. In M. Brooks-Gillies, E. G. Garcia, S. H. Kim, K. Manthey & T. G. Smith (Eds.), *Graduate writing across the disciplines: Identifying, teaching, and supporting*. The WAC Clearinghouse; University Press of Colorado. https://wac.colostate.edu/books/atd/graduate.

Lovitts, B. (2004). Research on the structure and process of graduate education: Retaining students. In D. Wulff & A. Austin (Eds.), *Paths to the professoriate: Strategies for enriching the preparation of future faculty* (pp. 115–136). Jossey-Bass.

Shapiro, E. (2008). Survival and failure, adaptation and acceptance. *ADE Bulletin, 146*, 18–27.

Whitesides, G. (2004). Whitesides' group: Writing a paper. *Advanced Materials, 16*(15), 1375–1377. http://www.ee.ucr.edu/~rlake/Whitesides_writing_res_paper.pdf.

The Space Between: MA Students Enculturate to Graduate Reading and Writing

Terri Fredrick, Kaylin Stravalli, Scott May, and Jami Brookman-Smith

EASTERN ILLINOIS UNIVERSITY

> **Abstract**: Written collaboratively by three master's-level students and a professor of composition, this article provides personal narratives of the enculturation experiences of students transitioning to graduate school. In the first section, Terri describes teaching a graduate composition seminar to incoming graduate students that incorporated activities related to enculturation. Jami explores how the emotional aspects of entering graduate school as a nontraditional student impacted her ability to write effectively in her classes. Kaylin discusses the enculturation challenges she encountered that ultimately led her to leave graduate school after the first semester. Finally, Scott discusses his transition from student to teacher and how he came to appreciate the in-between space he inhabited as a graduate student. The article concludes with some brief suggestions for how faculty might support students during this transitional period.
>
> **Keywords**: Graduate Study, Enculturation, Transition, Teacher-Student Relationship

Rosemary Perez (2016) argues that "early professional socialization experiences play a powerful role in shaping one's expectations of and commitment to [a] field" (p. 764). Graduate school is widely considered to be the stage at which students emerge as scholars and teachers in their own right, and for this reason, enculturation to graduate school has emerged as a topic of some interest across many disciplines. Drawing on research into communities of practice (Lave & Wenger, 1991; more recently summarized by Wenger-Trayner & Wenger-Trayner, 2015) and activity systems (Russell, 1995), we define "enculturation" as the process by which individuals are inducted into the values and practices of a community, including the practices of reading, writing, and creating knowledge. In this article, we argue that talking about enculturation has the potential to benefit all graduate students. Reading and writing as a member of a discipline is different than the reading and writing most students are asked to do as undergraduates. While graduate students are given more freedom to make connections across courses and to pursue interests, the "rules" and strictures that guide how that work can be done successfully are also subtler. Because the theoretical conversation is often removed from the actual lived experience of graduate students, it seems only right to us that graduate student voices play a major role in the literature on graduate student enculturation. Yet with notable exceptions (e.g., Good & Warshauer, 2000; Micciche & Carr, 2011; Simpson, Clemens, Killingsworth & Ford, 2015), publications on graduate student enculturation are all too often authored solely by faculty. This text, by contrast, is the work of three master's students and a faculty member, who came together in a composition studies pedagogy course:

- Terri is a professor of English, who has been teaching graduate composition classes for over a decade. Her Ph.D. is in Rhetoric and Professional Composition, and her research focuses on writing classroom pedagogy. During the writing of this article, Terri taught several additional graduate courses.
- Jami was a non-traditional graduate student. During the writing of this article, Jami completed coursework in literary studies and worked as a consultant and office manager for the Writing Center.
- Kaylin was a traditional graduate student in creative writing, who left the graduate program after her first semester. During the writing of this article, Kaylin worked as a communications manager and wrote in her spare time.
- Scott was a graduate student in Composition Studies. During the writing of this article, he wrote and defended his thesis on student responses to teacher evaluations and taught first-year composition at an area two-year college.

At our master's-granting public university, the MA in English offers concentrations in literature, creative writing, composition, and professional writing; most students take at least a few courses outside of their own concentration. The four of us met in Fall 2012 in Terri's introductory course in composition pedagogy; Jami and Kaylin were in their first semester of graduate school, while Scott had already completed a semester in the program. In some ways, the enculturation challenges we discuss in this article are exacerbated in the pedagogy course because, for many graduate students, this is their first introduction to Composition Studies as a discipline. Yet because the coursework is designed to be graduate-level, students are still expected to perform as emerging scholars/teachers. In other ways, however, Composition Studies—with its focus on the nature of teaching, learning, and writing—offers students the freedom to explicitly explore the difficult transitions they experience without losing credibility as an emerging scholar/teacher.

Perez (2016) argues that graduate students' socialization experiences are shaped by the ways in which students engage sensemaking and self-authorship in response to the "surprises, disruptions, or discrepancies" that occur during the first-year of graduate school. We approach this article, then, as individuals with varying perspectives: for example, at the end of the Fall 2012 semester, Scott changed his graduate concentration from literature to composition, while Kaylin left graduate school altogether. What we all share is a strong interest in the ways students make the disciplinary transition to graduate study and the supports professors can give students as they make that transition. For this reason, we present this text in a multi-vocal format. We find precedent in our approach in the *Literacy in the Raw* project, a web-based collection of narratives by English Studies graduate students on their literacy practices (Carr, Rule & Taylor, 2013). Like Carr et al., we believe "story can become a productive lens through which to explore graduate literacy practices," and we further believe telling our stories gives us some control over those stories. For this reason, we preserve our individual voices (albeit not in the "raw," unedited form captured in the narratives uploaded to the Digital Archive of Literacy Narratives) by letting a single person command each section. At the same time, we embrace the idea that knowledge is constructed through social interaction; in our several years working on this article, we came to better understand our own stories through long conversations on the issues we raise here. To give a sense of the ways our stories overlap and exist in dialogue with one another, we have included a type of marginal commentary in italics.

In the first section, Terri describes her efforts to design a graduate course that explicitly addressed enculturation. Jami explores the emotional dynamics she experienced as a non-traditional student navigating the transition from undergraduate to graduate study. Kaylin describes the stressors and frustrations that ultimately led her to withdraw from the program, leaving behind—at least for now—her goal of becoming an English professor. Finally, Scott discusses the positive and negative aspects of the unique situation graduate assistants find themselves in: not yet teachers but no longer only students.

Terri's Story, Part 1: Making Enculturation Explicit

Compared to my own experience teaching a stand-alone section of first-year composition during my first semester of graduate school, I tend to view the English graduate program at my current institution as a model of gentle enculturation. During their first semester, students enroll in a course designed to prepare them for the tasks of reading, writing, and presenting as an English Studies scholar. In addition, before teaching their own sections of first-year composition, graduate assistants (GAs) spend a year as consultants in the writing center and take three pedagogy courses: Writing Center Pedagogy, Composition Pedagogy, and a mentored teaching experience where they spend a whole semester co-teaching in the classroom of an experienced tenure-track or tenured faculty member. And yet despite coursework intended to ease the transition to graduate school, the students in my program continue to experience the "baptism by fire" that has long marked the entrance to graduate school.

So for the Fall 2012 composition pedagogy class, I decided to devote some class time to the practices of reading and writing in composition studies. In doing this, I hoped to ease students' transition to graduate-level scholarship. Specifically, I tried to create a space that:

- recognized the tension between what Paul Prior (1991) refers to as immediate socialization (the practices, communication strategies, and skills needed to succeed as a student) and anticipatory socialization (those needed to succeed as a professional) and
- encouraged vulnerability (Micciche & Carr, 2011), risk-taking (Burger, 2012), and exploration (Reid, 2009).

I engaged these issues of enculturation in several ways. Each week during class discussion, I asked the students to consider some aspect of the form and structure of the essays we'd read. In feedback on students' weekly responses to the assigned reading, I tried to point out examples of how someone steeped in the literature of Composition Studies might perceive the claims made in the articles. I pulled excerpts from students' own successful writing to model sophisticated ways of integrating source material and building toward a claim. In addition to these small changes, I introduced a "quality of failure" (QoF) component, which I developed after reading Edward Burger's essay "Teaching to Fail" in *Inside Higher Ed* (2012); here is the description from my syllabus:

> **Scott's take:** I'm a little embarrassed to admit I was unfamiliar with the term "enculturation" before Terri invited us to discuss the possibilities of this collaborative project. Only because of these explicit conversations over enculturation did I develop a better understanding of the stressors I experienced through our program—albeit, three semesters later than I would have liked. Having a discussion with students about the goal of socialization may be very helpful.

> **Quality of failure (5% of semester grade):** The knowledge of every discipline is based on a process that includes regular failure, reflection on that failure, and then adjustments made accordingly. Unfortunately, the nature of our educational system often makes the risk of failure seem too high for students; as a result, students may not develop risk-taking habits in their education and, subsequently, their careers. For most of you, this class intro-

duces you to a new discipline, a situation ripe with opportunities to fail. I encourage you to make high-quality mistakes: try out a new idea or approach in a reading response, share a partially formed idea, change your mind. And when you do, I will reward you for that in the currency of the university: your grade.

The impetus behind my introduction of this concept was two-fold: First, like Burger, I was looking for ways to productively challenge students' assertions and first efforts without shutting them down. Second, the composition pedagogy course introduces students to a range of theories about the teaching of writing. In previous experiences with the course, I'd learned that those students who too quickly or too thoroughly embrace a single theory tend to have only a limited grasp of subsequent theories and other issues. In addition, previous students' fear of being criticized for contradicting themselves sometimes prevented them from exploring potentially productive claims.[1] So this explicit encouragement that students should be willing to change their minds, or to "wallow in ambiguity" as the students and I came to call it over the course of the semester, was an important part of my effort to delay the solidification of their thinking on the issues in the course.

I was excited about the QoF component, but also nervous: Would students respond to this concept? How could I assess the quality of students' failure? Ultimately embracing the potential for failure myself, I decided to simply ask the students to evaluate themselves over the course of the semester in terms of their risk-taking and failure. Most of the students in the class responded positively to the quality of failure assignment, and several students described it as the most important element of the class in terms of building their confidence and/or opening pathways for them to create high-quality work. As this brief excerpt from Kaylin's QoF memo demonstrates, the QoF memo, written after the last class but before submission of the final paper,

> **Jami's take:** The QoF portion of our grade was instrumental in providing the "buffer" I needed in order to breathe a little easier. While it may not have made up for a poor paper grade, it was more about changing the way I approached the work of graduate school than just 5% of Terri's course.
>
> **Scott's take:** I agree with Jami that QoF did more as a gesture than it did in determining my grade. However, there was still a leap of faith that was required of me to take Terri up on the proposal. I didn't entirely trust that my failure would be rewarded. How does successfully failing really work? As I grew to understand it as an invitation to take risks, I thought better of it.

---

1   LaFrance and Corbett (this collection) also discuss how graduate students are "conditioned to avoid failure," thus "[missing] out on deeper learning opportunities."

provided a good opportunity for students to reflect on their experiences as learners and emerging teachers:

> Even as the semester comes to a close and I attempt to sum up my experience and defend it in my final papers, I wallow and I fail. I wallow in the fact that I still do not know exactly how I feel about all the pedagogies we studied. I feel drawn to some (expressive, feminist, process), but there is still so much I do not know about them because there is just so much theory to wade through in order for me to take a firm stand one way or the other. I fail in the fact that I have not mastered the language of the academy or the style in which to discuss these matters. I sometimes fail at grasping the material itself, which affects all of the above failure and wallowing.

Two students did not embrace the QoF component, primarily because they seemed to view the component as simply another assignment rather than as a philosophical way of approaching learning. For example, one creative writing student in the class wrote:

> 5% of one's grade is very little compared to the F we could get on a paper. The QoF element was a nice idea, but to me it was just something written on a syllabus. If I didn't take risks and produced more conventional work, my grade would be higher. It's hard to justify losing an assistantship over a creative risk.

In spite of these useful criticisms, I was pleased overall with the direction I'd begun taking with my graduate course; by the end of the semester, the overall quality of the students' written work had risen significantly, and the theory syntheses students wrote showed deeper engagement with the course concepts than I'd seen the previous time I'd taught the course. When the co-editors of this collection put out their call for articles on graduate student writing and reading, I was eager to contribute. I invited three people who'd had a range of positive and negative experiences during their Fall 2012 semesters to join me in writing the article. For me, this article was an opportunity to extend the conversations we'd had throughout the semester and in the students' QoF memos. Since we'd spent 15 weeks together explicitly exploring these issues, I believed I had a pretty good understanding of their experiences, but the stories they had to tell sometimes surprised me.

Jami's Story: Not a Fraud

Early in my first semester as a graduate student, I realized the workload and pacing of graduate school were going to require some serious adjustments—not just in how I performed the work, but in how I processed life as a graduate student. As a non-traditional student who completed my undergraduate degree at age 36, doing well had always been important to me, so I worried about grades and establishing good working relationships with my professors. I soon realized I needed to worry about just surviving the enculturation process of graduate school. The problem was I did not know how to "just survive," and in retrospect, I realize I was not given many of the tools to do so. The only explicit advice I was given as I began graduate school came from a professor who told me, "At some point you have to accept a certain amount of mediocrity in your work. You have to come to an understanding with yourself that you won't be able to do everything, and find a way to live with that." While I know my professor's statement was meant to make me feel better, I had always expected to perform at my best, so to be told my best was impossible actually increased my feelings of inadequacy. Rather than feel empowered, this statement led me to feel I was bound to fail. If that was the case, what I really needed was for someone to tell me how to accept specific academic failures without feeling like a failure as a person.

The methods of reading and writing I had perfected as an undergraduate just did not work anymore. There was so much information to be absorbed in such a short time it was impossible to get everything compartmentalized, and I did not know how to fix the problem. I remember sitting in my apartment one evening after my daughter had gone to sleep, thinking, "I do not belong here. I feel like a fraud." It seemed that, as a graduate student, I was expected to just *know* how to process the information and work through the demands of the program.

These feelings were amplified as I struggled in week two with the first paper of the semester for my literature elective. I was assigned to write a simple one-page, no-margin essay about a novel I was already familiar with. I was excited to find what I thought was an interesting link in the text; but, not only did the professor not see the link, she recommended I take the essay in a completely different direction. The feedback I received was kind, but I felt my work

> **Terri's take:** When I first heard this story from Jami, I thought it should be a success story: her professor found in just a single page of Jami's writing a topic worth pursuing. But as I listened to the emotion behind her experience, I was able to see it as she saw it: as a silencing and dismissal of her passion and ideas. How do we as teachers help students learn to identify the topics that will be of interest to the discipline without forcing them to abandon the issues and questions that draw them to the field in the first place?
>
> **Kaylin's take:** While Jami received overly-controlling suggestions on what to write, what I needed were specifics on how to say what I had already written within the strictures of the discipline.

had been dismissed in favor of the professor's vision. I was asked to revise that paper and every paper after it for that class, each time with the professor suggesting for me to change the topic. For example, my paper on female workers in the early British postal system turned into a paper on the development of the pneumatic tube system. In fact, every time I would think I had what the professor was looking for, I was told I did not. As the semester progressed, I began to worry I did not have what it took to write as a graduate student, and maybe I had never had it to begin with.

The result was that I no longer felt safe to write. I am not sure what I thought would happen if I just started putting words to the page, but panic had taken hold and, eventually, the words would not come at all. I would sit at the computer and think, *no I need to plan more*. I would second guess every decision; even my ability to punctuate a sentence became an issue. All of my thoughts, ideas, and assignments started interfering with the daily activities necessary for life. I was unable to sleep, not only because of the amount of work, but because I was too overwhelmed to shut down. When I did finally sleep, I would wake up in a panic, sure I had forgotten to complete something for the next day. The emotions created by sleep deprivation and a near constant state of panic led to tears—a lot of tears. Micciche and Carr (2011) have identified this as a common response to the enculturation of graduate school:

> It's no secret that graduate students (much like faculty) regularly encounter academic writing as an emotionally fraught, privately experienced hardship. [In my own program], the participants—some of whom specialized in literature or critical theory; others in rhetoric and composition—cried regularly in or after class, so overwhelmed were we by all that we had to know in order to create writing that made a contribution, no matter how minor, or just made sense. (p. 479)

The emotional toll caused by that first failure turned out to be greater than I realized as it spilled over into my other classes. My emotional response to the enculturation of graduate school was the result of a lack of confidence and not knowing how to accept and recover from what I perceived to be failure. What I needed was transparency rather than the "baptism by fire" feeling Terri mentions in her narrative. In the first week of the semester, I cannot remember one member of the faculty, either in the program orientation or classes, discussing the potential emotional and physical consequences of the program. Looking back, I have often wondered how the semester might have been different had these matters been discussed from the beginning.

It was the eventual sharing of that knowledge that finally allowed me the breathing room I needed to survive. One evening after class, Terri issued a firm challenge: I was no longer allowed to undercut my claims by saying "I'm probably not making sense" or "maybe I'm wrong" during class discussion or in weekly writing. Terri was attempting to help me see if I did not find some way to build my confidence, the professors would notice. Without that confidence, I had very little chance of earning their respect. This conversation was the turning point in that semester. Terri suggested I consider the phrase, "fake it until you make it." That phrase became my constant companion. I leaned on the "quality of failure" safety net Terri describes, and while that didn't mean I thought I could get away with writing garbage, I knew if an idea was not great, it would still be okay. The conversation also affected how I began reading for the class. I stopped worrying as much about being wrong and started rethinking the way I was approaching the reading. With the other mental clutter out of the way, I was able to focus on what was important—learning how to read pedagogical theory without letting my literature background get in the way. Instead of seeing the articles as a character list of theorists, I started seeing the ideas and putting them in practical context. Once I was able to see how each pedagogical theory might work in an actual classroom, it was easier to compartmentalize them. As a result, I gradually felt more comfortable expressing my views. Each week I looked forward to reading the feedback on my reflection papers, and eventually my confidence began to build, which was reflected in my ability to write for all my classes. I felt like a weight had been lifted.

> **Scott's take:** For me, a statement coming from an authority figure encouraging me to "fake it" would have been damaging to my performance and enculturation. A sense of pretending always lingers in academia, which most students resist and somewhat fear. I would not have valued my own work and efforts had I discovered my professors saw it as something built on the foundation of pretense. I would not have been able to take my work seriously had I thought that "faking it" was expected in the profession.

The first semester of graduate school was intellectually and emotionally difficult. Emotionally, there was no way to prepare for it without the transparency I can now see was needed. I went from thinking learning was neat and clean to knowing it can be unbelievably messy. My literary background didn't prepare me for reading the theory and pedagogies required in Terri's composition course. But, in the end, it was that course and Terri's willingness to say, "Fake it until you make it" that helped pull everything together and build the confidence I needed. It became a foundation on which to base new knowledge—what it means to learn, teach, and finally find the confidence to say I am not a fraud.

Kaylin's Story: Square Peg, Round Hole

Upon entering graduate school, I—like Jami—spent a semester struggling in ways I never expected in an academic environment. I began graduate school with the intention of pursuing a career as a college English professor. By mid-semester, I was reevaluating that pursuit. By the end of the semester, my plans had changed completely.

As a child, I struggled to learn to read, if only for a brief period of time. My reading teacher and my parents worked together and separately to turn that struggle into what became a lifelong passion. They gave me strategies to help me learn, and soon I had excelled so far that I skipped several reading levels and transferred from the basic reading class to accelerated honors. When I learned to write a short time later, I realized it came naturally and easily to me. It allowed me to organize my thoughts, feelings, and ideas in a way that made sense and entertained whomever read my writing.

When I went to graduate school, I quickly learned what had always come naturally and easily had become extremely difficult. I began to procrastinate until the last possible minute (by my standards, anyway) because I couldn't begin to fathom what I was supposed to write. So I did what experience had taught me to do when faced with a problem I could not solve independently — I asked for help. I sought advice from a few of my professors based on the feedback I received on my work. However, what I took as instruction on genre rules actually turned out to be the idiosyncrasies of individual professors, which while helpful in its own way, did not help me succeed on the broader spectrum.

I found the priorities and focus of the work (and even of the students) were grossly different from the private four-year research university where I completed my undergraduate degree. Whereas my undergraduate university focused on my well-being and growth as a student, my graduate school—a public MA-granting university—seemed to focus solely on the quality of my work. It missed the concept that one was intricately linked to the other.

Not only did I have to make the leap to graduate-level work, I also had to find my way in an entirely different academic culture than I was accustomed. But where was that transition supposed to occur? Was it the instant I graduated with my bachelor's degree or sometime in the first semester of graduate school? Either way, I was left to make the transition largely on my own, using only past strategies and knowledge to guide me as I built a shaky bridge from one level to the next. Enculturation required (or seemed to require) a lot of trial and error and a sink-or-swim mentality. I can tell you—I did not make that transition.

I had been lucky enough to have educators at every level up to that point who saw a natural talent in me and pushed me to foster it and progress beyond any limitations they or I set. They impacted my life so much, they unknowingly helped determine the path of my higher education and career. I wanted to write, to become a professor, and to be for my future students what they had been for me. I thrived under such educators who took the time to train me in the rules of the discipline, so I could then find my own ways of bending and playing with them as a writer. This is what I needed from the professors in my graduate program. This is what I asked of them, but it was not what I received.

As soon as I made progress in one class, I applied what I had learned to another course, and it was "wrong." What aid there was came in the form of feedback on papers, which ranged from helpful constructive criticism to vague statements that led me nowhere. In Terri's class, for example, I was not delving as deeply into the material as I should. I was not conversing with the text or its author(s) the way the assigned articles did with each other, and *that* is what I was supposed to be learning how to do. I was expected to have a certain level of knowledge and skill in academic writing. Yet, I was not being given the tools I needed to learn to read and write at the graduate or scholarly level. I was not being enculturated the way my previous educators taught me I should be. Navigating the waters of English Studies at the graduate level proved challenging and frustrating, that is, until Terri—like those before her—took the time to pass on a strategy or two.

In an effort to draw deeper analysis in and dialogue from my writing, for one assignment, Terri asked me to explicitly reference the reading material three times and flesh out those statements before I added in my thoughts. She took a few moments to mentor me as an individual, as a student, as a writer, and as a potential scholar. And it worked. I improved. I was able to move forward and apply that strategy and later mix it with my own style.

More common, though, were vague comments such as "This is too informal" or "Strive for a more academic tone," when I really needed to know exactly *where* I was being too informal and how I could make my tone more academic. The problem was not the quantity of comments but their specificity. Those ambiguous comments led me to realize something was "wrong" with my writing but only told me part of the problem. I wanted and needed more transparency. Had I been given that explicit information, my performance would have been better and my stress much lower.

The effect of knowing there was a problem and not knowing how to fix it started to take its toll; I felt I was spinning my wheels, unable to gain traction. I could not seem to get my professors to let me in on the secrets of the discipline or to enculturate me into the world of academia. Instead, my love and passion for reading, writing, and deep analysis were fading quickly. I dreaded the reading. I dreaded the writing. I found I took on these tasks with a combination of procrastination and panic—both new and unwelcome in my writing process. Suddenly, I felt I could not write. The pressure to be original, to bring something new, fresh, and different to the discussion was substantial. I also knew this pressure was not going to disappear if I pursued a career as a college professor. The words "Publish or Perish" were already ringing in my ears. In fact, this very fear came to life when I presented a paper in a department-wide literary seminar designed to help first-semester graduate students act as scholars. I was excited for this assignment and felt it was my chance to turn a corner in my graduate studies.

I was placed on a panel with two classmates with similar topics. After the presentations, everyone else on the panel received five or six questions, but I was asked just one: "So what's the purpose of your paper?" I was mortified. I had a sense of my topic when I first received the assignment and began writing, but the idea never took shape on paper the way it had in my mind. Even as I presented, I failed to bring to life what I had envisioned. Yet as I sat on the panel and listened to my peers, I heard my idea eloquently and seamlessly coming to life in someone else's paper.

E. Shelley Reid (2009) argues that new graduate teaching assistants should be challenged with writing assignments that push them just hard enough to excel but not so hard they run way. This concept spoke directly to me. It was as if she had written, "Kaylin, were you frustrated? Were you lost? Did you feel like you were stuck in limbo between the undergraduate and graduate level, graduate assistant and scholar?" Why yes, Reid. I was, and I did.

> **Scott's take:** As it was a professor who asked Kaylin the question that mortified her, I think it is worth mentioning that sincere inquiries can have an equally powerful impact on students' growth. Most graduate students want to know if the work they are doing is authentic, valuable, and interesting. Without Terri's interest in my advocacy of students' perspectives in composition pedagogy, I might not have changed my concentration from literary studies until it was too late.
>
> **Terri's take:** Reading Scott's comment, I'm struck that he does not call for praising students' work, but for finding what is authentic, valuable, and interesting in their work. That strikes me as much more difficult—and more important—than simply offering praise.

By this point in the semester, I had spent hours alone on my two-and-a-half-hour commute doing an immense amount of reflection and analysis of myself, of my goals, and of my life plan. I evaluated the work I was doing: I was getting by on work I was not proud of or satisfied with; I was certainly growing but not in the ways I had expected; I did not feel I was contributing much, if anything, of worth; and what had always been my passion, my joy, and my escape had become a prison sentence to endure. I observed my professors in and out of the classroom: I saw their lives—once believed to be ideal for their work, schedule, and ability to influence young lives and minds—and found it was not the life I wanted. That I was not being enculturated into this level of academia only exacerbated the fact that my values, goals, and life plan no longer coincided with that of a college professor but of something else I had yet to discover.

I felt like a square peg in a round hole, as if I would always be the one saying something shocking. For example, during one class, I voiced the opinion, "I don't believe everyone needs or should go to college, let alone continue beyond undergrad. We need people in trades. It takes all kinds to make the world go round." And everyone looked at me with eyes that said, "Did she *really* just say that?" It was the first in a long line of similar moments, where I knew my ideas, beliefs, and experiences would never align with the world I was attempting to enter. More importantly, I did not desire for them to do so. Simply put—try as I might, I was never going to fit into the life I thought I wanted.

It was at this point I knew I had a tough decision to make. I needed to leave the graduate program, but it did not make sense. I was doing well in terms of grades and participation. I had a graduate assistantship that provided me with a scholarship in the Writing Center, even in the first semester. I was studying in the discipline of my dreams. And yet . . . I was extremely disheartened, dissatisfied, and dispassionate. Ultimately, the experience of a semester of graduate school and my decision to leave the program did not boil down to "This is too hard; I can't hack it." Not by a long stretch. There were many more nuanced factors involved. Least of all was I sincerely felt someone else—who loved academia, who was willing to sacrifice and give more, who thrived in this environment—deserved to take my place in the program rather than me coast through stressed, miserable, and far from enculturated. I did not belong there, and I knew it.

My mind and heart had been in a constant battle for months until finally, I concluded, "Enough is enough. This isn't what I want." My plans had changed, and that was okay. A vast sense of peace settled over me once I made my final decision and told my professors (most of whom expressed shock at the news). Although I remain immensely grateful for the opportunity, for my professors and peers, and for the lessons in writing and in life that I would not have otherwise learned, the decision to leave graduate school is one I have never once regretted making.

Scott's Story: A Wonderful Position of Learning and Transition

In Terri's class, I did not like the concepts within the text or the subtext of what I was reading. Still a student myself with no teaching experience whatsoever, the ideas of cognitive process theory, the politics in teaching, and guarding the Ivory Tower left me with a sense of culture shock. As I moved from undergraduate- and graduate-level courses in literature to conversations about various teaching theories, I felt more like a student peering in at the world of writing instruction than a future educator. I thought the world of Composition Studies wouldn't much like me as I knew I didn't much like it. Somehow, the unveiling of the professional world I was working towards made me better understand myself as a student than as a teacher, and I'm sure this perspective came through in my writing. Although understanding my student self through the pedagogy material became a necessary first step to becoming a professional, it was a frustrating experience. In other words, before I could become a professional, I had to transition through hybrid roles of student and teacher. Prior (1991) says, "schools often manifest a tension between immediate and anticipatory socialization"; my socialization (or enculturation) came slowly. What I hope to convey here is that the act of socialization into the professional world of teaching through graduate school is a prime period within a student's development, and it should be acknowledged as a wonderful time to resist the material, take chances, and explore prior to becoming a part of the professional community. To celebrate such a period of learning is to accept and encourage the process in graduate-level writing.

As I failed to empathize with the theorists, I was (in my own way) challenging them for failing to empathize with me: the student. For example, The Connors and Lunsford (1993) essay "Teachers' Rhetorical Comments on Students' Papers" describes a scene where readers of 3,000 evaluated essays saw a "harder, sadder" (p. 210) image of graded writing than they ever imagined. The study gave me a glimpse at the larger picture of my profession, and it seemed rather morose. I couldn't understand how or why more composition scholars could not see the gloomy atmosphere I was seeing. On the side of the student, I was still beginning to engage with prominent minds within the profession.

Although part of me suspected I might be showing my ignorance or criticizing unfairly, I felt passionate about my harsh critique of the profession I was entering. My concern over my display of ignorance or stubborn attitude was at its peak when I had to write my term paper for Terri's class. It is one thing to express ideas during classroom discussions, but to include them in a thoughtful (and graded assignment) is quite another. Because of the Quality of Failure clause included in the syllabus for the class, I decided to test Terri's invitation by writing a paper criticizing the lack of scholarship that considered students' viewpoints, mainly in regards to grading and evaluations. In other words, I was still very much in the mind of the student, but I was beginning to see how I looked to a professional. During the class following our rough draft deadline, I distinctly remember Terri giving us a speech about how our papers should be written from our "perspectives as emerging teachers rather than as students." I sat back in my chair feeling defeated as if she had publicly called me out. However, she quickly amended her speech by saying, "Except for Scott." Then she described to the class how I was writing about the lack of concern writing pedagogy seemed to have in regard to students' perspectives. Still, she reminded me explicitly that I had to engage in the conversation through my paper from a scholarly position. At this moment, I should have felt like I was on the right track, that my rebellion had merit, and that I had just been invited into a professional conversation. Instead, I felt like a student who got lucky on a topic.

Still, Terri was treating my idea as if it had come from an emerging teacher, which made an impact on my socialization.

Regardless of my rebellious start, what I ultimately learned through the tough process of enculturation in Terri's class is that I did not have to relinquish my loyalty to students in order to become a part of the theoretical conversation. I learned I could maintain it, cultivate it, and merge it with the theories I had begun to engage. This synthesis of my ideas was the next step of my enculturation process. In order for me to take real academic and mental ownership of my position, be it in practice or in writing, I needed room to push against the text, and to some degree, against Terri's nudge to assimilate to the profession. Therefore, I believe allowing students the type of resistance I had to the material can be essential to enculturation and, in many cases, a significant part of immediate socialization that Prior discusses.

However, it took much more than Terri's reading list, writing lessons, class discussion, and the luxury of permission to explore through failure in order for me to continue my enculturation process. It took more hands-on experience. Outside Terri's class, I worked roughly 20 hours a week as a writing consultant. By working with students, I was able to begin enacting my student-centered philosophy (if it is even fair to call my resistance to enculturation a philosophy). I began to identify the problems with my (pseudo) scholarly thinking. For example, I was initially appalled by David Bartholomae's (1985) popular article "Inventing the University," which argues that college-level writing instructors should focus on academic writing as opposed to personal essays or expressive writing. As an admirer of Malvina Reynolds' (1962) song "Little Boxes," I believed Bartholomae's approach would turn the university into a "ticky tacky" factory where students are "put into boxes and come out all the same." However, as I put in hours in the Writing Center, I learned the necessity of teaching the academic genres advocated by Bartholomae. I also learned the importance of students practicing a level of composition beyond that of defining an individual's voice and identity through writing. By practicing what Terri was teaching me, I began my anticipatory socialization by beginning to think like a teacher—a necessary step regardless of my teaching values. Without this hands-on practice as a writing consultant outside her classroom, my one-dimensional perspective as a student may have persisted. Through this experience in the Writing Center, I began to empathize with professors' positions in composition just as I had held onto the

> **Kaylin's take:** I think Scott's connection to Malvina Reynolds' song describes exactly how I felt during my time as a graduate student. I felt as if I was being forced into a box I didn't fit quite right in and I, consequently, felt myself begin to resist that push and fight it to some extent. I didn't want to "come out all the same" as everyone else in the program. I wanted to find my own way and my own niche. Ultimately, that led me to look outside academia to find it.

empathy with students when I began Terri's class. Without this experience working in the Writing Center, my writing would have suffered, as my perspective on teaching would have remained shortsighted.

Working in the Writing Center might have started me thinking like a teacher, but it didn't give me a seat in the social circle of teachers, which is what I really wanted. While working with students in the Writing Center, I felt I had to side with professors' comments written on those students' writing. As a result, my own emerging beliefs as an educator were being inadvertently challenged by the professors at my university. For example, I worked with a student in the Writing Center who had used the phrase "chicken cordon bleu" twelve times within the short span of 200 words. The paper was a personal narrative, and the student was proud of his comical tone and word choice. I was, too. However, by looking at the remarks made by his teacher in early pages of the essay, I knew the teacher would not read the student's work with the same enthusiasm with which the student had written it. Because I envisioned twelve bright red circles drawn around each "chicken cordon bleu," I did not maintain my position. Instead, I forwent my philosophy and urged the student to "correct" the overusage of the phrase. Therefore, the Writing Center position did limit my approach to classroom lessons and essay writing.

> **Jami's take:** I had a similar situation in the Writing Center. A student had spent several hours researching a topic only to receive comments declaring how much the professor "hated" her topic on her early draft. She had to start her research over from the beginning, and this left her unable to write. I feel both of these students had the potential to create something unique and daring. However, like Scott, I felt that as the consultant, I had to appropriate the student's intentions (to a degree) in order to meet the professor's expectations.
>
> **Terri's take:** What strikes me about this brief example from Jami is how it is a mirror of the experience she describes in her narrative of having the very ideas of her paper co-opted by the instructor.

What I hungered for, and what I needed to push me to consider the context and content of my emerging philosophy, was real academic socialization as a teacher among teachers. I needed the ability to make my own teaching decisions and even some mistakes. I believed I needed a good pair of strong and worn professorial shoes and a tweed jacket (which I literally bought) to walk in around campus. After all, if I was meant to enculturate, then I should probably dress appropriately.

Not surprisingly, my final push into the teaching community came when I was given the opportunity to teach through my department's mentored teaching program. If not for this program, I do not believe I would have ever truly dressed the part of the professor at the university. Although I initially feared I would stand awkwardly in the corner of the classroom simply staring at students as I assumed another in-between role like that of the Writing Center consultant, the mentored teaching program acted as another necessary step in my enculturation. My responsibilities in the course gave me the opportunity to fully synthesize learning with practice. Moreover, my mentor was open to some of my teaching theories, which was confidence-building. I felt I had finally gained a foothold in the teacher's circle. I believe this stage allowed me to tackle classroom writing problems with the confidence and expertise my professors were looking for.

Although the positions between student and professional can feel artificial, I now believe graduate students should embrace the role. In programs like ours, where graduate students are offered opportunities for hands-on practice, students have an ideal place to begin a safe enculturation process, not unlike the invitation in Terri's Quality of Failure assignment. Furthermore, most of the undergraduate students I taught seemed to have an unspoken understanding that I was on the same side of the desk they were. The students seemed more at ease asking for my help and building rapport with me than with their professors. In other words, because I was not entirely enculturated to the practices of the "other side," I had a better relationship with students, which provided a more genuine approach to writing instruction—something I needed as I struggled to let go of being a student. Although my aim wasn't to improve my writing, I believe the context and content of my writing naturally improved as I experienced tensions within my microsociety, juxtaposition of authority as I experienced in the Writing Center, and my developing personal judgments (Prior, 1991). The position of the beginning graduate student, who is allowed the opportunity to practice their profession outside of the classroom, is an essential part of the enculturation process: a wonderful position of learning and transition. Without the opportunity to act like a teacher, I may still have been acting like a student, and my writing may have become stagnant as well.

Terri's Story, Part 2: Where Do I Go from Here?

Simultaneously unique and generalizable, the stories Jami, Kaylin, and Scott tell are, for me, the most important aspect of this article. Too frequently, we teachers speak *about* our students rather than listening *to* them. Several times as I submitted drafts of my section to my co-writers, they sent back notes saying, "No, what you describe when you talk about graduate students does not resonate with my experience." In responding to drafts of this article, however, reviewers were, perhaps not surprisingly, interested in hearing my response to the students' stories, particularly Kaylin's. So with the permission of my co-authors, I offer some additional thoughts.

In the end, most of the classroom strategies I so carefully planned and implemented did not register as important enculturation moments for my co-authors;

some did not register at all. Instead, when talking about my class, Jami, Kaylin, and Scott tended to focus on single "moments" between us that had a significant lasting impact on them. For example, all three students recalled as important my statement that they should be reading composition theories from their perspective as emerging teachers rather than as students. That was a significant moment for me as well, but not one I'd planned for the course. After reading a set of underdeveloped final project proposals, I was becoming frustrated with what I perceived to be students' too-glib responses to the articles we were reading. I spent the first half of the next class session listening closely to and mapping the students' discussion to pinpoint the source of my frustration, at which time I realized the majority of the class was reading and writing from the student perspective exclusively: For example, students responded to several articles on collaborative pedagogy with comments such as, "If a teacher asked me to work on a team project, I would hate it." During the ten-minute break following that discussion, I planned out a brief statement about learning to read with the mindset of a composition teacher and scholar. That brief statement stayed in my co-authors' minds far longer than many of the activities and assignments I spent hours, even days, crafting. Jami and Kaylin described in their narratives similar "moments" between us that had a significant impact on them; these interactions occurred outside of designated class time in one-on-one settings. None of these moments were ones I could have planned for at the beginning of the semester, but they reinforce my belief that what many graduate students need most is individualized, just-in-time mentoring that recognizes the enculturation processes students are engaged in.

But what about Kaylin? How does her story fit into my goal of helping students successfully enculturate to graduate school? As Kaylin describes, I intervened in her work during the semester when I found her writing was not at the level of most others in the class. Her academic writing improved over the course of the semester, but I knew much more work was necessary in order to bring her writing up to the level it would need to be for writing the thesis.

When Kaylin approached me to say she was not going to be staying in the program, I was impressed with her maturity and self-confidence, two traits I admit that I hadn't noticed during the semester. I've seen a lot of students limp through the graduate program or fade away slowly over time, but it's rare to see a student able to assess their work and their own emotional responses objectively enough to say, "This isn't working out." It was on the basis of that conversation—and her Quality of Failure memo, which was written in eloquent, engaging personal prose—that I decided to invite her to work on this article. My work with her in the nearly seven years since has shown me that those positive traits were there all along and my focus on scholarly reading and writing skills as the primary attributes of ability may have kept me from noticing the other strengths there: professionalism, organization, a direct writing style that communicates easily, and an ability to take constructive criticism unlike almost any student or scholar I've encountered. I agreed and still agree with

Kaylin's decision to leave the program. Like her, I don't believe graduate school is right for everyone, and I didn't see her decision to leave the program as a failure for her or me. I often tell students it is their responsibility to take control of their own education, and it is my responsibility to create an environment that facilitates student control. By that measure, Kaylin and I had a successful semester.

Through this project, I've learned so much about what James Scott refers to as the "hidden transcript" of my course, the discourse "that takes place 'offstage,' beyond direct observation by power holders" (as cited in Miller, 1998). In some cases, being granted access to the students' hidden transcripts has been surprising; in other ways, I've been gratified to learn more about how my students experienced the transition to graduate school and some of the most important moments for them, and to recognize, albeit in hindsight, other opportunities when I might have engaged directly students' experiences of enculturation. Ultimately, I've come away from this project committed to continue creating a classroom space that helps students transition to graduate-level reading and writing, but I realize now what I failed to do in my first attempt was to speak candidly and openly with my students about enculturation and to give them ample opportunities for reflection and dialogue. I still believe many of the enculturation activities I introduced were useful, and I have continued refining them in subsequent graduate composition courses. The Quality of Failure (QoF) component, in particular, gave students some space to explore and challenge course material and disciplinary conventions, as Jami and Scott discussed briefly in their narratives. With guidance from my co-authors and feedback from others in the class, I made small adjustments to the QoF, including increasing its value in relation to the semester grade while at the same time embedding its reflective elements into multiple aspects of the course. I reintroduced the QoF into my next graduate composition course, where it was widely embraced by the students, most of whom were full-time high school teachers eager to try taking their classroom material in new directions. The QoF assignment and other planned activities have improved my classroom environment, but based on my experience working with Jami, Kaylin, and Scott, helping graduate students through enculturation is now as much about getting to know the individuals in my classroom and encouraging them to talk about what they're experiencing as it is about teaching them particular strategies of reading and writing.

> **Kaylin's take:** The idea of Quality of Failure opened my eyes to possibility—inside the classroom and out. I began applying to all aspects of my life the process of taking a risk and then assessing what works, what doesn't, and what can be improved. The long hours commuting gave me the time to assess myself, my risks, my efforts, my heart, and my life as a whole. I found that the risk I'd taken by going to graduate school was not working for me the way I'd hoped, while the risk of leaving offered me endless possibilities to find where I fit.

Conclusion: Bringing Our Stories Together

As we conclude this chapter, we find our narratives do not lend themselves to a simple list of guidelines for the classroom. It is difficult to identify specific strategies that would accurately and adequately address the narratives we have presented here (and the 12 other stories from that composition pedagogy class in Fall 2012 not included but that lurk in the backs of our minds: What would our colleagues have added to this story of a semester of graduate reading and writing? How would their stories have changed what we have shared?). We hold firm in the belief asserted at the beginning of this chapter that it is the stories themselves—with their messy, context-specific details—that professors most need to hear as they consider their students' enculturation to graduate-level writing and reading.

Throughout our narratives, however, some common threads emerge. In their study of first-year master's students, Sato, Kozub, and Samalot-Rivera (2017) found that the "transition to graduate school created academic shock, social isolation, and adjustment to a new academic culture" (p. 632); the stories told here affirm that this transitional moment is a time of strong emotion—frustration, anger, resistance, loss of confidence, and fear. Terri went into the semester thinking that simply *showing* students the processes by which composition scholars read or write would reduce, perhaps even eliminate, many of these negative emotions. But Jami's, Kaylin's, and Scott's narratives raise the possibility that such strong emotions may be central to the enculturation process, and that enculturation may be as much about emotional transitions as it is about learning new practices. As Scott says, "Growth hurts. But for a graduate student to understand the purpose of that growth can make all the difference." Perhaps rather than seeking to mitigate students' emotional responses, professors would do more good by openly validating the emotional aspects of students' graduate experiences. Teachers might acknowledge that resistance and frustration are natural reactions of people struggling to find their place within a discourse community. In that way, the QoF assignment was valuable less for its own sake than for the space it created for instructor and students to engage in risky conversations—about not knowing, doubting oneself, resisting the discipline, or failing to enculturate.

Second, our stories attest to the fact that some of the most important enculturation moments happen outside of the formal classroom—in one-on-one conversations with students and in the spaces where a discipline does its work. For Jami and Kaylin, individualized mentoring from Terri carried greater impact than any planned activities or lectures. Professors would do well to remember that the lives, stresses, problems, and joys students bring to the classroom will impact how they experience the classroom. The classroom is just one of many spaces impacting the individual enculturation experience of each student. For students, the work of a particular course exists in dialogue with the work done in other classrooms; in their teaching or other workplaces; and in their conversations with peers, families, and friends. In truth, each professor plays only one part in a student's enculturation experience, so perhaps the best help to offer is transparency about what happens in the classroom, why it happens, and how and why that might differ from what students are likely to encounter in other spaces within the discipline.

Enculturation beyond the classroom also occurs when graduate programs give students more opportunities to engage in the professional work of the discipline. The importance of professional experience to enculturation is echoed in the other articles in this section: for example, the former graduate students surveyed in Lannin and Townsend (this collection) noted that work as a teaching assistant helped them to be more aware of their own writing and thus able to improve on their own writing abilities, while Shapiro (this collection) explores how teaching writing helps graduate students become better writers themselves. In Scott's narrative above, he describes well how his experiences as a writing consultant and composition teacher enabled him to find his own place within the discipline. And Kaylin poignantly describes her own professional presentation to English Studies colleagues, a largely negative experience, but an important one nonetheless. That same presentation confirmed for Jami that—despite the challenges of juggling graduate school, jobs, and parenting—she was finding her place within English Studies. Without that opportunity early in their graduate school careers, Kaylin and Jami might have taken much longer to make decisions about their futures in the discipline.

Finally, we argue that learning and talking about enculturation can help graduate students as they transition to graduate-level reading and writing. For most students, the practices of academic disciplines are not intuitive; they do not come naturally, and a "sink or swim" mentality through the experience may not lead to successful enculturation. For example, as Kaylin shared above, without guidance, a graduate student may be unable to distinguish standards of the discipline from individual teacher preferences. Examining students in literary studies courses, Laura Wilder (2012) argues that the genre conventions of literary analysis are rarely taught at any level from high school through graduate school even though these conventions "appear to play a significant role in instructors' evaluations of student writing, evaluations that frequently determine students' prospects for continued work in a discipline" (p. 108). Similarly, Boquet et al. (2015) found graduate students were often expected to write in genres they had not been exposed to as undergraduates, and the students interviewed in Fry et al. (2019), reported "their undergraduate work had not prepared them for the rigors of graduate writing, and that the graduate program had not yet clarified the expectations of what constituted 'good' graduate writing" (p. 2841). In our conversations about this project, the four of us returned over and over to the idea of transparency. It is only through exploring the concept of enculturation for this project that the student co-authors were able to recognize in retrospect what they experienced and needed during that

Fall 2012 semester. All three believe having a clear understanding of enculturation earlier would have helped them through that difficult first year of graduate school. Ultimately, graduate programs and professors need not make graduate school *easier*; rather the goal should be to normalize the process of enculturation by making it *clearer*.

References

Bartholomae, D. (1985). Inventing the university. In M. Rose (Ed.), *When a writer can't write: Studies in writer's block and other composing-process problems* (pp. 134–165). Guilford.

Boquet, E., Kazer, M., Manister, N., Lucas, O., Shaw, M., Madaffari, V. & Gannett, C. (2015). Just care: Learning from and with graduate students in a Doctor of Nursing practice program. *Across the Disciplines, 12.* https://wac.colostate.edu/atd/special/graduate.

Brooks-Gillies, M., Garcia, E. G., Kim, S. H., Manthey, K. & Smith, T. G. (Eds.). (2015). Graduate reading and writing across the curriculum [Special issue].*Across the Disciplines, 12.* https://wac.colostate.edu/atd/special/graduate.

Burger, E. (2012, August 21). Teaching to fail. *Inside Higher Ed.* http://www.insidehighered.com/views/2012/08/21/essay-importance-teaching-failure#.UhZ2h4Vdr_E/.

Carr, A. D., Rule, H. J. & Taylor, K. T. (2013). *Literacy in the raw: Collecting, sharing, and circulating graduate literacy narratives.* http://cconlinejournal.org/winter2013/literacy_raw/index.html.

Connors, R. J. & Lunsford, A. A. (1993). Teachers' rhetorical comments on students' papers. *College Composition and Communication, 44*(2), 200–223.

Good, T. L. & Warshauer, L. B. (2000). *In our own voice: Graduate students teach writing.* Longman.

Fry, S., Keith, M., Gardner, J., Bremner Gilbert, A., Carmona, A., Schroeder, S. & Kleinsasser, A. (2019). Entering a community of writers: The writing center, doctoral students, and going public with scholarly writing. *The Qualitative Report, 24*(11), 2832–2850. https://nsuworks.nova.edu/tqr/vol24/iss11/11.

LaFrance, M. & Corbett, S. J. (2020). Discourse community fail! Negotiating choices in success/failure and graduate-level writing development. In M. Brooks-Gillies, E. G. Garcia, S. H. Kim, K. Manthey & T. G. Smith (Eds.), *Graduate writing across the disciplines: Identifying, teaching, and supporting.* The WAC Clearinghouse; University Press of Colorado. https://wac.colostate.edu/books/atd/graduate.

Lannin, A. & Townsend, M. A. (2020). Graduate student perspectives: Career development through serving as writing-intensive GTAs. In M. Brooks-Gillies, E. G. Garcia, S. H. Kim, K. Manthey & T. G. Smith (Eds.), *Graduate writing across the disciplines: Identifying, teaching, and supporting.* The WAC Clearinghouse; University Press of Colorado. https://wac.colostate.edu/books/atd/graduate.

Lave, J. & Wenger, E. (1991). *Situated learning: Legitimate peripheral participation.* Cambridge University Press.

Micciche, L. R. & Carr, A. D. (2011). Toward graduate level writing instruction. *College Composition and Communication, 62*(3), 477–501.

Miller, R. E. (1998). The arts of complicity: Pragmatism and the culture of schooling. *College English, 61*(1), 10–28.

Perez, R. J. (2016). Exploring developmental differences in students' sensemaking during the transition to graduate school. *Journal of College Student Development, 57*(7), 763–777.

Prior, P. (1991). Contextualizing writing and response in a graduate seminar. *Written Communication, 8*(3), 267–310.

Reid, E. S. (2009). Teaching writing teachers writing: Difficulty, exploration, and critical reflection. *College Composition and Communication, 61*(2), W197–W221.

Reynolds, M. (1962). Little boxes. On *Sings the truth* [MP3 file]. Columbia Records.

Russell, D. (1995). Rethinking genre in school and society: An activity theory analysis. *Written Communication, 14*, 504–539.

Sato, T., Kozub, F. M. & Samalot-Rivera, A. (2017). Students' academic and social transition to new graduate programs in physical education teacher education. *Multicultural Learning and Teaching, 12*(2). https://doi.org/10.1515/mlt-2015-0018.

Shapiro, E. (2020). Towards an integrated graduate student (training program). In M. Brooks-Gillies, E. G. Garcia, S. H. Kim, K. Manthey & T. G. Smith (Eds.), *Graduate writing across the disciplines: Identifying, teaching, and supporting*. The WAC Clearinghouse; University Press of Colorado. https://wac.colostate.edu/books/atd/graduate.

Simpson, S., Clemens, R. Killingsworth, D. R. & Ford, J. D. (2015, August 25). Creating a culture of communication: A graduate-level STEM communication fellows program at a science and engineering university. *Across the Disciplines, 12*(3). https://wac.colostate.edu/docs/atd/graduate/simpsonetal2015.pdf.

Wenger-Trayner, E. & Wenger-Trayner, B. (2015, April 15). *Communities of practice: A brief introduction*. http://wenger-trayner.com/introduction-to-communities-of-practice/.

Wilder, L. (2012). *Rhetorical strategies and genre conventions in literary studies: Teaching and writing in the disciplines*. Southern Illinois University Press.

Creating a Culture of Communication: A Graduate-Level STEM Communication Fellows Program at a Science and Engineering University

Steve Simpson, Rebecca Clemens, Drea Rae Killingsworth, Jesse Priest, and Julie Dyke Ford
NEW MEXICO INSTITUTE OF MINING AND TECHNOLOGY

> **Abstract**: A flurry of recent research in writing studies has addressed the need for more systematic approaches to graduate-level writing support, though more research is needed into more organic models that account for graduate students' specific needs and that build infrastructure for writing support within university departments. This chapter reports on a graduate-level STEM Communication Fellows program at a science and engineering research university, in which graduate students in science and engineering fields help launch discipline-specific writing support in their home departments. The chapter begins with a discussion of program goals and departmental contexts. Then, two graduate STEM Fellows share their experiences developing support mechanisms in Earth and Environmental Sciences and Mechanical Engineering. Last, program assessment data from surveys and follow-up interviews are discussed. Findings from the STEM Fellows' narratives and assessment data demonstrate different degrees of success as fellows wrestled with intricacies of the different departmental cultures. Findings also indicate the need for more structured mentoring opportunities between advanced and incoming graduate students, more focus on unstructured writing support over writing courses, and more development of asynchronous methods of peer interaction.
>
> **Keywords**: Graduate Writing Support, STEM, Science and Engineering Writing, Writing Groups, Distance Education, Thesis and Dissertation Writing

As Mike Rose and Karen McClafferty (2001) argued nearly two decades ago, very little effort has been made in many universities to address graduate-level writing support in any "systematic" way. While a flurry of recent research in writing studies has addressed this issue (Aitchison & Paré, 2012; Simpson, 2012; Simpson, Caplan, Cox & Phillips, 2016; Starke-Meyerring, 2011), more research is needed to identify graduate writers' specific needs and to develop writing resources tailored to these needs. Two specific problems emerge as we discuss graduate writing program

DOI: https://doi.org/10.37514/ATD-B.2020.0407.2.07

design. First, as Steve Simpson (2012) argued, many of our existing WAC/WID models are designed with undergraduates in mind. The idiosyncratic and distributed nature of learning in graduate school requires us to rethink our "knee-jerk models of writing instruction (i.e., offering preparatory writing classes) and explore [. . .] models that better fit within students' existing academic networks and learning rhythms" (p. 102). Second, as Claire Aitchison and Anthony Paré (2012) have indicated, given the importance of writing to graduate students' professionalization, writing support should not be "isolated" within service entities on campus. Rather, universities should "suffuse the [graduate] curriculum with writing" (p. 20). Creating this pervasive emphasis on writing necessitates writing centers and WAC/WID programs developing critical cross-campus partnerships and helping build infrastructure for writing support within university departments.

This chapter reports on the development of a graduate STEM Communication Fellows program developed at New Mexico Tech. While based loosely on "writing fellows" programs implemented at the undergraduate level, this graduate-level program creates opportunities to develop organic, student-run programs catering to the writing activities most suitable for students' disciplines and to develop more community among graduate students both in our Writing Center and in students' home departments. Most significantly, this chapter is co-authored with two of the original graduate STEM Communication Fellows, one from Geology and one from Mechanical Engineering. Thus, we discuss the goals and logistics of our program design and foreground the students' own voices, allowing them to use their own words to provide their perspectives and describe successes and setbacks as they worked with peers to develop a community of writing in their home departments.

The chapter begins with a discussion of the program goals and institutional setting. We then include narratives written by the STEM Communication Fellows describing their work creating department-specific initiatives and navigating the intricacies of their home departments' cultures. We conclude with general program assessment data and recommendations for program design, which includes a call to rethink what "community" might mean for graduate students, and an update on the evolution of the program since the pilot project. Our goal is to challenge the field to address a demonstrated need by considering a wider range of program designs better suited for graduate students and to provide other WAC/WID researchers and administrators with ideas for implementing similar programs suitable for their own contexts.

Program Development at New Mexico Tech

The New Mexico Institute of Mining and Technology (NMT) is a small science and engineering research university in south-central New Mexico. While small

(1,563 undergraduates and 539 graduates), NMT has strong specialized programs in mechanical engineering, atmospheric and astrophysics, earth sciences, and petroleum engineering. Like many universities, NMT has become concerned with both the attrition and completion rates in its graduate programs and with the general quality of the graduate experience it provides. (For more on graduate education reform, see Council of Graduate Schools, 2010; Golde & Walker, 2006; Lee & Danby, 2012).

In 2009, NMT was granted a Title V: Promoting Postbaccalaureate Opportunities for Hispanic Americans (PPOHA) grant, the first Department of Education grant for graduate students. Among the initiatives proposed in the grant, NMT sought to provide a better range of graduate-level communication support and to encourage more community and peer-to-peer mentoring among graduate students. Despite NMT's small size, which in theory should encourage more community, NMT graduate students are still isolated in their labs and report receiving very little feedback on their writing projects from other graduate students.

Graduate program development occurred in stages and was built on cross-campus partnerships that Julie Dyke Ford had been nurturing between the Technical Communication program and the Mechanical Engineering Department, which started in response to ABET criteria for clear communication and feedback from alumni and employers. The initial stages of graduate program development at NMT involved collaboration between the Center for Graduate Studies, the Technical Communication program, and the Writing and Oral Presentation Center, and began in fall 2010 after Steve Simpson joined the faculty of the Writing and Oral Presentation Center. Initial writing and communication initiatives included three programs: science and engineering communication classes, which were initially linked with seminars in specific STEM disciplines; graduate student consultations in the Writing and Oral Presentation Center (which had previously only served undergraduates); and thesis and dissertation "boot camps," weeklong intensive thesis workshops for graduate students at the writing stage. More detailed descriptions of these programs can be found in Simpson's publications (2011, 2012, 2013; Simpson et al., 2016).

These initial programs succeeded in two important ways. First, they provided program developers with opportunities to work directly with faculty from STEM disciplines. Ford continued her work with Mechanical Engineering through a linked graduate communication in engineering, and Simpson partnered with Physics. The early success working with these programs led to collaboration with other departments, such as Earth and Environmental Sciences and Electrical Engineering. Second, these programs initiated numerous cross-campus dialogues on more organic communication models within university departments. Mechanical Engineering's interest in bolstering in-house communication resources led to Julie Ford taking a joint appointment between Technical Communication and Mechanical Engineering, and later a full appointment in Mechanical Engineering. (For more on Julie's transition into Mechanical Engineering, see Ford, 2012). The Physics Department started plans to revise a required graduate lab to include introductions to research and scientific communication. Further, faculty in the Earth Sciences Department had noticed how many graduate students participated in boot camp and likewise grew interested in encouraging similar activities in their department. As these discussions started, we found that a more flexible graduate resource was needed to nurture these budding programs within departments and to continue supporting students from other departments. Thus, in summer 2012, we began our STEM Communication Fellows program.

The STEM Communication Fellows act as a bridge between the original three initiatives and the academic departments, channeling students between the formal graduate initiatives and department-specific initiatives and filling in the gaps between the two. STEM Fellows are graduate students from STEM disciplines trained in tutoring peers in writing and oral presentations. They spend part of their time working with native and non-native English-speaking graduate students from all disciplines in the Writing and Oral Presentation Center and part of their time helping their home departments develop in-house communication resources. While we did not require prospective fellows to be expert communicators from the beginning, we previewed their writing for evidence of a strong communicative base and interviewed them to discern their awareness of their own writing processes. STEM Fellows participate initially in a two-part, four-hour training session that includes readings in peer tutoring and oral presentations and practice analyses of research posters and writing samples from NMT graduate students.

After the initial training sessions, STEM Fellows receive much of their training through informal mentoring sessions. Steve Simpson and Julie Ford met regularly with the first generation of fellows to address questions and concerns from conferences or to discuss recent relevant publications. After the first generation of fellows was trained, new fellows were mentored by more experienced fellows. Steve Simpson and Julie Ford also coached STEM Fellows in performing needs analyses of their home departments, encouraging fellows to speak with and survey department heads, faculty, and students about departmental communication needs.

The first year, we concentrated on developing programs in three of the largest graduate programs on campus—Earth and Environmental Sciences (58 students), Mechanical Engineering (60 total students, including 33 distance students), and Physics (32 students). Drea Killingsworth, the Earth Sciences fellow, worked with her department head to pilot a one-credit writing seminar focused on students' thesis proposals. She also became the go-to person in her department for help working with ESL students. Rebecca Clemens, the Mechanical Engineering fellow, assisted Julie Ford with an engineering communication course and helped develop an in-house thesis template as well as style guides. She worked individually with students in the engineering communication course and consulted with distance students in the program. The Physics fellow started a student-run writing group and worked with a faculty member piloting the new in-house graduate communication seminar. Along the way, fellows participated in other campus events. For example, Drea and Rebecca developed and delivered a series of three workshops on research posters, extended abstracts, and research presentations for the annual Student Research Symposium.

In the following sections, two of our STEM Fellows provide personal narratives of their experiences working in their home disciplines: Earth and Environmental Sciences (EES) and Mechanical Engineering. They recount their experiences wrestling with two vastly different departmental cultures and responding to additional needs that emerged while attempting to build community in their home departments. We then provide an assessment of our programs across all three of the initial disciplines: Earth Sciences, Mechanical Engineering, and Physics. Findings from the STEM Fellows' narratives and assessment data demonstrate different degrees of success as fellows wrestled with intricacies of the different departmental cultures. Findings also indicate the need for more structured mentoring opportunities between advanced and incoming graduate students, more focus on unstructured writing support over writing courses, and more development of asynchronous methods of peer interaction.

Building a Culture of Communication: Nuts and Bolts Drea, Earth and Environmental Sciences (EES)

Initially, my involvement as a STEM Fellow with the Earth and Environmental Science (EES) department focused on working with ESL graduate students in the Writing and Oral Presentation Center (WOPC) to revise articles for publication. I worked with students to review the language, organization, and clarity of their writing. This process improved the language and writing skills of the ESL students and benefited advisors by allowing time to focus on content with their advisees. This background fostered awareness in EES of the benefits to both students and faculty of working with a WOPC tutor, causing the department to be receptive to the idea of developing student-run graduate writing initiatives. In the beginning stages, I recognized that students were likely sharing resources and collaborating within their small research groups. Earth sciences' emphasis on fieldwork fosters the development of working and social relationships that encourage interaction and community among students. Despite this interaction, a larger peer-network is needed to provide information about available resources for data analysis and access to writing groups.

Developing an In-House Proposal-Writing Seminar

I conceived of the one-credit Graduate Writing Seminar with the help of both my advisor and the EES department head, who were concerned about the level of technical writing skills possessed by existing and incoming students. First-year graduate students from both Hydrology and G^3 (Geology, Geochemistry and Geophysics) complete a research proposal by their second semester for the purposes of either procuring funding or forming a thesis committee. We developed this seminar to provide scheduled, weekly time for students to work on thesis-related projects. Eight students enrolled in the pilot seminar, divided equally between incoming and existing graduate students and between Hydrology and G^3.

The participating students provided an initial writing sample to both their advisor and me to serve as a baseline for evaluation. In a brief survey, students were asked to give a description of the project they intended to work on, to describe their current stage in their project, to set reasonable goals for the semester, and to discuss their comfort level with graduate-level technical writing. Four students set goals to complete drafts of National Science Foundation grant proposals. The remaining students worked on sections of their theses or thesis proposals.

An atmosphere of disconnection exists between Hydrology and G^3, as students from these two programs take different core classes, use specialized labs and facilities, and even attend separate department-sponsored social events. Within the department, international students commonly feel isolated due to language or cultural barriers, non-traditional students have difficulties assimilating because of a difference in age and real-world experience, and both students and advisors are absent for extended periods of time for fieldwork.

At the beginning of each meeting, we discussed what each student had accomplished during the week and addressed any problems or questions students had. The remainder of each meeting was used for students to work on their projects and to meet individually with me to review drafts. The interaction between small groups of students created a more relaxed and open environment that not only facilitated discussion but also allowed students to get to know each other on a personal level through casual conversation. This comfort level encouraged students to approach each other for help both in and outside of the classroom environment and to discover parallels between their work.

Every two to three weeks, we used the scheduled meeting time for peer review. I asked the students to bring printed two- to five-page copies of the sections they were each currently working on to exchange with another class member. I was also given a copy to monitor progress and improvement in individual writing skills. The weekly meetings and group discussion in the PPOHA-sponsored graduate lounge greatly facilitated positive interaction between students of different disciplines, years, and backgrounds. One of the advantages of working with students from specialized fields within the same broad discipline is the ability to use peer review to answer questions such as, "Is your writing clear to someone outside of your specific discipline?" Grant proposals are directed to a wide, scientifically-educated audience, making it important to explain discipline-specific terms, emphasize the general relevance of the proposed project, and concisely describe detailed methodology. In the process of reading material aloud to another person, students evaluated their own work by listening to what they had written.

Common time and space resulted in the formation of mentorships between experienced and less-experienced students with similar fields of study. In two cases, students found a peer mentor within the seminar group. One incoming G^3 student was applying for funding from a grant that had been awarded to a current Hydrology student the previous year. This discovery made students realize that although the methodology of their individual research projects differs, the process of writing a proposal or thesis is similar. Although the second pair had different advisors and areas of focus, each used nearly the same methods to analyze samples in the geochronology lab. I asked the more-experienced student who was completing his master's thesis to work with the newer student on creating a template for a geochronology methods section. The more-experienced student gained insight into his own writing process by evaluating and teaching this process to others. The student being mentored benefited from seeing an example of how someone else had already organized similar material.

Mid-semester, I had the students use a discussion session to reevaluate and revise their project goals after they had more knowledge of the amount of work and time that goes into writing a thesis or proposal. Reevaluation allowed students to make more realistic plans for time management in the future, assess their resource needs, and recognize both their strengths and weaknesses throughout the writing process. Initially, one student had expressed that his previous project proposal was so heavily edited by his advisor that he no longer identified it as something he had written. Over the course of the seminar, he developed his "voice" by concentrating on only the methods section of his thesis. This focus allowed him to organize his data and improve his scientific writing skills through weekly revisions of a smaller volume of text. Eventually, he successfully presented his work to researchers, faculty, and students at the New Mexico Geological Society annual meeting, receiving high public praise from his advisor.

It was challenging to meet the different expectations of individual students. Despite the description communicated in the syllabus, incoming students were used to a more structured environment including lectures and regular assignments. The intent of this seminar was to provide a scheduled time during which students would be accountable to each other for making progress towards their writing goals. Graduate students are understandably overwhelmed by the daunting task of writing a proposal or thesis. This type of writing requires a longer time commitment, more in-depth knowledge of a highly-specific subject area, and more precise formatting than projects that students have previously completed. In many cases, students have the added pressure of being dependent on funding to continue their research. Part of the difficult transition into a graduate program is adapting to a framework of self-sufficiency in finding resources, developing projects, monitoring progress, and staying motivated. Importantly, classroom collaboration resulted in the formation of a sustainable peer-network beyond the scope and duration of the seminar, through which students can now share technical resources for methodology, such as data processing and analysis, encourage each other to stay motivated, or just express their frustrations.

After the Seminar

After participating in the pilot EES Graduate Writing Seminar, many students from both Hydrology and G^3 attended the thesis boot camp and afterward formed an informal thesis writing group that met twice per week in the PPOHA-sponsored graduate lounge. These students have expanded upon the pilot seminar structure to include longer, less formal meetings and have encouraged membership from additional students from within the department. An unexpected outcome of this initiative was the ability to observe student interaction and identify individuals who had the passion and knowledge of their own writing processes to succeed me as the department STEM Fellow.

Rebecca, Mechanical Engineering (MENG)

When I began as a STEM Communication Fellow in summer 2012, I had no familiarity with the MENG graduate student culture, which primarily involves students performing independent research, interacting mostly with their advisor rather than other students, and focusing on writing only in the last semester of their two-year graduate program. I did not consider how these attitudes of independence and postponement would affect my plans to increase participation in graduate student peer communication groups.

Herding Cats: Peer Review Groups in Mechanical Engineering

My original plan for the Fall 2012 semester in the department was to create a bi-weekly peer writing review session for MENG graduate students. I informally surveyed several faculty members about the areas of student writing they felt needed most improvement. The most common response was "structure and organization," and "clearly defining their ideas and their work's significance." These surveys gave me a starting point for areas to focus on in the proposed group sessions.

An online scheduling survey was sent to all on-campus department graduate students to see if there was interest in a bi-weekly or monthly peer review session. Initially, five students indicated an interest either through the survey or personal communications. I set up a date and time to have a group meeting with the five students, asking them to bring several pages of their most recent writing. Two students showed up; of the other three, one canceled prior to the meeting, and two simply didn't attend. This session was productive for the two who attended, so I tried scheduling a session for two weeks later. This time, no one came.

Trying to organize regular peer writing review sessions in the MENG department was problematic for several reasons. To begin, students tend to think they only need to take the communication in engineering course to develop good writing habits and skills. MENG students work independently on research, which carries over to their writing approach. Most MENG students have historically started writing the bulk of their thesis in their last semester, an attitude that reflects engineers' tendency to view communication products as an afterthought to technical work (Winsor, 1990). Students often consider the thesis itself to be peripheral to the main focus of their graduate school experience—their research work—and often comment that they aren't ready to write until they've completed all research, analyzed all data, and reviewed their conclusions with their advisor. Then, when they start writing, they feel they "don't have time" to spend on activities away from the computer (even ones that may help with their writing).

Further, the structure of the Mechanical Engineering program complicates the community building necessary for peer review groups and encourages students' natural inclinations toward working independently. The four MENG degree specializations (Explosives, Fluid and Thermal Sciences, Mechatronics Systems, and Solid Mechanics) require different core and elective classes, separating students into smaller, regularly interacting groups. Department laboratories are located in several buildings around campus, further segregating students. Each specialization has multiple advisors, and even if two students have the same advisor, each student's research differs, and he or she may interact regularly only with the advisor, not other students in the research group.

A Different Approach: The Communication for Engineers Course

My next approach was to work more directly with Julie Ford's Communication for Mechanical Engineers. I enrolled in this class myself in spring 2013 to fulfill one of my outside-the-department class requirements. This course allows students to use their own research work as the technical content for written and oral presentation assignments. All assignments are graded by Julie Ford and also peer-reviewed by classmates, which is a good introduction to the peer review process. Many students choose their thesis literature review as their major written assignment, and by the end of the semester they have a polished piece of writing to incorporate in their thesis. One interesting new assignment Ford added was a "Three Minute Speech," based on a competition at the University of Queensland (for more, see http://threeminutethesis.org/). Nine class members presented their research in front of an audience of NMT faculty, staff, and students, with only one static PowerPoint slide and three minutes of presentation time. One of the audience members organizes the annual NMT Student Research Symposium (SRS), and was so interested and engaged that a Three Minute Speech category was added to the April 2014 SRS. Ford encouraged students to contact me (as a STEM Communication Fellow) outside of class, and some classmates did take advantage of the opportunity. I met several times with one student to help clarify his understanding of writing assignments and to work on his organization, flow, and grammar. I met with another student more than once to discuss the basics of literature reviews: finding and cataloging relevant literature, what information should be included, and how it should be organized. One drawback, however, was that most students assumed that the class is the only writing "group" they will need or want to participate in during their time in graduate school.

Building Community Remotely: The Distance Education Factor

One unexpected area of increasing participation in our programs is with Distance Education (DE) students, who often miss out on the opportunities to build community with peers on campus. New Mexico Tech offers Master of Science degrees in Science Teaching (MST) and Engineering Management that are conducted mostly or entirely as distance courses. All MENG graduate courses are offered online, as well, and, in fact, there are more distance MENG graduate students than resident students. In the Fall 2012 semester, a professor asked me to work with an Engineering Management student who was struggling with his report. The student emailed me his reports, and, over the next two weeks, two review sessions were conducted using Skype. Due to poor connection capability at the time, the Skype sessions were not very successful, and we switched to using the "track changes" and commenting features of Microsoft Word software, then emailing the updated versions back and forth. I have worked with several distance students since then, some from Engineering Management and some from MENG. I initially offer students the option of using Skype, but to date all have chosen the email and document "track changes" route. One student, working overseas in Afghanistan, found this method extremely helpful, as the time difference (10 hours) and his work schedule made it almost impossible for him to schedule live meetings. After several weeks of working together, he completed his thesis and submitted it to his committee. He successfully defended (by Skype) and has graduated.

There are several drawbacks to using email communication only: It is time consuming for the reviewer, as all comments and questions must be typed in; written comments or questions may be misinterpreted by the student as criticism, as it is hard to clearly indicate tone of voice and attitude in typing; and it limits the relationship that can develop between the student and reviewer even after several "sessions" are conducted. I worked, on and off, with one student for about 12 weeks, and had to repeatedly explain that I wasn't criticizing her approach or style in my questions. In the future, I plan to offer only the Skype option to start with, as the connection quality has improved; this will provide clearer understanding of questions asked and comments made and allow us to develop a "face-to-face" relationship.

Reflections on my Time as a STEM Fellow

After my first year working as a STEM Fellow, six NMT MENG students went through the defense and graduation process during the Spring 2013 semester, four on-campus and two distance. Of those, three of the on-campus and one distance student contacted me for individual thesis review and feedback. Two of the on-campus students also engaged in informal peer review of each other's writing. I am a STEM Communications Fellow through the 2013–2014 academic year and am continuing to build community in my department, particularly in promoting the improved capabilities of the Writing Center's online assistance.

Program Assessment

As Drea and Rebecca discussed in their narratives, our STEM Communication Fellows program chalked up numerous successes in its first year. Departmental cultures can often be resistant to change, however, which has created numerous obstacles. In this section, we present some initial findings from our assessment of the STEM Communication Fellows Program and analyze the programs' effects to date. Assessment for the STEM Communication Fellows program is ongoing. Thus, assessment data included in this chapter are preliminary and focus on a small population—19 student respondents (of 21 enrolled) and 11 advisors (out of 12). Nonetheless, tentative findings shed an interesting light on our STEM Communication Fellows' personal observations and suggest directions for future program design in our own context and in others. All narrative and survey data collection in this study has been approved by our university's Institutional Review Board (IRB).

Program assessment consisted of follow-up surveys with students and advisors (administered via SurveyMonkey) and 30-minute follow-up interviews with select student participants from all three participating programs. Surveys utilized a "retrospective pre-post" design, an instrument used in educational research to account for "response shift bias"—that is, when respondents rank themselves higher on pre-tests before fully understanding what is being assessed (Moore & Tananis, 2009). Student participants were recruited from three initiatives: Drea's one-credit writing seminar, the graduate communication in engineering course with which Rebecca assisted, and the Physics writing group. In keeping with the "retrospective pre-post" survey protocol, student participants were given surveys after participating in the program and asked to rank their perception of their communication abilities before and after participating in these initiatives on a scale of 1–5 (1 being "poor," 5 being "excellent"). Students were also asked their likelihood of soliciting feedback from peers before and after participating and were asked to indicate their likelihood of participating in other writing initiatives (e.g., writing groups, thesis and dissertation boot camp, communication courses, etc.). Advisors were asked to rate their students' communication abilities before and after participating in these initiatives. Last, students were contacted in the semester following their involvement in these activities for short follow-up interviews to elicit more nuanced responses on students' experiences and to see how many of the writing practices they learned continued with students after formally participating in a class or workshop.

Overwhelmingly, students and advisors indicated improvement in students' communication abilities, though interesting differences emerged among the three groups of students (Earth Science [EES], Physics [PHYS], and Mechanical Engineering [MENG)]). As seen in Table 7.1, EES students reported the most improvement in academic writing, moving from a 3.33 to a 4.42, an assessment echoed to some degree by faculty respondents. PHYS students noted no change in the surveys, though in the optional explanation box one indicated that it was simply "too early to tell." As we will see later, Physics students indicated other ways in which the initiatives helped. MENG students, as a whole, indicated some improvement (in most cases moving from a "3" to a "4", or a "4" to a "5"), though their self-reported skills were higher than EES students' and much higher than how MENG advisors ranked them. These rankings confirm what many of us observed: EES students seemed to be more aware than MENG students of what writing skills they needed. Further, and perhaps more interestingly, the EES student group consisted of both first- and second-year master's students, and the PHYS group consisted of doctoral students, some of whom have already participated in previous writing initiatives and have experience publishing. The MENG group consisted almost exclusively of first-year master's students, many of whom had only started working on their theses.

In addition to assessing student and advisor perceptions of growth in communication skills, we also assessed whether students participating in these initiatives were more likely to seek help from peers on writing, and whether they were inclined to continue participating in other Title V graduate writing programs. Students in all three programs identified being much more likely to seek out peer response after participating in these programs. Of 19 total respondents, 13 indicated that they "rarely" or "never" sought out peer response beforehand. However, 17 of 19 students indicated that after participating in these initiatives they would "definitely" (8) or "probably" (9) seek out peer assistance. All seven mechanical engineer respondents indicated that they would "definitely" (1) or "probably" (6) seek peer assistance.

Table 7.1. Student and advisor rating of communication skills before and after participating in STEM Communication Fellows initiatives

Participants	Ratings (Number of Responses)					Rating average
	1	2	3	4	5	
All Students (n=19)						
Before	0	0	10	9	1	3.47
After	0	0	1	15	3	4.11
EES (n=9)						
Before	0	0	6	3	0	3.33
After	0	0	0	8	1	4.11
MENG (n=7)						
Before	0	0	3	4	0	3.57
After	0	0	0	5	2	4.28
PHYS (n=3)						
Before	0	0	1	2	0	3.67
After	0	0	1	2	0	3.67
All Advisors						
Before	0	3	4	2	0	2.89
After	0	1	3	4	2	3.70
EES (n=4)						
Before	0	1	1	1	0	3.00
After	0	0	1	2	1	4.00
MENG (n=5)						
Before	0	2	2	0	0	2.50
After	0	1	1	2	0	3.25
PHYS (n=2)						
Before	0	0	1	1	0	3.50
After	0	0	1	0	1	4.00

However, these groups diverged in their responses to participating in future initiatives. EES and PHYS students were emphatic in their wish to participate in boot camp (8 of 12 were "definitely," 2 were "probably") and writing groups (4 "definitely," 6 "probably"). MENG students were much more noncommittal, 6 of 7 indicating that they would "maybe" participate in a writing group, 4 of 7 indicating that they would "maybe" participate in boot camp. Thus, at least as far as the survey responses are concerned, most of the 19 students developed good impressions of peer feedback. MENG students, while in theory more receptive to the notion of peer response, were reluctant to participate in any of the formal mechanisms created through our graduate program design.

The follow-up interviews shed more light on the dynamics of student interaction within these initiatives and how the programs evolved to better fit the diverse departmental cultures. In particular, these interviews revealed quite a bit of activity in the Physics writing group despite participants' hesitance to indicate improvement over the semester. In the fall 2010 and spring 2011, Steve Simpson had partnered with a physics professor to help physics students set up student writing groups with little success, mostly because students had trouble finding common meeting times. The Physics STEM Communication Fellow had more success, as he adopted a more flexible plan that did not require synchronous meetings. One participant described the setup as such:

> It was pretty casual. It was a group of about five or six of us who all expressed an interest in not only improving our writing but helping others to improve theirs. When we started out, we sort of met in person, and we tried to figure out a good online way to pass the information, and we settled on Google Drive, which has been pretty useful for this purpose.

In most cases, participants explained, the group would email each other when they needed feedback and upload the document to Google Drive. Participants mostly provided comments using either the Google or Word commenting features. Participants wanting to provide further explanation on comments would stop by the writer's office or lab and provide extra explanation if necessary. In some cases, such as when members of the group were preparing research posters for a regional American Physical Society meeting, the group arranged a physical meeting time. Otherwise, most feedback was given asynchronously.

As participants explained in interviews, the informal nature of the writing group worked in this case, as many of them had common deadlines, which provided incentive to work together:

> Actually, [name removed] and I helped each other on the New Mexico Space Grant. She asked if the writing group would review hers. I go, "Oh, this is a good idea." If there's a bunch of essays and proposals of your research they go, "Yeah, I'll send you myself then too." I think it's just because in our department everyone's schedules are so different. I know other departments are the same. It seems that when there was a writing sort of, task

that we all had to do because we're all in the same kind of, field we're all sort of, focused then.

More significantly, starting the writing group through the STEM Communication Fellow helped provide a forum for students who wanted such assistance but felt awkward about initiating such contact, as one participant explained:

> For me, the hard part was initially asking for other students to help me review. That's why the student writing group was perfect because now there was a small subset of my classmates that I knew I could go to ask for that help.

As with the physics writing group, the EES seminar was informally constructed and catered to students' different schedules. Perhaps more interesting, however, was the unique blend of students from both G^3 (geology, geophysics, and geochemistry) and Hydrology backgrounds, as Drea explained earlier, and the mix of beginning and advanced students in the program. In follow-up interviews, one of the more advanced students indicated that he joined the seminar specifically because it gave him an opportunity to share his knowledge with incoming students;

In other words, both departments had students who were more naturally inclined to provide peer feedback but did not have formal mechanisms through which to do so. In this sense, the initiatives "got the ball rolling," creating precedent for future peer partnerships. This opportunity benefited some of the newer students in the class. One such student admitted in an interview that she was so new to the field and to the research process that she hardly had anything to write for the first part of the class. Much of this time was spent observing more advanced students talk about their writing. Thus, by the time she got around to working on her own writing (a short NSF grant proposal), she felt that she had some direction.

Discussion

The goal of our STEM Communication Fellows program is to take positive steps toward developing a more pervasive, large-scale culture of communication in our graduate programs on campus and to develop more community among graduate students. Naturally, institutional contexts vary widely. While our particular program design might not transfer directly to other institutions, we believe that our thought processes might be useful to other WAC/WID program administrators developing similar initiatives elsewhere.

As seen in both our STEM Fellow narratives and our assessment data, we experienced different degrees of success across the three departments with which we worked. Our EES and Physics STEM Fellows experienced reasonable success developing more informal, peer-based writing support mechanisms within their departments. While Rebecca made significant headway in Mechanical Engineering—particularly in support for distance students—she reported some difficulties getting students to commit to writing groups outside the confines of a class. Numerous factors account for her experiences with these students, some of which are simply out of her control (e.g., some students simply have numerous work or family obligations to balance with school work). Further, both Julie Ford and Rebecca Clemens have noted in their interactions with MENG students that they tend to be more focused on their core coursework and more independent-minded than other students at New Mexico Tech.

However, as Julie Ford reported reflecting on these experiences, other contributing factors might be addressed more easily. Ford mentioned that many of the graduate students in the Mechanical Engineering program also completed undergraduate degrees at New Mexico Tech (unlike the vast majority of students in EES and Physics) and had already taken a required undergraduate technical communication course in addition to the graduate-level Communication for Mechanical Engineers, which many advisors strongly recommend. Thus, some students might have developed the impression that they had "their bases covered" in terms of communication, rather than seeing writing as something to address throughout their graduate and professional careers. Further, as noted earlier, the MENG students who participated all tended to be first-year students, as opposed to the PHYS writing group, comprised exclusively of upper-level students, and the EES initiatives, which included a mixture of first-year and advanced students. Quite possibly, the first-year students were not as aware of what writing skills they would need as they progress toward the thesis and did not have the benefit of interacting with more advanced students within the context of the class who could alert them to these needs.

These findings have several important implications for program design. First, they underscore the importance of facilitating conversation among beginning and upper-level students in graduate programs. Our initial program designs with the Title V grant focused almost exclusively on acculturating and retaining new graduate students, an ill-fitting hold-over from many retention efforts at the undergraduate level. In graduate program design, we must consider that students will have a variety of needs at different levels of their academic progress, and many graduate students might not fully appreciate the complexity of graduate-level writing until they are at the thesis-writing stage. Further, facilitating discussion on writing between advanced and beginning students builds an architecture of apprenticeship into the program, wherein more advanced students are given opportunities to share their knowledge with newcomers. Not only is such student-centered design potentially more sustainable, but it is potentially more persuasive to graduate students, who might be more resistant to support mechanisms that seem to be imposed on them from faculty. To an extent, we saw this phenomenon in the Physics Department initiative, where a student-initiated writing group experienced more success than previous attempts at faculty-initiated groups. Second, these findings emphasize the importance of coupling graduate-level classes with other forms of support. Drea Killingsworth, in her writing seminar, established a link with the thesis boot camp from the start: students were generating proposals of projects they would later work on in boot camp. And, in fact, four of the students with whom she worked participated in boot camp afterward. The Communication for Mechanical Engineers graduate course filled a critical need in that department, though Ford, upon reflection, indicated the need to better emphasize the need for further forms of support beyond the class.

Further, these findings raise questions about how and when one attempts to change a local department culture. On the one hand, program designs that fail to account for local student attitudes are naturally limited in their potential effectiveness; in fact, these elements of local department cultures can often be harnessed in useful ways. For example, our MENG students, while extraordinarily independent-minded, are also competitive. Thus, Ford experienced great success with a "3-minute speech" competition with cash prizes in her communication course. On the other hand, one cannot just assume that departmental cultures are immutable. The rift between G^3 and Hydrology students that Drea recognized in the EES program is long-standing and stubborn, but students from these programs can benefit from more interaction with each other. Similarly, many professors in the Mechanical Engineering program would attest that the students—and the department—would benefit from more peer collaboration, particularly since peer collaboration is an essential component of one's future professional life in engineering. Meeting this type of resistance means that more efforts are needed to demonstrate the value such programs might have for them.

As indicated earlier, a central focus of our Title V programs has been to create better community and peer mentoring among graduate students. Our program design efforts, however, have required us to challenge our assumptions of what "community" entails. Our initial program designs assumed much more face-to-face interaction among graduate students. Graduate students' lives, however, are complex, and giving our STEM Fellows the reins to partake in the program design afforded them the opportunity to show faculty what forms of community might better suit their needs. In the case of Physics students, the community that developed was almost entirely online and asynchronous. In Rebecca Clemens' experiences with DE students, the community that she developed had to be online and, in some cases, asynchronous. Drea's course design included a mixture of face-to-face and online interactions. Some of the ESL students with whom Drea has worked have preferred face-to-face interactions, though other students preferred other means.

After the conclusion of the PPOHA grant in 2014, the STEM Communication Fellows program was sustained by linking it with a quarter-time graduate student minority scholarship through the Center for Graduate Studies. Students become STEM Fellows through a competitive application process which has afforded the position an unexpected prestige among graduate students on campus.

Epilogue: An Incoming Writing Center Director Reflects on the STEM Communication Fellows Program

Jesse Priest

Reading about the challenges and rewards of developing the STEM Fellows program at its inception is humbling and inspiring. As a new director, I have inherited a program that now, a few years later, seems like an obvious and organic part of the NMT Writing Center environment. WPAs and WAC coordinators would do well to continually investigate institutional histories and contexts as a constant reminder of what Jackie Grutsch McKinney (2013) calls "the material realities of our centers" (p. 36). In doing so, as this chapter has reminded me, I can see the STEM Communications Fellows program as *not* obvious and organic, but rather an institution full of the history of individuals who designed it as a response to specific contextual needs. As an incoming director, I can make a few observations to update readers on the progress of the STEM Communications Fellows program a few academic years into its growth.

During last academic year, the Writing and Oral Presentation Center tutored an average of 130 unique student visitors each semester, with graduate students accounting for nearly 25 percent of our tutees. By New Mexico Tech standards, this means we are now tutoring more graduate students per semester than the WOPC was seeing for total student visitors in 2005. As an incoming director, it is easy to see the crucial role the STEM Communications Fellows program has played in that expansion and will continue to have as we expand even further.

The original authors of the *Across the Disciplines* article (Simpson et al., 2015) cited the continual need to "identify graduate writers' specific needs and to develop writing resources tailored to these needs," (p. 1) and I believe the STEM Communications Fellows program has grown into a practical realization of this earlier call. For a new director, the STEM Fellows provided me with de facto assistant directors: engaged graduate tutors who came qualified to combine burgeoning disciplinary expertise with graduate student writers' perspectives. The variety of STEM Communications Fellows I have already worked with—including graduate students from Materials Engineering, Biology, Mineral Engineering, and Chemistry—has given me an apparatus for campus outreach and understanding different departments' faculty and graduate student needs. For a now returning director entering my second year, the STEM Communications Fellows continue to provide me with a finger on the pulse of different departments each semester, keeping my perspective fresh and aware of changing needs. I am a firm believer in Writing Program Administration that seeks to create sustainable institutions that do not rely on one individual director's vision to function, and the STEM Communications Fellows program models that kind of sustainability.

Including individual students' voices in the institutional histories of our writing centers and WAC programs is an ongoing necessity. The resonance of these voices exists regardless of whether we recognize them or not: Drea's earlier observation that graduate students' two "primary difficulties" are finding resources and knowing how to begin writing, hold true today and is clearly a part of the pedagogical onus behind the STEM Communications Fellows program that I inherited. Similarly, both Drea and Rebecca comment on students struggling with expectations of linear writing processes or separations between thesis-writing and research in similar ways that our current Biology STEM Fellow reflects on how working as a STEM Communications Fellow has improved her own writing process:

> I would say my biggest accomplishment as a STEM Fellow was broadening my teaching skills by learning to listen to what a student expects from a tutoring session at the Writing Center. This helps guide the rest of the session and makes the session more valuable to both parties involved. Additionally, it was important to learn that it is okay to have limitations set for your session, for example, going through X pages of a thesis together rather than a whole thesis in a one hour session.

This reflection resonates with Mary Jane Curry's (2016) observation that graduate students benefit from "speaking with an authorial voice" (p. 87) in their transition from knowledge receivers to knowledge producers. Being a STEM Communications Fellow allows graduate students to inhabit roles of authority concurrently with their process of becoming experts in their own disciplines.

The WOPC and the STEM Communications Fellows continue to have an expanding role in the Student Research Symposium, a connection which I now know can be at least partially traced back to Julie Ford piloting a new assignment in her 2013 Communication for Mechanical Engineers course that Rebecca took part in. Our Biology STEM Fellow this year helped redesign the Student Research Symposium presentation templates, an initiative that she pioneered, which I am going to make an annual part of the STEM Communications Fellows' involvement with the SRS.

We continue to work on developing reliable modes of assessing graduate students' experiences. Currently, our STEM Communications Fellows perform weekly check-ins and an informal exit interview with me, which I am working on formalizing to help me design training and professional development for future STEM Communications Fellows. In doing so, I seek to experiment with program design that fosters intersections across success and retention initiatives on campus. The STEM Communications Fellows and similar programs foreground individual graduate student experiences within program development and help directors and other WPAs create historically-aware institutions.

Acknowledgments

Funding for these initiatives was provided in part by a Department of Education Title V grant (PPOHA: Promoting Postbaccalaureate Opportunities for Hispanic Americans). However, the content of this article does not necessarily represent the policy of the Department of Education, and you should not assume endorsement by the Federal Government.

References

Aitchison, C. & Paré, A. (2012). Writing as craft and practice in doctoral education. In A. Lee & S. Danby (Eds.), *Reshaping doctoral education: International approaches and pedagogies* (pp. 12–25). Routledge.
Council of Graduate Schools. (2010). *Ph.D. completion and attrition: Policies and practices to promote student success.* Council of Graduate Schools.
Curry, M. J. (2016). More than language: Graduate student writing as "disciplinary becoming." In S. Simpson, N. A. Caplan, M. Cox & T. Phillips (Eds.), *Supporting graduate student writers: Research, curriculum, and program design* (pp. 78–96). University of Michigan Press.
Ford, J. D. (2012). Integrating communication into engineering curricula: An interdisciplinary approach to facilitating transfer at New Mexico Institute of Mining and Technology. *Composition Forum, 26.* http://compositionforum.com/issue/26/new-mexico-tech.php.
Golde, C. M. & Walker, G. E. (2006). *Envisioning the future of doctoral education: Preparing stewards of the discipline.* Jossey-Bass.
Lee, A. & Danby, S. (Eds.). (2012). *Reshaping doctoral education: International approaches and pedagogies.* Routledge.
McKinney, J. G. (2013). *Peripheral visions for writing centers.* Utah State University Press.
Moore, D. & Tananis C. A. (2009). Measuring change in a short-term educational program using a retrospective pretest design. *Journal of American Evaluation, 3*(2), 189–202.
Rose, M. & McClafferty, K. A. (2001). A call for the teaching of writing in graduate education. *Educational Researcher, 30*(2), 27–33.

Simpson, S. (2011). Graduate learning communities? Integrating language support for ESL and native-English speaking graduate students. *SLW News: The Newsletter of TESOL's Second Language Writing Interest Section, 5*(3). http://newsmanager.comm partners.com/tesolslwis/issues/2011-02-28/1.html.

Simpson, S. (2012). The problem of graduate-level writing support: Building a cross-campus graduate writing initiative. *WPA: Writing Program Administration, 36*(1), 95–118.

Simpson, S. (2013). Building for sustainability: Dissertation boot camp as a nexus of graduate writing support. *Praxis: A Writing Center Journal, 10*(2). http://www.praxis uwc.com/simpson-102.

Simpson, S., Caplan, N. A., Cox, M. & Phillips, T. (Eds.). (2016). *Supporting graduate student writers: Research, curriculum, and program design.* University of Michigan Press.

Simpson, S., Clemens, R. Killingsworth, D. R. & Ford, J. D. (2015, August 25). Creating a culture of communication: A graduate-level STEM communication fellows program at a science and engineering university. *Across the Disciplines, 12*(3). https://wac.colo state.edu/docs/atd/graduate/simpsonetal2015.pdf.

Starke-Meyerring, D. (2011). The paradox of writing in doctoral education: Student experiences. In L. McAlpine & C. Amundsen (Eds.), *Supporting the doctoral process: Research-based strategies* (pp. 73–95). Springer. https://doi.org/10.1007/978-94-007-0507-4.

Winsor, D. A. (1990). Engineering writing/writing engineering. *College Composition and Communication, 41*(1), 58–70.

PART 3: "Help each other. Find a writing group!" OR Collaborations and Programs 'Alongside' Curriculum

Marilee Brooks-Gillies
INDIANA UNIVERSITY–PURDUE UNIVERSITY INDIANAPOLIS

I vividly remember gathering in a small conference room in Olds Hall on Michigan State University's campus in August of 2008. The newest Rhetoric and Writing doctoral student cohort, Graduate Director Malea Powell, and an array of snacks were taking up all the space in the room, which had an air of eager anticipation. Malea reassured us that we would be supported in this program, and she urged us to also care for one another. She stressed that this was a graduate program where we helped each other. That moment has stuck with me, and there were multiple times throughout my first year in the program when various faculty members mentioned that creating a study group or writing group would be productive. At that point, I was in coursework, and the most meaningful kind of support I could think of would be to discuss the dense and extensive reading we were asked to complete for courses. Occasionally a group would come together for a week or two, sometimes to share our thoughts about course-assigned material, sometimes to discuss a well-known text in the field that had not been assigned in its entirety for class. These groups, though, had little staying power.

It was in my second year at MSU and my second year as a graduate consultant in MSU's Writing Center that I was introduced to more structured writing groups to support graduate students. I had the good fortune to become The Writing Center's graduate writing group coordinator and had the opportunity to first undergo training as a group facilitator and later facilitate training sessions for other graduate consultants who were interested in guiding groups of graduate writers. That summer, Elena and I also took on the responsibility of facilitating The Writing Center's Navigating the Ph.D. Workshop. In both of these roles, I was struck by how important it was to address and consider issues that seemed unconnected to writing in order to support writing. We worked with writers to plan out their semesters: What are your primary writing goals? What other commitments in your life need to be considered when planning the semester? What are your known writing strengths and limitations? Who do you seek out for support?

We'd discuss how difficult it was transitioning into graduate school, too. I remember hearing stories about how small concerns made focusing on larger concerns difficult. For example, upon moving to East Lansing, a student was frustrated by small things like trying to find a place to get their hair cut and the need to continually get quarters from the bank to do laundry. It is easy to dismiss these small, everyday tasks, but they have a real impact on the ways we organize our lives: How long is your commute? Do you have childcare? Are you getting enough sleep? Are you staying active? Are you taking care of yourself?

During the Navigating the Ph.D. Workshop, we spent a lot of time discussing support networks, stressing that students shouldn't expect any one mentor to be able to provide all the different kinds of support that they might need. Instead, they should consider the multiple mentors in their lives—some acting in official capacities, like advisors and committee mentors, some more informal mentors, often professors not on the student's committee as well as colleagues in their Ph.D. program—and recognize that support from non-academic settings—such as a local choir, craft group, running club, or informal gatherings with friends—were of equal importance.

My experience coordinating and facilitating graduate writing groups and the Navigating the Ph.D. Workshop emphasized just how important it is for graduate students to find support outside the classroom. In this section, contributors share a variety of programming and experiences outside but alongside the classroom such as writing centers, writing groups, and writing camps to emphasize the importance of attending to graduate writing needs in structured ways beyond the curriculum.

Making Do by Making Space: Multidisciplinary Graduate Writing Groups as Spaces Alongside Programmatic and Institutional Places

Marilee Brooks-Gillies
INDIANA UNIVERSITY–PURDUE UNIVERSITY INDIANAPOLIS

Elena G. Garcia
UTAH VALLEY UNIVERSITY

Katie Manthey
SALEM COLLEGE

> **Abstract**: Graduate students are often students, teachers, consultants, mentors, and facilitators all at once. Their knowledge is utilized in teaching and administration, yet they are not fully credentialed and their decisions are under higher scrutiny than those of full-fledged faculty. Given the in-between position of graduate students, we argue that there is a great need for spaces that are free from the judgment of institutional assessment (*outside* departmental places) while still meeting institutional writing needs graduate students have (*alongside* the more official places). In two focus groups of graduate writing group members, we asked participants to tell us about their motivations for joining these groups, the benefits they gained through the groups, and the ways the groups were limited. In this chapter, we illustrate why such writing groups are important spaces for graduate education in that they provide support and community, structure and accountability, and multidisciplinary perspectives to their participants.
>
> **Keywords**: Graduate Writing, Graduate Writing Education, Graduate Writing Groups, Writing Groups, Writing Centers, Space and Place, Communities of Support, Multidisciplinary

Each of us spent three-to-five years working with and mentoring graduate students in graduate writing groups at Michigan State University (MSU) while completing our own graduate degrees.[1] Our experiences with the graduate writing groups, as well

---

1   During the publication process, each author earned their degrees and began working at different universities.

DOI: https://doi.org/10.37514/ATD-B.2020.0407.2.08

as our own experiences as graduate students, have taught us that graduate school is a personal and emotional experience that has a significant impact on student identity and well-being. During graduate school, students become disciplined into fields of study seen as esoteric and elusive to their friends, acquaintances, and colleagues who work in different environments. For many graduate students, earning their degree isn't just about achieving a higher level of education, but about challenging themselves and contributing to and changing the world. Like other creative people, these individuals hope "to bring order to experience, to make something that will endure after one's death, to do something that allows humankind to go beyond its present power" (Csikszentmihalyi, 1997, p. 38). The movement between their pre-graduate school identity and their degree-holding identity, like any movement "is rarely just about getting from A to B. The line that connects them, despite its apparent immateriality, is both meaningful and laden with power" (Cresswell, 2006, p. 9).

In "Introduction: (E)Merging Identities: Authority, Identity, and the Place(s) In-Between," Melissa Nicolas (2008) describes graduate school as an in-between space; we would contend that all *space* is similarly in-between and that graduate school is an excellent example of space. Nicolas writes:

> In-between spaces are murky, stressful, overwhelming, exasperating, challenging, exciting, hopeful, and full of potential. Inhabiting an in-between place, whether professionally or personally, puts our minds in over-drive. . . . During this in-between time, we often experience moments of great clarity about who we are and what we want, quickly followed by moments of intense self-doubt and questions about our identity. Being in-between causes us to assess our situation and reflect on our strengths and weaknesses in order to accept or reject roles and to negotiate this liminal space. (p. 1)

Graduate students are often students, teachers, consultants, mentors, facilitators, and administrators all at once. Their knowledge is utilized in teaching and administration, yet they are not fully credentialed and their decisions are under higher scrutiny than those of full-fledged faculty. They question their own abilities; they question whether they have what it takes to finish the process. The spaces graduate students make alongside the formal place of the academy influence their confidence and success within their graduate programs. Despite the many roles graduate students play in their everyday lives, it is writing that often determines their progression through degree programs. Coursework, comprehensive exams, and dissertations—as well as publications—are predominantly written products; the assessment of these products determines whether students' progress through their graduate programs and is linked to advisor and instructor judgment of students' academic capabilities. Yet, writing instruction and support at the graduate level is primarily dependent upon individual advisors and committee members.

Many of these instructional and supportive spaces and places tend to be rife with the same high stakes—assessment and judgment—as the final written products.

In this chapter, we focus on a very specific space: multidisciplinary graduate writing groups at Michigan State University.[2] We also focus on a specific context, that of a university writing center. We see the graduate writing groups facilitated through MSU's Writing Center as one of the spaces that graduate students make alongside the institutional places of their graduate programs, departments, and disciplines. We conducted two focus groups with participants of the MSU Writing Center's graduate writing groups to learn more about how they understood and used the groups as spaces alongside institutional places. Our questions centered on several key themes: why the students joined these groups, the benefits they gained through the groups, and the ways the groups were limited.

The purpose of this chapter is to provide working definitions of space and place that convey in-between-ness as a quality of space in particular and to show that the writing groups at Michigan State University are important spaces of writing support for graduate students because they function alongside places of institutionalized assessment and judgment. We use data from our focus groups to show how participants, as members of graduate writing groups, make spaces alongside and within institutional places that positively influence their academic abilities and identities. In particular, we discuss how graduate writing groups are informal spaces of writing and professional development that are important resources for graduate students precisely because they function alongside *and* within institutional places.

A Theory of Space and Place

It's important to note that space and place are relative terms. In general, place is more fixed and stable, and space is more flexible and fluid. However, what is a place to one person might be a space to another. For instance, as teachers we might have memories and experiences in particular classrooms that we have taught in for several semesters. We can connect multiple experiences, people, objects, and practices to a particular classroom. However, a student taking her first class in the same room will not immediately attribute any special feelings or memories to this classroom. For her, the classroom is likely associated abstractly with other classrooms in her life,

---

2   Additional research on MSU's graduate writing groups is available in Garcia, Eum, and Watt's "Experiencing the Benefits of Difference within Multidisciplinary Graduate Writing Groups" (2013) and Kim and Wolke's "Graduate Writing Groups: Helping L2 Writers Navigate the Murky Waters of Academic Writing," found in this collection. Each study focuses on different elements of the groups and worked with different participants, but there is overlap across the pieces that could be of particular interest to readers developing or researching graduate writing groups on their own campuses.

but it doesn't at first contain any distinctive meaning for her. Doreen Massey (2005) defines space as a "meeting-up of histories" (p. 4), as "stories-so-far" (p. 130), while places are stabilized collections of these stories. Rules and orders that limit practice and membership characterize places, while spaces tend to have less definition and regulation. Place is more stable than space and is given meaning through artifact, language, and practice. Spaces are made to change, adapt, and manipulate places.

To graduate students, programs, departments, and/or disciplines are sometimes seen as monolithic entities or places with static conventions and rules in which they "cannot find" or "have no" place. They appear as places in that they are fixed with stable rules and practices that maintain their boundaries. On the other hand, spaces are openings alongside and within these places that graduate students find and make in order to belong, in order to make room for themselves. Graduate programs, disciplines, and even genres themselves can be understood as places (Bawarshi, 2001) in that they feature rules and orders that limit who can take part in writing/making and reading them. Writing, then, is a practice that can open up and make space and/or create and maintain the boundaries of place.

Writing Center programming has less firm boundaries than disciplines and is more space-like than place-like, making writing centers easier for students to navigate. Muriel Harris (1995) points out that the tutorial instruction in writing centers "is very different from traditional classroom learning because it introduces into the educational setting a middle person, the tutor, who inhabits a world somewhere between students and teacher" (p. 28). These writing tutors and consultants are often undergraduate and graduate students themselves. The writing groups we discuss in this chapter were facilitated by graduate writing consultants at a writing center. Graduate students in a writing group, like students in a writing center session, "can also offer other useful information they would be less willing to give teachers" (p. 29). That is, the graduate writing groups we focus on also have softened boundaries and are spaces of negotiation around what "writing" is and what "good writing" means in the contexts writers discuss and experience both in and outside the groups.

The groups allow for a rhetorical understanding of writing that recognizes "writing as a site of long-term socialization or 'disciplining' of doctoral students into the discourses and genres of their fields—the repeated discursive practices that have evolved in specific research cultures through repetition over time" (Starke-Meyerring, 2014, p. 66). The groups, then, become spaces of support that provide graduate students with opportunities to negotiate their scholarly identities in relation to institutional norms and conventions.

This is particularly important since the discourses and genres that graduate students are learning about and engaging in

> regularize and regulate what can, must, or must not be said, thought, or acknowledged; what and whose knowledge (e.g.,

indigenous knowledge, practitioner knowledge, etc.) or evidence counts or not; which conversations to take up and how; how to work out and position one's contribution amidst competing epistemological, ontological, and ideological factions of a given research culture; whom doctoral scholars are being asked to become as researchers through their writing; what disciplinary orthodoxies are to be reproduced; and much more. (Starke-Meyerring, 2014, p. 67)

Like Starke-Meyerring, we recognize that institutional environments created within higher education are maintained through daily practice that has often been made invisible and normalized as "common sense" and "how things are done," without critical reflection. In particular, this normalization has silenced and marginalized conversation around academic writing. Spaces like writing centers and programs such as graduate writing groups and writing process camps (Busl, Donnelly & Capdevielle, this collection) make explicit the implicit and encourage daily practices that create a space of opportunity to make disciplinary and institutional practices more visible, which in turn allows graduate students to enter into institutional realities with a clearer understanding of how the institution operates.

Our Groups

The Writing Center at Michigan State University hosts graduate writing groups. Each group is facilitated by a graduate writing consultant, and all groups are overseen by one graduate student coordinator. Like many other opportunities The Writing Center provides, the graduate writing groups are completely voluntary, with students requesting participation and leaving the groups when they determine participation is no longer necessary. In order for the groups to be useful and successful, the Center asks that writing group participants dedicate themselves to participating in writing group work for three hours a week for a full semester. A graduate writing consultant, often a Ph.D. student but sometimes an MA student, facilitates each group's two-hour weekly meeting, with the third hour dedicated to reading the work of other group members to prepare for the meeting. Groups vary in size from three to six members. In larger groups, members can expect to have conversations about their own writing every other week, while in smaller groups, discussions about each member's writing every week are possible. The number of groups varies semester to semester, typically with three to six active groups per semester, each with three to six members.

Although there is an attempt to group students together by discipline, availability becomes the most important consideration when scheduling a group. As a result, most groups are multidisciplinary. Multidisciplinary groups have been selected more purposely by other researchers such as Cuthbert, Spark, and Burke (2009), who write, "The decision to run multi- rather than single-discipline groups was based partly on practical concerns, including the diverse backgrounds of participants—for instance there was only one person from Italian Studies, compared with ten from the predominantly social science disciplines housed within the School of Political and Social Inquiry" (p. 142). Cuthbert et al. also emphasized that multidisciplinary groups could more easily encourage "participants to focus primarily on writing, rather than on the discipline-specific details of content. In addition, it was felt that supervisors would (or should) be filling the role of 'expert' content readers" (2009, p. 142). Like Cuthbert et al. (2009), we came to see the multidisciplinary aspect of the writing groups as a strength.

When a group is first organized, the facilitator spends time with the group introducing a writing center approach to peer response to the group members. Participants discuss the difference between higher-order and lower-order concerns and how to provide productive feedback on structure and organization as well as sentence-level error. In addition to a foundation of productive peer response methods, the facilitator works with students to determine their writing goals for the semester as individuals and as a group. It is expected that group members will read the writing of selected group members prior to the weekly meeting and prepare some feedback. During each group's weekly meeting, the first 15 minutes are spent with group members checking in about their writing progress for the week and any personal updates they would like to share. The bulk of the meeting is spent providing spoken peer response about group members' writing. On occasion, the group will participate in a planning or writing activity during the group meeting, such as preparing a strategic plan for writing goals for the semester. The facilitator sees their role as to respond to writing in supportive and constructive ways and guide members to engage in this practice as well. The facilitator works with participants to focus on higher-order concerns, provide guidance on genre and disciplinary conventions, and build community.

Our Participants

Curious about the influence of the graduate writing groups on participants, we began developing an IRB-approved set of studies as part of a research cluster focused on graduate writing within Michigan State University's Ph.D. program in Rhetoric and Writing. We designed a survey with Soo Kim and Shari Wolke (see Chapter 9, this collection) and emailed it to all former and current graduate writing group participants for the years of 2009–2011. The survey asked participants to provide information about their participation in the graduate writing groups, including their motivation for joining and satisfaction with the experience. They were also asked for information about their familiarity with writing instruction, access to writing assistance and resources, and self-perceptions of their writing ability. We received 28 responses; 21 respondents answered all of the survey questions. The survey responses, for us, were primarily used to develop questions for our focus groups and to recruit participants for our focus groups. We sent a focus group request to everyone who completed the survey. Five people responded to the focus group requests. We held two focus group meetings, which each lasted around 90 minutes. Each of us transcribed and reviewed the interviews for patterns and themes in the responses.

Four graduate writing group members volunteered to participate in our focus groups: Angela, Lindsey, Adrienne, and Adam.[3] Angela was a Ph.D. student in Organizational Psychology and joined one of Elena's groups in 2010. She was a member of a writing group that stayed together for more than a year; members of this group had a relationship prior to joining a Writing Center graduate writing group, which likely contributed to the longevity of the group, even after a Writing Center facilitator was no longer requested by the group. Lindsey and Adrienne both joined one of Elena's groups in the summer of 2011. Lindsey was a Comparative Religion major who was not an official MSU student—her husband was hired as a professor in the university, and she came to East Lansing with him. Adrienne was a Literature student who actively participated in writing groups both within her discipline and through other support services on campus, and she was interested in writing pedagogy at the graduate level. Adam—a Public Health Administration student who, like Lindsey, attended a different university but had moved to the East Lansing area—participated in another facilitator's group.

During our focus groups, we were primarily interested in learning about why participants sought out graduate writing groups, the benefits of being a member of a graduate writing group, and the limitations of these particular graduate writing groups. Throughout the focus groups, participants noted that the qualities they associated with the space of the writing groups are different than the qualities they associated with the place of their programs, departments, and disciplines. Three major themes linked to these differences arose: support and community, structure and accountability, and the strength of a multidisciplinary approach.

Support and Community

The participants reported that they found the groups helpful not just as a source of writing knowledge and practice but as a space of emotional as well as intellectual support. The groups provided community and helped participants feel that they were not alone. In these groups, students supported one another; they learned

---

3   Pseudonyms have been used by request of the participants.

about writing and mentoring through practice within the group. The most-cited need for a writing group mentioned by the students we talked to was a consistently available support system and community of peers.

Two of our participants were not technically MSU students—they were displaced students from other universities, in the area of East Lansing because of work, for themselves or their spouses. Lindsey explains her experience as follows:

> I am a displaced graduate student. I don't go here for graduate school, but I moved here because my husband is a professor here. So, I was kind of writing to a void and had lost my community and needed a group to sort of stay productive and also remember that there is an audience out there.

Adam defined his similar experience as being "displaced" because he, too, was a graduate student from a different university. Students who were MSU students, like Angela, also expressed a sense of isolation: "I thought, I'm going to be writing. I had just lost a lot of support in my graduate program, and I wasn't sure how I was going to get it done, so having any group to write with sounded like a good idea." Because they had lost their previous support systems either through leaving their home institutions, finishing coursework, or because many of their disciplinary peers were not easy to connect with, they were most in need of some way to stay connected to other students.

The group members we spoke with emphasized the importance of getting support from their peers instead of authority figures. Angela shared:

> I really liked that it felt like there was no judgment about my character as a graduate student. It was accepted that you're a doctoral student, you're trying to get somewhere, and we're trying to help you with your writing and trying to make it better. That's all the focus was on and I really liked that that was it. There was no other stuff brought into the room.

Her sentiments were echoed by others, which line up with this understanding of interacting with peers who were not understood as authorities, judges, or evaluators: "People 'just playing' at pool, or at math, or at coming up with clever rebuttals to arguments, do better than those who are trying to impress an evaluator—unless they are already highly skilled at the task" (Gray as cited in Wolfsberger, 2014, p. 183). Our participants expressed that the groups allowed them to develop confidence in a safe environment.

The group members also expressed that because the group felt safe and supportive, they felt comfortable sharing and learning from one another, which enabled them to build confidence and knowledge around writing strategies and in using writing terminology.

Adrienne: . . . getting more confidence for myself: I think because there are lots of mentoring structures in place in my department, it makes me feel more confident about sharing that advice. Since I feel more confident about my writing, . . . I can say, well, I struggle doing this. I feel confident enough to admit that I struggled and got out of it. And so sort of passing that on to other people through various means.

Lindsey: There was a person in our group, and she always talks about interventions and what her intervention is in the literature. And to me, what she means is what she's doing different. And the sort of original thinking that's going on. And so I was able eventually to say, well, what's your intervention here?

Because of the informal and peer-focused environment, group members felt comfortable sharing their thoughts and supporting each other without the sort of scrutiny they perceive as associated with working with faculty advisors.

Our findings regarding support and community as an important benefit of graduate writing groups are not unique. Cahill, Miller-Cochran, Pantoja, and Rodrigo (2008) note of their own graduate writing group that they had "become a community of support for one another and the support goes beyond writing. As our friendships have grown significantly, so has our commitment to one another's professional and personal success" (p. 155). The writing groups at MSU, then, are once again similar to those studied by Starke-Meyerring (2014), who writes, "Doctoral students may well organize into groups to discuss writing, without necessarily identifying these arrangements as 'writing groups,' because for them writing may be inseparable from their academic life, positionalities, and the related politics of writing in institutions" (p. 71). While conversations about writing practices and specific writing projects were the main focus of the groups, group members also spent a lot of time discussing work-life balance, teaching concerns, problems with advising, and other topics that, while not directly about their writing, inform their writing situations and their professional lives. As Smith, Molloy, Kassens-Noor, Li, and Colunga-Garcia (2014) note of a similarly-organized faculty writing group, "We share not only writing pieces but also our stories, successes, joys, and frustrations with each other" (p. 182). This kind of sharing and connection beyond and around the writing itself was a motivator for sustaining the groups.

Structure and Accountability

One of the most consistent and powerful practices of a graduate writing group for these participants was, very simply, consistent and structured meeting times.

For all four participants, there was a clear need for the community of working regularly with other graduate students. Participants were especially interested in how the groups could help them with structure, deadlines, and accountability. In coursework, weekly classes, required homework, and the regular availability to talk with faculty provide structure and consistent accountability. Readings and responses are due each week; seminar papers are due at the end of the semester; there are clearly scheduled deadlines, and the student has to work diligently to keep up. Once coursework is complete "many graduate students find they need structured writing support in order to succeed" (Phillips, 2012). Time can be particularly difficult to manage, and there are few, if any, resources on college campuses that can provide the kind of regular, weekly support that our graduate writing groups did.

An isolated graduate student, for example, might go weeks, even months, without talking to their advisor or other committee members, who are not expected to actively keep track of each student. This is particularly the case when a student is in a situation like Angela's where her department was hands-off and she was entirely responsible for completing her work. Angela revealed:

> Since I'm sort of on my own these days, this will be great to have people to at least give me some feedback. Because I knew that the chair that I had moved to was a very hands-off person and he just expected you, just like the other faculty, to figure it out. It's just that I knew that going into that relationship with him, so I was prepared to deal with it. And so when this idea came up, it's like, I think this will fill the void of having constant feedback. I think that was about all I had thought about it, in terms of expectations of the group.

Angela's response clearly and strongly articulates the need that many graduate students have to "fill a void" left when coursework ends. All four participants were in the exam or dissertation stage of their Ph.D. programs when they decided to join one of the Writing Center's graduate writing groups. They had lost their previously-structured writing environments and sought an alternative.

Concerns about structure and accountability are often brought up in larger conversations regarding Ph.D. completion and retention rates, since the dissertation process can drag on for many years. Adam and Lindsey, in their focus group interaction, addressed this difficulty:

> *Adam:* people, when they get to that level, when they have no more classes, they have—all they have to do is write. There's a group of them out there that's, I don't want to use the word

lonely, but I mean, I've been getting by with it, but it's like it would have been a little easier.

Lindsey: It's very isolating.

In her study of doctoral graduate writing groups, Claire Aitchison (2009) identified that the writing group participants she interviewed and observed "pointed to the greater regularity of the group meetings, compared to their difficulties accessing busy supervisors . . . [and] the sense of reciprocity and mutual obligation they shared" (p. 909) as primary benefits of working consistently with a writing group. Preparing for exams and especially writing the dissertation can be very lonely and isolating activities, and a writing group helps to mitigate that situation.

One of the most powerful roles the graduate writing groups can play in the life of an isolated or lonely student is that of providing a regularly-meeting support system through which students not only receive feedback on their work but also work through other difficulties and concerns they have about grad school and life more generally. The writing groups provide consistent scholarly, human contact which, when combined with the knowledge that they are being held accountable to others, can help students completing exams and dissertations maintain productivity.

Multidisciplinary Perspectives

Graduate writing groups offer unique opportunities for students to form different types of relationships than they have in their departments because multiple disciplines are represented in each group. Since students bring different disciplinary knowledge to the table, less emphasis is placed on knowledge linked to a particular discipline, and students can perform as experts within their own disciplines instead of the more traditional role of mentee noted above. While there have been calls for discipline-specific graduate writing groups, the multidisciplinary nature of the graduate writing groups can be beneficial for group members. Starke-Meyerring (2014) indicates that treating writing and research as arhetorical creates a paradox:

> On the one hand, the demands placed on doctoral students were, of course, deeply rhetorical: students were expected to perform in the highly contextualized and historically evolved discursive practices of their research cultures. On the other hand, given the non-research-based assumptions about writing as a universal skill, these discursive practices remained shrouded in silence and therefore difficult to access for doctoral scholars. (p. 68)

Multidisciplinary writing groups can mitigate that paradox by showing participants the rhetoricity of writing. That is, that writing in different contexts for different disciplines requires different approaches, genres, and vocabularies.

Our participants indicate that they experienced first-hand how important context, audience, and purpose are to writing through their interactions in the groups.

> *Adrienne:* I think that articulating how your discipline thinks about ideas is part of becoming disciplined; being able to say that.
>
> *Angela:* (continuing the conversation from Adrienne) That's why this is English, that's why this is anthropology, this is why it's—
>
> *Adrienne:* And that the terms are specific to those disciplines and they need to be thinking outside of them. So when the engineer asks what do you mean by "queer," it has a really specific development within humanities or within these other disciplines. And then just articulating that for yourself makes you feel smarter. Oh, I know what that is and I know all these problems and I know how it's developed over the last 30 years, and being able to get that information out is, I think, just so productive . . . it does make you feel like an expert.
>
> *Andy:* What I came to realize that those folks from other disciplines and similar disciplines, they were really my audience because my advisor and I, we get it. But if they don't get it, it means others won't get it, too, because we wrote for two people and we both agree with what we're getting at. But I think that was something that I learned that they don't understand it. And you kind of step back, and you look at it and say, maybe I can say that differently or I'm not making myself as clear as I could in that particular—or I expanded too much or I didn't expand.

Multidisciplinary groups tend to focus on learning about writing rather than only focusing on content and one discipline's way of making arguments.[4]

Learning ways to talk about writing and think about it differently became necessary when working with writers from various disciplines. Sometimes the simple fact of not really understanding the content put the emphasis back on the writing and required the group members to really think about writing structures.

---

4 The previously-presented chapter by Garcia, Eum, and Watt, "Experiencing the Benefits of Difference within Multidisciplinary Graduate Writing Groups" in *Working with Faculty Writers* (2013), focuses entirely on the multidisciplinary benefits of the graduate writing groups at MSU. While there are some similarities between the content of that chapter and this section of our chapter, the different focus group participants lend additional insights.

Adrienne: There was still that sort of basic impulse of explaining the [content] idea to someone outside of the discipline, which is a different mode of creating interdisciplinary work. But no matter what the limits of that were, English was never thermodynamics. So reading people's work that I literally couldn't read— like I couldn't read a sentence because I didn't know, had to talk through the formula. So that, in a way, makes you focus on basics, like how was this paragraph put together. Even though I don't know what this sentence says, I know what this paragraph is about, it's comparing these two things. I have no idea what these two things are or their relationship is, but it just takes you down to the most basic level of sentence structure or paragraph structure. So that was one sort of positive aspect of the interdisciplinarity and my interest in doing it.

Recognizing that content and writing cannot be separated, as Adrienne describes, provided confidence to writers providing feedback to other writers, even though they were in different disciplines.

Lindsey: It was a big confidence builder to be able to give feedback to people in different fields about their writing and to be able to see what I thought about what they were writing was able to impact their writing for the better, even though I know nothing about whatever topic it was.

Readers were able to see that even though the topic and discipline of the writing may be unfamiliar, they could provide useful input about the ways they understood the messages in the text and how clear those messages were.

In multidisciplinary groups, graduate students are exposed to "different individual and disciplinary writing styles, conventions, practices, approaches, and strategies" (Garcia, Eum & Watt, 2013, p. 266–67) and are able to practice being an expert. Perhaps because "individual participants may be the only representative from their disciplines in the group," there was the opportunity to "foster disciplinary confidence and concomitant sense of authority" (Cuthbert et al., 2009, p. 145).

Lindsey: You own your stuff in a way that you can't when you're talking to, for instance, your advisers or to people who are— know a lot about your field. I mean, I think in the rest of the world outside of the group, it's one of the hardest things for me is believing that I am an expert. And outside of the group, it's really terrifying to do those same things and say, well, I really do know this thing.

Cuthbert et al.'s (2009) research on graduate writing groups has similar findings; they wrote that the groups "provided an opportunity to develop an 'authoritative voice' in speaking—and, importantly, writing—on her specialty, political theory, within a group with only general knowledge about the discipline and its key debates" (p. 145) and that the experience "enabled participants to 'try out' the role of disciplinary specialist in a supportive, rather than competitive, context" (p. 145). It shouldn't be surprising that multidisciplinary groups enhanced the confidence of writers about their knowledge of their own disciplines.

Group members also found the multidisciplinary approach as something that would benefit them as faculty members sitting on college- and campus-level committees.

> *Andy:* I also feel it would be helpful if you were ever on a job search committee. You need to understand things from outside of the field and ask people in a pleasant, polite way when it doesn't make sense. And also help you when you are applying for a job and need to make sense of your own work to people who are very much outside the discipline.

Andy's reflection indicates that group members saw the practices they were learning outside the completion of their high-stakes writing projects as applicable to other considerations that have an impact on their future lives as faculty members, such as being in the academic job market, sitting on search committees, and arguing their own promotion and tenure cases at the college and campus levels to multidisciplinary audiences.

Before becoming members of the graduate writing groups through the MSU Writing Center, three of our four focus group participants commented that they were aware of the multidisciplinarity of the groups and that this was an aspect that was specifically desired.

> *Adrienne:* I liked the idea of it being interdisciplinary.[5] I'm actually in two writing groups right now. One is through the Writing Center but discipline-specific and one is this interdisciplinary one that meets at the Writing Center. And I like the idea of having people ask really basic questions about your writing that people in the discipline might not ask and so giving you a

---

5   In general, we see the groups as "multidisciplinary" more so than "interdisciplinary." Interdisciplinary speaks to work in which disciplines are meshed together and intertwined. Multidisciplinary, instead, implies that multiple disciplines are represented and work together, but the work created by individual members still pertains to a particular discipline. In some cases, interdisciplinary work is done in a multidisciplinary writing group.

chance to think through some of the assumptions that you make in your own writing.

In another segment of our conversation, Adrienne reiterated this desire to join an interdisciplinary group. She explained that her dissertation work is actually going to be fairly interdisciplinary in nature, utilizing psychoanalytic concepts to discuss literature, and so she had hoped to be placed in a group that included someone from a psychology background. This didn't actually happen, but her experiences in her own multidisciplinary group still seemed positive, as shown above.

Lindsey, too, commented that she wanted to work in a multidisciplinary group. She explained that her own work is very interdisciplinary in nature, so obtaining feedback from a wide variety of readers was important for her. She specifically explains her desire for such a group:

> I personally feel like I'm working in an interdisciplinary field. I'm in comparative literature, but I also do comparative religion, and I'm hoping to be in a Jewish studies department—so I'm interested in being able to speak a language that does reach people in fields as different as ethnomusicology on the one hand and history on the other hand and English on the third hand.
>
> And so being able to communicate with all of those people in our writing group who are in different fields was I think a high priority for me. I don't want to be somebody who writes with such disciplinary conventions that I can't communicate with the other people who might actually end up being in my same department.

Lindsey and Adrienne were both doing interdisciplinary work, and so they sought the multidisciplinary environment our groups provided. Adam, however, did not want to work originally in a multidisciplinary group because he wanted feedback that would help him write in an explicitly scientific manner. Due to the constraints of the group, his desire was not possible to meet, and while later we discuss his positive experiences with his group, Adam's situation highlights some of the limitations of multidisciplinary graduate writing groups.

In addition to the desires for inter- and multidisciplinary contact that Adrienne and Lindsey emphasize, Angela points out one more benefit to the diversity of these writing groups. She'd had some fairly negative experiences in her own department and described the non-departmentally-located groups as a chance for reprieve from the existing stress, which she describes in the following statement: "I really liked the fact that none of them knew any of my advisors, none of them knew, really, the history of what I had been through until I think I lost it in one of our meetings." Being part of a multidisciplinary writing group, for Angela, meant she did not have to deal with departmental politics. She was able to reveal her struggles when she felt comfortable with the relationships she had formed with her group members.

Making Space: Limitations and Strengths

Ultimately, this is a story of the everyday. Our daily lives as teachers, scholars, and ordinary people are affected by the spaces we work in as well as the spaces we're from and the spaces we live in. All of these spaces are made and maintained through particular practices. These practices are limited by rules as well as by physical boundaries. In many circumstances, workers in the academy must often make spaces for themselves, spaces alongside places of power. As Michel de Certeau (1984) would say, "People have to make do with what they have" (p. 18). Graduate students, especially, need to "make do"—with advisors and committee members, with the time allotted by those individuals, and, sometimes, with a lack of educational and emotional support.

Despite all the positive aspects of graduate writing groups we've discussed in this chapter, there are certainly limitations. In particular, participants lamented the lack of discipline-specific feedback. Adam described the need for group members with "some particular expertise," explaining that while the other graduate students in the group had similar professional development experiences, at the end of the day, no one else understood his work. He explained, "I have nobody else except my advisor" and recommended having professors join the groups to offer "that other level of feedback." This was echoed by other participants at first.

The desire for expertise highlights the need each graduate student has for multiple kinds of writing support. Graduate writing groups are not a panacea for all that ails graduate writers. That said, in both focus groups, the participants seemed to talk themselves out of the idea of wanting more "experts" in the groups and settled back on the idea that the groups were the most beneficial as is. According to another interviewee, "discipline-specific [groups are] still interdisciplinary." This seemed to be the ultimate consensus of both focus groups, and the benefits of the interdisciplinary groups compensated for the lack of "expert" authority.

While the multidisciplinary graduate writing groups we've described cannot provide specialized expertise like a student's dissertation advisor can, the groups provide a particular kind of space: one in which graduate students from across disciplines can talk about their writing, their advisors, their classmates, and their non-academic lives without the stress of assessment and disciplinary judgment. Our participants, after some reflection, decided they preferred the multidisciplinary approach. For Angela, in particular, the graduate writing group provided her with a space to discuss some of the personal and academic struggles she was having in her own department.

To further support this benefit of multidisciplinarity, Angela shared a complex situation in which her advisor needed to leave while she was developing her dissertation proposal, and she began working with another faculty member. Unfortunately, the change was very rough, as this new faculty member pretty much told her she should stop pursuing her Ph.D.. She explained that it was a relief to work with students outside of her department because of the fact that the other writing group members didn't know the history of what she had been going through. She added:

> I really liked that it felt like there was no judgment about my character as a graduate student. It was accepted that you're a doctoral student, you're trying to go somewhere, and we're trying to help you with your writing and trying to make it better. That's all the focus was on and I really liked that that was it. There was no other stuff brought into the room.

Angela's reflection highlights the importance of having a space alongside but outside the place of her department to contemplate her professional work and get feedback on her writing.

Like interactions in traditional peer consulting at a writing center, work in graduate writing groups flattens hierarchies. The mentoring that happens in graduate writing groups has a very different power differential than that associated with mentoring by faculty members. Jenn Fishman and Andrea Lunsford (2008) explain the traditional role of mentee:

> Regarded as a novice, a mentee is someone who undergoes an extended process of initiation and assimilation in order to learn duty and obedience alongside the rudiments of a discipline and/or profession. Construed as an apprentice, a mentee is not only a student or pupil (roles associated more with childhood than with professionalization), but also someone socially as well as intellectually subservient to a master or mentor. (p. 28)

The mentoring relationships in graduate writing groups, however, are more akin to Dianne Rothleder's "friendships of play," which are "more truly concerned about the emotional well-being both of the group as a whole and each individual in the group" (as cited in Ashe & Ervin, 2008, p. 90) than "traditional, product-oriented mentoring relationships [, which] can generally be categorized as friendships of utility." These relationships, Rothleder writes, bring out the best in people because they "make space for stories to be told, for people to feel connected" (as cited in Ashe & Ervin, 2008, p. 90).

The location of the writing groups in the Writing Center and their facilitation by trained Writing Center consultants helped to create the kind of space where Angela could feel safe with and respected by her peers. Writing centers have a standing tradition of working with students at their point of need, whether that need is focused on what's written on a page or if that need is for emotional support and security. In addition, many writing centers employ students as consultants, so the very nature of the interactions that take place between consultant and client exist outside the traditional assessment and grading authority that exists within classes and departments.

The graduate writing groups at the MSU Writing Center create rather unique institutional spaces, spaces that exist outside of traditional institutional authority yet inside the institution itself. Because of their nature, they provide graduate students with an important "bubble" in which those students can more objectively examine the practices expected by their departments, classmates, and especially advisors. Like Thesen (2014), though, we want to caution: "It must be said that the circle sometimes feels very fragile, and the flattened hierarchy of the group does not solve all problems" (p. 165). The groups allow students to come together to share and compare experiences, departmental and disciplinary practices, and of course writing knowledge with the hope that such exposure helps everyone become better scholars and professionals

References

Aitchison, C. (2009). Writing groups for doctoral education. *Studies in Higher Education 34*(8), 905–916.

Ashe, D. & Ervin, E. (2008). Mentoring friendships and the "reweaving of authority." In M. F. Elbe & L. Lewis Gaillet (Eds.), *Stories of mentoring* (pp. 83–97). Parlor Press.

Bawarshi, A. (2001). The ecology of genre. In C. R. Weisser & S. I. Dobrin (Eds.), *Ecocomposition: Theoretical and pedagogical approaches* (pp. 39–56). State University of New York Press.

Busl, G., Donnelly, K. L. & Capdevielle, M. (2020). Camping in the disciplines: Assessing the effect of writing camps on graduate student writers. In M. Brooks-Gillies, E. G. Garcia, S. H. Kim, K. Manthey & T. G. Smith (Eds.), *Graduate writing across the disciplines: Identifying, teaching, and supporting*. The WAC Clearinghouse; University Press of Colorado. https://wac.colostate.edu/books/atd/graduate.

Cahill, L., Miller-Cochran, S., Pantoja, V. & Rodrigo, R. L. (2008). Graduate student writing groups as peer mentoring communities. In M. F. Elbe & L. L. Gaillet (Eds.), *Stories of mentoring* (pp. 153–158). Parlor Press.

Cresswell, T. (2006). *On the move: Mobility in the modern world*. Routledge.

Csikszentmihalyi, M. (1997). *Creativity: Flow and the psychology of discovery and invention*. Harper Perennial.

Cuthbert, D., Spark, C. & Burke, E. (2009). Disciplining writing: The case for multidisciplinary writing groups to support writing for publication by higher degree by research candidates in the humanities, arts, and social sciences. *Higher Education Research and Development, 28*(2), 137–149.

de Certeau, M. (1984). *The practice of everyday life.* (S. Randall, Trans.). University of California Press.

Fishman, J. & Lunsford, A. (2008). Educating Jane. In M. F. Elbe & L. L. Gaillet (Eds.), *Stories of mentoring* (pp. 18–32). Parlor Press.

Garcia, E., Eum, S. H. & Watt, L. (2013). Experiencing the benefits of difference within multidisciplinary graduate writing groups. In A. E. Geller & M. Eodice (Eds.), *Working with faculty writers* (pp. 260–278). Utah State University Press.

Harris, M. (1995). Talking in the middle: Why writers need writing tutors. *College English, 57*(1), 27–42.

Kim, S. & Wolke, S. (2020). Graduate writing groups: Helping L2 writers navigate the murky waters of academic writing. In M. Brooks-Gillies, E. G. Garcia, S. H. Kim, K. Manthey & T. G. Smith (Eds.), *Graduate writing across the disciplines: Identifying, teaching, and supporting.* The WAC Clearinghouse; University Press of Colorado. https://wac.colostate.edu/books/atd/graduate.

Massey, D. B. (2005). *For space.* Sage Ltd.

Moran, J. (2010). *Interdisciplinarity.* Routledge.

Nicolas, M. (2008). Introduction: (E)Merging identities: authority, identity, and the place(s) in-between. In A. D. Smith & T. G. Smith (Eds.), *E(Merging) identities: Graduate students in the writing center* (pp. 1–10). Southlake, TX: Fountainhead Press.

Phillips, T. (2012). Graduate writing groups: Shaping writing and writers from student to scholar. *Praxis: A Writing Center Journal, 10*(1), 1–7.

Smith, T., Molloy, J., Kassens-Noor, E., Li, W. & Colunga-Garcia, M. (2014). Developing a heuristic for multidisciplinary writing groups: A case study. In A. E. Geller & M. Eodice (Eds.), *Working with faculty writers* (pp. 175–188). Utah State University Press.

Starke-Meyerring, D. (2014). Writing groups as critical spaces for engaging normalized institutional cultures of writing in doctoral education. In C. Aitchison & C. Guerin (Eds.), *Writing groups for doctoral education and beyond: Innovations in practice and theory* (pp. 65–81). Routledge.

Thesen, L. (2014). 'If they're not laughing, watch out': Emotion and risk in postgraduate writers' circles. In C. Aitchison & C. Guerin (Eds.), *Writing groups for doctoral education and beyond: Innovations in practice and theory* (pp. 162–176). Routledge.

Wolfsberger, J. (2014). A weekly dose of applause!: Connectedness and playfulness in the 'Thesis Marathon.' In C. Aitchison & C. Guerin, (Eds.), *Writing groups for doctoral education and beyond: Innovations in practice and theory.* Routledge.

Graduate Writing Groups: Helping L2 Writers Navigate the Murky Waters of Academic Writing

Soo Hyon Kim
University of New Hampshire

Shari Wolke
Lansing Community College

Abstract: The present study examines how second language (L2) graduate writers are socialized into the academic discourse practices of a U.S. graduate school via Graduate Writing Groups (GWGs) sponsored by the university writing center. More specifically, it sheds light on how the discourse and interactions within a peer-based GWG affect L2 graduate writers' identities, as well as their socialization into academic disciplines and cross-disciplinary academic conventions. Results of the study revealed that, unlike the simple portrayal of L2 graduate writers as novices and their enculturation into academia as linear and unidirectional, L2 graduate writers have multi-faceted identities as writers, depending on academic task, context, and previous academic literacy experiences. The study suggests that despite the potential challenges inherent in multidisciplinary GWGs, they offer valuable opportunities for L2 graduate writers to enact the identity of disciplinary expert. Furthermore, the peer-based, extracurricular nature of these groups supports graduate writers' socialization into academic discourse communities.

Keywords: Graduate Writing Group, Writing Center, Multidisciplinary, Multilingual Writers, Identity, Enculturation, Language Socialization

> Usual representations of writing collapse time, isolate persons, and filter activity . . . Actually, writing happens in moments that are richly equipped with tools (material and semiotic) and populated with others (past, present and future). When seen as situated activity, writing does not stand alone as the discreet act of a writer, but emerges as a confluence of many streams of activity: reading, talking, observing, acting, making, thinking, feeling as well as transcribing words on paper. (Prior, 1998, p. xi)

Unlike the common assumption that graduate student writers come to graduate school equipped with the literacy skills needed to succeed, learning how to read and write in graduate school is a complex and gradual process. "Literacy is learned through use across contexts and over a lifetime" (Michigan State University Writing Center, n.d.), and graduate reading and writing is no exception; graduate writing is an extension of literacy learning that involves enculturation into a new academic community as well as the acquisition of specific academic writing skills.

Golde (1998) characterizes this as "an unusual double socialization" (p. 56) process in which graduate students must simultaneously learn how to be a graduate student as well as become socialized into the academic discipline and profession. Thus, graduate students, according to Golde (1998), are required to accomplish four distinct yet interrelated tasks: "intellectual mastery, learning about the realities of life as a graduate student, learning about the profession, and integrating oneself into the department" (p. 56). And while this may be challenging for all graduate students, it is particularly difficult for second language (L2) writers, as they must cope with what Golde calls "triple socialization" (p. 3). That is, L2 graduate writers carry the additional burden of being socialized into a new language and culture in which their L1 counterparts have most likely been immersed throughout their lives.

In response to these issues, there have been increasing efforts made in recent years to support graduate students as they navigate the murky waters of academic writing. Graduate writing support has received a great amount of attention, especially in the field of second language (L2) writing, where research on graduate writing support has spanned English for Academic Purposes (EAP) courses, dissertation writing support, graduate support in writing centers, graduate writing in the disciplines, and advisor and advisee mentoring (e.g., Casanave, 2008; Costley, 2008; Fujioka, 2008; Hedgcock, 2008; Phillips, 2012, 2013, 2016; Rogers, Zawacki & Baker, 2016; Simpson, 2012, 2016; Tardy, 2005, 2009).

The present study builds upon this growing body of research on graduate writing support. It takes a close look at how L2 graduate writers are socialized into the academic discourse practices of a U.S. graduate school via Graduate Writing Groups (GWGs) sponsored by the writing center. More specifically, the study sheds light on how the discourse and interactions within a peer-based GWG support L2 graduate writers' socialization into their disciplines and cross-disciplinary academic conventions. The study also uncovers ways in which GWGs afford L2 graduate writers the opportunity to not only learn specific academic writing skills, but to also co-construct and negotiate their academic identities.

Academic Literacy

Although academic literacy has previously been narrowly defined as having the ability to read and write the various texts assigned in the university setting (Spack, 1997), in this study, we utilize Ferenz's (2005) expanded definition of academic literacy which adds that academic literacy within graduate school and for L2 writers of English "encompasses knowledge of the linguistic, textual, social and cultural features of academic written discourse as well as knowledge of English as used by their academic disciplines" (p. 340). That is, this study considers the idea that socialization into academic discourse is not solely dependent on the acquisition of the jargon of the field, but includes mastering a complex matrix of practices surrounding literacy events within the institution. Schneider and Fujishima (1995) confirm this idea in their study which followed one L2 graduate writer's experiences with entering a graduate professional school in the U.S. Through an analysis of the L2 graduate writer's journal entries, interviews with instructors, and classroom writing samples, the study revealed how "achieving success at the postsecondary level involves more than control of the English language; it also involves familiarity with the writing conventions of the university culture and disciplinary subcultures in which the second language learner participates" (p. 4). This notion is echoed in a recent study by Wette and Furneaux (2018), who examined international graduate students' challenges and coping strategies in relation to their socialization into academic discourse communities at English-medium universities. Among the challenges that were reported by international graduate students were "their unfamiliarity with aspects of source-based, critical, and writer-responsible writing" (p. 186). Rather than seeing these as the lack of specific linguistic or writing skills, the authors interpret them as "challenges of establishing an authoritative (but modest) identity in accordance with Anglo-western norms" (p. 191). That is, these challenges stem from the lack of awareness of writing conventions that are affected by specific cultures and disciplinary conventions.

Language Socialization

The studies discussed above show that the acquisition of academic literacy occurs within an environment consisting of people, institutional settings, and learning materials (Braine, 2002). That is, they view academic literacy as an inherently social practice. Likewise, in the present study, we adopt language socialization as our theoretical framework to examine the ways in which graduate students are socialized into academic discourse communities. Language socialization theory views learners as novice members in a community of practice who, through engagement with and scaffolding of expert members of the community, acquire legitimate practices of the community. In this sense, it is similar to situated learning (Lave & Wenger, 1991), but emphasizes how novice members are socialized into using language through language. Language socialization, however, is not a simple one-way process by which students unproblematically "enter" a discourse community (Prior, 1998). What is often depicted as a simple, linear process of enculturation is, in fact, "conceptualized as experiences that are necessarily partial, diverse, conflicted and fragmentary" (Casanave, 2002, p. xiii).

Prior's (1998) case studies of graduate students' socialization into their academic discourse communities found that, "graduate students are not entering the autonomous social and cognitive spaces of discourse communities, but engaging in active relations with dynamic, open, interpenetrated communities of practice" (p. xxi). Prior's case studies brought to light the idea that graduate students are not simply being enculturated into the practices of graduate school, but that they also have a dynamic relationship with these practices. That is, even as they are inducted into the norms of a community of practice, L2 writers of English, as do all graduate students, retain the right to contest and negotiate the relations of power that are inherent in that community.

Language Socialization and L2 Graduate Writers' Identities

Like Prior (1998), Casanave and Li (2008) also note that socialization into academic disciplines "is not a one-way assimilation through which the dominant social, cultural, and historical forces impose their values and practices on hapless individuals" (p. 6). They point out that the chapters in their collection demonstrate how participants in academic discourse communities simultaneously prompt change by resisting conventions and by bringing their own identities and practices into their academic communities (Casanave & Li, 2008). In this sense, the process of academic socialization is closely intertwined with graduate writers' identities; graduate writers transform their scholarly identities through participation in their disciplinary communities, and these communities are also changed by the diverse experiences and identities brought by graduate writers.

This view of graduate writers' identities is in line with the conceptualization of identity in the fields of applied linguistics and L2 writing in which identity is viewed as a socially-situated, multifaceted, and dynamic construct (Norton, 1995, 1997, 2013; Norton & McKinney, 2011; Racelis & Matsuda, 2015; Varghese, 2004; Wenger, 1998). Previous research in these areas of study show how language learners' various language and literacy backgrounds—as well as their social contexts—affect the way they construct and negotiate their identities within and across communities of practice (e.g., Belcher & Connor, 2001; Matsuda, Snyder & O'Meara, 2017; McIntosh, Pelaez-Morales & Silva, 2015). L2 graduate writers are no different in this respect in that they also continuously construct and (re)construct their identities as readers, writers, and scholars within their disciplinary communities as they participate in a range of academic literacy practices.

GWGs as Graduate Writing Support

In the introduction to their edited collection on writing groups for doctoral education, Aitchison and Guerin (2014) situate GWGs among a host of new approaches to doctoral education (e.g., workshops, seminars, conferences, masterclasses, courses) that have sprouted as a response to the changing realities of doctoral education in a competitive global market. While they point out that writing groups have thus far been discussed in relation to academic writing and publications, specific program types, benefits of peer review and learning, development of scholarly identities, and pedagogical practices in writing groups, there is a need to more carefully assess these pedagogical interventions, and that academic scholarship on writing groups is "still fragmented and under-theorised" (p. 6). The following studies illustrate an effort towards bringing together several of the above themes on writing groups by examining how "writing groups explicitly address the questions of knowledge, textual practice and identity in a context of peer relations" (Aitchison & Lee, 2006, p. 266).

Noting that recent literature on writing groups in higher education has focused on institutional efforts to improve writing or assess writing group participants' satisfaction and productivity, Aitchison (2010) instead focused on the pedagogy of graduate writing groups. Using semi-fictionalized writing group stories based on her research, theory, and practice (Aitchison, 2003, 2009; Aitchison & Lee, 2006; Lee & Aitchison, 2009), she examined how doctoral students learn how to write for publication by working in writing groups and what role the facilitator plays in this process. Through an analysis of her transcripts, Aitchison highlighted how the discourse surrounding graduate writers' texts played an important role in their socialization, and how "coming to know and the articulation of that knowledge are intimately entwined" (p. 87).

Cuthbert, Spark, and Burke (2009) examined the perceived strengths and weaknesses of multidisciplinary writing groups by analyzing focus group data from four writing groups designed to support graduate student publication. The authors note that the participants were predominantly L1 writers of English with the exception of a few L2 writers. An important theme that emerged from their results was that the GWGs provided an environment in which graduate students were able to develop a professional academic identity and to "'try out' the role of disciplinary specialist in a supportive, rather than a competitive, context" (p. 145). They also found that the multidisciplinary nature of the groups provided writers with "a level playing field in which postgraduates may approach the writing process as a shared methodology, encompassing a suite of specialised but generic skills that cross-disciplinary boundaries" (p. 137).

Unlike the writing groups described in the previous studies, Li's (2014) writing group was specifically designed to support international L2 graduate writers as they wrote their graduate theses at an Australian university. In response to the needs of L2 graduate writers, who are often socially isolated and generally lack confidence in expressing complex ideas in academic English, Li created an ongoing writing group for L2 graduate writers to meet weekly and discuss short excerpts of their writing.

She drew on the process approach to writing, rhetorical genre research, and cultural perspectives on L2 writing to form the central pedagogies for her graduate writing group for L2 writers. As a group, the L2 graduate writers engaged in constant negotiation of meaning by collaboratively restructuring phrases and experimenting with language during the revision process.

Studies like Aitchison (2010), Cuthbert et al. (2009), and Li (2014) are important to the understanding of GWG pedagogy, as they show how, through engaging in discourse surrounding writing, graduate writers "not only develop self-awareness of linguistic forms, but also critical awareness of disciplinary discourses and rhetorical genre knowledge related to their field of study" (Li, 2014, p. 150). In addition, they also demonstrate how participating in graduate writing groups, more specifically, engaging in discourse surrounding texts, has an impact on graduate student writers' identity construction and socialization into their academic discourse communities.

Present Study

Building on previous research, the present study closely examines GWGs as an avenue of academic discourse socialization for L2 graduate writers implemented alongside the university curriculum. Research on learning spaces such as GWGs are invaluable in that they could complement our current understanding of more traditional, curricular means of socialization such as writing courses. While GWGs exist in many shapes and forms with varying routines and practices (Haas, 2014), GWGs are often a unique component of the graduate school experience that provides graduate writers with a means to not only gain assistance with writing in academic genres, but to also establish an academic persona and disciplinary orientation in a *peer-based* writing space. In the absence of a true "expert" or "novice" among participants, this peer-based setting complicates the boundaries of socialization and enculturation (Prior, 1998), and may afford graduate student writers opportunities to engage in discourse and interactions that promote socialization into academic discourse communities. In this sense, GWGs are a particularly fitting context within which to explore and challenge the "unidirectional assumptions of learning behind an apprenticeship-style model . . . by documenting the complex interactional nature of participation in academic literacy practices" (Casanave & Li, 2008, p.5).

In addition, while there are several practical resources that provide guidance for GWG facilitators regarding the logistics of running writing groups (e.g., Amaton, 2006; Moss, Highberg & Nicolas, 2004; Reeves, 2002; Rosenthal, 2003), few of these texts explicitly address what Aitchison (2010) aptly describes as the "less-often-told accounts of the pedagogical practices of writing groups" and "the real life of writing groups that is frequently flattened out in analysis" (p. 83). Also, the aforementioned resources on GWGs are mostly geared towards supporting L1 graduate writers; few of them focus on L2 graduate writers or the relational dynamics between L1 and L2 writers and how these interactions within the group may affect graduate writers' language socialization and acquisition of academic discourse.

Thus, the present study explores the following question: How do the discourse and interactions within multidisciplinary Graduate Writing Groups (GWGs) with both L1 and L2 English speakers affect L2 graduate writers' identities and socialization into academic discourse communities? In exploring this research question, we viewed the communities into which the GWG participants were being socialized as twofold: (1) their specific disciplines, such as Chemical Engineering, Journalism, or Sociology, and (2) the broader context of the academic community which has a shared language across fields and disciplines. While we understand that there may be some overlap between the two contexts, we believe it to be important to distinguish socialization into a specific discipline from socialization into the broader and more universal identity of "graduate student" and "academic."

Methods

Setting

Research was conducted at Michigan State University, which had an undergraduate population of approximately 36,000 and a graduate student population of approximately 11,000 as of fall 2010 (Michigan State University, 2011). The number of international students in these two groups (undergraduate and graduate students) was 3,341 and 2,166, respectively, in the fall of 2011 (Michigan State University Office for International Students and Scholars, 2011). The significance of this project at this specific institution was that the proportion of international graduate students to the overall graduate student population was much higher than the same proportion for the undergraduate population, yet the group that received the most writing help in the form of ESL writing courses was the undergraduate student population. The graduate student population, while having petitioned for elective courses on English writing, did not have a graduate-level course in writing, and were also not allowed to enroll in an undergraduate writing course. Their other opportunities for help with writing in coursework or one-on-one instructor feedback were also limited according to our interview data.

The Graduate Writing Groups (GWGs) we examined were affiliated with the university's Writing Center (also see Brooks-Gillies, Garcia & Manthey, this collection), whose mission is to help support writers in all disciplines and fields across the University. While we recognize that there may be graduate writing groups that are more organically organized within the university context, we chose to study those organized by the Writing Center, as these groups have the most potential for institutional implementation and change.

Participants

Interviews were conducted with three current GWG members (Bao, Mahsuri, and Sintia), two former GWG members (Dao-Ming and Jiaqui), and four current and former GWG facilitators (Phil, Sam, Meghan, and Emma).

Our focal participants for the study were Bao, Mahsuri and Sintia, as they were L2 writers of English who had the most diverse experiences. These students were those from whom we were able to obtain the most comprehensive responses about their experiences as L2 writers in a GWG, in that we observed their group sessions and conducted interviews with them.

The three focal participants (Bao, Mahsuri and Sintia), while all L2 writers of English, had varying degrees of experience with English as an L2. In examining their stories, we considered Birla's (2010) imploration to think about the multi-dimensional nature of the study of "others," in this case, L2 graduate student writers. As Birla (2010) writes,

> This question of particularity—how to address the particular situation and relations that inform and constitute the basis for any study concerned with culture, political economy, history—is a multidisciplinary problem that structures how the study of "others" is institutionalized in the North American academy. (p. 95)

That is, while we include brief stories of our focal participants below, we understand the complexity of representing individuals and their experiences in short synopses of a few lines, and recognize that these are not the only or primary lives our participants lead.

All names included in the text are pseudonyms with the exception of the first names of the researchers, Shari and Soo. This was done to both protect the anonymity of participants as well as acknowledge our involvement in the GWGs. In Shari's case, this was in the roles of both a facilitator and researcher, and for Soo, this was in the roles of a former facilitator and researcher. As we were simultaneously graduate students and past or present GWG facilitators ourselves at the time of the study, we were not unchanged by the experience nor were we objective observers of the GWGs.

Focal Participant Profiles

Bao was a member of Shari's GWG and was a participating member of this group from the summer of 2011 to mid-spring of 2012. As Bao indicated in his interview, he was highly versed in writing in his L1, Vietnamese, as he had written an undergraduate thesis of "more than 100 pages." However, none of his academic writing prior to beginning his Ph.D. at MSU had been done in English.

Mahsuri, however, had a much more complex relationship with academic writing in English. Mahsuri, who was a third-year Ph.D. student at the time of our interview, was a member of Phil's GWG. During our interview, Mahsuri stated that her L1 was Tamil, though the official languages of her home country, Malaysia, are English and Malay. Thus, her formal instruction was in Malay and English, and all academic writing she had done was in these two languages.

Sintia, who was from Portugal, was a D.V.M. (doctor of veterinary medicine) who returned to academia to complete a Ph.D. She was a member of Phil's GWG, and was a fourth-year doctoral student in the Department of Clinical Sciences in the College of Veterinary Medicine. Sintia explained that while her L1 is Portuguese, all of her higher-level academic writing, and more specifically, the form of writing that she had learned to do as a graduate student in the sciences, had been in English.

The L1 writers of English who are included in analyses below are Kathy, a Philosophy major studying the ethics of public health and Shawn, a mathematics educator who had graduated from a master's program and was interested in large-scale changes to education, including No Child Left Behind. Shawn was applying to doctoral programs in educational policy during the course of this study. Both of these writers were in Shari's GWG. Also ancillary to most of the analysis but present in some of Sintia's references was Craig, a member in Phil's GWG who was in a Public Policy program and was interested in legal issues, including underage drunk driving laws. The composition of both groups changed week-to-week over the course of the study. Shari's group included, at one point or another over the course of the study: Kathy, Shawn, Bao, Samanya, Kagiso, Ibrahim, Nadya (who only came to one session), and Dan. Phil's group included, at one point or another over the course of the study, Sintia, Mahsuri, Craig, and Phil, who himself submitted writing to the group at times.

Procedures

Data for this study was collected via an online survey of past and present GWG members[1] (collaboratively created and shared with Brooks-Gillies, Garcia & Manthey, this collection), participant observation of group sessions which included audio and video recordings of group sessions, and semi-structured interviews with

---

1 Participants for the study were recruited after receiving approval from the Institutional Review Board at MSU. Information about the study and participants' rights were presented via email along with a link to the online survey. GWG members who also chose to participate in semi-structured interviews and observations read and signed additional consent forms before data collection.

both the GWG facilitators and group members. Potential participants were chosen because they were former or current members of one of the GWGs facilitated by the Writing Center at MSU.

For the survey, participants were asked to fill out a preliminary online survey that asked them for basic background and geographical information, their experiences with GWG(s), their reasons for leaving the group if they were not currently a member, their perspectives on writing, and other questions relating to the GWG experience. Those for whom English was not their first language were asked to answer an additional set of questions about their language learning backgrounds so that we might have a more accurate understanding of the role that GWGs played in language issues or development of their L2. The survey was emailed to the list of current and former GWG members compiled by the Writing Center. This survey generated a total of 28 responses, with 21 of those 28 completing the entire survey. For the purpose of our study, this survey data was used to better inform us of our participants' backgrounds and to form a basis for our semi-structured interview questions.

Group observations were conducted in two GWGs, those facilitated by Phil and Shari, and included observations which were both video and audio recorded. Soo and Shari also took notes on the members' interactions with each other and any other significant aspects of the meeting. Six GWG sessions of Shari's group were recorded, and one session of Phil's was recorded. GWG sessions are generally two hours long, although the sessions we recorded often lasted anywhere from an hour to a little over two hours depending on the amount of discussion generated from the writing that was being reviewed. The group observations were also followed up by semi-structured interviews with the L2 graduate writers during which we asked these writers their perceptions of the writing group and attempted to specifically garner information about their experiences as a GWG member. Further, we conducted these interviews to shed light on significant issues that were brought up in the online survey results. Four approximately hour-long one-on-one interviews were audio recorded. In addition, four hour-long, audio-recorded interviews with present and past facilitators of GWGs (Phil, Sam, Meghan, and Emma) were conducted in order to complement data collected from observations of and interviews from GWG members. The interviews with GWG facilitators elicited their understanding of how L2 writers of English and L1 writers of English interacted in the group space. These interviews were also conducted to understand the contributions of facilitators to L2 writers' interactions and socialization in the peer space of GWGs.

The interview data were then transcribed for qualitative analysis during which the transcripts were examined for recurring themes that emerged. This cyclical process involved conducting multiple rounds of content analysis and building upon and/or merging the initial themes that were identified. While we did not adopt an a priori scheme of analysis in this process, the central concepts we discussed in our theoretical framework (e.g., legitimate peripheral participation, language socialization, identity) did inform our analysis and discussion. The transcripts from the GWG observations were also analyzed in a similar manner, and results from all sources of data were compared to examine possible convergences or divergences.

Results and Discussion

Potential Challenges in the Inherent Complexity of GWGs

Here, we introduce the major themes that emerged from this study by contemplating the following survey response from a previous GWG participant; it reflects the two most frequently cited challenges of implementing and participating in diverse graduate writing groups:

> . . . no one showed up to my group after the first week so [the writing group] was canceled, which was fine because everyone was a non-native English speaker in a field that was not science so I didn't think they could help much anyway.

As noted here, the GWGs in this study involved members from diverse disciplinary and linguistic backgrounds. Each group member brought with them unique literacy histories and professional experiences. Also added to this mosaic of experiences were the complexities that came from each member's perceptions of self and others, as well as the unique group dynamics that developed among the members of each group.

While there is no doubt that the complexity that arises from the diversity of these groups can be difficult to navigate, we argue that it is this complexity and diversity that creates a fertile environment for graduate socialization and learning to take place within GWGs. Unlike the negative perceptions reflected in the survey response, diverse GWGs can make a wealth of experiences and expertise available to their members when their potential is harnessed into productive group dynamics. As Aitchison (2010) notes, writing groups composed of members with diverse disciplinary orientations and language backgrounds have the potential to be "one of the most useful pedagogical triggers" (p. 97) for graduate learning and socialization.

In the following section of this chapter, we discuss the major themes that emerged from our study: (1) the interaction and discourse surrounding writing that occurs in GWGs contribute to graduate students' language socialization, and (2) the multidisciplinary, multilevel composition of peer-based GWGs enable L2 graduate writers to explore and enact different identities as writers which, in turn, helps with socialization into the academic literacy practices of graduate school.

Graduate Writer Identity

The L2 graduate writers we meet through our extant research literature are often depicted as struggling to simultaneously improve their English proficiency while also trying to socialize themselves into the culture of graduate school (e.g., Bitchener & Basturkmen, 2006; Cadman, 1997, 2000; Cotterall, 2011; Ryan & Zuber-Skerritt, 1999; Tang, 2012; Wang & Li, 2008). The challenges that these L2 graduate writers face range from adjusting to a different set of academic writing conventions than that with which they are familiar, clearly expressing complex content in academic English, maintaining confidence and a positive self-image regarding their academic performance, seeking academic support and interacting with advisors and peers, and lacking a sense of community in their social lives (Li, 2014). Interviews and transcripts from our study showed that while, to a certain extent, these portrayals of L2 graduate writers were true, they did not provide the whole picture. The L2 graduate writers in our study constructed complex and dynamic identities as writers, graduate students, and learners/users of English.

For example, Bao, who was in Shari's writing group, commented that he preferred having both L1 and L2 speakers of English in the GWGs due to his identity as an L2 writer:

> Actually I prefer both (native and non-native speakers in the group). Because Natasha [another L2 writer] is also very helpful and I think in the class some . . . I need someone who is the same with me because if I only one Vietnamese guy and uh ((laughs)) and all other guys speak English, I become so, so bad. (Bao, semi-structured interview)

Yet, Bao had also cultivated different identities as writers in his L1 and L2. When asked about how he perceived himself as a writer, he first responded that his "writing is very bad." But then, he clarified, saying, "Um actually, [when] I write in my—in my own language . . . I believe I'm very good in writing in my own language" (Bao, semi-structured interview).

His writerly identities also differed depending on the genre of writing in which he engaged. He was confident about doing informal types of writing; he was a prolific writer in his L1 who published blog posts online and maintained a journal in which he regularly wrote. He felt he was a good writer in this context because he felt he could express exactly what he intended. When it came to academic writing, his beliefs about what constitutes good writing in his L1 seemed to transfer to his academic writing in English. As an undergraduate student in Vietnam, he had written an undergraduate thesis which he had been confident about because, "when you write something you need to have something to write. I mean, for example, when you write thesis, it is based on some results you already conduct, and if you have good knowledge and if the result is really good, it is a basement for writing something really good" (Bao, semi-structured interview).

However, Bao learned that this approach to writing did not seem to work for academic writing in English. He spoke about his first experience writing an academic paper in his graduate program at MSU, which was five months prior to the time of the interview. Bao commented that initially he had been confident writing the analysis paper. Explaining that, at the time, he didn't "clearly understand how to write a really good paper," he said he wrote a long analysis "with lots of reference" and was met with negative feedback from his advisor: "Your writing is so bad!" (Bao, semi-structured interview). This became the catalyst for him to visit the Writing Center for one-on-one sessions and to participate in the GWGs to improve his writing.

Meanwhile, our interview with Sintia painted a distinctively different picture of L2 graduate writers in the U.S. academy. During our interview, Sintia explained how English had become her "academic first language":

> Oh, even in Portuguese, I have difficulty to write at this point, I mean—because I haven't—Now, only time I do speak Portuguese is when I call home, and I read news in Portuguese; that's it. But English, I think it's easier for me to write my th- work in English because all the vocabulary, all the terms, it's just—I read in English, so it's easier. (Sintia, Semi-structured interview)

She went on to say that if she were to try to explain her research in Portuguese, she wouldn't have the vocabulary necessary to succeed: "If you ask me about my research in Portuguese I don't know all the words." She felt that "neither Portuguese nor English is perfect at this point," and even though she recognized that, in general, it is more difficult to write in a second language, she had come to associate English with her academic work and identity.

Bao and Sintia's descriptions of their academic and language backgrounds are significant in that they disrupt the notion of L2 writers of English having a fixed and linear relationship with English as their second language. While, like Bao, some L2 graduate student writers may begin writing in English academically once they start their graduate programs, others, like Sintia, may only know how to write for academic audiences in English. This complicates the notion of who L2 graduate writers are and their relationship with academic discourse in a U.S. graduate school environment as well as their experience with disciplinary vocabulary and jargon. Through Sintia's example, we can see that L2 writers embody a far more complex population than the simplistic label *L2 writer* would suggest, such that it would be difficult to make sweeping generalizations about them. In Sintia's case, the simplistic picture of L2 writers as novice writers struggling to acquire the linguistic competency and disciplinary conventions of academic writing would be misleading.

Multi-Disciplinary, Peer-Based GWGs and L2 Graduate Student Identity

Earlier, we discussed how language socialization does not occur as an unproblematic one-way process by which students enter and then follow in a linear progression from novice to expert within a discourse community (Casanave & Li, 2008; Prior, 1998). Instead, L2 graduate writers negotiate their own identities as they take part in their communities of practice (Lave & Wenger, 1991). This was made possible within the GWGs in this study, in part, due to the "flattened hierarchy" within the group members and to a certain extent, the GWG facilitators. Phil refers to this aspect of the group when he states,

> And I think—I think there is something valuable in in having— in being a part of the group that you coordinate . . . I like being able to share my writing and get the same questions. I think it gives you an additional investment in the group as well, which is nice. And there's the whole thing about no one's perfect and everyone's kinda—you know, you get to—you get to flatten the hierarchy of you as the authority figure and that you are just a part of the group as well. (Phil, GWG facilitator, semi-structured interview)

Phil's sentiments here about the flattened hierarchies within multidisciplinary GWGs are shared by Aitchison (2010) as well, who stated that "[t]he student-teacher and peer relationships are horozontalized [sic] (Boud & Lee, 2005) and power and responsibilities are diffused, resulting in a more fluid and responsive curriculum and pedagogy" (p. 97).

In addition to this peer-to-peer dynamic, analysis of the transcripts of GWG sessions and interviews with L2 writers in this study suggests that the multidisciplinary nature of GWGs improve L2 graduate student writers' sense of agency within GWGs, as L2 writers in these contexts are considered experts in their field, bringing their disciplinary knowledge into the groups. It places the L2 writer in the position of "expert" and therefore mitigates power relationships which could potentially exist based on a native speaker/non-native speaker divide. Kathy, with regard to Bao, the only L2 graduate writer participating in Shari's group, observed,

> There was the potential for there to be a dynamic [with Bao] . . . and . . . for us to perceive that as an inequality, but I think that the fact that he was constantly teaching us about his research methodology constantly undermined that.

We could see how this played out among the members in Phil's GWG as well. The following excerpts come from transcripts of a GWG observation during which

Craig and Sintia take turns sharing their work with the rest of the group members. There was one other group member, Mahsuri, who was present, as well as the GWG facilitator, Phil. The first excerpt comes from an exchange that emerged from Craig's choice to use the word "bias" to report on his study results.

> *Sintia:* And should [it] be "a gender bias" or should [it] be "modified by gender"? Because bias is something—it's giving— you know what I mean? When I say "bias" [it means] something like there is error and you cannot control for that error in your study.
>
> *Craig:* Yeah, I try to be—
>
> *Sintia:* So just—is it just a type of opinion, is it a gender effect, a gender association? You know there is that difference among males and females, so it's like—
>
> *Craig:* Right, gender effect too. Oh, yeah . . .
>
> *Sintia:* "Effect modifier" or "interaction," or "effect," or "the risk is modified by gender." Something like that words.
>
> *Craig:* By using the word "bias," I was just trying to be a little cute.
>
> *All members:* ((laugh))
>
> *Sintia:* Mmhm. But bias is—when you say something . . . "there is a bias," "their study has a bias," it seems like, oh, we know there is error associated to gender, not that there is an effect associated to gender.
>
> *Craig:* Right.
>
> *Phil:* Ok, so you—I see. So it makes it sound—I see—like an error instead of the phenomenon.

After spending some time discussing the nuances of the word "bias" in Craig's paper, the group comes to a consensus that in the context of Craig's paper, "gender" should be a "mediating factor" or a "modifier." Subsequently, Phil leads the group in a discussion considering the importance of word choices such as these in disciplinary writing at the graduate level.

> *Phil:* I would—I would never think about that, so that's interesting. But I can see your point. Absolutely.
>
> *Sintia:* It's just uh terminology. Well—
>
> *Phil:* Yeah, it is. 'Cause I don't think of bias in that way. But I can see from the scientific field that bias would be considered (an error) . . .

> *Craig:* Well, sometimes—like—I mean especially if you're a statistician, and you see the word significant. I mean, well, you know, you always think of it as statistically significant, whereas . . . just important to that study.
>
> *Phil:* Right! Yes! Yes!
>
> *Craig:* Yeah. "This is very significant," and it's like—then you go back to the tables and look at- No, this wasn't significant; what are they talking about.

As seen in the above excerpt of Phil's GWG session, the power dynamics in GWGs are shifted in that there is no true "novice" in this peer-to-peer interaction. The expertise in the group was based on discipline-specific knowledge, unlike in spaces where the power dynamic is often evident, such as classroom spaces or a consultant-client interaction. That is, "participants are positioned as the primary 'content' experts, further disrupting traditional . . . hierarchies" (Aitchison, 2010, p. 98). We see this play out in the excerpt above, where Sintia is an L2 writer of English, but she is much more versed in the norms of her scientific academic community and is therefore implicitly socializing the other members of the group into her mode of academic discourse.

According to Sintia, the multidisciplinary nature of the groups made it easier for L2 writers to "question [other GWG members about] their research." That is, because writers in these groups are from different fields, it was easier for an L2 graduate writer to question—or contest—another graduate student's structure, methodology, or writing. This, in turn, allows for a space for L2 writers to explore, test, and enact identities other than "the L2 writer." They are given the opportunity to question the work of L1 writers and engage in discussions focused on language-specific issues if they please, or they may decide to abstain from the focus on language altogether and read for organization and meaning instead. Sam, a former GWG facilitator, notes,

> Just . . . like—for non-native speakers—they feel confident, more confident in their own field. Right? Because they have that professional knowledge; they have that professional language; they are more used to, you know, communicating, talking about something in their field. (Sam, former GWG facilitator, semi-structured interview)

Interestingly, we found that not all GWG discussions concluded with a satisfactory answer or plan for revisions. Similar to what Li (2014) found in her study, sometimes the collaborative revision process in the GWGs required group members to experiment with language as they restructured or reworded words and sentences. For example, another discussion occurs when Phil's GWG engages in collaborative wordsmithing of a sentence in Sintia's research article. Sintia reported that she was having trouble finding the right word to describe her research results in which there were a small number of cells present in each experimental group. The group members suggest, contest, and explore alternatives for the word "sparse," provide metalinguistic explanations of the word's usage (e.g., its part of speech), explore referential and inferential meanings of alternative words, and discuss possible perceptions and nuances of words from a disciplinary (hard science) perspective. As a result, the group comes up with alternatives such as *paucity, thin, very little data, not many, thinly scattered, thinly distributed, scattered data, dearth, sporadic, all over the place,* and *lack of consistency.* After a great deal of back and forth, the group comes to the conclusion that it would be best for Sintia to present the research results graphically. Others also suggest checking with her advisor or other members of her disciplinary community, to find the most disciplinary-specific word that accurately conveys the complex ideas of Sintia's research results.

Comments from the GWG members toward the end of the session reveal that failure to come up with a satisfactory alternative to the word, "sparse," does not necessarily have to be seen as a failure of the GWG's goal or mission. As the GWG session slowly wraps up, Sintia states to the group,

> Well, my experience was . . . because English is my second language, so I thought I had the double problems. I have that . . . struggling a lot, and I imagined an English speaker will not struggle as much, but I realize, actually, that all of us struggle . . . different way, kind of, to express ideas. And not just because of English. Well, it's a requirement, but . . . writing is . . . just hard.

In response, the group members comment on how writing is a humbling process for both L1 and L2 writers, and how focused discussions around language issues in writing can be beneficial because they require GWG members to practice explaining the concepts in their field to those in other disciplines. As Li (2014) explains, "the specific questions raised in the writing group become the starting point of learning that further engages the research students beyond the writing group, and within the disciplinary context of their research" (p. 150). In other words, by engaging in discourse surrounding disciplinary writing within a multi-disciplinary GWG setting, the graduate writers were able to raise their awareness of expectations of their immediate audience (i.e., the GWG members) as well as their disciplinary discourse communities.

Multi-Level GWGs and L2 Graduate Student Identity

Another feature of the GWGs that added a layer of complexity was that the graduate writers in the group were at different stages in their academic careers. Some members had just gotten started in their programs, others were in the process of writing their dissertation prospectus, and still others were finishing up their dissertations, working on publications, and/or preparing to go on the academic job market.

When asked about his perceptions about working with GWG members at different stages in their studies, Bao responded positively, saying,

> I prefer something diversity. Because it uh help to improve some weak points, strong points . . . And I think it's very useful for example, for people who prepare for dissertation who—they have their own problem, but we could see the problem in the future. I mean . . . maybe in the next several years, when I write thesis, I could see my same problem again. (Bao, semi-structured interview)

While it was evident that Bao appreciated the opportunity to anticipate potential challenges he might face in the writing of his own dissertation in the future, he was also aware how the multi-level composition of the GWG offered him the opportunity to make solid contributions to the group as well. During the first observation of Shari's session, Shawn had brought in a statement of purpose he was drafting for his application to a Ph.D. program in Education. Among the group members present during that GWG session, Karen was furthest along, having completed her dissertation, and Shari and Shawn were the most novice members in that they were preparing to apply for doctoral programs. During this session, Bao noticeably took a stronger leadership role, more frequently offering comments and suggestions, and often referring back to his own experiences writing statements for doctoral programs. When asked to describe his perceptions of the interactions that occurred during that GWG session in a post-session interview, he commented,

> Shawn, he prepare for Ph.D. program, and I see his problem is the same as I- my problem one years ago when I prepare for statement of purpose, and . . . so we could learn and we could share. I think it's useful. (Bao, semi-structured interview)

This theme came up again during a second interview with Bao when asked to describe his greatest strengths and contributions to the GWG as a group member:

> I think knowledge . . . I have knowledge something about Ph.D. life like . . . recently in our second class, I bring some good idea about how to prepare for a statement of purpose. Because I already apply for graduate school and I have some experiment in academic life, academic writing. (Bao, semi-structured interview)

Bao's interview revealed that in addition to disciplinary expertise, the multi-level nature of the GWGs also served to complicate the potentially uneven power dynamics between L1 and L2 writers in the group. It seemed that L2 graduate writers who had gained more experience in the academy and acquired general knowledge on "how to be a graduate student" felt that they had more to contribute to the group. Sam, a former GWG facilitator, also spoke about how this intangible graduate student knowledge played a role in the multi-level GWGs:

> You can see some people were more clear about what they want to accomplish, and they know what the process that is coming forward and some people are like still not sure. But that set up a good example for those people who have no idea what is going to happen. (Sam, former GWG facilitator, semi-structured interview)

When asked about the multi-level composition of the GWGs, several GWG facilitators noted that depending on the task at hand during a particular GWG session, the members that were further along in their studies would naturally take the lead in the interaction: "I think if they're further along, they're more ready to perform expert roles" (Phil, GWG facilitator, semi-structured interview). Another former GWG facilitator concurred that graduate students at more advanced stages in their degree "see themselves as more of a resource" (Meghan, former GWG facilitator, semi-structured interview).

And while the scaffolding that the more "expert" members perform can generally be helpful for the other more "novice" members, GWG facilitators acknowledged that the facilitators in the group had an important role in moderating the interactions at times, so that the novice members of the groups also felt encouraged and equipped with discursive strategies to contribute to the group discussions. Speaking about his group, in which two members were in more advanced stages of their studies, Phil noted,

> It just so happens that the two people are in the dissertation-type stage. I feel like the level of conversation is very different, and on the days when the early people—the people who are in their first year—share, there's way more advice given by everybody. Whereas when the folks that are further along, the folks that are early on are like, "I like it." And so trying to, like, pull them out.

Sam also talked about helping GWG members at different stages in their studies bring out their greatest strengths in the writing group setting:

> And so some people know, have more experience writing paper, managing time and setting goal, and accomplish, and they know the process. Some people are less experienced. So, you—that's something you want to pull out of your member, you know,

what kind of strengths, what kind of, they can bring in to this group. (Sam, former GWG facilitator, semi-structured interview)

As an example, Sam shared how he previously worked with a GWG member named Yvonne, who was an L2 graduate writer and who had joined Sam's GWG right at the beginning of starting her degree program. Yvonne seemed reluctant to offer feedback on other members' writing.

> . . . if you are communicating in English with these professional people in different field, it's intimidating. And I think you need to do extra work to make sure, to kind of, that she's valuable to this group. And people can definitely benefit from her comment, her feedback. (Sam, former GWG facilitator, semi-structure interview)

Noticing this reluctance to actively participate, Sam took some time during his GWG to discuss reader response questions, and how these questions were valuable in helping authors to reconsider how their writing was coming across to the reader, especially in the academy, where it is likely that your writing may have to be comprehended by a general but well-educated audience. He found that Yvonne was gradually able to incorporate reader response comments and questions into her repertoire and use them effectively during GWG meetings, even when the piece of writing being discussed would be from more-experienced members of the group:

> She [Yvonne] was able to provide reader's comment, and when she's not sure, she asks. I mean, that's something she can do and that's something that you can reinforce. "Okay, that's a good question. Okay, yeah I have the same kind of question, too," and you have the writer respond. (Sam, former GWG facilitator, semi-structured interview)

In sum, what we found in our study was that GWGs composed of graduate writers at different stages in their academic trajectories can create an environment in which newer, peripheral members of the academic discourse community can participate (Aitchison, 2010).

Role of GWGs in Graduate Academic Literacy Acquisition

Acquiring academic literacy (Ferenz, 2005) at the graduate level involves not only the development of academic reading and writing skills but also the cultivation of an identity as a graduate student and scholar. Thus, graduate socialization encompasses both the cognitive and affective aspects of acquiring academic literacy (e.g., learning the disciplinary conventions of research writing vs. learning how to engage with critical feedback from reviewers). This process of graduate socialization often occurs within an intricate web of people, resources, and settings, within which we found GWGs also play an invaluable role by complementing more traditional sources of graduate writing support and providing a sense of community and emotional support.

A prominent theme that emerged during participant interviews was that GWGs complemented some of the more conventional means of graduate writing support and mentorship. We found that the mentorship and advising that GWG members received in their disciplinary programs was predominantly centered around the one-on-one advising relationships that graduate students had with their research/academic advisors. In fact, at the time of the study, several of the participants (Sintia, Bao, Craig) were co-writing manuscripts for publication with their advisors, and when discussing these manuscripts during GWG sessions, frequent references were made to the interactions with and feedback from their advisors. Interestingly, GWG members seemed to view their research advisors as a source of helpful feedback on the content of their research and rarely expected to get detailed feedback on the writing of a manuscript. Sintia, for example, commented,

> My advisor, she was really happy that I joined this group, and she can see the difference. So now she is part of the committee Ph.D., my friend that's from Costa Rica, and she says I'm going to advise her to join the group too ((laughs)). (Sintia, GWG group observation)

Thus, one of the most common reasons that GWG members initially joined the writing group was because they wanted to receive feedback on their writing from others before sending it to their advisor for further input. As Craig explained, "My advisor's very busy and I would like—you know, I'd like to maybe cut out some of those things—find it and then send it to her" (Craig, GWG group observation).

Meanwhile, the GWGs also served as a space for graduate writers to gain a sense of community in a collaborative and supportive environment from peers outside of their disciplines, away from the traditional—and often competitive/stressful—confines of their own disciplinary programs. When asked about different resources available to obtain writing feedback, Bao discounted feedback from peers in his program because he felt uncomfortable taking time away from them:

> It's really hard to get help from the person in the same class or something because actually they are very useful—I mean they are very busy. And it's so—it's so shame to ask them, hi, could you please read my writing and fix the—I don't wanna take

their time in detail to fix my problems. (Bao, semi-structured interview)

He indicated that he felt more comfortable soliciting feedback from peers in the GWG setting because

> . . . all of us want to improve writing. And uh we are ready to say, ready to share experience with each other, so I could learn a lot from them and each people could learn from other people. (Bao, semi-structured interview)

However, it was not only this shared goal and commitment to helping improve each other's writing that encouraged Bao to participate in the GWG. He also noted that being among other graduate students from different disciplines who are more or less grappling with similar challenges with graduate writing provided a sense of camaraderie, because, in Bao's words: "We're the same." This idea came up during an observation of Phil's GWG session as well. Throughout the session, members often shared their insecurities as novice researchers, to which other members offered words of reassurance and validation such as "That's not too unusual, though" (Craig, observation) or "That is like every graduate student ever" (Phil, observation). Towards the end of the session, Phil offered some encouragement, saying,

> I think that on some level, one thing that I see more is that—pretty much to a T—every member that we've had here has said, 'Man, I don't feel like I'm a good writer,' and then everyone else, when the first time they see their writing has been, 'Man, you're a really good writer!' Every time. And that's a good thing. To think of the encouragement is really nice. I mean, you know, we comment on Sintia and her science amazing craziness, and Craig has organization, and you [Mahsuri] have beautiful writing yourself, and so we're able to have this kind of motivation and encouragement that's pretty awesome.

In many ways, the GWG had become "much more than just the writing group" (Phil, observation). It became a social activity where members could talk about their work in a more informal and relaxing environment, enjoy each other's company, and help them keep momentum in their writing. According to Phil's GWG members, this helped with the loneliness that often comes with conducting research and writing in graduate school (see, for example, Aitchison, 2010; Ferenz, 2005; Li, 2014), especially at advanced stages when graduate students have completed coursework and have little interaction with their peers. In other words, the GWGs became a space in which members cultivate "a sense of connectedness and belonging to an academic community" (Aitchison & Guerin, 2014, p. 12) as they develop and nurture their scholarly identities.

Phil's GWG session ended with a cheer when Craig stated, "And the last paper—I haven't published it yet; it's to be published—I acknowledged the Wednesday MSU M—Wednesday writing group" (Craig, observation). The GWG had given its members a collaborative space to give and receive writing feedback, but perhaps more importantly, fill a void in terms of the affective and emotional support that graduate students need to not merely become socialized into graduate school practices, but to thrive.

Multidisciplinary, multi-level GWGs, however, are not without potential challenges. While the benefits abound, as described above, it is uncertain whether the format and implementation of these groups is the most *efficient* method for graduate writers' acquisition of specific disciplinary knowledge and genres. Having the opportunity to explain and clarify disciplinary conventions to an audience, thus, raising one's own awareness of these disciplinary conventions, is undoubtedly one of the greatest benefits of multidisciplinary GWGs. Interactions from Shari and Phil's GWG in this study, as well as those in previous literature (e.g., Aitchison, 2010; Cuthbert et al., 2009; Li, 2014), show that when "peers test and extend . . . [each other's] conceptual knowledge as well as their capacity to communicate this knowledge through writing," (p. 87) to a broader audience, they are more likely to develop the necessary skills to effectively communicate with both those within and outside their own disciplinary discourse communities.

However, not all features of academic writing easily cross disciplinary boundaries, resulting in occasions in which GWG members are forced to spend valuable time justifying language choices that are widely accepted in their specific area of study. The following quote by Sintia illustrates this issue:

> It's good to explain your research when someone is not in your field, but uh, sometimes their approach will be things that I know that [those in my field] will not question . . . I feel like—sometimes (I spend) my time explain things I will not have explain to someone in my field. (Sintia, semi-structured interview)

She went on to explain that she and the other GWG members would often engage in conversations about what audience expectations might be in terms of the organization of her writing or what may or may not be considered common knowledge and unnecessary to explicitly explain in their papers. This may be perceived as a disadvantage, as providing these explanations to group members outside of one's discipline may take away valuable meeting time. It was also found that, due to the stark differences in disciplinary knowledge and conventions, sometimes members were unsure about what they would be able to contribute through feedback (see also, Boud & Lee, 1999; Brooks-Gillies et al., this collection; Cuthbert et al., 2009).

Conclusion

Our study shows that multidisciplinary, multi-level GWGs may present potential challenges in their implementation; however, they are also invaluable for the language socialization and identity development of graduate writers, especially L2 graduate writers. The flattened hierarchies and diversity inherent in GWGs' extracurricular, peer-based space give these L2 graduate writers the opportunity to explore and enact identities that are not limited to their language proficiency. Rather, they are invited to perform roles of disciplinary expert, fellow academic, peer reviewer, and support group. We call for further research to be conducted on questions that are crucial to understanding the complex interactional dynamics in multidisciplinary, multi-level peer groups such as GWGs. Some questions that we find essential to a more thorough understanding of these spaces are:

- Do disciplinary (as opposed to multidisciplinary) spaces have an equally leveled hierarchy in member interactions?
- How do disciplinary GWGs contribute to the identities of L2 graduate writers?
- What additional improvements to the organization and implementation of GWGs would be most beneficial for both L1 and L2 graduate student writers' identity development and socialization?

Considering how graduate student writers are socialized into their academic disciplines is timely, as shifts in the population of L2 writers, particularly L2 graduate writers, have garnered much interest from language researchers and teachers in terms of the best ways to serve these students. As part of this effort, we have explored in this chapter ways in which GWGs assist in the socialization of L2 writers into the larger academic discourse community. We found that the simple portrayal of all L2 graduate student writers as novices and their enculturation into academia as linear and uni-directional can be limiting to our understanding of L2 writers' socialization into academia and also to the ways in which we can facilitate this process. Based on these findings, we call for a reexamination of how graduate student writers' identities vary and also change across time and contexts. We also suggest that the complexity inherent in mixed groups of L1 and L2 graduate writers from different disciplines and at different stages in their academic career can create a favorable environment for socialization into graduate writing discourse communities. Our hopes are that further research efforts that expand the inquiries in this study will help to identify the ways in which educational institutions are serving the academic needs of L2 graduate student writers and contributing to the multifaceted socialization that occurs within the academic community context.

References

Aitchison, C. (2003). Thesis writing circles. *Hong Kong Journal of Applied Linguistics, 8*(2), 97–115.

Aitchison, C. (2009). Writing groups for doctoral education, *Studies in Higher Education, 34*(8), 905–916.

Aitchison, C. (2010). Learning together to publish: Writing group pedagogies for doctoral publishing. In C. Aitchison, B. Kamler & A. Lee (Eds.), *Publishing pedagogies for the doctorate and beyond* (pp.83–100). Routledge.

Aitchison, C. & Guerin, C. (Eds.). (2014). *Writing groups for doctoral education and beyond.: Innovations in practice and theory*. Routledge.

Aitchison, C. & Lee, A. (2006). Research writing: Problems and pedagogies. *Teaching in Higher Education, 11*(3), 265–278.

Amaton, C. J. (2006). *How to start and run a writers' critique group*. Stargaze.

Belcher, D. & Connor, U. (Eds.). (2001). *Reflections on multiliterate lives*. Multilingual Matters.

Birla, R. (2010). Postcolonial studies: Now that's history. In R. Morris (Ed.), *Can the subaltern speak?: Reflections on the history of an idea* (pp. 87–99). Columbia University Press.

Bitchener, J. & Basturkmen, H. (2006). Perceptions of the difficulties of postgraduate L2 thesis students writing the discussion section. *Journal of English for Academic Purposes, 5*(1), 4–18. https://doi.org/10.1016/j.jeap.2005.10.002.

Boud, D. & Lee, A. (1999). *Promoting research development through writing groups*. Paper presented at the Australian Association for Research in Education Conference, Melbourne, Australia. http://www.aare.edu.au.

Boud, D. & Lee, A. (2005). "Peer learning" as pedagogic discourse for research education. *Studies in Higher Education, 30*(5), 501–516.

Braine, G. (2002). Academic literacy and the non-native speaker graduate student. *Journal of Academic Purposes, 1*(1), 59–63.

Brooks-Gillies, M., Garcia, E. G. & Manthey, K. (2020). Making do by making space: Multidisciplinary graduate writing groups as spaces alongside programmatic and institutional places. In M. Brooks-Gillies, E. G. Garcia, S. H. Kim, K. Manthey & T. G. Smith (Eds.), *Graduate writing across the disciplines: Identifying, teaching, and supporting*. The WAC Clearinghouse; University Press of Colorado. https://wac.colostate.edu/books/atd/graduate

Cadman, K. (1997). Thesis writing for international students: A question of identity? *English for Specific Purposes, 16*(1), 3–14.

Cadman, K. (2000). "Voices in the air": Evaluations of the learning experiences of international postgraduates and their supervisors. *Teaching in Higher Education, 5*(4), 475–491.

Casanave, C. P. (2002). *Writing games: Multicultural case studies of academic literacy practices in higher education*. Lawrence Erlbaum Associates.

Casanave, C. P. (2008). Learning participatory practices in graduate school: Some perspective-taking by a mainstream educator. In C. Casanave & X. Li (Eds.), *Learning the literacy practices of graduate school: Insiders' reflections on academic enculturation* (pp. 14–31). University of Michigan Press.

Casanave, C. P. & Li, X. (Eds.). (2008). *Learning the literacy practices of graduate school: Insiders' reflections on academic enculturation.* University of Michigan Press.

Costley, T. (2008). "You are beginning to sound like an academic": Finding and owning your academic voice. In C. Casanave & X. Li (Eds.), *Learning the literacy practices of graduate school: Insiders' reflections on academic enculturation* (pp. 74–89). University of Michigan Press.

Cotterall, S. (2011). Doctoral students writing: Where's the pedagogy? *Teaching in Higher Education, 16*(4), 413–425.

Cuthbert, D., Spark, C. &Burke, E. (2009). Disciplining writing: The case for multi-disciplinary writing groups to support writing for publication by higher degree research candidates in the humanities, arts and social sciences. *Higher Education Research and Development, 28*(2), 139–149.

Ferenz, O. (2005). EFL writers' social networks: Impact on advanced academic literacy development. *Journal of English for Academic Purposes, 4*(4), 339–351.

Fujioka, M. (2008). Dissertation writing and the (re)positioning of self in a "community of practice." In C. Casanave & X. Li (Eds.), *Learning the literacy practices of graduate school: Insiders' reflections on academic enculturation* (pp. 58–73). University of Michigan Press.

Golde, C. M. (1998). Beginning graduate school: Explaining first-year doctoral attrition. *New Directions for Higher Education, 101*, 55–64.

Haas, S. (2014). Pick-n-mix: A typology of writers' groups in use. In C. Aitchison & C. Guerin (Eds.), *Writing groups for doctoral education and beyond* (pp. 30–48). Routledge.

Hedgcock, J. (2008). Lessons I must have missed: Implicit literacy practices in graduate education. In C. Casanave & X. Li (Eds.), *Learning the literacy practices of graduate school: Insiders' reflections on academic enculturation* (pp. 32–45). University of Michigan Press.

Lave, J. & Wenger, E. (1991). *Situated learning: Legitimate peripheral participation.* Cambridge University Press.

Lee. A. & Aitchison, C. (2009). Writing for the doctorate and beyond. In D. Boud & A. Lee (Eds.), *Changing practices of doctoral education* (pp. 87–99). Routledge.

Li, L. (2014). Scaffolding the thesis writing process: An ongoing writing group for international research students. In C. Aitchison & C. Guerin (Eds.), *Writing groups for doctoral education and beyond: Innovations in practice and theory* (pp. 145–161). Routledge.

Matsuda, P. K., Snyder, S. E. & O'Meara, K. (Eds.). (2017). *Professionalizing second language writing.* Parlor Press.

McIntosh, K., Pelaez-Morales, C. & Silva, T. (Eds.). (2015). *Graduate studies in second language writing.* Parlor Press.

Michigan State University. (2011). *The Graduate School annual report* [Data file]. http://grad.msu.edu/.

Michigan State University Office for International Students and Scholars. (2011). 2011 statistical highlights [Data file]. https://oiss.isp.msu.edu/about/statistical-report/.

Michigan State University Writing Center. (n.d.). *About.* Retrieved January 21, 2020 from http://writing.msu.edu/about.

Moss, B. J., Highberg, N. & Nicolas, M. (2004). *Writing groups inside and outside the classroom*. Lawrence Erlbaum.

Norton, B. (1995). Social identity, investment, and language learning. *TESOL Quarterly, 29*(1), 9–31.

Norton, B. (1997). Language, identity, and the ownership of English. *TESOL Quarterly, 31*(3), 409–429.

Norton, B. (2013). *Identity and language learning: Extending the conversation*. Multilingual Matters.

Norton, B. & McKinney, C. (2011). An identity approach to second language acquisition. In D. Atkinson (Ed.), *Alternative approaches to second language acquisition* (pp. 73–94). Routledge.

Phillips, T. (2012). Graduate writing groups: Shaping writing and writers from student to scholar. *Praxis: A Writing Center Journal, 10*(1). http://www.praxisuwc.com/.

Phillips, T. (2013). Tutor training and services for multilingual graduate writers: A reconsideration. *Praxis: A Writing Center Journal, 10*(2). http://www.praxisuwc.com/.

Phillips, T. (2016). Writing center support for graduate students: An integrated model. In S. Simpson, N. Caplan, M. Cox & T. Phillips (Eds.), *Supporting graduate student writers: Research, curriculum, and program design* (pp. 159–170). University of Michigan Press.

Prior, P. (1998). *Writing disciplinarity: A sociohistoric account of literate activity in the academy*. Lawrence Erlbaum.

Racelis, J. V. & Matsuda, P. K. (2015). Exploring the multiple identities of L2 writing teachers. In Y. L. Cheung, S. B. Said & K. Park (Eds.), *Advances and current trends in language teacher identity research* (pp. 203–216). Routledge.

Reeves, J. (2002). *Writing alone, writing together: A guide for writers and writing groups*. New World Library.

Rogers, P. M., Zawacki, T. M. & Baker, S. E. (2016). Uncovering challenges and pedagogical complications in dissertation writing and supervisory practices: A multimethod study of doctoral students and advisors. In S. Simpson, N. Caplan, M. Cox & T. Phillips (Eds.), *Supporting graduate student writers: Research, curriculum, and program design* (pp. 52–77). University of Michigan Press.

Rosenthal, L. (2003). *The writing group book: Creating and sustaining a successful writing group*. Chicago Review Press.

Ryan, Y. & Zuber-Skerritt, O. (Eds.). (1999). *Supervising postgraduates from non-English speaking backgrounds*. Buckingham, UK: Open University Press.

Schneider, M. L. & Fujishima, N. K. (1995). When practice doesn't make perfect: The case of a graduate ESL student. In D. Belcher & G. Braine (Eds.), *Academic writing in a second language: Essays on research and pedagogy* (pp. 3–22). Ablex.

Simpson, S. (2012). The problem of graduate-level writing support: Building a cross-campus graduate writing initiative. *Writing Program Administration: Journal of the Council of Writing Program Administrators, 36*(1), 95–118.

Simpson, S. (2016). Essential questions for program and pedagogical development. In S. Simpson, N. Caplan, M. Cox & T. Phillips (Eds.), *Supporting graduate student writers: Research, curriculum, and program design* (pp. 286–298). University of Michigan Press.

Spack, R. (1997). The acquisition of academic literacy in a second language: A longitudinal case study. *Written Communication, 14*, 3–62.

Tang, R. (Ed.). (2012). *Academic writing in a second or foreign language: Issues and challenges facing ESL/EFL academic writers in higher education contexts*. Continuum.

Tardy, C. M. (2005). The role of English in scientific communication: Lingua franca or Tyrannosaurus Rex? *Journal of English for Academic Purposes, 3*(3), 325–338.

Tardy, C. M. (2009). *Building genre knowledge*. Parlor Press.

Varghese, M. (2004). Professional development for bilingual teachers in the United States: Articulating and contesting professional roles. In J. Brutt-Griffler & M. Varghese (Eds.), *Re-writing bilingualism and the bilingual educator's knowledge base* (pp. 130–145). Multilingual Matters.

Wang, T. & Li, L. (2008). Understanding international postgraduate research students' challenges and pedagogical needs in thesis writing. *International Journal of Pedagogies and Learning, 4*(3), 88–96. Wenger, E. (1998). *Communities of practice: Learning, meaning, and identity*. Cambridge University Press.

Wette, R. & Furneaux, C. (2018). The academic discourse socialisation challenges and coping strategies of international graduate students entering English-medium universities. *System, 78*, 186–200.

Appendix A: Intake Survey

In this security-enabled survey, participants will provide information about their interest and/or participation in the MSU Writing Center's Graduate Writing Groups. They will also provide information about their motivation for joining the groups, satisfaction with the writing groups, familiarity with writing instruction, access to writing assistance and resources, and self perceptions of their writing ability. The responses will help us get a sense of what motivates students to access writing assistance such as the MSU Writing Center's Graduate Writing Groups. This survey will be distributed to all students who have shown interest in joining a graduate writing group as well as current graduate writing group members. The survey should take around 15 minutes to complete.

Demographic Information

1. Name:
2. Gender:
3. Department/program and year of study:
4. First language:
5. If you are fluent in any other languages, please list them here:
6. Please add any comments you may have about your language use: (explanation box)
7. How long have you been at MSU?
8. (For doctoral students) Have you advanced to candidacy in your program? (yes/no)

9. Have you begun working on your doctoral dissertation/master's thesis? (yes/no)
10. If so, where are you in the process? Check all that apply.
    - Brainstorming
    - Literature review
    - Data collection
    - Data analysis
    - Write-up
    - Revision
    - Formatting
    - Other: _____

Graduate Writing Group Interest

11. How did you learn about the Writing Center's Graduate Writing Groups (GWGs)? (explanation box)
12. When did you express interest in the Writing Center's Graduate Writing Groups? (month/year)
13. Did you join a Graduate Writing Group? (Check yes or no)
14. If so, when did you join a Graduate Writing Group? (month/year)
15. If not, why did you decide not to join a Graduate Writing Group? (explanation box)
16. Why did you/did you want to join a Graduate Writing Group? (explanation box)

Self-Perception of Writing Ability

17. Do you feel prepared to write in the academic genres your program expects of you? (yes/no/other)
18. Do you enjoy academic writing? (yes/sometimes/rarely/never/other)
19. I consider myself a/an _____ academic writer. (excellent/good/satisfactory/poor/other)
20. Do you enjoy non-academic writing (e.g., creative writing, blog writing, etc.)? (yes/sometimes/rarely/never/other)
21. What are your writing strengths? (comment box)
22. What are your writing limitations? (comment box)
23. How comfortable are you going to your advisor/chair for assistance with your writing? (extremely/mostly/sort of/not/other)
24. How available is your advisor to assist you with your writing? (extremely/mostly/sort of/not/other)

25. Describe the assistance and guidance your advisor provides.
26. How comfortable are you going to another committee/faculty member for assistance with your writing? (extremely/mostly/sort of/not/other)
27. How available are your committee members to assist you with your writing? (extremely/mostly/sort of/not/other)
28. Describe the assistance and guidance your committee members provide.
29. How comfortable are you going to peers within your program for assistance with your writing? (extremely/mostly/sort of/not/other)
30. How available are your peers to assist you with your writing? (extremely/mostly/sort of/not/other)
31. Describe the assistance and guidance your peers provide.
32. Describe the assistance and guidance your graduate writing group provides.
33. How does your experience in the graduate writing group differ from your experiences with other forms of writing assistance?

Familiarity with Writing Instruction and the Writing Center

34. Have you had any explicit writing instruction? If so, in what context? (Select All that Apply)
    - Composition class at Michigan State University
    - Composition class at another institution
    - Workshop or short-term seminar on writing
    - Individual instruction from a tutor
    - Individual instruction from faculty member
    - Other: (please explain)
35. How did you learn about the Writing Center?
36. What Writing Center experiences have you had besides Graduate Writing Groups? (Select all that apply)
    - Classroom workshops as faculty
    - Classroom workshops as student
    - Navigating the Ph.D.
    - One-to-one consulting
    - Other (Please describe): _____
37. If so, did this experience occur before or after you joined a Graduate Writing Group?
38. Have you ever been part of a writing group that was not organized by the MSU Writing Center?
    a) no

b) yes, please indicate the type:
- informal disciplinary group
- class-based writing group
- group developed by faculty
- other (please describe):

39. If yes, was the other writing group something you took part in before or after your participation in the writing center graduate writing group? (explanation box)

Access to Writing Resources

40. What writing resources have you used/do you use in addition to participating in a Graduate Writing Group? Check all that apply and explain in the space provided below.
    - People (an advisor, colleagues in your department) (comment box)
    - Texts (writing handbook, research articles, websites, etc.) (comment box)
    - Coursework (comment box)
    - Workshops (comment box)
    - Other: (comment box)

41. What makes these writing resources helpful for you? (Please explain):

42. What writing resources have you used/do you use in your Graduate Writing Group? Check all that apply.
    - People (guest speakers, etc.)
    - Texts
    - Activities/exercises
    - Other: _____

43. What writing resources are made available by your graduate program? Check all that apply.
    - Advisor office hours/appointments (comment box)
    - Texts (for example, handbooks) (comment box)
    - Workshops (comment box)
    - Other (comment box)

44. Would you be willing to participate in an individual interview about your graduate writing group experiences?

45. Would you be willing to participate in a focus group about graduate writing groups?

46. If you are willing to participate, please provide a way for us to contact you (email, phone, etc.) (comment box)

Appendix B: Interview Questions for GWG Members and Writing Consultants

Interview Questions for GWG Members

1. For ESL students: What is your L1? Your L2? Any other languages?
   - How do you feel about writing in each of these languages?
   - What is your greatest concern with regard to your L2 writing?
2. How important do you think is the role of writing in your academic field?
3. What kind of assistance does your GWG provide?
4. Describe the interactions between L1 and L2 writers in your Graduate Writing Group.
   - Can you tell us about the specific types of feedback that you give and receive?
   - Do you feel more comfortable with certain types of feedback than others?
   - What is the most frequent form of feedback in your Graduate Writing Group?
   - Do you tend to value comments from certain members more than others? Why? (e.g., similarity in disciplines, L1 vs L2 speakers)
5. What do you think can be your greatest contribution to the group? What aspects of writing do you feel most comfortable helping others with?
6. How does your experience in the GWG differ from your experience with getting writing assistance from advisor/committee member/peer/WC/other? (several different questions)

Interview Questions for Writing Consultants

1. What were your expectations when you signed up to facilitate Graduate Writing Groups at Michigan State University?
   - Did you expect to work with L2 writers of English?
   - How do you feel about facilitating a Graduate Writing Group which is composed of L2 writers of English?
2. What was the most difficult or challenging thing to you about facilitating a Graduate Writing Group at MSU?
3. What is your perception of the interaction between the writers whose first language is not English and the native English writers in your Graduate Writing Group?

Camping in the Disciplines: Assessing the Effect of Writing Camps on Graduate Student Writers

Gretchen Busl
Texas Woman's University

Kara Lee Donnelly and Matthew Capdevielle
University of Notre Dame

Abstract: In the past ten years, an increasing number of universities have begun organizing writing "camps," or full-week immersion experiences, in an effort to address the increased need to support graduate student writing. Outside of anecdotes and testimonials, we have previously had very little data about these camps' success. This study, conducted over the course of three such camps, attempts to address this lack of data by measuring graduate student writing confidence levels and self-regulation efforts both before and after attendance. An analysis of our preliminary results suggests that writing camps that include process-oriented programming result in small but meaningful improvements in attitudes and behaviors that positively affect graduate student writing.

Keywords: Graduate Student Writing Camps, Graduate Student Writing Process

As this collection attests, over the last decade, our field has seen an increase in the attention given to the unique writing challenges facing graduate students. Also within the last ten years, but not necessarily keeping step with emerging research into graduate writing challenges, we have seen graduate schools devoting more resources to supporting graduate students as writers, supplementing departmental training with interdisciplinary instruction and support. One significant innovation is the writing camp, a full-week immersion experience modeled on the "Dissertation Boot Camp" that began at the University of Pennsylvania in 2005 (Lee & Golde, 2013). Many schools across the country offer similar camps, often run by partnerships of graduate schools, writing centers, libraries, and other support units. Camp participants and administrators are generally positive about these writing immersion experiences, and there is extensive anecdotal evidence of these camps' positive results. However, with a few notable exceptions (Locke & Boyle, 2016; Simpson, 2013), we have very little data about the success of these camps outside of anecdotes and testimonials. Still less is known about how these camps affect writers over the long term and whether their impact varies across the disciplines. This is partly because, in spite of the growing body of research into graduate student writing, to which this collection contributes significantly, we still lack sufficient data on the behaviors and attitudes of graduate student writers in general and on how these behaviors and attitudes typically differ across disciplines.

This chapter adds to the discussion of graduate student writing support by offering a report on preliminary research into the short- and long-term impact of writing camps. Our emerging results highlight important design considerations for the construction of effective graduate writing camps. The chapter begins with an overview of research on graduate student writing camps and the positive attitudes and behaviors about writing that we teach in our camps. We articulate our hypothesis that instruction regarding these behaviors and attitudes will make students more confident and better able to manage their writing process. In the following section, we describe the camps we hold and the study that we performed during our camps. The data for this study is drawn from several camps conducted over the mid-semester and summer breaks at the University of Notre Dame. Using surveys and focus groups to measure camp participants' writing behaviors and attitudes, we work to assess the short- and long-term impact of the camps on those behaviors and attitudes and to determine continuities and differences across disciplines. Working from a hypothesis that writing camps that offer programming can improve the soft skills required to complete a long-term project like a thesis or dissertation, our pilot study sets out to measure graduate student writing confidence levels and self-regulation efforts both before and after attendance at a writing camp. In the results section, we trace the trends we see emerging in our responses, suggesting that writing camps that teach students strategies for managing their writing processes may result in small but meaningful improvements in student attitudes and behaviors. Students who attended such camps tended to feel less anxious when they sat down to write and felt more confident that they had the abilities and tools to complete the writing task at hand. We close this chapter with suggestions for further research into systems of support for graduate student writing across the disciplines.

Do Graduate Student Writing Camps Affect Attitudes and Behaviors?

Graduate student writing camps are an innovation in ongoing efforts to support graduate student writers, and accordingly, there is currently little research, analysis, or theory devoted to them. Mastroieni and Cheung (2011) provide a broad survey and retrospective of these programs, while Smith and Kayongo (2011) explore the collaboration between libraries and other support units in terms of senior thesis writing camps. Locke and Boyle (2016) offer a qualitative inquiry into the dissertation boot camp model as an instrument of intervention for dissertation writers who have stalled in their writing process. Allen (2015) discusses learning outcomes for writing camps through a personal account of her experience as a participant in a dissertation boot camp. In one of the most useful analytical approaches, Lee and Golde (2013) divide dissertation boot camps into two curricular models: "Just Write" camps and "Writing Process" camps.

"Just Write" camps provide students with a physical space that is deemed conducive to writing. The theory behind these camps is that graduate students have the necessary skills and behaviors to write successfully, and they simply need to be provided a dedicated time and space to actually get down to the business of writing. The location is quiet, has adequate table space, and provides sufficient power outlets for students to use laptops and other electronic devices. Students are provided with set hours during which they are encouraged to use this space, for example 8:00 a.m. to 4:00 p.m. every day for a week. In many of these camps, students are also provided with refreshments of some kind, such as breakfast and coffee in the morning and snack in the afternoon; some camps with enough funding also provide lunch. In "Just Write" camps, there is no specific instruction on writing or on the writing process.

In contrast, "Writing Process" camps encourage "consistent and on-going conversations about writing" in addition to providing time and space (Lee & Golde, 2013). The theory behind these camps is that attendees have not fully mastered the skills and behaviors necessary to complete a dissertation or other long writing project. Consequently, these camps offer focused instruction on the writing process, for example on maintaining a dissertation log or on generative writing strategies to help overcome writer's block. They also frequently offer the services of a writing consultant or tutor. Lee and Golde strongly encourage a "Writing Process" orientation and the involvement of writing centers in graduate student writing camps. Simpson (2013) has also advocated for "Writing Process" camps. This is in part because he seeks to create "outward-focused camps," or camps that are primarily a tool for developing writing initiatives across the university. Simpson has found that camps can serve as an important launching pad for deeper cross-campus involvement in writing and can draw graduate students into campus writing centers.

While we also encourage "Writing Process" camps, this study is aimed at testing the hypothesis that process-oriented camps are preferable to "Just Write" camps. We must assess if "Writing Process" camp participants are actually better able to manage the writing challenges they face, both during the camp and after it has ended. In particular, this pilot study asks how the two models of writing camps improved graduate students' thoughts about writing and their behaviors as writers. In the realm of their thoughts about writing, we considered their *perceived self-efficacy* and their *motivation*. Perceived self-efficacy in writing describes how confident a writer is that he or she will be able to complete a given writing task to the necessary standard. Perceived self-efficacy can be determined in part by past performances on similar tasks, but it can also account for differences in performance among individuals with similar abilities (Bandura, 1989). Educational psychologists argue that perceived self-efficacy influences motivation (Pret-Sala & Redford, 2010; Pret-Sala & Redford, 2012). Writers with higher perceived self-efficacy are more likely to persevere in the face of obstacles and to see them as challenges rather than roadblocks. They are also less likely to respond to failure with maladaptive behaviors. This may be why writers with high self-efficacy perform better than writers with low self-efficacy regardless of writing ability.

In addition to examining students' thoughts about writing, we examined their writing behaviors. Specifically, we focused on their methods for *self-regulation*. Self-regulation is a set of behaviors that are correlated with self-efficacy and motivation (Pintrich, 1999; Zimmerman & Bandura, 1994). Self-regulated learners are diligent and resourceful; they tend to plan, set goals, and monitor their own progress towards achieving those goals (Zimmerman, 1990). In short, our study sought to determine whether writing camps affected perceived self-efficacy, motivation, and self-regulation in graduate student writers. In "Writing Process" camps, we teach specific behaviors that will help with self-regulation (e.g., maintaining a writing log, pre-scheduling writing times, setting short-term goals). We also foster cross-disciplinary discussion about writing and offer process-improvement tools that we hope will change students' levels of self-efficacy and motivation. For this reason, we hypothesize that students in "Writing Process" camps will increase their adaptive beliefs and behaviors, while students in "Just Write" camps will not.

Methodology

This study examines graduate writing camps held at the University of Notre Dame, a mid-sized private research university. Since 2011, university entities such as the Library, the Writing Center, and the Graduate School have worked together to hold weeklong graduate writing camps during both fall and spring breaks. Our initial research in spring 2013 took place within the context of these existing camps, and in June 2013, we added an additional camp that was designed specifically for the study.

Spring Data Collection

In the writing camp offered during spring of 2013, we began our initial study of graduate student writing camps. Two camps ran concurrently, one for students working on a dissertation or thesis, and one for students working on articles. Because the camps had already been established, we designed the spring component of the study to create minimal impact on the existing structure of the camps. Each camp had been designed to feature a daily morning workshop, a morning goal-setting session, free-writing time, and a daily group wrap-up session (see Appendix A). All students registered for the camps were asked upon arrival on the first day to participate in the study. Of 40 students who attended the dissertation/thesis camp, 17 agreed to participate in the study; of the 18 students who attended the publications camp, 10 agreed to participate in the study. Of the participants, four were enrolled in a master's program, and 23 were enrolled in a Ph.D. program. Eleven were in the humanities, seven were in the social sciences, and nine were in STEM fields.

Data from these camps was collected primarily through surveys and daily writing logs. At the opening of the camps, all students who participated in the study filled out a pre-camp survey that asked them about their writing practices. The survey was designed to collect information about general student attitudes towards the writing process, as well as to better understand their writing processes, including their self-regulation efforts. Participants were asked about their feelings towards writing (to measure confidence, enjoyment, and anxiety) according to a Likert scale. They were also asked about how frequently they worked on their writing project, engaged different writing strategies (e.g., brainstorming, outlining), set goals, tracked their writing, and sought help from various sources (e.g., advisor, other faculty or peers in their department, a Writing Center tutor, etc.). Our questions arose from our desire to get a better picture of graduate student writing processes—a necessary baseline in order to understand how camps could affect those processes. They were based on our collective experience working with graduate student writers and observing the challenges they faced.

During the camps, all students filled out daily logs in which they noted how many hours they were on-task during the day, how many words they wrote, and whether or not they achieved their writing goal. At the end of the weeklong camp, students filled out a post-camp survey. This survey asked them about their attitudes towards writing, using questions similar to the pre-camp survey. The post-camp survey also asked students about their plans for writing after the camps, including how frequently they intended to write, to seek help from various sources, and to engage various strategies for writing and for managing their productivity. Three months after the camps, students were asked to complete the same questions found on the pre-camp survey; the goal of re-administering the survey at the three-month mark was to determine if and how students' writing attitudes and practices had changed following the camp. Six students completed the three-month survey and participated in focus groups or answered focus group questions over email four and a half months after the camps.

Summer Study

In summer of 2013, we continued the study with modifications to better analyze the impact that graduate writing camps have on the attitudes and practices of graduate student writers. In particular, we investigated the impact of programming designed to improve students' self-efficacy and self-regulation. In other words, we sought to test the claim made by Golde and Lee (2013) and by Simpson (2013) that "Writing Process" camps are more effective than "Just Write" camps at supporting graduate student writers. This camp comprised 26 graduate students, though not all students completed the camp or consented to participate in the study.

In order to assess the impact of programming that seeks to develop techniques for writing and for self-regulation, half of the students experienced "Writing Process" programming, while the other half followed the "Just Write" model for writing camps. The students in the "Writing Process" cohort attended a morning session to introduce them to different writing strategies (e.g., analyzing models, setting long- and short-term goals) and to set and share goals on a public whiteboard. They also attended an afternoon wrap-up session to discuss challenges and report on whether or not they met their goals, in addition to crossing their completed goals off the whiteboard. The students in the "Just Write" cohort did not attend instructional or goal-setting sessions, though they were welcome to talk with each other about writing. Students' names and project titles were removed from their registration materials, and then camp participants were evenly sorted by college and department into either camp. All students—those with programming and those without—took the same pre-camp and post-camp surveys and filled out the same daily writing logs as the students in the spring study did. Seven students from both the "Just Write" and "Writing Process" camps completed both pre- and post- surveys, for a total of 14 students. Nine students from the summer camp participated in focus groups or answered focus group questions over email a month after the camp.

Results and Data Analysis

While the small sample size of this initial study prevents us from making broad claims about the effectiveness of writing camps, our data does offer some interesting insight into both the highly individualized nature of the writing process and general trends that can be observed. Comparing our pre-camp surveys, which emphasized current attitudes and behaviors, with the immediate post-camp surveys, which addressed current attitudes and *expected* behaviors, it is clear that the writing camps which incorporated daily programming influenced the students' perceptions of their own writing ability, the value of process-management techniques, and the value of seeking external assistance. Writing camp programming clearly has the potential to influence student intentions toward making positive changes in their writing habits.

Influence of Writing Camp Programming on Graduate Student Attitudes and Process-Oriented Behaviors

By comparing the pre- and post-camp answers from the 21 complete survey sets for camps that included programming, we can see a measurable change in students' feelings towards writing. Each question was assigned values on a scale of 1–5 (completely disagree to completely agree), and the data was compared to assess areas of positive or negative change, in relation to the nature of the question. For example, in response to the statement "I am confident in my skills as a writer," 29 percent of students reported at least a one-point shift towards more strongly agreeing with the statement (see Figure 10.1).

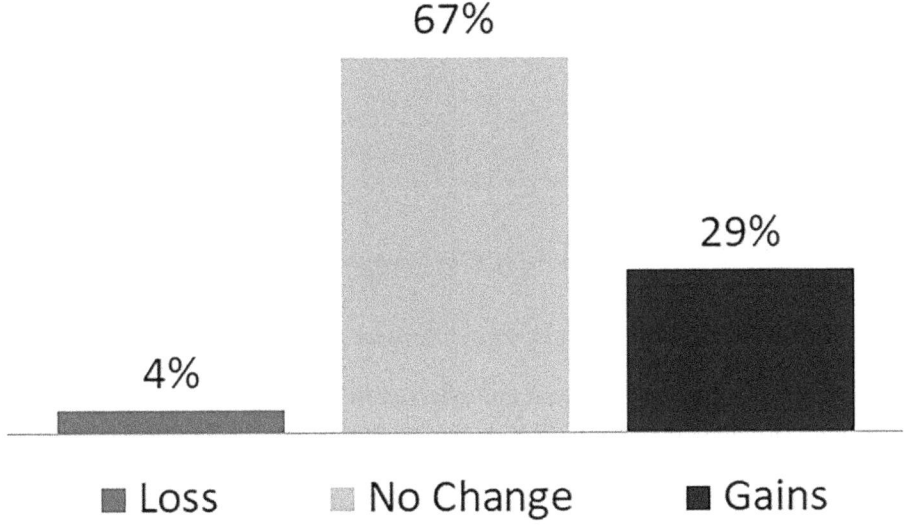

Figure 10.1. Participants experiencing a change in confidence level.

Answers to other related questions indicate positive gains that relate or correspond to measures of confidence. For example, 33 percent of students more strongly identified with either the statement "I enjoy writing" or "I have a positive attitude towards writing" (see Figure 10.2).

Focus group discussions confirm that many students felt an increase in their confidence during the camp for a variety of reasons, including an increased ability to focus on the writing process, exposure to new strategies for managing time and goal-setting, and engagement with peers across the disciplines. This corresponds with findings of Fergie, Beeke, McKenna, and Crème (2011), which found that graduate students who participated in a group writing instruction module identified "thinking about writing, developing new writing and reading processes, and increased interaction about writing . . . as factors contributing to an increase in confidence" (p. 241).

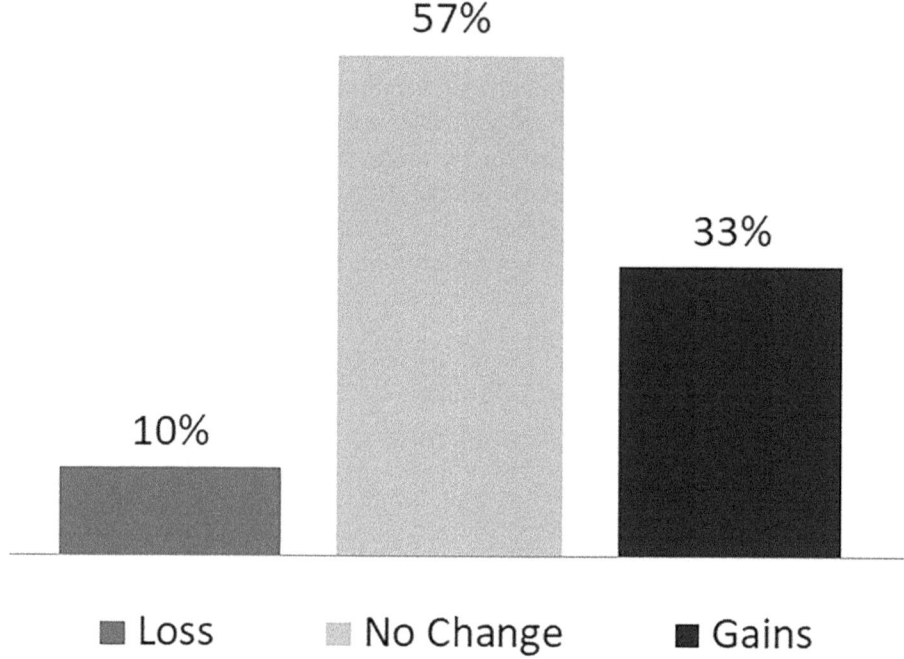

Figure 10.2. Participants experiencing other positive attitude changes.

Even more significant changes are reflected in students' post-camp intentions for process-oriented behaviors. Before the programming-oriented camps, participants were asked to rate on a 5-point scale how often (never, rarely, sometimes, frequently, and often) they engaged in behaviors that contribute to self-efficacy and self-regulation, such as brainstorming, outlining, setting and sharing goals, tracking productivity, and analyzing disciplinary models. After the camps, students used the same scale to rate how often they *intended* to engage in such behaviors.

Many students were more willing to take on strategies that the writing camp programming had promoted: 57 percent indicated they were more likely to share their goals with others, 67 percent indicated they were more likely to write goals for each writing session, 71 percent indicated they were more likely to use a journal to track their productivity, and 76 percent indicated that they were more likely to analyze model writing products within their field (see Figure 10.3). Focus group discussions indicate that these process-improving changes are highly individualized: students are apt to be drawn towards one or two particular strategies that were presented during camp programming, and to make a conscious decision to implement them on a more regular basis. Students reported employing a number of different post-camp strategies that would affect motivation and self-efficacy, such as starting a dissertation notebook to track ideas and writing progress, creating a spreadsheet of hours spent writing and number of words set to the page, and finding a group of students to meet with weekly in order to share goals and written drafts.

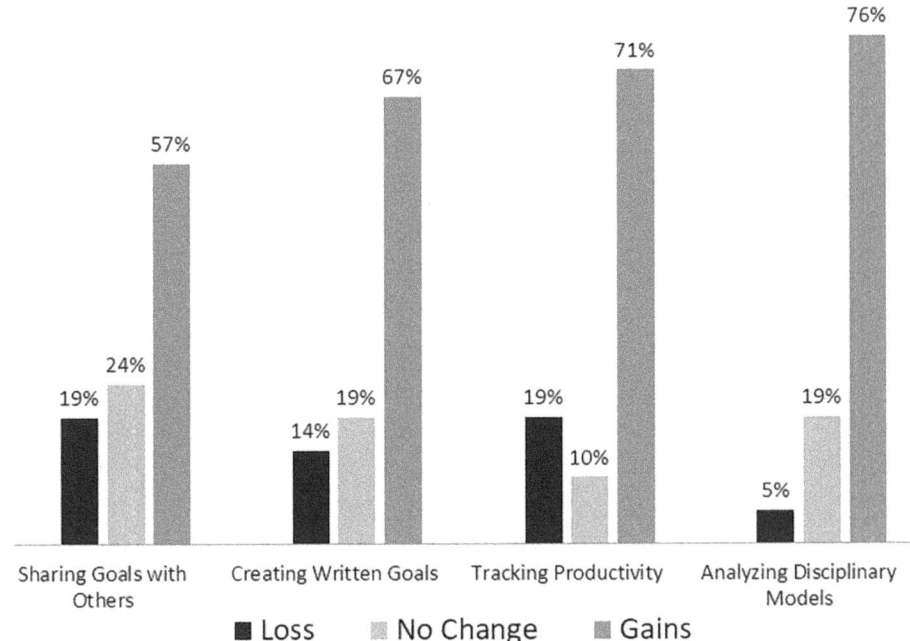

Figure 10.3. Participants intending to engage in process-improving behaviors.

The survey results also indicate that at the close of the camps, over half the students expressed a greater willingness to seek external help with their writing, either more frequently than previously or from a greater variety of sources. Fifty-seven percent showed a willingness to work more frequently with their advisor, 52 percent indicated they would more frequently seek help from other faculty within their discipline, and 57 percent indicated they would work more often with peers in their department (see Figure 10.4). In addition, 52 percent of the students indicated that they would be more likely to visit the Writing Center for assistance with their projects (see Figure 10.4). This willingness to interact with others about writing may be a reflection of students' increased confidence, as well as an important factor contributing to it.

Nurturing this desire represents an excellent opportunity to increase graduate student traffic in often predominantly undergraduate-focused centers. Most significantly, the interdisciplinary atmosphere of the camps contributed to 71 percent of students indicating that they would seek support from fellow students outside their discipline (see Figure 10.4). Participants appear to have considered the interdisciplinary atmosphere and programming activities (such as public goal setting and wrap-up sessions) designed to create a sense of community with other students to be highly valuable, a notion that post-camp focus group responses bear out.

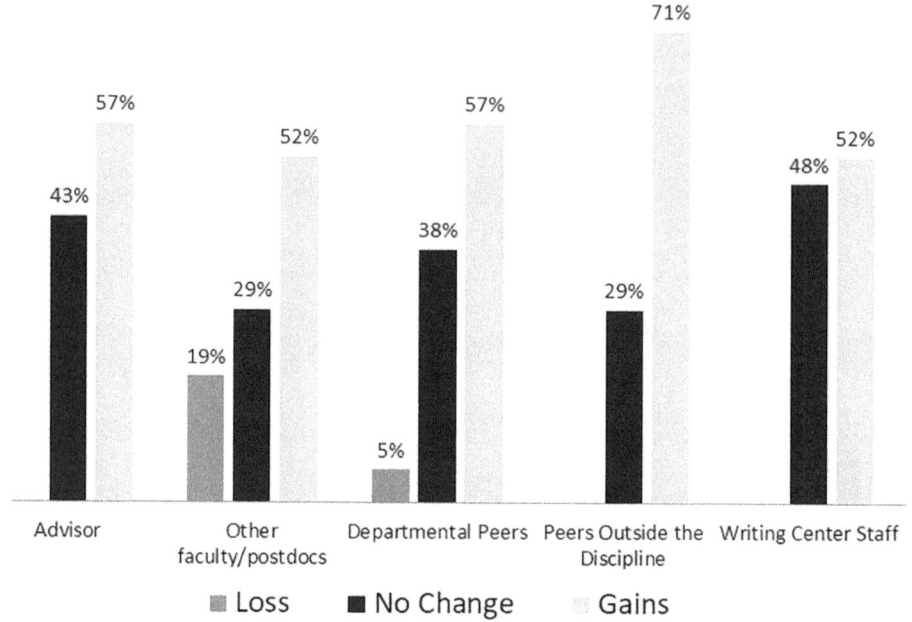

Figure 10.4. Participants willing to seek support from external sources.

Programming Camps vs. "Just Write" Camps

As stated above, in order to test whether or not the change in student attitudes and intended behaviors was simply the experience of writing within a camp environment or the specific programming, we held two camps in June 2013, one with programming (a "Writing Process" camp) and one without it ("Just Write" camp). Half of the students were located in the University's Writing Center and took part in process-oriented programming and shared their goals with other students. The other half of the students were in a similar space in the same building but were largely left to their own devices. Writing Center staff interacted with the students only to collect daily writing logs and to furnish refreshments. A comparison of the data from the 14 respondents who completed both pre- and post-camp surveys indicates that programming is, in fact, necessary to make significant changes in student attitudes and intended behaviors.

Camping in the Disciplines | 253

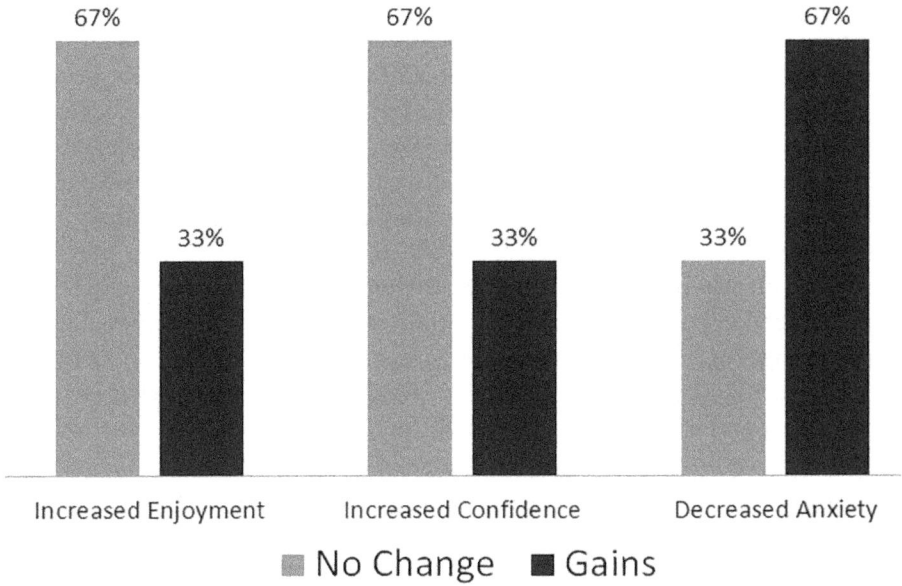

Figure 10.5a. Participant attitude shifts after "Writing Process" camp.

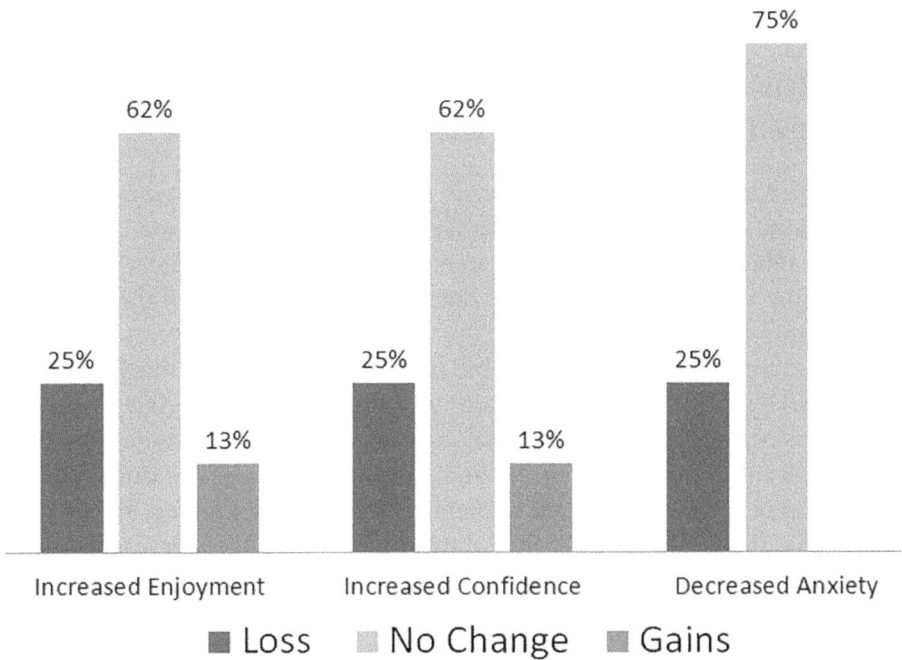

Figure 10.5b. Participant attitude shifts after "Just Write" camp.

Sixty-seven percent of the students who engaged in writing camp programming reported a decreased level of anxiety at the close of the camp, while none of the students in the "Just Write" section of the camp reported such a decrease. Overall, the majority of attitude shifts displayed by the "Just Write" students were negative (see Figure 10.5b). Students *with* programming did not show any negative shifts in their attitudes towards writing; in fact, they showed positive changes in three categories, including enjoying the writing process, feeling confident in writing skills, and feeling less anxious (see Figure 10.5a).

As with the previous participants, students in the June 2013 camp also reported on their intended post-camp behavior. While students in both sections indicated positive changes in a number of categories, only the students in the "Just Write" section reported a significant *decrease* in their willingness to engage in behaviors related to motivation and self-regulation. Overall, the group that did not have access to programming reported *more* negative changes in *more* categories, from pre-camp to post-camp surveys, while the students who engaged in the programming saw more positive changes in more categories. This trend does seem to indicate that writing camps have a more positive effect on student attitudes and intended behaviors when they involve at least some group programming. It also indicates that programming should be at the minimum instructive, but camps will see greater results if students are asked to engage in specific self-regulatory and motivational techniques.

Improved Behaviors Three Months After Programming-Oriented Camp

The trends present in this small data set do seem to indicate that writing camps are, in fact, able to change student attitudes about their own writing and their perception of the value of process-improving strategies. However, data from a survey given three months after the camp indicates that student expectations of their behaviors may be higher than the actual pay-off.

For the nine students we were able to track successfully through the three-month mark (six from the spring camps and three from the summer camp), we saw an interesting trend in their actual implementation of the strategies emphasized during camp programming. By and large, at the end of the camp, students indicated an increased desire to set written goals for writing sessions. Survey results indicate that three months after the camp, students did indeed set written goals, but did not do so as frequently as they had planned to immediately following the camp. Six of the nine students did indicate that they used writing goals more frequently than they had before the camp, which does represent a significant effect. Other camp programming intended to increase student accountability also seemed to have a small, but sustained effect at the three-month mark.

Camping in the Disciplines | 255

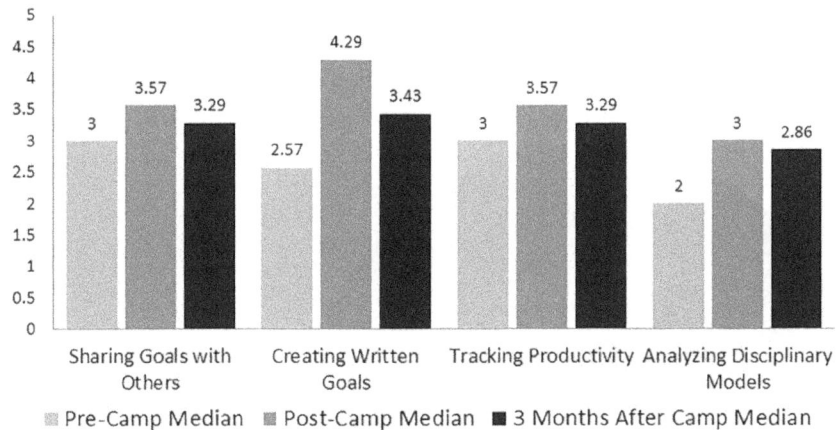

Figure 10.6. Participant engagement in process-improving behaviors.

Overall, three months after the camp, students did not maintain the level of engagement in sharing goals, setting written goals, tracking productivity, or analyzing disciplinary models that they anticipated at the end of the camp, but they did report a greater level of engagement than before attending the camp (see Figure 10.6). A number of students who took part in a focus group four and a half months after completing a "Writing Process" camp indicated that, while they experienced an immediate change in their writing routine after the camp, their increased writing productivity had started to wane.

These results indicate a positive effect on student behaviors, at least for a short period of time. Writing camp programming that engages students in process-improvement strategies leading to increased self-efficacy and self-regulation certainly seems to improve willingness to undertake such activities after the close of the camp. Students then need to negotiate the integration of such strategies into their regular routine, away from the "artificial" environment of the writing camp—a fact that begins to account for the gap between students' expectations of their behaviors and actual results. A longitudinal study would be necessary to suggest whether students can maintain such behaviors past the three-month point without a "refresher" camp. These results also suggest that there is room for innovation within graduate writing camp design: camp designers should work to develop strategies for helping students maintain the positive changes they make during camp once they return to their normal routines.

Breakdown of Attitudes and Behaviors by Division

Beyond a better understanding of the potential effectiveness of writing camps, this study also gives us limited but useful insight into graduate student attitudes towards writing. If we look for general trends in the pre-test feelings of the 38 students for whom the March or July camp was their first experience at a writing camp, we can make a few observations. Overall, these students, who self-selected to attend a writing camp, display a somewhat low confidence in their writing ability.

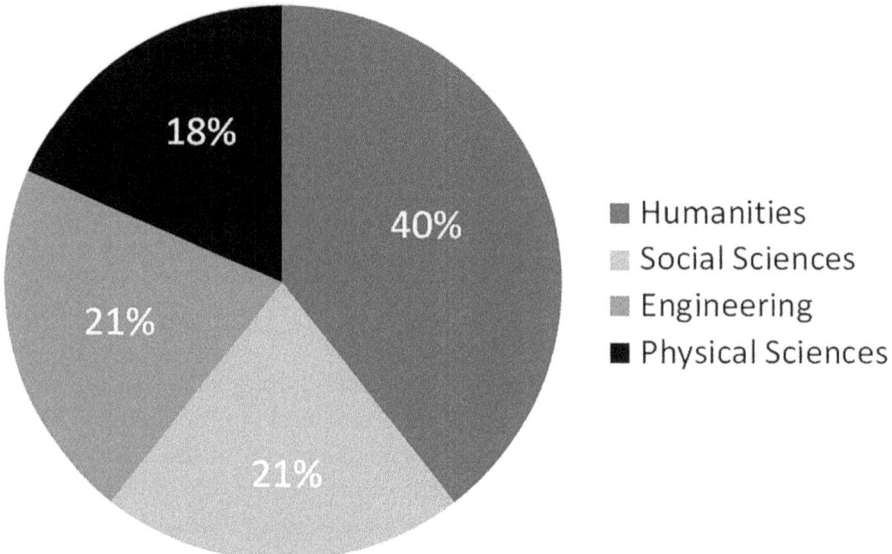

Figure 10.7. Participant breakdown by division.

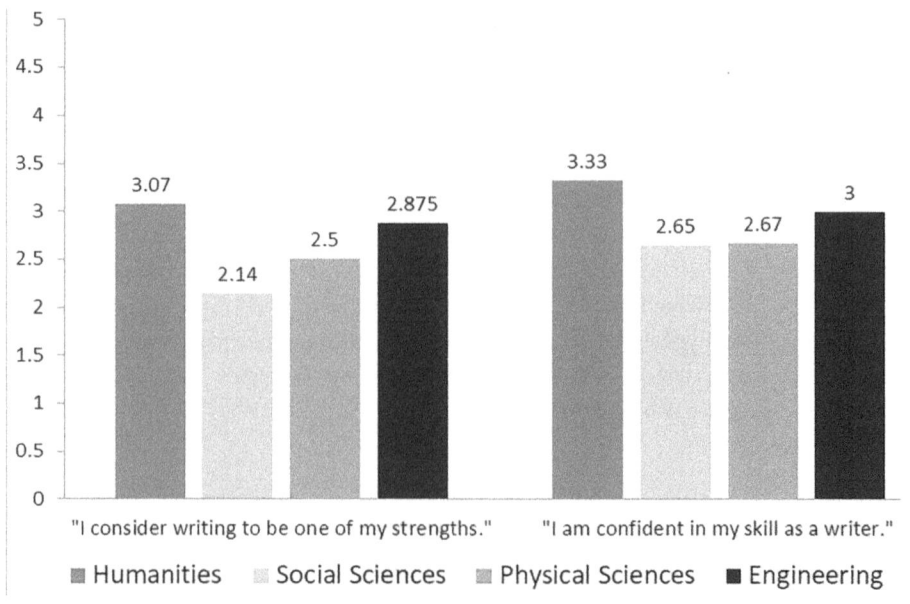

Figure 10.8. Pre-camp positive attitudes by division.

Humanities students displayed the most confidence in their writing skills, while social science students displayed the least confidence in their skills. Social science students also displayed the lowest level of agreement with the statement "I enjoy writing."

These numbers, along with enrollment statistics, seem to indicate that humanities students are more likely to attend a writing camp, but they begin the camp with a somewhat more positive outlook than students in other disciplines. For this reason, organizers may want to consider more aggressively recruiting students in STEM and social science fields to participate in writing camps. During the camp and in the post-camp focus groups, students indicated that a mix of disciplines is highly desirable: the students found it particularly useful to understand how diverse the writing process is for students outside their own discipline. Their own confidence may be increased by hearing about the broad spectrum of challenges that others face.

In regard to student behaviors, at the pre-camp stage, students across the board report a fairly low frequency of activities that might contribute positively to their self-regulation. Students in different divisions do, however, report varying degrees of frequency in process-improving behaviors that may influence self-efficacy.

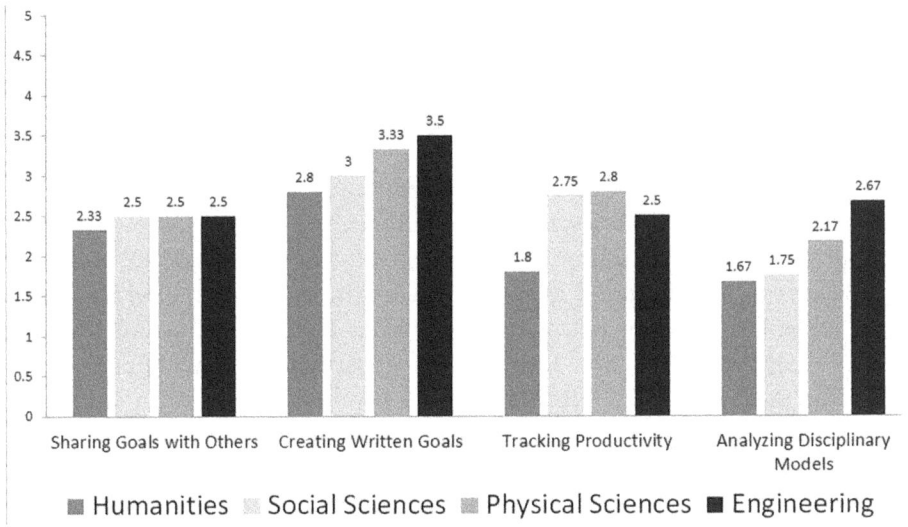

Figure 10.9. Pre-camp process-improving behaviors by division.

There is no appreciable difference between divisions in the frequency of sharing goals with others, but other process-improving behaviors show interesting trends. Students in the STEM divisions tend to engage more frequently in process behaviors like creating quantifiable goals and tracking productivity (see Figure 10.9). This could be the result of a number of factors, including the quantitative focus of their research and the greater emphasis on collaborative writing products. In general, it is clear that disciplinary practices and department protocols vary widely, and they likely have differing impact on student self-efficacy.

Conclusion

Our preliminary studies on graduate writing camps indicate that camps can positively affect the beliefs and behaviors of graduate student writers, but that there is room to improve current models for camps and to conduct further research. First, our research suggests that in order for camps to improve self-efficacy, motivation, and writing processes, they should include programming that emphasizes discussion, collaboration, and process-improving behaviors. We encourage additional research on these camps since our small study size limited our results. Second, since our research suggests that positive changes in graduate students' beliefs and behaviors decrease over time, researchers and teachers should work to improve the curricula of writing camps and to develop supplementary programs to help graduate student writers to maintain improvements after the camp ends. The development of improved curricula and programming would be supported by our third recommendation for future research: cross-institutional analysis. While graduate student writing camps are a new innovation, they have been adopted by a large number of universities in a relatively short period of time. However, each institution modifies the basic model to fit their students' needs and their available resources; we suspect that there is a great deal of diversity from camp to camp. We recommend that future research seek to discover the prevalence of graduate writing camps and to describe and analyze the various models different institutions have employed in the hope that we can learn from one another. A further promising line of inquiry lies in the pedagogical ground shared between writing groups and writing camps. As we see in Chapter 8 of this collection (Brooks-Gillies, Garcia, and Manthey), the writing group can occupy a unique space that holds a tremendous potential for writers to flourish. Research into ways of combining the writing camp experience with semi-structured writing groups may yield insights into both of these support approaches, particularly in better understanding how writing camps and groups can help socialize graduate students into different discourse communities and integrate them into their profession. In Chapter 9, Kim and Wolke go far towards illuminating this process for L2 students. Finally, we recommend more basic research on graduate students as writers, building on the work represented in this collection. Further, with studies such as those presented by Simpson, Caplan, Cox, and Phillips (2016), our knowledge continues to grow concerning graduate students' behaviors, beliefs, and attitudes about writing and the role it plays in their disciplinary and professional training. A better understanding of graduate student writers is necessary if we wish to improve graduate student writing support.

In general, our study and the other studies in this collection offer a glimpse into the beliefs and behaviors of graduate student writers. The picture that emerges illustrates a number of writing challenges facing graduate students. Among those examined in this study are lack of self-efficacy, negative attitudes toward writing, struggles to learn disciplinary norms, and difficulty at managing an appropriate writing schedule. Writing camps are not a panacea for all that ails graduate education, but they can offer specific and targeted instruction to reduce the challenges graduate students face in their writing. Each student responds differently to camps, and his or her attitude towards writing is linked to many factors outside the camp environment, such as the stress caused by impending deadlines and the unpredictable nature of academic research. However, camps that provide direct instruction on strategies for managing the writing process and a collaborative, supportive environment that fosters positive attitudes towards writing do lead to incremental but meaningful improvements in the beliefs and behaviors of graduate student writers.

Epilogue

This study has informed our practice of providing writing support to graduate students in camp and retreat formats at our respective institutions. Busl brought the model to Texas Woman's University, where she has been offering dissertation and thesis boot camps and continuing to collect data to inform her camp design for the past five years. As a public, minority-majority institution, this new context for dissertation and thesis boot camps allows for a broader study of how different educational, socio-economic, and ethnic backgrounds affect graduate student writing processes. Along with her research partner, Dr. Sally Stabb, Busl is currently collecting data to examine how camps may affect graduate student persistence and time-to-degree. At the University of Notre Dame, Capdevielle has continued to offer the camps in collaboration with the library and the graduate school. He has also begun to investigate the role of disciplinarity in the long- and short-term effects of the camps by offering discipline-specific camps at Notre Dame. In addition, he has sought to address the long-term difficulty in sustaining the positive writing process changes introduced by the camp experience, which we noted in our study. To address this difficulty, along with his institutional partners, he developed a cohort-model dissertation support system called the Integrative Dissertation Proseminar, a ten-month program for a small group of dissertation writers, including two boot camp experiences during the academic year along with monthly social events and monthly lunch-and-learn seminars on topics relevant to the writing project. They continue to build writing support programs, drawing from the insights generated by this study.

References

Allen, J. (2015). Graduate school–facilitated peer mentoring for degree completion: Dissertation-writing boot camps. In G. Wright (Ed.), *The mentoring continuum: From graduate school through tenure* (pp. 23–48). Syracuse University Press.

Bandura, A. (1989). Regulation of cognitive processes through perceived self-efficacy. *Developmental Psychology 25*, 729–735.

Brooks-Gillies, M., Garcia, E. G. & Manthey, K. (2020). Making do by making space: Graduate writing groups as spaces alongside programmatic and institutional places. In M. Brooks-Gillies, E. G. Garcia, S. H. Kim, K. Manthey & T. G. Smith (Eds.), *Graduate writing across the disciplines: Identifying, teaching, and supporting*. The WAC Clearinghouse; University Press of Colorado. https://wac.colostate.edu/books/atd/graduate.

Fergie, G., Beeke, S., McKenna, C. & Crème, P. (2011). "It's a lonely walk": Supporting postgraduate research through writing. *International Journal of Teaching and Learning in Higher Education, 23*, 236–245. http://www.isetl.org/ijtlhe/pdf/IJTLHE1016.pdf.

Kim, S. & Wolke, S. (2020). Graduate writing groups: Helping L2 writers navigate the murky waters of academic writing. In M. Brooks-Gillies, E. G. Garcia, S. H. Kim, K. Manthey & T. G. Smith (Eds.), *Graduate writing across the disciplines: Identifying, teaching, and supporting*. The WAC Clearinghouse; University Press of Colorado. https://wac.colostate.edu/books/atd/graduate.

Lee, S. & Golde, C. (2013). Completing the dissertation and beyond: Writing centers and dissertation boot camps. *Writing Lab Newsletter, 37*(7–8), 1–5.

Locke, L. A. & Boyle, M. (2016). Avoiding the A.B.D. abyss: A grounded theory study of a dissertation-focused course for doctoral students in an educational leadership program. *The Qualitative Report, 21*(9), 1574–1593. http://nsuworks.nova.edu/tqr/vol21/iss9/2.

Mastroieni, A. & Cheung, D. (2011). The few, the proud, and the finished: Dissertation boot camp as a model for doctoral student support. *NASPA Excellence in Practice, 3*–6.

Pintrich, P. R. (1999). The role of motivation in promoting and sustaining self-regulated learning. *International Journal of Educational Research, 31*, 459–470.

Prat-Sala, M. & Redford, P. (2010). The interplay between motivation, self-efficacy, and approaches to studying. *The British Journal of Educational Psychology, 80*, 283–305.

Pret-Sala, M. & Redford, P. (2012). Writing essays: Does self-efficacy matter? The relationship between self-efficacy in reading and in writing and undergraduate students' performance in essay writing. *Educational Psychology, 32*, 9–20.

Simpson, S. (2013). Building for sustainability: Dissertation boot camp as a nexus of graduate writing support. *Praxis: A Writing Center Journal 10*(2), 1–8.

Simpson, S., Caplan, N. A., Cox, M. & Phillips, T. (2016). *Supporting graduate student writers: Research, curriculum, and program design*. University of Michigan Press.

Smith, C. & Kayongo, J. (2011). Senior thesis camp: partnership in practice at the University of Notre Dame. *The Journal of Academic Librarianship 37*, 437–442. https://doi.org/10.1016/j.acalib.2011.06.008.

Torrance, M., Thomas, G. V. & Robinson, E. J. (1993). Training in thesis writing: An evaluation of three conceptual orientations. *British Journal of Educational Psychology, 63*, 170–184.

Zimmerman, B. J. (1990). Self-regulated learning and academic achievement: An overview. *Educational Psychologist, 25*, 3–17.

Zimmerman, B. J. & Bandura, A. (1994). Impact of self-regulatory influences on writing course attainment. *American Educational Research Journal, 31*, 845–862.

Appendix A: Sample Camp Schedule

	Monday	Tuesday	Wednesday	Thursday	Friday
9:00	Breakfast	Breakfast	Breakfast	Breakfast	Breakfast
9:30	*Goal Setting*	*Time Management*	*Analyzing Models*	*Getting Feedback*	*Editing and Revising*
10:00	Quiet writing time	Quiet writing time	Quiet writing time	Quiet writing time	Quiet writing time
12:00	(Lunch)	(Lunch)	(Lunch)	(Lunch)	(Lunch)
1:00	Quiet writing time/tutoring	Quiet writing time/tutoring	Quiet writing time/tutoring	Quiet writing time/tutoring	Quiet writing time/tutoring
2:30	Snack	Snack	Snack	Snack	Snack
4:30	*Daily wrap up*	*Daily wrap up*	*Daily wrap up*	*Daily wrap up*	*Daily wrap up*

Appendix B: Participant Surveys

Pre-Camp/Three Month Post-Camp Survey Sample Questions

1. I write most frequently:

At home, in a public space	At home, in a private space	On campus, in a public space	On campus, in a private space	Off campus, in a public place	Off campus, in a private place

2. Please rate your agreement with these statements on a scale of 1 (completely disagree) to 5 (agree completely).

	1 Completely disagree	2 Disagree	3 Neither agree nor disagree	4 Agree	5 Completely agree
I understand the standard features of writing in my field.					
I am confident in my skill as a writer.					
I enjoy the process of writing.					
I consider writing to be one of my strengths.					
I have generally positive attitude towards writing.					
When I sit down to write, I feel anxious.					
I feel unable to manage distractions and focus on my writing.					
I procrastinate on my writing.					

3. In the past six months, how often have you:

	1–3 times a month	3–6 times a month	7–10 times a month	10–20 times a month	More than 20 times a month
Gone two days without writing					
Gone one week without writing					
Written at least five of seven days in a week					
Written for more than four hours in one day					

Spent more than 20 hours in one week writing				
Spent more than 40 hours in one week writing				

4. Which of the following strategies do you currently employ in the writing process?

	Never	Rarely	Sometimes	Often	Frequently
Brainstorming/ thought mapping/ Free writing					
Outlining					
Setting written goals					
Tracking productivity in a journal or application					
Analyzing disciplinary models					
Sharing your goals					
Scheduling specific times to write each week					
Employing specific strategies to help avoid distractions (headphones, website blocking software, focus apps, etc.)					

5. How often do you seek help with your writing (Once a month, twice a month, three times a month, once a week, more than once a week)?

	Once a month	Twice a month	Three times a month	Once a week	More than once a week
From your advisor					
From another faculty member or postdoc in your field					

From graduate student peers within your discipline					
From people outside your discipline					
From the writing center					

6. How often do you avoid writing or are you distracted from your writing by the following?

	Always	Frequently	Sometimes	Rarely	Never
Social Media on my computer (Facebook, Twitter, blogs, etc.)					
Research-related tasks (reading in the field, meeting with collaborators)					
Teaching-related tasks (lesson planning, grading, meeting with students)					
General work (checking work email, doing paperwork, reading in the field)					
My phone (for emailing, texting, talking, playing games)					
Other distractions away from my computer (chatting with a friend, getting a snack, doing chores)					

Think about a big writing project that you are working on or have just completed.

6. How long is the typical gap between two consecutive writing episodes on your project (in other words, if you write on a given day, how long is it you typically return to that project to continue writing)? Check one field.

Less than one day	One day	Two days	Up to one week	More than one week

7. How long is your typical writing episode (without a break in which you disengage and do something else)? Write in the duration in **hours**, rounded to the quarter hour (e.g., 2.25 hours) _____

8. How many hours a week do you typically write on this project? Write in the duration in **hours**, rounded to the quarter hour (e.g., 2.25 hours) _____

One Week Post-Camp Survey Sample Questions

1. Please rate your agreement with these statements on a scale of 1 (completely disagree) to 5 (agree completely).

	1 Completely disagree	2 Disagree	3 Neither agree nor disagree	4 Agree	5 Completely agree
I understand the standard features of writing in my field.					
When I sit down to write, I feel anxious.					
I enjoy the process of writing.					
I consider writing to be one of my strengths.					
I have generally positive attitude towards writing.					
I am confident in my skills as a writer.					

2. How often do you intend to employ the following strategies in your writing process?

	Never	Rarely	Sometimes	Often	Frequently
Brainstorming/ thought mapping/ Free writing					
Outlining					
Setting written goals					
Tracking productivity in a journal or application					
Analyzing disciplinary models					
Sharing your goals					

3. How often do you intend to seek help with your writing:

	Once a month	Twice a month	Three times a month	Once a week	More than once a week
From your advisor					
From another faculty member or postdoc in your field					
From graduate student peers within your discipline					
From people outside your discipline					
From the writing center					

1. How long do you plan to make the typical gap between two consecutive writing episodes on your project (in other words, if you write on a given day, how long is it you typically return to that project to continue writing)? Check one field.

Less than one day	One day	Two days	Up to one week	More than one week

6. How long do you plan to make your typical writing episode (without a break in which you disengage and do something else)? Write in the duration in **hours**, rounded to the quarter hour (e.g., 2.25 hours) _____

7. How many hours a week do you plan to typically write on this project? Write in the duration in **hours**, rounded to the quarter hour (e.g., 2.25 hours) _____

Daily Productivity Report

How many words did you write today?	
How many hours (in .25 hour increments) did you spend on-task today?	
What goal(s), if any, did you set for today?	
Did you meet your goal(s)?	

Crossing Divides: Engaging Extracurricular Writing Practices in Graduate Education and Professionalization

Laural L. Adams
VIRGINIA COMMONWEALTH UNIVERSITY

Megan Adams
UNIVERSITY OF FINDLAY

Pauline Baird
KANAZAWA TECHNICAL COLLEGE

Estee Beck
THE UNIVERSITY OF TEXAS AT ARLINGTON

Kristine L. Blair
DUQUESNE UNIVERSITY

April Conway
UNIVERSITY OF MICHIGAN

Lee Nickoson
BOWLING GREEN STATE UNIVERSITY

Martha Schaffer
CASE WESTERN RESERVE UNIVERSITY

Abstract: This collaborative chapter describes how we find that participation in strategic extracurricular writing experiences—experiences beyond those that formal, course-based graduate inquiry provide—benefit students and faculty in meaningful ways through contextualized and critically self-aware social practice. The chapter provides eight different perspectives on extracurricular writing experiences from both students and mentors and argues that these create and facilitate social spaces and interactions that contribute significantly to graduate education.

DOI: https://doi.org/10.37514/ATD-B.2020.0407.2.11

Keywords: Extracurricular Writing, Graduate Education, Identity, Enculturation, Reflection

> In graduate education, professional practices circulate as embedded, implied, and mystifying 'lore'. . . . [and] students attempt to glean professional expectations from peers and professors in patchworked ways—piecing together through time a sense of how to "do" reading, writing, collaborating, and professionalizing.
>
> —Carr, Rule & Taylor, 2013

Academics come to inhabit professional identities through a series of attempts to know the unknown, as Carr, Rule, and Taylor (2013) reveal in their richly situated study of graduate student literacy. The forging of professional identities happens not only through formal, course-based graduate inquiry, but also through participation in strategic extracurricular writing experiences such as collaborative research and publication opportunities (such as this chapter), which benefit students and faculty in meaningful ways as contextualized and critically self-aware social practice. As the larger collection demonstrates, much consideration has been given to traditional means of educating and professionalizing graduate students. While the chapters in the preceding sections focus on coursework and pedagogy for graduate student writing, this chapter delves into the formative social interactions that occur in and around the graduate curriculum, extracurricularly, through writing and collaboration among graduate students and faculty, as they are shaping and being shaped by the discipline.

Through a series of reflections from six former graduate students and two graduate faculty, we demonstrate how academics grow and change by building bridges across spaces traditionally regarded as separate and binary: student and teacher, classroom practices and professional scholarship, being and doing. These bridges, whether disciplinary, institutional, or personal are forged through socially constructed curricular and extracurricular writing experiences and play central roles in the development of graduate and faculty professional identities. The chapter embodies this bridge-building through the practice of an extracurricular writing experience as a socially situated act in both its impulse toward collaborative writing and revision and presenting readers with a cohesive reflection on the topic by retaining the multivocality that arises from a collection of unique graduate and faculty perspectives. This tension between thematic cohesion and multivocality is common to any vibrant field and its professionalizing practices. Traversing this tension fruitfully is at the heart of disciplinary enculturation: on the one hand, new members model their professional practices after disciplinary conventions while seeking, on the other, to bring something of themselves, something novel, to their participation. Casanave (2008, 2016) notes the importance of sharing stories of "invisible struggles" in this process as a way to alter the literacy practices of the academic community. With this in mind, the contributors here share their struggles with professionalizing, such as the performance anxiety associated with writing for publication along with the demands of occupying the dual roles of student and teacher, and the ways scholarship on graduate writing has addressed these struggles and enabled students to grow into their disciplinary identities.

This chapter presents reflections that arise out of three distinct vantage points: the deeply emotional links between writing and identity, writing that enhances the development of key elements of professional academic life, and faculty-sponsored extracurricular writing opportunities. Each reflection is founded on the idea that we build bridges to our disciplinary communities through social interaction that often (and increasingly) arises from extracurricular writing, and these practices enable us to reach our greater potential. The first three student reflections reveal deeply personal anxieties and experiences that often spur developing academics to begin the process of forging links to their academic communities through extracurricular writing. Megan Adams gives voice to the novice writer's deep desire for writing-related mentorship that supports early, tentative steps toward professional growth. April Conway reflects on the ways in which her extracurricular work as a poet informs an emerging disciplinary identity by stimulating creative thinking and writerly aesthetic. Pauline Baird shares how writing to learn with knowledgeable others enables her to cross into an unfamiliar, overwhelming expanse of disciplinary content, arguing that writing engenders mastery which then gives rise to professional identity. The next three reflections in the chapter explore ways in which specific extracurricular writing experiences enhance professional development in teaching, creating scholarship, and sustaining opportunities for deep thinking. Martha Schaffer explores written exchanges that inform graduate teachers' professional development, enabling graduate students (and their undergraduate pupils) toward fuller potentiality. Estee Beck describes the richness of extracurricular mentorship in the production of scholarly work, and suggests these opportunities are critical in the face of pressures to publish. Laural Adams considers the value of deep disciplinary engagement, arguing that students and their mentors must use extracurricular writing experiences to develop new scholars' thinking and to maintain their fields' vitality.

In the final reflections, two graduate educators and mentors describe how extracurricular projects—collaborative writing and multimodal writing—benefit not just students, but themselves and the institutions in which they serve. Lee Nickoson offers collaboration between teacher and student as a mode that enables each to work across such identities towards the other. Kris Blair describes how an online publication, *Computers and Composition Online*, enables her students to develop aptitudes outside the space of the classroom. The social nature of these projects opens up terrain for exploration and growth that is unavailable to students and faculty working in isolation or constrained by traditional student-teacher roles.

In closing, we hope that readers find the following provocations extend conversations on, and possibilities for, extracurricular writing experiences in their own academic lives.

Learning to Jump: Overcoming Anxiety in Graduate Student Writing through Extracurricular Mentoring (Megan Adams)

As I moved from a career in broadcast journalism to graduate school, I became increasingly tense about my writing. I was shifting genres as I crossed fields. This meant that while I felt like an expert in audio-visual composing, I was a novice in composing for academic audiences. The shift from expert to novice filled me with anxiety. Although support within the classroom, feedback from coursework, and reflective readings helped me become more aware of "imposter syndrome," and provided methods for improving my writing, the readings and discussions were not enough to dispel my self-doubt. Had it not been for the relationships built and strengthened outside the classroom with faculty mentors, I would not have been able to find my voice as an academic. The social interactions I experienced, along with the extracurricular support I received, allowed me to move past anxieties and grow as a writer in the discipline.

As I reflect on the experience, I am reminded of a moment from my childhood. When I was eight years old, my family and I hiked on an island in the middle of a lake, surrounded by steep rock cliffs. Somehow, I broke away from my family, climbed to the top of a cliff, yelled, "Watch me," and, without hesitation, jumped. Years later, writing for academic audiences felt similar: there is a feeling of wanting to be noticed, of forcing oneself to have no fear, and in the end, blindly jumping.

In their 2011 article, "Toward Graduate-Level Writing Instruction," Laura Micciche and Allison Carr, reported similar feelings of uncertainty among graduate students whose writerly identities are still being composed. Micciche describes a graduate course where she explores graduate students' highly emotional experiences of learning to write: "When I taught. . . this course for the first time, two accomplished well-respected graduate students in our program wept when asked to introduce themselves and narrate their writing processes to the class" (p. 479). Although these experiences point to the value of classroom experiences to help students "leap from the cliff," in my experience, it is the relationships I have formed with faculty members and colleagues that have helped me overcome fears of failure that paralyzed my ability to write. I am not alone in such feelings; recent efforts to make the literacy practices of graduate students more visible (Carr, Rule & Taylor, 2013) indicate that the ability to enter into scholarly conversations still eludes many graduate students. Overcoming this sense of paralysis requires openness and a willingness to fail. Students need more spaces where it is okay to be wrong, to explore, to share, and ultimately, to fail in order to become better writers, an observation also made by Michelle LaFrance and Steven Corbett in Chapter 12 of this collection, "Discourse Community Fail! Negotiating Choices in Success/Failure and Graduate-Level Writing Development."

These spaces can only be cultivated by faculty members who are sensitive to the fears that may prevent graduate students from speaking or writing, thus stalling, or even foreclosing altogether on student opportunities for rich learning experiences. While the classrooms I entered at Bowling Green State University provided some of these opportunities, the most profound and formative conversations occurred in alternative spaces. One of the most significant ways I learned to overcome my own self-doubt occurred through discussions with faculty that my anxieties were not uncommon. I recall a conversation with Kris Blair during her office hours in the first semester of my Ph.D. program, in which she detailed her own struggles with imposter syndrome at each step of the process, but how, by focusing on one project at a time, she made it through. There were many moments throughout my tenure as a graduate student where I would hear Kris' voice in my head, and the knowledge that a successful scholar had similar fears helped me to forge on in my studies.

Without voices of encouragement and constructive criticism, I wonder how long I would have continued to agonize in front of a computer screen thinking that nothing I could say was worthy of reading. I wonder how long I would have stood on the edge of the cliff, peering over but too fearful to jump, too fearful to risk falling flat. In order to bridge the divide between my identity as an expert in one field and my status as a novice in another, I had to make a proverbial "leap of faith." I had to reach out to my mentors and, thankfully, they reached back. As Carr so eloquently notes, "To become better writers, we must become more careful, more deliberate, and daring writers" (Micciche & Carr, 2011, p. 484). This means conquering the inner voice telling us we have nothing to say and could not possibly say it well if we did. With help though, over time, these leaps of faith in ourselves grow more graceful, and more regular. Then it is our turn to reach out to the next novice.

Writing as an Extracurricular Space for Language, Creativity, and the Social (April Conway)

When I began a Ph.D. program in rhetoric and composition after completing an MFA in poetry, I recognized that I was about to embark on a path that hinged on my strengths in academic prose, a genre I had only dabbled with since earning my BA. In my new academic life, I would leave behind, as poet Louise Glück (1994) wrote, "those poems that seemed so small on the page, but that swelled in my mind" (p. 4) for essays that would stretch out across pages, forsake lyrical tones, and leave behind imaginative realms—or so I believed. After all, I assumed, writing poetry is not done in the curricular spaces in my new discipline, nor did I see that it might inform my development. Yet, like rhetoric and composition, poetry is a socially structured discourse that belongs to a specialized community. Poets have been writing to and with each other for as far back as the craft goes. We build bridges with each other through language. In a very real sense, I collaborate with the contemporary poets with whom I share my work, those whose published work I devour, and those whose work stretches back through time and space. Rhetoric and composition, my new field, is also inherently social through and by language. As Gwendolyn D. Pough (2011) put it, however one identifies as a writer, "We all *do* language" (p. 302). It is precisely this assertion that has empowered me to be, as Pough said, "*un*disciplined," particularly as I write *across* disciplines. In other words, I learned that it is my attention to and training in language that allows me to write across disciplines.

Writing itself is in essence an extracurricular space, one not confined to the classroom in which students explore their burgeoning relationships to new fields and new communities. I share my experiences moving from creative writing to rhetoric and composition to demonstrate that students who are learning to write for new disciplines must be encouraged to attend to the social nature of writing as well as to the level of language with care and passion, because it is in this way that creative thinking and artful communication in academic discourse emerge. In this way, new members build bridges with disciplinary communities while also retaining their unique aptitudes and identities, and by extension, their capacities to contribute creatively.

The histories of poetry and rhetoric and composition have been explored before and accounts often highlight overlaps in their linguistic, social, and creative emphases. Douglas Hesse (2010) pointed to the "rhetorical force" found in belles-lettres, and noted they "carry information and ideas" while demonstrating aesthetic prowess (p. 48). Indeed, when I draw upon the training I received in studying poetry, including an understanding of the precision of word choice, the impact of structure, the musicality of language, and the power of metaphor, my writing in my new discipline becomes richer.

Furthermore, I can relish in the pleasure of the "process of language itself" (Said as cited in Smith, 1999, B9) to explore ideas through writing. With digital compositions, I use my ear for the sonic elements of language to explore aural modes (Halbritter, 2004; Yancey, 2004). For example, in a computer-mediated writing class taught by Kris, I created a technology autobiography in a video format and chose to "narrate" the video through music. As a result, spoken language was communicated through the moods represented in each featured song. (I should note here that, like the extracurricular relationships with mentors that Megan writes about, I felt comfortable exploring this sonic form of communication in part due to my extracurricular relationship with Kris. This is because, as editor of *Computers and Composition Online*, Kris worked with me as I published a book review for the journal).

Finally, as I am steeped in a new discipline, the creative expression I learned to develop as I worked in an earlier discipline can be turned towards mastery in my new field, especially in adopting and working with its foundational theories. Physicist David Bohm is noted for resisting narrow disciplinary specializations and synthesizing the thinking from disparate fields, such as physics, biology, and philosophy, in order to arrive at profound insights. He believed that creativity is at the root of theorizing (1998). Poet Richard Siken (2013) observed, ". . . poetry is the language of the imagination," and language and imagination is key to all academic disciplines, since through language imagination allows a writer-scholar to explore and develop new theories in and across fields. My background in poetry, then, provides a foundation for me to struggle with and to unlock the creative processes necessary to advance ideas I am beginning to shape, and it is foundational for enabling me to write myself into my new community. As graduate students, each of us arrives at the edge of our fields with our own disciplinary histories from which we might draw creative energies, theoretical perspectives, and unique relationships to language and writing.

Our pasts serve as extracurricular writing spaces and the ground from which—through care and passion—we bridge into new communities. This socio-historic backdrop accompanies us even while we draw on contemporaries, on emerging and experienced writers in our new disciplines, creating webs of relationships in which we write, thus highlighting the social nature of all writing.

Graduate Knowledge-Building with a "Write to Learn" Approach (Pauline Baird)

Early in my graduate studies, I encountered a wall: while I knew a lot about Teaching English to Speakers of Other Languages (TESOL), I knew little about the field I was drawn to—rhetoric and composition. I stood at the intersections of two fields, TESOL and rhetoric and composition, wondering not only how to become knowledgeable about the latter discipline, its methodologies and paradigms, but also about how to amass enough knowledge quickly to cross-pollinate these two disciplines for my own research interests. I thought conducting independent classroom research would help me learn more about both fields. What I did not expect was that my extracurricular writing (experiences) relationships would reorient my research of writing practices and perspectives on what writing in the discipline looks like.

When I think of the "burgeoning relationships" formed in extracurricular writing endeavors, as April notes in the previous reflection, I think of relationships in which knowledgeable others—colleagues and editors—in extracurricular communities challenge graduate writers' knowledge about writing. Here is a story: In the years after earning my TESOL MA, while teaching in Japan, colleagues and conference submission editors became part of my extracurricular writing network. I recall a more experienced colleague challenging my fledgling attempts at conducting research on how ESL learners compose by asserting, "But you are not doing 'real' research." In her view, I did not have charts and numbers to warrant my claim to "real" research. She was not alone in this view, for in an attempt to publish an article on my research, an anonymous peer reviewer said of the paper, "This thing must never see the light of day!" These experiences not only highlighted my lack of requisite knowledge of disciplinary research methodologies, but also, they triggered deep self-doubt—a feeling not alien to the more than ten Ph.D. professors I have interviewed on their own publishing experiences. I think of Micciche and Carr (2011), who have noted similarly that graduate students and scholars alike experience apprehension, personal shame, inadequacy, emptiness followed by terror, and even feel as if they "sweat blood" over their writing (p. 486). Clearly, the angst of solitary writing attends each generation of novice writers often throughout their careers, but *kairotic* moments also attend those who persevere. This perseverance is often fostered in extracurricular spaces through the act of writing and conversations about writing.

Here is another story: After submitting an article for publication, a reviewer asked me to reconsider changing the word "traumatized" to "apprehensive" when I described my writing anxieties, arguing that I would project an image of myself to posterity that I might regret later. I deferred to him and changed the word, not because I believed he was right, but because I recognized his act as care for me, someone he only knew through writing. The mentoring and collaborative spirit in this exchange happened outside the classroom through the medium of writing, and it happens often enough that we must regard extracurricular writing as fundamentally social, even at its most solitary. It is in these spaces that we build bridges to our new communities and locate our writing selves within or alongside others.

For example, I recall my recognition of the deep significance of audience when I shared some notes on an assignment I had written in my local Guyanese dialect. I defied the usual conventions. The reader, a fellow graduate student, seemed puzzled and asked, "Who is your audience?" I said, "Me," and in that instant, the idea of "owning one's voice" became important. My choice to speak in the vernacular helped me build a sense of my own ethos, my confidence in the ability to claim expertise and make an argument. Unbeknownst to me, I had been practicing the "write to learn" process. For me, writing to learn is an extracurricular practice that continues to link me with the disciplinary community, even when I am my only audience. The write to learn approach has the potential to foster writers' knowledge of complicated textual content and unfamiliar disciplinary ground, and even one's sense of self emerging and growing in a new disciplinary context.

When we write to learn, we write for ourselves, and the language we use becomes a "tool for discovering, for shaping meaning, and for reaching understanding" (Fulwiler & Young 1982/2000, p. x). Richard Gebhardt (1977) advised aspiring teachers to include the write to learn approach in their repertoire of "productive methodologies to help students . . . write" (p. 137). Gebhardt promoted the write to learn process in his courses for would-be composition teachers *by writing*, by having them use writing to master the content.

I continue to engage this practice on my own outside the classroom. For example, in a log I keep of my conversations with professors and scholars, it has become clear to me that most have learned to write *by writing*. In essence, even the most experienced writers write to learn. And whether they write alone or write collaboratively, they engage the insights of peers (Olsen & Raffeld, 1987; Reeves, 1997). But the write to learn approach simply cannot be made regularly available to students through coursework and seminars. Graduate students must be encouraged to use the practice extracurricularly, and though it seems solitary, paradoxically, write to learn bridges the individual to the discipline through deeply personal disciplinary knowledge-making.

Extracurricular Writing in Graduate Teaching Mentorships (Martha Wilson Schaffer)

While Megan, April, and Pauline describe their use of extracurricular writing as a way of attending to their personal experiences of coming to a discipline as new graduate students, my reflection considers how extracurricular writing can help graduate students resolve the tensions of their dual roles as student and teacher. Jessica Restaino's (2012) *First Semester* sheds light on the conflicted space occupied by graduate teaching assistants (GTAs) as she follows four graduate student composition teachers struggling with process theory, day-to-day classroom practices, student resistance, and grading—the "struggle to survive" as Restaino describes it (p. 22). Not only does Restaino (2012) reveal the intellectual, emotional, and professional tensions inherent in this "middle ground," she emphasizes the peril of not acknowledging these tensions. Her argument is for a GTA experience that is both pedagogically and academically rich through programs and professors working "to nurture students' and teachers' collective potential for making change by giving them a space for experimentation. . . that makes change likely and possible" (p. 104). Having been a graduate student who mentored new GTAs, I can attest to the value of using extracurricular writing to experiment not only with the practicalities of teaching, but also the affective experience of teaching. In other words, extracurricular writing can help graduate students across the disciplines respond to the intellectual and emotional challenges of being teacher and student simultaneously.

Our institution provided bi-weekly, semester-long courses to new GTAs who will be teaching first-year composition (FYC), but we also arranged for new GTAs to have individual weekly meetings with an experienced peer mentor. While the course and the meetings provided GTAs with practical classroom activities, theories of writing instruction, and sample essay prompts and syllabi, there was simply not enough time for affective matters such as working through frustrations with students, balancing teaching and coursework, or handling feelings of vulnerability in the classroom. Discussions between GTAs and mentors must be supplemented by writing that originates beyond the curricular context, often circulating in the heart of the night or the middle of the weekend when lessons are prepped and papers are graded.

For example, email exchanges between me and my mentees constituted rich extracurricular writing experiences, particularly as new GTAs strove to provide composition students written feedback on their essays, feedback that struck the delicate balance between critique and encouragement. It is a particularly personal, and yet deeply social, element of teaching (and writing), and GTAs struggle with their own emotional and intellectual reactions to student ideas and expressions as well as with the impact that their own words have on students. GTAs wrote to me: Am I being too harsh? Am I being too easy? It is a good paper, but it was late; what should I tell the student? I know what she is trying to say, but she just isn't getting there; how do I help her? Am I saying too much or too little to my students? And I wrote back with suggestions for revision, questions to provoke further reflection, and my own words of encouragement. These private written exchanges were about more than the practicalities of providing useful feedback; they were about interaffectivity.

Megan Watkins (2009, 2010) defines interaffectivity as "a process of mutual recognition realized as affective transactions that at one and the same time can cultivate the desire to learn and the desire to teach" (2010, p. 271). This mutual recognition occurs as social interaction between students and teachers (or between GTAs and their mentors) and enriches the process of teaching and learning. In order to help give rise to this form of relating, the GTAs and I relied on extracurricular writing spaces. The GTAs also used similar spaces with their own students toward the same ends. Engaging in this interaffectivity was a powerful experience for me, the GTAs, and the students, all of us drawing strength and energy from these mutual exchanges of ideas, inspirations, and intentions. Sharing feelings and thoughts through extracurricular writing enables GTAs to "try things on": to experiment with affects (their own and those of their students), forge relationships with other novice teachers and scholars, and explore social practices that shape us as we struggle with our roles in new academic communities. Through this form of extracurricular writing, it is possible for GTAs to experience graduate school as a "bloom-space" (Gregg & Seigworth, 2010), fragrant and stimulating, from which they are gathering the affective energies to be writers, scholars, teachers, and the deeply personal desire to contribute to the discipline, to society, and to each other.

The Role of Extracurricular Mentorship in Transforming Graduate Students' Seminar Papers to Publications (Estee Beck)

The vibrant space of extracurricular writing experiences provides graduate students with opportunities to learn how to write for and with disciplines—to enter into the unique contours of the discourse and register and respond to the fluctuations of scholarship and research. In turn, this gives students the opportunity to sample what it means to have a productive scholarly life. Additionally, teachers and scholars in English studies have explored how to mentor graduate students into disciplinary conversations responsibly (see Olsen & Taylor, 1997). These discussions focus on practical advice for all members entering into their professions, but also examine the role of graduate student publishing (Lauer, 1997) and the role of scholarship to teaching (Boyer, 1990). Mentorship plays a strong role for graduate students learning how to enter such conversations. Thus, I offer my journey of engaging with extracurricular scholarship, which led to the acceptance of a journal article, but only through mentoring relationships was I able to keep moving in the face of rejection.

As a graduate student, I have felt both uncertain about publishing my work in professional venues and enthused as I enjoy the messiness of the writing process. I have been fortunate to receive mentorship from faculty at my home institution through formal coursework, informal mentoring, and advice from peer colleagues. These mentoring relationships have allowed me to engage in extracurricular scholarship and projects; however, like countless other graduate students, I struggle with anxieties about publication, recognizing that entering scholarly discourse is a recursive process of trial and error.

I have come to see conversations about writing involve not only demystifying publishing practices, but also deeply reflecting upon the values, habits, and persistence that writers carry with them into writing spaces. For example, early in my doctoral coursework, I wrote a seminar paper exploring the ethical considerations in using student real-life identities in class blogs and wikis. Then in another course on publication—a curricular space for learning how and where to publish—I had the opportunity to revise this paper. As my ideas developed, so did a persistent sense of imposter syndrome that lurked at the edge of my thoughts: I wasn't a writer. I wasn't a scholar. What could I possibly have to contribute? I went to my professor with these doubts, and she assured me that the feelings were common, that I should push them aside, and challenge myself—prove I could participate in scholarly discussions. Like Megan, I took a leap of faith, and I submitted my work to a journal.

A few months later, I received a rejection letter with reviewer feedback. I felt disappointed—*in myself*, for sending a manuscript that I could now see needed more research, better organization. Despite the self-criticism that the rejection engendered in me, the submission process yielded two encouraging events. First, the reviewers were generous with their feedback. One had taken care to point out places where I could refine the argument and had suggested additional sources. The other had attended and responded to the overall organization of the article. After my initial disappointment in myself, I revisited their comments and saw them for what they were: mentoring. Their feedback was an act of generosity extended to a fledgling member of the field. I felt encouraged.

The second event that enabled me to move forward with the project occurred when my professor offered to reread the work with the reviewers' feedback in mind. The course had ended, but she made herself available outside its bounds, and helped me reflect on their advice and devise a revision plan based on it. The words of unfamiliar reviewers, of experienced members of the discipline I hoped to join, made more sense when they were restated—"translated"—by a mentor with whom I am familiar into a language with which I am familiar. From this feedback, I completed a deep revision of the manuscript—the kind of deep revision William Germano (2013) discusses in *From Dissertation to Book*.

I submitted the work again, and after a revise and resubmit, and additional revisions on my part, the peer-reviewed journal accepted it. Through mentorship, I entered an extracurricular space, scholarly publishing, and crossed divides from seminar paper to journal article, from *student writer* to *writer*.

This personal example illustrates not only the importance of persistence, but also the range of mentor-related practices that take place in a disciplinary community. Once I experienced this community as fundamentally supportive, it gave me the strength to persist with my writing. My faculty mentor was a lynchpin in that process, helping me situate feedback from experienced reviewers, helping me learn their language. Her mentorship helped me see the reviewers as mentors and sustained me through the writing process. Without knowing it, these people formed a support network for me and helped me gain confidence in my abilities to write for scholarly audiences.

However, while scholarly publishing was a place for me to build a bridge into the academic community, publishing in graduate school is not necessarily right for all students. In a special issue of the profession in *College Composition and Communication*, Doug Hesse (2013) reflects on the changing nature of scholarly expectations for newly-minted Ph.D.s as compared to those when he entered the profession in the 1980s, and he questions the sustainability of such expectations. Instead, we must recognize the complexities associated with these new demands and foster mentorship in extracurricular spaces, such as in interactions between students and established colleagues. Such mentorship amounts to a generosity of spirit that keeps disciplines thriving despite ever-mounting pressures to publish.

Extracurricular Spaces for Deep Disciplinary Engagement in Graduate Education (Laural Adams)

Graduate students yearn to be part of the "conversation," whether that means interacting with a community of peers writing and presenting at conferences to work through a discipline's difficult issues or contributing with other symbolic acts, such as teaching, to make an impact. Disciplines constantly evolve, and as they change, so too do the methods by which new members come to know them. Curricula reify approaches which serve as bridges between new members and their disciplinary communities, and graduate educators assess and modify these approaches in response to the shifting needs of new students in shifting educational contexts. Eventually, the discipline's new members participate with more experienced members to instantiate their discipline through its communities, infusing them with vitality and innovation. As Martha points out earlier, disciplines offer new members a wide variety of modes of participation (e.g., teacher-researcher, researcher, teacher, administrator, adjunct). However, every discipline needs some part of its body dedicated to deeply engage the discipline's conversations in order to advance its scholarly questions and concerns.

In today's academy, taking on disciplinary questions and concerns through scholarship is a role that increasingly goes to a privileged few with the luxury of time and energy to consider them. Graduate programs are increasingly pressed to demonstrate sufficient "completion rates," and to retool programs so that students who might not find jobs in the academy can find them elsewhere. Across the disciplines, curricular spaces that had traditionally engendered deep immersion are modified to make room for other emergent aptitudes and literacies. For example, as Kris points out in a later section in this chapter, digital literacy is critical for graduate students, whether they aspire to work in the academy or forge their professional identities elsewhere. Ultimately, shrinking opportunities for a range of new members to deeply engage their discipline's scholarship limits its potential for growth and creativity. Unfortunately, to make matters worse, graduate students are inclined to forgo deep immersion in the face of pressures to publish *before* graduating in order to compete for increasingly limited academic positions. Those who feel they must secure several quick publications can find it difficult to spend time deliberating on core ideas or fundamental debates. For me, the pressure to finish my program with a lengthy CV left me anxious that I might have to forgo the deep disciplinary engagement that had traditionally been found by those who came before me and, through their engagement, made my discipline such fertile ground.

I was to discover, however, that deep disciplinary immersion need not occur in curricular spaces. For example, students in my program devised a forum to regularly inquire about common interests among us and to organize extracurricular study groups to explore them. For me, writing book chapters has been the extracurricular experience that has offered the greatest opportunities for deep disciplinary engagement. However, these were not simple projects that I could publish quickly. They were interdisciplinary, a key component in stimulating the deep immersion I was seeking and also responding to the contemporary university's call for relevancy by spanning disciplines. These projects required that I learn in whole new terrains and make links across disparate bodies of scholarship. For example, in one chapter, I linked Herman and Chomsky's (2008/1988) "propaganda model" to activity theory (Engeström, 1987), arguing that together these lenses could explain the "green" discourse now so prevalent on university websites. In another chapter, I argued that my field's response to open educational resources should be informed by a "deep ecology" perspective where all stakeholders recognize and foster mutual interests, and most importantly, do not exploit those to whom access to education is so critical. These projects provided me with opportunities to explore not just the issues in my own field, but to experiment with "interdisciplinarity." Later, I would fuse an interest in cognitive psychology research on mental models (Johnson-Laird, 1983) with the notion of writing ecologies (Cooper, 1986) for my dissertation.

Through these projects, I have developed the ability to creatively link ideas across fields, enter new discourse communities, navigate my way to their foundational resources, and address questions in my own field by looking beyond it. And what a delight to experience the mentoring relationship that book editors have with their junior contributors! From these projects, I have forged lasting professional ties and endorsements beyond the scope of my dissertation committee or my program's faculty on the value of my academic contributions. Book chapters, often regarded as the ugly stepchild among the possible publishing venues, require intense focus, the courage to explore unfamiliar ground, and the patience to wait for a book's publication, even while one's peers celebrate the rapid turn-around of publications in other forms.

Retaining spaces for deep disciplinary engagement has not come without other costs, as well. For example, I have yet to produce scholarship for the multimodal outlets where some of my field's most innovative work is emerging, such as *Computers and Composition Online* and *Kairos: A Journal of Rhetoric, Technology, and Pedagogy*, despite my love of their encompassing spirit and innovative approaches to sharing—even enacting—knowledge. But the deep engagement I had with the book chapters has nonetheless inched me toward my version of "a contributing member" of the field. The climate in higher education increasingly pressures graduate students through curricular structures to forgo deep engagement and favor marketability and job placement, but students who want to cultivate deep immersion can through extracurricular opportunities such as these. Taking responsibility for one's own professional enculturation by exploring extracurricular spaces requires independence, curiosity, courage, and stamina, because as a graduate student, you worry you may not fit the mold set forth by your programs' design. This can be discomfiting when the ultimate aim is to be part of the community that gave you your start, took you under its wing. Yet, disciplinary communities, and most of their members, recognize the importance of divergence in fostering innovation and growth. Moreover, academics do most of their "disciplinary work" outside of curricular spaces, so it makes sense that professors encourage their students to view these spaces as integral to their development, and when such development feels personal, this is the kind of deep engagement that produces deep personal identity and the sense of standing in relation to a community. These spaces for personal and professional growth are often constituted by writing, whether a student is commenting on a scholar's recent blog post or composing a book chapter. When we are deeply engaged, these spaces are personal spaces, and they link us to our communities. Graduate students should be encouraged to forge such spaces and also to build bridges to others out of them because identity, both professional and personal, is ultimately communal.

Working in the Spaces Between: Engaging the Extracurricular (Lee Nickoson)

Carr et al. (2013) forward digital literacy narratives as a method for graduate students to engage similarly critical self- and group reflections. Reflections such as these, they go on to argue, ready students to consider their place in a complex disciplinary ecology. The preceding six narratives perform the transformative reflection Carr and her co-authors describe, and, as Laural's narrative persuasively argues, readiness and self-advocacy brought each to purposeful action through engagement in extracurricular collaborative writing projects. Beyond the formal space of the graduate seminar, participation with and reflections on extracurricular writing establish students as makers. These spaces—the spaces between coursework and visible, required/expected sites of academic performance and assessment of those student-based performances—have become powerful points of reflection and connection for me as well as for the students. I learn most about graduate students as new(er) members of my own field. Such learning opportunities invariably bring me to (re)consider my own position in the discipline. When faculty and graduate student scholars elect to write alongside one another, we expand our knowledge *about* and place(s) *in* this ecology. We learn (about) ourselves when we write with each other; we write (with) each other in part to learn who we are and who, as writers, researchers, teachers, and even tenured faculty members of the discipline, we might (still) want to become.

Like many of my program faculty colleagues, I often collaborate with graduate students outside the classroom. These collaborations, which can take the form of articles, book chapters, or conference presentations, seem to grow organically from conversations—engaged, curious exchanges—that may originate in a seminar classroom, in a crowded hotel hallway during a busy conference, or in the department mailroom. In these extracurricular spaces, I have opportunities to learn about my graduate student colleagues' intellectual wonderings, and these conversations result in collaborations with them.

Because the projects arise organically, they enable me to interact with students in less structured ways than the graduate seminar affords. Collaborations with students introduce me to new scholarly conversations, methods, genres, and modes of delivering writing scholarship. The process keeps me energized and curious in ways that writing on my own, or even with other faculty, simply does not. Extracurricular student-faculty collaboration also allows spaces for deepened, often sustained professional relationships with co-authors or co-presenters. Collaborative scholarship introduces occasions and purposes for graduate students and faculty to work—and to work *differently*—together.

Of course, such collaborations also present very real demands on each participant. The greatest demands I experience revolve around issues of time, labor, and collaborator resistance. The first two are not likely to surprise any academic, faculty, or graduate student. As faculty, I must manage multiple professional responsibilities, some of which are visible to my graduate-student collaborators—such as classroom teaching. However, committee work, advising, and developing my own scholarly projects are less visible, and students may need help understanding my time constraints, just as I may need to understand theirs. Also, collaborations require significantly more time than solo efforts. Planning, drafting, reading, revising, revising yet again with one or more collaborators is messy. Lastly, I must consider how my participation in any collaborative writing project will be perceived by institutional merit and promotion committees, which may or may not recognize their value.

Student-faculty collaborations are most productive when each author brings their full skillset to the table. Collaboration asks students and faculty alike to develop working relationships that value and, in fact, rely on all collaborators as active contributors to achieving the end goals of any multi-authored project. Often, however, I find I must respect graduate student colleagues' seeming reluctance to, or even their active resistance to assuming a position of authority or the role of scholarly expert in our collaborations. I constructively challenge my colleagues' reluctance. It is this tension, which arises from displacing the power dynamics of the more formal, traditional student/teacher relationship, I find to be simultaneously the most limiting and most rewarding aspect of graduate student-faculty collaborations. In contrast to hierarchical collaboration, this collaboration is rewarding and fruitful when each person feels they can openly assume the position of engaged, curious collaborator: co-researcher, co-author, co-learner. This "dialogic collaboration," as Lisa Ede and Andrea Lunsford (1990) described it, is "loosely structured," and collaborators engage "multiple and shifting roles as the project progresses" (p. 275). Despite the fact that students have not yet completed their formal enculturation, they have insights that contribute to disciplinary conversations, thus helping to shape the field.

Kris Fleckenstein, Clay Spinuzzi, Carole Clark Papper, and Rebecca Rickly (2008) argue that researchers and their "active involvement in and contribution to a research ecosystem" contribute to the construction of the very ecologies they aim to study (p. 395). Student and faculty collaborations, too, share in this ecology formation. When successful, student-faculty collaborations also allow the faculty collaborator opportunities to experience disciplinary conversations, and indeed the discipline itself, (once again) anew.

Extracurricular Multimodal Composing (Kris Blair)

Even as various fields refigure their definitions of writing and literacy from the alphabetic to the multimodal, my longstanding concern is that graduate students' literate practices are too frequently overlooked in these discussions, based on the false presumption that they already possess sufficient confidence and expertise (Carr et al., 2013) to compose in digital spaces. As a result, another presumption is that integrating multimodal composing in the classroom is an undergraduate, rather than a graduate, goal. Yet without the opportunity to develop online professional identities, and to do so in extracurricular ways that extend beyond the classroom, graduate students are doomed to privilege the very alphabetic literacies and academic borders with their future students that many scholarly conversations, including this one, attempt to subvert.

One example of such extracurricular opportunity is through *Computers and Composition Online*, a fully online, multimodal journal that I have edited since 2002. Once it moved to Bowling Green State University, the journal was largely run by graduate student editors, with whom I collaborated to secure submissions and then shepherded them through the digital composing process toward eventual online publication. That a number of my co-authors find the Carr, Rule, and Taylor webtext a meaningful touchstone in discussing the anxieties graduate students face in developing disciplinary literacies is significant to me in that the piece appears in *Computers and Composition Online* as both a rhetorical and multimodal example of "unlocking creative processes," something April contends in her earlier narrative.

Indeed, as I have learned during my time as editor, involving graduate students in the online editorial process has the potential to foster scholarly publication models that encourage new voices in new media and foster a form of graduate writing that is both extracurricular and collaborative. For our team of student editors, this occurs in several ways:

1. **Design.** Very often authors, including more established voices, have limited experience in digital composing. Thus, our section editors have served

not only as consultants but also as mentors and co-designers, in some cases receiving design and author credit as they oversee development of submissions that include the use of web-authoring, digital imaging, video, and audio-editing tools. This role ultimately enables that particular contributor to undertake future projects in ways that are more socially aware of the highly collaborative nature of the digital composing process and that also impact the future digital collaboration of the section editors as well. In my own digital collaborations with Estee and alumna Mariana Grohowski, for instance, we often worked side by side in a computer lab, late into the evening or over a holiday break, each playing varying, but always co-equal roles with code, design, and image/text editing.

2. **Networking.** As an editor, I have encouraged graduate students, even as they work with online authors, to view these conversations as networking opportunities, perhaps enabling future collaborations and fostering an emerging professional reputation and identity for our students as digital scholars. For example, section editors and other students have interviewed leading scholars such as Kathleen Blake Yancey, Chris Anson, and Cynthia Selfe & H. Lewis Ulman about the role of new media and multimodality on the teaching of writing. These connections have in several instances fostered invitations to participate in professional development forums and editorial partnerships, such as Ohio State University's annual Digital Media and Composition Institute and the separate Computers and Composition Digital Press.

3. **Authoring.** For both graduate student editors and other students in our graduate program, there are ample opportunities to experiment with digital composing, often leading to shorter multimodal publications such as book or software reviews that appear in the journal. Frequently, our Reviews Editor works with fellow students as a coach, helping them to improve the design, accessibility, and navigability of these early submissions. These initial experimentations with remediating a traditional academic genre can lead to larger projects as well, allowing students to circulate their scholarship more widely. Moreover, I am delighted not only that April, Estee, and Megan have published such reviews in the journal, but also that as a result of these extracurricular publishing processes, the relationship I have with these women and other former graduate students has evolved from mentor-mentee to co-equal members of a community of digital writing scholars.

4. **Mentoring.** Although I have focused upon the mentoring that occurs within a specific extracurricular, digital writing space, another important type of mentoring occurs through the role graduate students play in fostering digital composing among their own colleagues and students once they leave BGSU. For me, such efforts represent a form of sustainability, as these new

faculty engage in the same digital composing processes and social practices that lead to submissions to *Computers and Composition Online* and other online journals, including *Enculturation* and *Kairos: A Journal of Rhetoric, Technology, and Pedagogy*. Notably, the digital collaborations I have since engaged in with both Megan and Estee in particular have involved reciprocal mentoring in which they contribute as much to my growth as a digital scholar as I have to theirs during our shared time at BGSU. As much as digital literacy specialists advocate multimodality across the undergraduate writing curriculum, that goal is dependent on multimodality across the graduate curriculum not only in classrooms but also in other extracurricular, professional development spaces. A forum such as *Computers and Composition Online* has played a substantial role in fostering that goal. For Kathleen Fitzpatrick, "Writing and publishing in networked environments might require a fundamental change not just in the tools with which we work, or in the ways we interact with our tools, but in our sense of ourselves as we do that work" (2011, p. 55). Sustaining academic relevance across the disciplines, and my relevance as a graduate educator and journal editor, depends on this shift in professional self to view the multimodal literacy acquisition of graduate students as a social process of extracurricular mentoring and modeling. Inevitably, this process helps, as Estee powerfully notes, move graduate students from "*student writer* to *writer*" and shapes their critical self-awareness of technology's impact both on their emerging faculty identities and on the literate identities of the undergraduate students they serve.

Conclusion

Each of us has reflected upon what it means to cross divides between curricular and extracurricular spaces. At best, the liminal space within which graduate students operate allows a sense of becoming—a fostering of growth and development as writers, scholars, and teachers. Here, extracurricular support and mentorship enables graduate students to bridge the space that separates them from their burgeoning identities as writers in new disciplines. Graduate students need opportunities to be composers through reciprocal mentoring models that translate to what they will do as future faculty. While extracurricular writing need not be collaborative, we argue it is always social. We also find (for example in the writing of this chapter) that a collaborative model between graduate students and faculty enables us to celebrate our own metamorphoses as we learn about and participate in the rich writerly lives of both our lesser and more experienced colleagues. Ultimately, by taking advantage of extracurricular writing experiences, graduate students and faculty alike learn together to cross the material, social, and cultural constraints of writing that shape academic life.

In her book *Women Writing the Academy* (1993), Gesa Kirsch contends that much of academic writing "reflects male forms/norms of discourse because it is based on notions of competition and winning, and it privileges formal, reasoned arguments" (p. 19). Kirsch relies specifically on the observations of Cynthia Caywood and Gillian Overing (1987), who noted that the academy values the expository over the exploratory, the argumentative over the autobiographical, and the impersonal over the subjective, and thus called for "attention to the social, cultural, and political dimensions that shape writing and academic life" (p. 126). The perspectives shared in our chapter and throughout this collection reflect that call to "pay attention" (Selfe, 1999) to the material and ideological conditions that enable and constrain our identities as writers across genres, modalities, and disciplinary contexts.

Clearly, we are not alone. Kirsch's initial work, along with those we have cited throughout this chapter, particularly Carr et al. (2013) as well as Micciche and Carr (2011), foreground the need for graduate programs to more consistently mentor their students, a process that requires engaging them beyond the confines of the classroom. But how and where can we provide extracurricular space and time for students, and their faculty, to experiment with authorial voice and to understand the ways in which those voices can transform what it means to compose? As we discovered through our writing process on this chapter, it is important to understand collaborative composing as an affective enterprise in which graduate students, professors, teachers, and scholars can reciprocally impact one another in ways that promote the potential of each participant to *become*. Enabling collaboration has the potential to disrupt the hierarchy among these participants to better equalize identities, perspectives, and voices, and to sustain disciplines that need the creative input that their members can generate under the right conditions. To that end, mentors and graduate program administrators should help students recognize the disciplinary and larger academic environments, which lie beyond the classroom, so that they can more proactively craft and reflect upon their own identities in ways that balance scholarship, teaching, and service, and allow them to assume formative roles in their fields.

Graduate students and their mentors should embrace shifts in literate practice, from the creative to the expository to the multimodal, that will in turn shape the future of the discipline and its professionalization practices. Embracing change often requires students and faculty to participate beyond the classroom, where curricula struggle to keep pace with the changes occurring in the disciplines. It requires faculty to nudge their graduate students into the places where disciplines are actually constructed and instantiated, and these tend to be extracurricular writing spaces. As the adage suggests, the only constant is change, both inside and outside the academy. Indeed, John Trimbur (1993) wrote in his foreword to Kirsch's book, "higher learning is not just about disciplining its practitioners . . . but that the practitioners themselves . . . can seize the academic tools of production for their own ends" (p. xi). Our ends have been, as Trimbur described it, "to make academic work into socially useful knowledge" (p. xi). For us, that use value extends beyond this chapter and into our current and future roles as colleagues and mentors committed to providing and calling for extracurricular spaces that enable sustained reflection among diverse voices about the challenges of developing writerly lives that cross curricular and extracurricular divides.

References

Bohm, D. (1998). *On creativity*. Routledge.
Boyer, E. L. (1990). *Scholarship reconsidered: Priorities of the professoriate*. Carnegie Foundation for the Advancement of Teaching.
Carr, A. D., Rule, H. J. & Taylor, K. T. (2013). Literacy in the raw: Collecting, sharing, and circulating graduate student literacy narratives. *Computers & Composition Online*. http://cconlinejournal.org/winter2013/literacy_raw/index.html.
Casanave, C. P. (2008). Learning participatory practices in graduate school: Some perspective-taking by a mainstream educator. In C. P. Casanave & X. Li (Eds.), *Learning the literacy practices of graduate school: Insiders' reflections on academic enculturation* (pp. 14–31). University of Michigan Press.
Casanave, C. P. (2016). What advisors need to know about the invisible 'real-life' struggles of doctoral dissertation writers. In S. Simpson, N. A. Caplan, M. Cox & T. Phillips (Eds.), *Supporting graduate student writers: Research, curriculum, and program design* (pp. 97–116). University of Michigan Press.
Caywood, C. & Overing, G. (1987). *Teaching writing: Pedagogy, gender, and equity*. State University of New York Press.
Cooper, M. M. (1986). The ecology of writing. *College English, 48*(4), 364–375.
Ede, L. & Lunsford, A. (1990). *Singular text/plural authors: Perspectives on collaborative authoring*. Southern Illinois University Press.
Engeström, Y. (1987). *Learning by expanding: An activity-theoretical approach to developmental research*. Orienta-Konsultit Oy.
Fitzpatrick, K. (2011). *Planned obsolescence: Publishing, technology, and the future of the academy*. NYU Press.
Fleckenstein, K., Spinuzzi, C., Papper, C. C. & Rickly, R. (2008). The importance of harmony: An ecological metaphor for writing research. *College Composition and Communication, 60*(2), 388–419.
Fulwiler, T. & Young, A. (Eds.). (2000). Introduction. In *Language connections: Writing and reading across the curriculum*. (pp. i–xiii). The WAC Clearinghouse. https://wac.colostate.edu/books/landmarks/language-connections/ (Original work published 1982, National Council of Teachers of English).
Gebhardt, R. C. (1977). Balancing theory with practice in the training of writing teachers. *College Composition and Communication, 28*(2), 134–140.
Germano, W. (2013). *From dissertation to book*. University of Chicago Press.
Glück, L. (1994). *Proofs and theories: Essays on poetry*. Ecco Press.
Gregg, M. & Seigworth, G. J. (2010). *The affect theory reader*. Duke University Press.

Halbritter, S. (2004). *Sound arguments: Aural rhetoric in multimedia composition* [Doctoral dissertation, University of North Carolina at Chapel Hill]. ProQuest Dissertations & Theses (305168799).

Herman, E. S. & Chomsky, N. (2008). *Manufacturing consent: The political economy of the mass media*. Bodley Head.

Hesse, D. (2010). The place of creative writing in composition studies. *College Composition and Communication, 62*(1), 31–52.

Hesse, D. (2013). Sustainable expectations? *College Composition and Communication, 65*(1), 16–18.

Kirsch, G. (1993). *Women writing the academy: Audience, authority, and transformation.* Southern Illinois University Press.

Johnson-Laird, P. N. (1983). *Mental models: Towards a cognitive science of language, inference, and consciousness*. Harvard University Press.

Lauer, J. M. (1997). Graduate students as active members of the profession: Some questions for mentoring. In G. Olson & T. W. Taylor (Eds.), *Publishing in rhetoric and composition* (pp. 229–235). State University of New York Press.

Micciche, L. R. & Carr, A. D. (2011). Toward graduate-level writing instruction. *College Composition and Communication, 62*(3), 477–501.

Olson, G. A. & Taylor, T. W. (1997). *Publishing in rhetoric and composition*. State University of New York Press.

Olson, M. W. & Raffeld, P. (1987). The effects of written comments on the quality of student

Pough, G. D. (2011). It's bigger than comp/rhet: Contested and *un*disciplined. *College Composition and Communication, 63*(2), 301–313.

Reeves, L. (1997). Minimizing writing apprehension in the learner-centered classroom. *The English Journal, 86*(6), 38–45.

Restaino, J. (2012). *First semester: Graduate students, teaching writing and the challenge of the middle ground*. Southern Illinois University Press.

Selfe, C. (1999). *Technology and literacy in the 21st century: The importance of paying attention*. Southern Illinois University Press.

Siken, R. (2013). *Why*. University of Arizona Poetry Center. https://poetry.arizona.edu/library/history-of-readings.

Smith, D. (1999, Feb 27). When ideas get lost in bad writing; Attacks on scholars include barbed contest with 'prizes.' *The New York Times*. https://www.nytimes.com/1999/02/27/arts/when-ideas-get-lost-bad-writing-attacks-scholars-include-barbed-contest-with.html.

Trimbur, J. (1993). Foreword. In G. Kirsch, *Women writing the academy: Audience, authority, and transformation* (pp. ix-xi). Southern Illinois University Press.

Watkins, M. (2009). Teachers' tears and the affective geography of the classroom. *Emotion, Space, and Society, 4*, 137–143.

Watkins, M. (2010). Desiring recognition, accumulating affect. In M. Gregg & G. J. Seigworth (Eds.), *The affect theory reader* (pp. 267285). Duke University Press.

Yancey, K. B. (2004). Made not only in words: Composition in a new key. *College Composition and Communication, 56*(2), 297-328.

PART 4: "Stop reading. Start writing. The best dissertation is a done dissertation." OR Examining Discourse Communities and Genres

Soo Hyon Kim

University of New Hampshire

I could feel her eyes anxiously search my face as I looked through the thesis proposals my graduate advisee had brought in—three different proposals, on three different topics. The problem she was wrestling with didn't, in any way, stem from incompetence. This graduate student was not only exceptionally bright and dedicated, but also creative, critical, and passionate. The challenge she was facing was identifying and committing to a research project that she felt was equal measures interesting and meaningful.

As a graduate student, I had also spent many an afternoon at my local coffee shop during the summer I wrote my dissertation proposal, avidly reading all the scholarship I could find that was even tangentially related to my area of interest. Although reading and writing in that sun-drenched coffee shop was definitely one of the most blissful moments in my graduate school career, it wasn't one without its own frustrations. As a graduate student, I often felt lost in the vast sea of literature, and struggled to learn how to make space for myself among the authoritative voices of renowned scholars I came across in print. I grappled with ways to effectively situate my research questions in the interdisciplinary field of Second Language Writing by connecting ideas in the various disciplines of Applied Linguistics, Composition, and Education.

Now, sitting face to face with a graduate student advisee who was in the depths of navigating her own sea of literature, the challenge that I faced as her advisor was to enthusiastically support her mission to explore a question she was passionate about, and at the same time, help rein it into the scope and format of a master's thesis—a thesis that would meet the requirements of our graduate program and also make a sound contribution to the field of Second Language Writing. Faced with this role reversal, I found myself repeating some of the sage—albeit cliché—comments I had encountered as a graduate student which, at the time, seemed cryptic and out of reach: "I see where you're coming from, but there's no need to reinvent the wheel. You know what they say: A done dissertation is the best dissertation."

As I continue to mentor graduate student writers in our program, I have found that some questions are more or less expected from MA students coming to the program with little research experience and who are learning new and unfamiliar genres of writing: How do I format a research paper? What methods do I use to collect data? How do I write an IRB application? Answering these types of questions is relatively straightforward, and I can often provide models or point students to resources on MA thesis requirements, research methods, and APA style guidelines. Other questions, however, are more complex: What is the purpose of a literature review? Can I critique this author's research in my literature review even though it is often-cited and well known in the field? Should I use first-person pronouns when writing my thesis? Why or why not? Who is the audience for my thesis? How do I draw from a different discipline while still anchoring my study in the field of Applied Linguistics? Can I explore a research question for my thesis that may have few pedagogical implications but is personally meaningful to me?

As I work through these complex (and necessary) questions with my graduate students, it has become clearer to me that learning how to write in graduate school does not only involve learning the textual features of a new genre. To write effectively, graduate students must also learn the underlying values and disciplinary expectations that are inextricably linked to the textual features of each new genre in which they write. Learning the rhetorical moves performed in literature reviews is only useful to the extent that graduate student writers understand and appreciate that they are engaging in broader conversations in the field through these moves in their writing (see Blazer & DeCapua, this collection; Caplan, this collection). Similarly, the intertextuality in graduate students' research papers has as much to do with the scholarly identities and positionalities of these writers as it has to do with accurate and effective citation practices (Abasi, Akbari & Graves, 2006). To become more purposeful, deliberate, and effective writers, it's imperative that graduate student writers learn *how* to write in new genres as well as *why*. This takes time and perspective.

The challenge that I face, now in my position as a graduate student advisor, is to be able to clearly articulate the often opaque expectations of writing in graduate school. What are some effective ways for graduate students to learn the values and norms in their disciplines? How can advisors and mentors provide clear signposts and expectations for graduate students to move towards, while encouraging them to be creative, explore their scholarly identities, and pursue their interests? The following three chapters in this section of our collection speak to these questions.

References

Abasi, A., Akbari, N. & Graves, B. (2006). Discourse appropriation, construction of identities, and the complex issue of plagiarism: ESL students writing in graduate school. *Journal of Second Language Writing, 15*(2), 102–117.

Blazer, S. & DeCapua, S. E. (2020). Disciplinary corpus research for situated literacy instruction. In M. Brooks-Gillies, E. G. Garcia, S. H. Kim, K. Manthey & T. G. Smith (Eds.), *Graduate writing across the disciplines: Identifying, teaching, and supporting*. The WAC Clearinghouse; University Press of Colorado. https://wac.colostate.edu/books/atd/graduate.

Caplan, N. A. (2020). Genres and conflicts in MBA writing assignments. In M. Brooks-Gillies, E. G. Garcia, S. H. Kim, K. Manthey & T. G. Smith (Eds.), *Graduate writing across the disciplines: Identifying, teaching, and supporting*. The WAC Clearinghouse; University Press of Colorado. https://wac.colostate.edu/books/atd/graduate.

Discourse Community Fail! Negotiating Choices in Success/Failure and Graduate-Level Writing Development

Michelle LaFrance
GEORGE MASON UNIVERSITY

Steven J. Corbett
TEXAS A&M UNIVERSITY, KINGSVILLE

Abstract: If there is a better way to become an effective academic writer, many of us don't ever find it. In our experience, we become better writers by failing, sometimes abysmally, at the writing tasks set before us. But few scholars have made the importance of learning from failure their primary focus. Our goal in this autoethnographic essay will be to bring implicit assumptions about the productivity of failure to the surface of the discussion about learning to write as a graduate student.

Keywords: Productive Failure, Transfer, Queering Failure, Risks

I would hurl words into this darkness and wait for an echo, and if an echo sounded, no matter how faintly, I would send other words to tell, to march, to fight, to create a sense of hunger for life that gnaws in us all.
—Richard Wright, American Hunger, 1977

I try my best to be just like I am,
But everybody wants you to be just like them.
—Bob Dylan, "Maggie's Farm," 1965

If there is a better way to become an effective academic writer, many of us don't ever find it. In our experience, we become better writers by failing, sometimes abysmally, at the writing tasks set before us. Even so, few among us like to talk about failure, let alone admit to the ways we have failed. For graduate students—especially in light of the pressures to professionalize, publish, and negotiate a demanding job market—the desire for professional acceptance often precludes any admission of struggle, difficulty, or self-doubt (Corbett & Decker, 2012). In today's educational climate, students—particularly graduate students—are conditioned to avoid failure at all costs (Wardle, 2012), and the stakes for educators who allow failure in their classrooms are high. Yet, novice writers may miss out on deeper learning opportunities in their own writing development if they neglect to reflect upon complex task completion, *particularly when it is unsuccessful*. As Edward Burger (2012), mathematician and learning theorist, notes,

> Individuals need to embrace the realization that taking risks and failing are often the essential moves necessary to bring clarity, understanding, and innovation. By making a mistake, we are led to the pivotal question: "Why was that wrong?" By answering this question, we are intentionally placing ourselves in a position to develop a new insight and to eventually succeed. (para. 3)

Current discussions of transfer research (Ambrose et al., 2010; *Critical Transitions*, 2013; Donahue, 2012; Driscoll & Wells, 2012; Wardle, 2012) have often similarly implied that *failure* is a quintessential part of "robust" learning. Christine Casanave and Xiaoming Li (2008) also argue that most graduate students accrue skills slowly and without a clear sense of progress. Moreover, our current theories of writing seem to call for a discussion of the learning potentials in failure. Post-process theories (Kent, 1999; Smit, 2004) have pushed against generalized or overdetermined notions of writing; these discussions foreground the indeterminate and ephemeral nature of producing complex writing within disciplinary communities. For graduate students, tasked with using writing as a vehicle to enter a professional field, the indeterminacy—and high stakes—of writing tasks like the dissertation (Pantelides, 2015) can often contribute to further confusion and anxiety around writing.

But few scholars have made the importance of learning from failure their primary focus. Our goal in this autoethnographic essay will be to bring implicit assumptions about failure to the surface of the discussion about learning to write as a graduate student (also see Fredrick, Stravalli, May, Brookman-Smith, this collection). Autoethnography, a form of critical ethnography, poses personal experience as a rich site for analysis, as it reveals the everyday impact of social forces upon the individual. Researchers who use autoethnography typically pose their own finely-grained personal accounts as sites that reveal the commonalities of experience across quite different situations, locations, and contexts. Drawing on discussions of transfer and productive failure (particularly discussions of metacognition, discourse communities, and the importance of attitude and motivation); theories of writing and writing-development; queer theory; and our own experiences as graduate student writers, writing program administrators, and instructors working with graduate student writers, this essay will discuss diverse theories and lived experiences in order to highlight why coming to terms with failure is important for writers. *Failure, we contend, offers rich opportunities for understanding the writing process and writing development for graduate student writers—it is part and parcel of processes of socialization into professional communities and learning to contribute to the knowledge-making activities of the discourse communities where we seek to belong.* We will end by calling for more intentional awareness of the concept of failure, particularly at the graduate level.

Too Little to Succeed? Even Strong Writers Struggle in "Discourse Communities"

As college writing instructors, we have often used the concept of the "discourse community" to explain the rigors of academic writing to students new to—and frequently struggling to master—writing for college coursework. For academics, language use and community belonging exist in a reciprocal sort of tension, or as Patricia Bizzel (1992) explains, "[f]orms of language use [are] shaped by their own social circumstances" (p. 108). This definition of discourse community shows us that what we might call "expertise" in writing—or refer to more monolithically as "good writing"—is actually situationally dependent. In short, we use the term discourse community with students new to college to reassure them that learning to write effectively in a college context will take time and focused effort. The same is true for graduate students, particularly those who have been away from school for a bit of time before returning or who have switched disciplines and interests.

But we fail to understand the complexity of these working organisms if we do not also recognize their dynamic and ever-changing nature. In their study of how undergraduates work toward becoming more proficient writers within the disciplines, *Engaged Writers and Dynamic Disciplines: Research on the Academic Writing Life* (2006), Chris Thaiss and Terry Myers Zawacki explain further that discourse communities, academic disciplines, and even academic genres "evolve and change in response to a complex range of variables, including the motives underlying their production, the contexts in which they are produced, and the institutional and ideological agendas that help to shape both motive and context" (p. 18–19). Writers who know that the expectations for effective communication in one situation may differ substantially from those in another are set up to be more attentive learners in the writing situations they step into. Following this ideal, writers who keep their eyes open for signposts that indicate new or unfamiliar norms of language usage will be more aware, and as such, more effective, when entering an unfamiliar writing situation.

Unfortunately, this is easier said by writing instructors than it is learned by writers, even at the graduate level. And so, even as we find this discourse crucial to our work with writers at all levels, we also recognize that the majority of writers we speak with will learn—as we did—through trial, error, *and persistence in the face of failure*. A number of educational theorists and voices in the popular press have begun to call this quite typical experience "productive failure" (see Kapur & Bielaczyc, 2012). We see a concern for avoidance of failure in the increased attentions writing researchers are giving to theories of learning transfer, particularly active in relation to the pedagogical design and value of first-year writing. But these issues and realizations are not relegated to the first-year writing classroom by any means, and are just as pressing, we contend, for our pedagogical approaches to work with graduate student writers.

Of course, for graduate students, the stakes feel much, much higher. In the introduction to their collection *Learning the Literacy Practice of Graduate School* (2008), Casanave and Li eschew the term "discourse community" for the broader term "community of practice," in part to recognize the breadth and diversity of abilities necessary for success in graduate school and as a newly professional academic. While both terms—discourse community and community of practice—call up the ways that writing is situated within and informed by an array of professional expectations, Casanave and Li use "communities of practice" to illustrate the ways that learning academic writing is a process bound up with any number of shifting and frequently undefined expectations particular to each graduate program. "[L]earning to become a member of a graduate school academic community requires that students become familiar with new cultural, literacy, and sociopolitical practices while under the pressure of time, financial hardship, and possibly unclear authority relationships with faculty members," they write (p. 3). Financial hardship coupled with the sometimes unclear mentor-mentee relationship with faculty, alone, is enough to cause great stress. But the vagaries and indeterminate nature of the larger learning process for graduate students often contribute to further confusion, anxiety, and self-doubt around writing.

"Students enter programs knowing that the dissertation looms on the horizon, though 'it' is rather ambiguous," Kate Pantelides (2015) notes as but one example of the lack of explicit training for the writing graduate programs require (p. 1). Often grad students have to face the high-stakes writing event that is dissertating as a trial and error gauntlet. If the problem of graduate student writing-performance confusion and anxiety is such a ubiquitous problem, then what steps can or might be taken to work toward possible solutions? "What graduate school did not do was teach me to read or write through the explicit means that I had anticipated," John Hedgcock lays out plainly in his essay "Lessons I Must Have Missed: Implicit Literacy Practices in Graduate Education" (2008, p. 43). The stories shared with us over our years of being and working with graduate students, as well as a number of the essays in the Casanave and Li volume (and the essays in this collection), also attest to this point: graduate classes as a rule require writing, yet few graduate-level courses explicitly set out to explain what may constitute "good" writing within the context of a course or field.

This has led some educators to argue that graduate programs need to be thinking more programmatically about their students as writers—offering explicit instruction in the genres and professional heuristics central to their disciplinary practices. In her article "The Need for Curricular Writing Models for Graduate Students," (2001) Carol Mullen argues that too often graduate programs and instructors incorrectly presume that becoming a published writer will be a "natural" outcome of graduate work. The difficulty with this assumption is that "[g]raduate study is not typically shaped to socialize graduate students into the world of academic publishing; to many graduate students research and especially publication appear to be activities reserved for scholars" (p. 119). Learning to write for publication, according to Mullen,

> is a research project in itself, and some students may need guidance and support. Many students are unaware of the level of detail they need to familiarize themselves with in regard to such aspects of the publishing world as electronic clearinghouses, appropriate journals and other outlets, submission requirements, and the review process. They can also benefit from instructor's stories that offer advice about developing writing habits, preparing works, and getting published. Students may need support for making final revisions beyond formal course timelines. (p. 121)

As Adams et al. also make clear in Chapter 11 of this collection, these social interactions—modeling, advice, feedback, mentorship—are the social keys to student success in disciplinary communities. Without explicit instruction in writing for their courses and for professional publication, Mullen and Adams et al. argue, graduate students may accrue skills too slowly and without a clear sense of progress. The inattention to written norms of practice may be setting graduate students up to experience forms of failure that are not, in the end, as productive as anyone would like.

"Much of my knowledge emerged incipiently, without conscious awareness on my part," Hedgcock confides (p. 32). As such, Hedgcock argues that some of his struggle might have been mitigated or averted if he and other graduate students were more intentionally introduced to the expectations and processes of writing for their fields as part of their graduate training. The gains here may be larger than simply producing better writers in the short term. Hedgcock describes a typical emotional reaction to the difficulties he faced as a writer: "I have never viewed academic writing as anything but difficult, if not torturous; my attitude hasn't changed appreciably since my student days. Even after nearly 15 years of full-time employment in the academic ranks, I seldom find writing to be a natural or organic process" (p. 32). Whether more attention to writing in graduate school could avert the negative relationship some writers develop with their craft or offset the darker emotions that come to be associated with writing is left to be seen. Hedgcock, Casanave, Li, Mullen, and others, however, believe strongly that explicit attention to norms of written practice can only be beneficial. Struggling with writing on top of trying to figure out all the other elements of success as a graduate student and an academic can feel pretty miserable.

Perhaps because of these widespread graduate school experiences, failure and the field of writing studies have always realized a mutually sustaining relationship. Writing process pioneer Donald Murray (1968/1982) argued that the most important experience of all for a writer is the experience of failure, as the process of writing is laden with failure: "the writer tries to say something, and fails, and through failure tries to say it better, and fails, but perhaps, eventually, he says it well enough" (p. 119). This led Murray to claim that the writing course should be an experimental one,

> a course in practicing, a course in trying, a course in choice, a course in craft. Failure should not be accepted passively, but failure should never be defeat. The student should learn to exploit his failures as he rediscovers his subject, re-searches his information, redesigns his form, rewrites and edits every sentence. (p. 119–120)

We might just as easily argue, then, that the graduate course curriculum in writing studies must therefore also be a curriculum with the notion of failure at its core, but one wherein students learn to metacognitively come to terms with the concept of failure, to manage their own experiences with failure, and to exploit the notion for its full worth. The work of queer theorists can aid us in these complex calls to personal exploitation as personal growth, offering foundational insights into our own experiences of writing development.

To "queer" something can mean to take an alternate path, to disturb the order of things, to "fail" in or "dis" traditional orientations (Ahmed, 2006). Judith Halberstam, in her book *The Queer Art of Failure* (2011), offers what might be called a theoretical blueprint for how graduate students often learn to balance exactly the tensions they experience between needing to conform to conventions and expectations in order to succeed and the desire to resist and take risks. Taking risks is an important piece of the growth of a writer; planning for more purposeful failures can then be a part of our intentional and strategic growth as learners and writers. For Halberstam, failure offers its own rewards: "Under certain circumstances failing, losing, forgetting, unmasking, undoing, unbecoming, not knowing may in fact offer more creative, more cooperative, more surprising ways of being in the world" (p. 2–3). Halberstam believes that one can realize a state of being "in but not of" (p. 11) the university, that even though we are—indeed by choice—part of the socially engineered world of the modern university, we might still realize our own local, esoteric knowledges, and that these unbridled knowings might just do their part to push the boundaries of the serious, stuffy academy where any sort of resistance by force may seem futile.

What might it mean to negotiate the often fuzzy interstices of choice in failure, adversity, and success in relation to conformity, resistance, or boundary-pushing? Building on Morten and Harney's "Seven Theses" of the "subversive intellectual," and informed by Michel Foucault and others, Halberstam posits three ways graduate students and teachers might consider "queering" their learning and teaching and, by extension, challenging the dominant paradigm of Conformist U. One, resist mastery: Halberstam believes that the counternarratives of "stupidity" in relation to mastery might open the doors to more salutary *conversation* that questions the boundaries of knowledge through "multilogue." She gives the example of ethnographic research that approaches a study with a very fixed set of assumptions, assumptions that can close-off the process of learning that overflows the original framework the researcher enters (p. 11, 88). Two, privilege the naïve or nonsensical: in championing stupidity and ignorance, we might just be also acknowledging the limits of our own mastery or expertise. Halberstam invokes Paulo Freire's famous "banking concept of education" and other pedagogical scenarios to argue for resistance to or outright rejection of the dominant attempts at intellectual colonization by the all-knowing discourse community "masters" (pp. 12–13, 120). And three, suspect memorialization: while implicitly acknowledging the value of memory in building discourse communities, Halberstam counterintuitively argues for the equally or (because it is so infrequently employed) even more important role of forgetting and erasure. She uses Toni Morrison's *Beloved* as an example of a text that works against the grain of tidy histories of slavery (p. 15, 83). Holding memory in suspect can release the power of alternate ways of knowing and experiencing that can help graduate students make choices in what memories to hold on to even as they consider what knowledge will necessarily supplant or compliment previous understandings. In short, Halberstam urges academics to make choices in how they "fail" to be "normal."

In the following sections, we offer some of our own intimations—some more assimilative and others more resistant—of learning to negotiate the vagaries of the discourse community of Writing Studies/Composition and Rhetoric through our ongoing writing successes and failures.

Finding My Way as an Academic Writer: Michelle's Story

"Failure is a bruise, not a tattoo"
—Jon Sinclair

All of my life I have struggled with proofreading.
There I said it. Out loud. (An English professor—especially a writing teacher and writing program administrator—should have "perfect" grammar and spelling, right?)
I am a lousy typist.

I am sometimes stumped by the spellings of fairly common words.
I have to look up some of the academic terms others take for granted.
Sometimes, I look them up more than once.
Sometimes, I look them up more times than I can keep count.

I get lost in my thoughts and lose my way in just about every lengthy writing project I have ever taken on. I sometimes . . . with patience and persistence . . . find my way out of those thorny, dark places.

Yes. I said this. Out loud. To you.

But I am not alone.

At a backyard barbecue, I mentioned to a colleague—a junior professor like myself—that I was working on an article about the difficulties many graduate students face as they work toward becoming professional academic writers. Her eyes immediately darkened, and I knew she had a story to tell—a story not that different from the many I've heard from graduate students and new professionals working toward becoming published academic writers. A story not so different from my own. "It was so hard," my colleague confided in a low voice. Another colleague overheard us and jumped in at this point, eager to share her own similar experience. "Asking for help sometimes felt like an admission that I couldn't cut it," the second colleague admitted. "It was really frustrating," the first agreed, looking grim. "I just had to figure it out on my own." These professionals feared failure as much as I did.

Anyone who has worked with graduate students around issues of academic writing has undoubtedly heard the same sorts of laments with some regularity. As a graduate peer tutor in a university writing center, I often encountered graduate students who found themselves befuddled by the norms of writing they were asked to adhere to for their graduate coursework: the young woman in the social sciences crushed that her professor did not appreciate the poem that she had written to conclude her first grad-level seminar paper. The middle-aged businessman returning to school for his theology doctorate, who struggled to make claims (over simply summarizing), focus, and organize his scholarly papers. The dissertator in ethnomusicology who produced evocative descriptions of the community events she had attended, but who drew a blank when trying to connect those events to the theories of belonging and social organization that were active in her field. The numerous international students who could think with complexity and purpose in their native languages, but who struggled to cope with the steep learning curve of writing in accepted forms of polished Standard American English, let alone Academic English.

Like Hedgcock, Casanave, Li, and Mullen, I tend to agree with a need for more explicit attention to writing skills on all levels of study and across the disciplines for students, graduate and undergraduate alike. As Henderson and Cook demonstrate in Chapter 2 of this collection, "student self-expectations, and even self-doubt" often lend enormously to our impressions of ourselves as writers. Explicit training in the work of graduate writing has the potential to broaden this sense of self and to clarify writing situations for graduate students. The students that I've referenced above frequently *felt* like failures until they had begun to master the rhetorical and communicative situations they found themselves in. Some were openly discouraged from continuing in their graduate programs by their mentors. Others were deeply wounded by professors' comments; they carried those wounds into the next writing task—but the comments made that task *harder, not easier*, to carry. Some dropped out—in my eyes, prematurely. It's only those who developed resilience—who kept writing despite the setbacks—that then moved from this place of uncomfortable confusion.

A frank discussion about failure is an important but missing piece of our approach to working with graduate students. We must present the possibilities and potentialities of failing to meet the expectations of others as part of the process of becoming a professional writer. While Writing Studies' current interest in learning theory and discourse communities, especially in terms of knowledge transfer, is commendable and can add to conversations involving failure, the field still has much to learn about how to coach students to a stronger understanding of these often difficult and sometimes emotionally charged experiences. Here, scholars in Writing Studies can take important cues from thinkers in other fields, particularly queer theorists who have long negotiated outsiderness and challenges to their academic and everyday belongings. In the struggle for recognition, a number of queer theorists have taken quite bold and sophisticated journeys into the notion of what it means to "fail" or "succeed." If we, as a field, were to openly address these moments of failure in graduate student education (and their close cousins: struggle, confusion, disillusionment, abjection, and rejection), we would come closer to the ideals already espoused by central discourses in our field, enacting a safer place for experimentation, intellectual growth, and identification for graduate student writers, bringing to life further opportunities to understand writing as a process and the ways writing development coincides with professional development. The first step in this process would be to pedagogically reconceptualize failure. It is currently read as a mark of outsiderness—we may re-see it as the very means by which we come to belong.

Like Halberstam, I believe that we need to change the grounds of our work—allowing writers at every level to resist and refuse the stiff models of belonging as perfection traditionally offered, clearly announcing that most of our own projects are unfinished, imperfect products of where we are at *now*.

As you may have guessed, however, my entrance into the discourse community of my graduate program was often marked with an enormous fear of failure: anxiety, dread of writing *at all*, and a pressing sense that others thought I wasn't really good enough to be in my program or to get a doctorate. (Some people call this "imposter syndrome" [e.g., Corbett & Decker, 2012]. Others say that graduate students in the humanities are particularly plagued by it.) I should note here that it took me a long time to get to grad school—on the way, I was a crisis counselor for run away and homeless teenagers, worked in women's shelters and group homes for learning-disabled/developmentally delayed adults, and provided administrative support in a number of professional capacities (most notably assisting health-sciences researchers with publication in national medical and behavioral-health journals). So, I applied to graduate school a confident writer—I had published poetry; written for newsletters, regional newspapers, and on the job; and had once presented at an academic conference as an undergrad. My undergraduate professors praised the creativity and risk-taking in my writing. (They also consistently reminded me that typos and misspellings were distracting for readers, but were more encouraging than tyrannical about sentence-level correctness.) My employers occasionally noted that I struggled to edit my own work, but typically we worked in teams, so I usually had built-in readers for the final drafts of important written communications.

In my new graduate discourse community, the rules for writing had changed dramatically. (As Henderson and Cook note in Chapter 2 of this collection, the expectations for writing tend to change in the transition between undergrad and graduate programs). Suddenly none of my previous experiences seemed to matter at all. I was baffled, then, when my graduate instructors barely mentioned how to write . . . or what they wanted as readers and arbiters of my work. Their expectations were a screen of mystery. Most included one or two lines about the final assignment for their classes on the syllabus, describing it simply as a "seminar paper" or a "journal-length essay suitable for publication."

I was surprised when no classmates asked about these expectations. And, when I asked in class about these expectations, I could feel a level of impatience rise amongst my mentors and classmates. I asked questions anyway and my mentors answered—like zen-masters, speaking in koans:

"You need as many sources as you need."

"Sit with your questions."

"Push on the text."

"Interrogate the text."

"You need to clearly articulate the stakes for your argument."

"It's all about exegesis."

"A graduate student should know about these expectations . . ."

My classmates smiled and nodded. I smiled and nodded, all the while thinking that I had *no idea* what they meant. They were speaking in riddles to me—an insider language that everyone else had and that I was ashamed to admit I didn't.

At home, on my own, I'd spend half an hour on a single sentence. Rewording, reworking. Spinning. Trying again. And again. I couldn't hear myself think. Texts felt like an impenetrable fog. What was worse, my work simply didn't cut it. My professors' end comments called me out. I was not "modeling the sorts of conventions necessary for an academic conversation." Why had I begun so many paragraphs with quotations? Why hadn't I laid out my argument more clearly in the introduction? I needed to really focus, really grapple with the ideas. *Did I know that I wasn't producing graduate-level work?*

After a graduate mentor described my writing as "a string of blinking Christmas lights with no real substance"—which I translate now as meaning that I had not made clear the connections between what I believed were related ideas—I confided my frustration and fear to a small group of peers at a departmental social gathering. I was working harder than I had ever worked before to no clear advantage.

One of my friends visibly ducked her head and scrunched her shoulders around her ears, lowering her voice: "You should be careful talking about this. You never know who is listening."

As if, should we be discovered talking about the negative feedback I had received, *something we could not even name might happen to us*. As if admitting that I was failing despite my best efforts was itself taboo.

I fell silent.

I stayed silent.

For years, I have been terrified to tell others about how hard this work is for me . . . how frequently I find myself backed into corners, faced with a project that just isn't working . . . thinking that admitting this to others somehow signifies that I am poorly suited to this work. That I don't deserve to stand among my colleagues and peers.

But—as I have learned—the most fruitful projects develop over time.

Quality work takes time.

Sometimes it's the lengthier process that yields more thoughtful results.

It's okay to fail. Our goal should be to fail miserably and to fail often—as long as we keep learning from those failures and keep moving toward the goal we have set.

Failure is a bruise, not a tattoo.

A necessary part of the process.

Coaxing a vision into life takes time. Good work is not always convenient or entirely pretty or even half-way happy-making. I sometimes must coach myself into the patience and energy required to cope with my own processes. Those moments of realization—the recognition that what I'm doing *isn't working* and that I will have to start over or think more about what I see that others don't—are the bread and butter of my academic life.

I am always teaching myself to think the problem through.

And to think it through on my own terms. In my own way.

It is not always very fulfilling.

I'm thinking again about Halberstam's call to queer the academy—and LGBT activists in the 80's and 90's who shouted in the streets that *silence is death*. As professionals in Writing Studies—a special brand of professional writers, no less—we must recognize the danger in allowing the moments of silence that inevitably arise when we engage in the social process of learning to take on such power over "novice" writers. Most of us enter graduate school aware that it will ask us to challenge ourselves and to remake our writing as much as it remakes our lives. And, there is something about the process of becoming an effective academic writer on the graduate and professional level that also often triggers deep anxieties, uncertainty, difficulty, and a sense of failure or inadequacy in otherwise confident and accomplished writers. Real personal gains for a writer can be recognized and capitalized upon in exactly those moments when a project feels most like it will fall apart—if only for the ways these moments teach us patience, perseverance, and dedication to the development of our best ideas.

If my enculturation into academic writing rarely ever felt as if it was actually *on purpose*—my accumulation of awareness and skill with the conventions of the scholarly essay was too gradual and too openly agonizing for that sort of descriptor—somehow, I did learn to be a more effective writer. I did this the same way most writers do, through reading and writing and revising and reading and writing and revising some more. Listening to readers, thinking forward as I wrote my first draft, trying to stay in moments of uncertainty so that I could slowly articulate a new idea, and coming to accept that failure—those moments that sapped my confidence, made me rethink, and got messy-messy-messy—were as important as any triumph.

It is important that we say these things to one another.

Out loud. In our writing. In our research.

As Halberstam notes above, we have to let go of the postures that stifle us as learners and as appointed mentors within an academic field. Failure must be recast as one of our most important sites of learning.

It signifies our belonging, not our defeat.

Processes of Authorial (Un)Becoming: Steven's Story

"Failure" can be somewhat of a relative term, and it can mean different things for different people at different times. As Michelle discussed above, oftentimes what seem to be crushing defeats can—in time—prove themselves really only minor setbacks. Something I'm trying to get better at is negotiating how to make my work "fit" into various venues, while at the same time choosing when to fail to be too normal. When I originally wrote an essay for the collection *On Location: Theory and Practice in Classroom-Based Writing Tutoring* (2005), I had purposefully composed it as a very hyper-stylized piece that addressed the issue of classroom-based tutoring on a rather broad and cross-disciplinary level. When I spoke with one of the editors, Candace Spigelman, however, she wanted a very specific focus that would fit precisely with what she felt she needed for her collection. She asked me to research a bit on the directive/nondirective instructional continuum, an important and often talked about methodological concept in peer tutoring. We talked about texts that would help support this new focus. She also wanted me to eliminate most of the playful stylistics (the type you are experiencing right now!) to match the tones and styles of the other authors in the collection. Yet, I still got to have my "creative" moments. I was able to sneak in both a Bob Dylan and Walt Whitman quote to bring a smidge of color and personality to my essay and the collection. I usually carry this sort of "bend but don't break" authorial attitude into most writing situations. (Hint: After an essay has been vetted by an editor or commented upon by reviewers, you can frequently sneak in just a bit more color if you want. Shhh . . . don't tell the editors of this piece though.) I want to find those moments where even the nonsensical side comment can find its fitting place.

But, years later—when I failed my qualifying exams—I wondered what it would take to get those oh-so-serious Ph.D. exams up to academic snuff. At the time, it felt like the biggest failure of my life, like there was something really wrong with me. That I had been unmasked, finally found out . . . But what I really needed to understand was the loose baggy monster that is the genre of the exam essay. I needed to realize that it wasn't just ME (the actor), it was also YOU (the scene). It is well-understood in Writing Studies that students unfamiliar with a new writing situation or genre will fall back (regress) often on summary rather than argumentation and analysis. What my committee wanted were smart, sophisticated argumentative essays. Sure, they wanted lots of evidentiary support, but when I started to really study other people's exams, what I noticed was that they might only have 10 or 15—strategically well-chosen—sources for each essay, rather than, say, the 30 or 40 I had ridiculously tried to stuff in. The lesson here? When faced with an unfamiliar writing situation, I study models of the genre I am about to write in. I don't just peruse—I study. After meeting with my dissertation chair, I realized I should have also talked more with all my committee members about precisely what they would be looking for. How much summary did they want? How much argumentation did they want?, etc.

Then came the new rhetorical situations of the job search. First off, let me preface a more detailed discussion of the preparation that went into my job search materials with a brief idea of the sort of attitude I took and still take into these sorts of communicative rhetorical situations. Coming from the "nonmainstream" background I do, I carry a bit of a chip on my shoulder. I feel like I constantly must mask my working-class upbringing with all the intellectual showmanship I can muster. I recently told a couple of close colleagues at my previous institution that (before accepting their offer) I interviewed with several big schools and those schools didn't want to have anything to do with me. (I was being hyperbolic of course. Sort of.) I went on to say that "I want to show them that I can teach two courses per term, administer the writing program, *and* out-publish all of them!" Arrogant? Sure, maybe. But I was and still am learning . . . humility.

I learned a hard lesson during my exams, one that I won't soon forget. In preparation for the job search I did all the things right, textually, that I did wrong during the exams. I took all the sample materials I could get and studied them, especially the cover letter. The first draft of my cover letter was very vague about my experiences, publications, and accomplishments. Too much "aw shucks" and not enough "look at this!" perhaps. But after studying, especially my chair's cover letter from his uber-successful job search eight or so years before, I knew exactly what I needed to do. (The ancient rhetorical art of imitation in the service of invention must never be taken for granted.) I noticed that he didn't hold back in describing the details of his publications, presentations, administrative positions, and research activities in his cover letter—the significance of them, what they mean to our field, what they did for his teaching and learning, what they could mean for the institution he was trying so skillfully to persuade that they needed him. Once I felt I had a stronger draft of the letter, I asked all my committee members to read it and give me feedback. I took it through several successive drafts; I babied it and compulsively worked every paragraph, every sentence, every word, until I felt satisfied. And as the job search progressed, I tweaked it as I tried to better fit the needs of the particular audience I felt I was writing for. And there is that word "fit" again. Such an important concept in writing and academia in general.

Another strategy, suggested above while working my way through composing the job search materials, is letting as many readers in on the revising action as possible. Now that I've found myself in a position of authority, you'd think I might think it's ok (finally?!) to trust in my own editorial skills, right? Wrong. Now, more than ever, I rely on my colleagues to proofread any sensitive written correspondences I want to send out, including emails. (The "e-" means "electronic" not "emergency," I have to tell myself). I once sent an email to a prospective employer, referring to her as "Ms. ____." She emailed me back with a very curt reply along the lines of "I did not spend 8 years earning a Ph.D. to be referred to as 'Ms.'" Needless to say, I failed to get any consideration, let alone the job. When working with situations that often involve people's jobs, their lives, the wrong words put the wrong way can be devastating. The one minute it takes to compose a well-intentioned, but perhaps hurried, email to an adjunct instructor—telling them that you don't have a course to offer them next term—needs to be followed by about 15 minutes of wait time before being sent. I am learning much about tact and diplomacy from far more seasoned colleagues who have had to do this many times before, chairs, deans, other program leaders. Often what I end up discovering is that some of the sensitive writing situations I find myself in—while relatively simple-seeming on the surface—are actually quite complex, often unique enough that they require some collaborative and collective rumination with intelligent council. Sometimes these situations are even new for the veterans and really require some creative, multi-perspective problem-solving before we can even attempt a written response.

I am learning that many communications I used to take for granted—emails, memos, queries—can be just as important as any major essay, letter, or grant application. So I am trying to train myself to approach the composing process of these written communications the same way I would any important essay or letter. The more important the email, the longer I let it sit in my outgoing mailbox. My offices are the studios of an artist. I have many writing projects going on at once, all in different stages, and I come back to draft after draft over time, always thinking about my audience, always wondering about the consequences of my words-as-action, constantly seeking advice for what I may not be (fore)seeing clearly. I often wonder "what would so-and-so think?" And, when possible, I *ask* so-and-so what they think. I don't want to have to face the consequences of another failed communication—if I can do whatever I can in advance to forestall such (unintended or not) failure.

Further, I am finding other connections between the training I received in grad school and the professional writing I've performed on a daily basis. For example, at my former institution, in preparing my yearly renewal file (building toward my eventual promotion and tenure [P&T] review), I found myself performing many of the same sorts of rhetorical show-and-tells I did while on the job search. The cover letter I spoke of above is very similar to the rationales I had to provide for the four categories of renewal and eventual P&T: teaching and professional competence, creative activity, productive service to the department and university, and professional attendance and participation. As I prepared the rationales for these files, I found myself doing similar detailing of teaching and administrative philosophy, publication and presentation venues and respective merits, and service to my academic community and to other people and institutions outside my university.

In all of these situations above—the Ph.D. exams, the job search, and the multifarious on-the-job communications—I made deliberate choices to toe-the-line, to conform. I made conscientious choices in my attempts to *avoid failure* by studying and performing more "expert," "smart" communicative moves that would not shock the minds and memories of my various audiences. I tried my best to act in ways becoming of a budding teacher-scholar. Then I prepared myself to fail at making everyone who read my materials love me and need to hire me.

Yet while performing all of these attempts to conform, especially for my former institution, gnawing at my conscious was that very question of "fit," of "normal." As I mentioned above, even though my former institution is considered a teaching school with a 4/4 teaching load, I stubbornly (even proudly) refused to ease up on my research and creative activity. I knew very well that—in the scrutinizing eyes of my P&T reviewers, those masters of that particular discourse community—much of my creative activity was considered surplus and almost unnecessary. But this is where the force of my own image of a college professor queerly diverged from my colleagues' and institution's cemented notion of the role of a professor at a teaching college. In short, and in some sense, I purposefully chose to "fail" at being a good teaching-college professor, opting instead to remember and hold true to the (counter)memory of the types of professors my graduate school mentors modeled for me: perhaps I proved "unteachable" in some ways for my new institution. Maybe, in the long run, all the lessons I learned from graduate school actually resulted in "negative transfer" to my new institution—albeit with what I believe to be my full understanding and consent in my own (un)becoming processes.

Conclusion: Exploring the Value of the Negative

> The message is familiar: Abundant success lies on the other end of failure. Could guiding our students through their own failures inspire the next groundbreaking physicist, talk-show star, or iPhone inventor? Possible . . . but not likely. Even if the results end up being a little less grandiose, I think they are just as important. Learning to fail could help our students become more resilient, self-aware, innovative, and compassionate. Not bad for a bunch of "failures."
> —Ann Sobel, 2014, "How Failure in the Classroom Is More Instructive than Success"

We will briefly conclude this essay with our thoughts on how our field(s) and graduate students themselves might consider the implications of failure in relation to (un)becoming the best teachers, learners, and researchers of writing we possibly can. We couch these thoughts within learning theory's notion of failed or negative transfer.

Any professional or performer—although they may not always like it—inherently understands the key role of learning to deal with failure in order to succeed. That's why athletes, dancers, actors, cooks, etc. spend countless hours watching, considering, and critiquing their own and their peers' performances, good and bad. In her notably cogent article "Transfer, Portability, Generalization" (2012), Christiane Donahue offers a succinct review of the literature on writing and transfer drawn from education, psychology, sociology, and composition studies. While much has been made about the power of metacognition in the successful transfer of learning from one situation to another (e.g., Donahue, 2012), we know relatively little, especially in composition studies, about what phenomenon might contribute to failed moments of knowledge transfer. Learning procedures without an understanding of the accompanying underlying concepts, a-contextualized learning, and the learner's pre-existing conceptions can all interfere with and prevent successful transfer. Relating back to the notion of "discourse community" we discussed above, Donahue claims this very notion in itself can lead to failed transfer because the idea of "the university as a discourse community into which students must enter, and then disciplines as more specialized versions of that community, seem now to be reductive and overly linear understandings of the negotiation students take on" (p. 157). Rather,

Donahue points to the work of activity theorists like David Russell and Patrick Dias in her claim that meta-awareness of the various functions of writing as ways of thinking and knowing in and through various activities must be painstakingly gained through time-intensive processes of enculturation and apprenticeship. Donahue goes on to discuss studies and texts that offer "boundary-crossing" scenarios as productive exercises in experimenting with what might work in one situation versus another (cf. Feldman, Csikszentmihalyi & Gardner, 1994). And this notion of boundary-crossing brings us back to those queer theories of divergent, multivoiced, multiperspectival, and even resistant, realizations discussed above.

If Michelle were to offer any advice to graduate students, she would offer four points:

- The first is to keep all feedback in perspective. Ultimately, the work any writer produces in graduate school or professional situations is the work of that writer. One of Michelle's favorite tips for writers is from popular speculative fiction author Neil Gaiman, who says, "Remember: when people tell you something's wrong or doesn't work for them, they are almost always right. When they tell you exactly how to fix it, they are almost always wrong" ("Ten Rules," 2010). This maxim holds true whether the respondent is one of our peers or our favorite (revered) graduate mentor.
- Michelle also recommends asking mentors about their work habits and struggles—processes, difficulties with writing, and revision strategies. As a graduate student, Michelle cannot remember a single instance where a faculty member discussed these real-life/real-work issues with her. She knows now, as a faculty member at a major institution, that most faculty have at least one useful story about learning how to solve a writing problem, rejection of their work, or institutional misunderstandings about the nature and value of their work. (Though, yes, only a few are actually forthcoming about their own painful experiences—and many believe that such sharing is a breach of professionalism. Writing is an affective as well as cognitive and social process, so it serves no one at all to pretend these things didn't happen or that a writer's negative emotional associations with a project aren't something that can become a "professional" problem at some point.) It can be enormously helpful to hear our mentors talk about these things, humanizing a process that often feels alienating, intimidating, and cold.
- The real goal for any learner (qua graduate student writer) is to embrace the process—and that means keeping failures in perspective. For most of us, (even incredibly painful) moments of failure are necessary and instructive opportunities for deeper reflection that allow us to move to the next level. Take the time to stop and study what went wrong, what went right, what can be or was done to recover.

- Surround yourself with a small group of close colleagues who you can confide in when the work becomes difficult, who will listen to you as you talk your ideas through, who can tell you about their own struggles, and who can remind you to embrace the difficulty, the work, and the process. We're all in this together, after all.

If Steven were to offer any advice to graduate students on negotiating choices in success/failure he might include:

- Decide how far you are willing to go in conforming or boundary pushing/breaking in any given professional performance. He frequently likes to follow the advice of an old Cheap Trick song: "surrender, surrender, but don't give yourself away."
- Like Picasso did with painting, learn the formal aspects of various professional genres—emails, cover letters, CVs, book chapters, articles in the pertinent academic journals, etc. But also find your moments to bring (or develop) those nonconformist attitudes and actions. These can set you apart and keep you true to who you really are and want to become.
- All writers begin to thrive when they are able to coordinate the previous two suggestions as closely as possible with what they believe are their own creative strengths. It is in this integration that a writer finds their unique voice and begins to see the specific contributions to the ongoing conversations that only they may make. Search out venues that will foster your unique qualities: if you are a natural speaker or performer, seek out presentation venues; if you love interacting with people, seek out qualitative field research venues; if you like journalistic writing, try composing articles for your school newspaper or online sources like The Chronicle of Higher Education or Inside Higher Ed. Or, more modestly, consider contributing to or starting a blog where you write to whoever will listen: the point being that you write, practice, write, experiment, write, sometimes fail, sometimes succeed . . . whenever possible on your own terms.

And, finally, we both recommend that all writers at all stages of development talk to others as candidly as possible about when and where they struggle, their failures, and what they can learn from these experiences. And above all, keep working, even if the gains do not feel so readily apparent. As Brian Ray (2015) notes in his article "The Lessons of Failure," we are always making choices, trade offs, and strategizing as researchers—it takes time to watch our own patterns, habits, and processes over time. It often takes many years until we begin to see what many would call "success." We know from our own experiences and our work coaching and mentoring others that we can help ourselves and our students come to terms with the crucial role of systematic experimentation and boundary-pushing. The most fundamental aspect of our development as professionals is this relationship:

learning to and from failure. When our pedagogies and mentoring strategies begin to account for the complex opportunities failure offers, we offer ourselves, and our students (and our colleagues), an invaluable gift.

Then, *plan* to fail early and fail often.

References

Adams, L., Adams, M., Baird, P. F., Beck, E., Blair, K. L., Conway, A., Nickoson, L. & Schaffer, M. (2020). Crossing divides: Engaging extracurricular writing practices in graduate education and professionalization. In M. Brooks-Gillies, E. G. Garcia, S. H. Kim, K. Manthey & T. G. Smith (Eds.), *Graduate writing across the disciplines: Identifying, teaching, and supporting.* The WAC Clearinghouse; University Press of Colorado. https://wac.colostate.edu/books/atd/graduate.

Ahmed, S. (2006). *Queer phenomenology: Orientations, objects, others.* Duke University Press.

Ambrose, S. A., Bridges, M. W., DiPietro, M., Lovett, M. C., Norman, M. K. & Mayer, R. E. (2010). *How learning works: Seven research-based principles for smart teaching.* Jossey-Bass.

Bizzell, P. (1992). *Academic discourse and critical consciousness.* University of Pittsburgh Press.

Burger, E. (August 21, 2012). Teaching to fail. *Inside Higher Ed.* http://www.inside highered.com/views/2012/08/21/essay-importance-teaching-failure.

Casanave, C. P. & Li, X. (2008). *Learning the literacy practices of graduate school: Insiders' reflections on academic enculturation.* University of Michigan Press/ELT.

Cheap Trick. (1978). Surrender. On *Heaven tonight* [MP3 file]. Epic.

Corbett, S. J. & Decker, T. (October 15, 2012). Impostors, performers, professionals. *Inside Higher Ed.* http://www.insidehighered.com/advice/2012/10/15/essay-feeling -being-impostors-academe#ixzz2XdYD41r9.

Critical transitions: Writing and the question of transfer. (2013). Elon University Center for Engaged Learning. https://blogs.elon.edu/criticaltransitions/.

Donahue, C. (2012). Transfer, portability, generalization: (How) does composition expertise "carry"? In K. Ritter & P. K. Matsuda (Eds.), *Exploring composition studies: Sites, issues, and perspectives* (pp. 145–166). Utah State University Press.

Driscoll, D. L. & Wells, J. (Fall 2012). Beyond knowledge and skills: Writing transfer and the role of student dispositions. *Composition Forum,* 26. http://compositionforum.com /issue/26/beyond-knowledge-skills.php.

Dylan, B. (1965). Maggie's farm. On *Bringing it all back home* [MP3 file]. Columbia Records.

Feldman, D. H., Csikszentmihalyi, M. & Gardner, H. (1994). *Changing the world: A framework for the study of creativity.* Praeger.

Fredrick, T., Stravalli, K., May, S. & Brookman-Smith, J. (2020). The space between: MA students enculturate to graduate reading and writing. In M. Brooks-Gillies, E. G. Garcia, S. H. Kim, K. Manthey & T. G. Smith (Eds.), *Graduate writing across the disciplines: Identifying, teaching, and supporting.* The WAC Clearinghouse; University Press of Colorado. https://wac.colostate.edu/books/atd/graduate.

Halberstam, J. (2011). *The queer art of failure*. Duke University Press.

Hedgcock, J. (2008). Lessons I must have missed: Implicit literacy practices in graduate education. In C. P. Casanave & X. Li (Eds.), *Learning the literacy practices of graduate school: Insiders' reflections on academic enculturation* (pp. 32–44). University of Michigan Press; ELT.

Henderson, B. R. & Cook, P. G. (2020). Voicing graduate student writing experiences: A study of cross-level courses at two master's-level, regional institutions. In M. Brooks-Gillies, E. G. Garcia, S. H. Kim, K. Manthey & T. G. Smith (Eds.), *Graduate writing across the disciplines: Identifying, teaching, and supporting*. The WAC Clearinghouse; University Press of Colorado. https://wac.colostate.edu/books/atd/graduate.

Kapur, M. & Bielaczyc, K. (2012). Designing for productive failure. *Journal of the Learning Sciences, 21*(1), 45–83.

Kent, T. (1999). *Post-process theory: Beyond the writing-process paradigm*. Southern Illinois University Press.

Mullen, C. (2001). The need for curricular writing models for graduate students. *Journal of Further and Higher Education, 25*(1), 117–126.

Murray, D. M. (1982). The process of teaching. In D. M. Murray (Ed.), *Learning by teaching: Selected articles on writing and teaching* (pp. 115–120). Boynton/Cook. (Reprinted from *The Leaflet*, Nov. 1968)

Pantelides, K. (2015, August 25). Dissertation genre change as a result of electronic theses and dissertation programs [Special issue on graduate writing across the disciplines]. *Across the Disciplines, 12*(3). https://wac.colostate.edu/atd/special/graduate/.

Ray, B. (2015, Jan 07). "The lessons of failure." *The Chronicle of Higher Education*. http://www.chronicle.com/article/The-Lessons-of-Failure/150967.

Smit, D. W. (2004). *The end of composition studies*. Southern Illinois University Press.

Sobel, A. (2014, May 5). How failure in the classroom is more instructive than success. *The Chronicle of Higher Education*. http://www.chronicle.com/article/How-Failure-in-the-Classroom/146377.

Spigelman, C. & Grobman, L. (Eds.). (2005). *On location: Theory and practice in classroom-based writing tutoring*. Utah State University Press.

Thaiss, C. & Zawacki, T. M. (2006). *Engaged writers and dynamic disciplines: Research on the academic writing life*. Boynton/Cook.

The Guardian. (2010). Ten rules for writing fiction. https://www.theguardian.com/books/2010/feb/20/ten-rules-for-writing-fiction-part-one.

Wardle, E. (Fall 2012). Creative repurposing for expansive learning: Considering "problem-exploring" and "answer-getting" dispositions in individuals and fields. *Composition Forum, 26*. http://compositionforum.com/issue/26/creative-repurposing.php.

Wright, R. (1977). *American hunger*. Harper and Row.

Disciplinary Corpus Research for Situated Literacy Instruction

Sarah Blazer
Fashion Institute of Technology (SUNY)

Sarah E. DeCapua
University of Connecticut

Abstract: In this article, the authors demonstrate one example of how corpus research can prepare disciplinary outsiders to support faculty and students engaged in graduate-level reading and writing of disciplinary genres. The corpus study answers the question: What are the most common high-frequency phrases that appear in a corpus of public health (PH) research articles, and what do they mean? Because students often struggle as much or more interpreting the phrases that make up the connective tissue of a text—its subtechnical language—as they do with content or specialized vocabulary and phrases, the former are of particular interest in this study. Students pursuing graduate-level disciplinary study need precise understanding of the language their field most frequently uses to express relationships among key terms and concepts. The authors discuss concrete pedagogical applications for their corpus research findings and connect sociocultural theory to corpus linguistics (CL) research and materials development to discuss how the latter can assist in students' mediation and internalization of discipline-specific linguistic and conceptual knowledge.

Keywords: Public Health (PH), Literacy Development, Subtechnical Language, Disciplinary Discourse, Writing Center, WAC, WID, Corpus Linguistics (CL), Concordancing Program, AntConc, Sociocultural Theory (SCT), Mediation, Internalization

Writing Across the Curriculum (WAC) and writing center scholars engaged in supporting student literacy development are often recruited across disciplinary contexts to guide faculty in their development of course materials and curriculum as well as to develop and teach workshops or courses for students. Outsiders to a field may be challenged to determine what disciplinary genres and discourse conventions could be taught to students and how to provide appropriately situated instruction (Curry, 2016), as advocated for by Chris Thaiss and Terry Zawacki (2006), David Russell (1995, 2002), and others. When possible, one might prepare to guide or teach outside of familiar disciplinary territory by following models like Stoller, Jones, Costanza-Robinson, and Robinson (2005); this team of applied linguistics and

DOI: https://doi.org/10.37514/ATD-B.2020.0407.2.13

chemistry faculty at Northern Arizona University employed corpus research in a lengthy project to systematically explore writing in chemistry and redesign curriculum and instructional materials (see, as well, Caplan, this collection; Tribble & Wingate, 2013). However, when time or budget constraints result in the absence of opportunities for such rich, extended collaboration, engaging in smaller-scale research can support investigation of unfamiliar genres and discourses. Digital corpus research[1] is an accessible, flexible way for writing center and WAC/WID faculty to generate knowledge and teaching materials in support of discipline-specific literacy instruction for the purposes of course or workshop design.

In this chapter, we provide an overview of corpus research in literacy teaching and situate corpus-informed teaching as compatible with sociocultural theories (SCT) of language learning. We find SCT provides a useful framework for understanding how corpus research helps us facilitate graduate students' development of insider discourse knowledge in the discipline of public health. We then demonstrate how one small corpus study helped Sarah Blazer develop discourse and genre knowledge, as well as inquiry-based exercises relevant to the needs of graduate students enrolled in a Public Health graduate reading and writing course at Lehman College, The City University of New York.[2] For the Masters in Public Health (MPH) program at Lehman, we focused our corpus study and materials development on research articles representative of those that students in this program were expected to gain facility reading and producing. Within a corpus of research articles from the *American Journal of Public Health*, we focused on subtechnical language, a feature of disciplinary discourse characterized by abstract, low-imagery vocabulary and phraseology used to create logical connections among concepts (Baker, 1988; Heltai, 1996).

Corpus Research for Teachers of Reading and Writing

Discourse knowledge is developed in part through participation in a community, but individuals learning in an academic setting also benefit from explicit literacy instruction situated within disciplinary and genre contexts (Aull, 2015; Curry, 2016; LaFrance & Corbett, this collection; Samraj, 2002; Swales & Feak, 2012; Tribble & Wingate, 2013). Corpus research can and does inform situated literacy instruction; for example, researchers may use an existing corpus like the Corpus of Contemporary American English (Davies, 2012) to investigate language patterns, or they may create a corpus to target a particular register. The latter may be more appropriate for

---

1 A corpus is a principled collection or database of texts compiled from naturally occurring examples of written language or language transcribed from recorded speech. Electronic corpora can be studied quantitatively and qualitatively using corpus software (Hunston, 2002).

2 Lehman College's MPH program has since merged with other CUNY Public Health programs and is now housed at another site.

classroom teaching (Krieger, 2003), as was the case in our study designed to develop instruction and materials for a graduate course in public health (PH).

Digital corpus research tools allow us to study corpora of any size with precision and efficiency. Through a concordance program like the one we used (AntConc; Anthony, 2011), researchers can produce and analyze data in various ways. For example, as we will later illustrate, one might first search a corpus for its most frequent words or phrases with various parameters for length. From the list produced, a word or phrase can be selected and viewed in concordance lines; the number of surrounding words is set by the search to show each instance throughout the corpus with the degree of context needed. It is also possible to view the word or phrase within the entire original text to provide maximum context. Analysis of concordance lines is a basic and pragmatic approach to processing corpus data when the goal is to inform day-to-day teaching (Hunston, 2002).

Daniel Krieger (2003) summarized corpus-derived language investigation for teaching purposes: researchers can look at many language patterns from morphological to lexical to discourse, and they do so with varying agendas. For example, Mona Baker (1988) discussed teaching applications for corpus-derived collocations with a focus on collocations that function rhetorically in a particular genre. From her corpus of medical journal articles, she found that in Discussion sections, "findings" is frequently preceded by "our" and followed by language like "extend" and "raise a question" to convey authors' evaluative commentary. Baker suggested that learners be made aware of frequent collocations and the genre and sections of text in which such phrases frequently appear to help learners gain facility with "whole stretches of language" (p. 104), as opposed to individual words.

From their study of a large corpus of chemistry research articles, Stoller et al. (2005) created a guide to passive voice, past participle verbs frequently seen in Methods sections. Such a list provided advanced chemistry students with access to discipline- and genre-conventional options for varying their use of verbs. This explicit list—including, among others, "was assigned," "was performed," "was filtered," "was washed" (Appendix B)—may expose students to vocabulary they have not yet learned, as well as invite meaning-making questions from curious novices about why particular phrases are so frequent in a particular section of chemistry research articles. Approaching materials development from a different direction, Christopher Tribble and Ursula Wingate (2013) argue that corpora of student writing may be optimal for the development of pedagogical materials that allow students to gain facility understanding and controlling target genres.

In *Academic Writing for Graduate Students*, John Swales and Christine Feak (2012) suggested that students explore academic phraseology of interest by performing basic internet searches and employing digital corpus tools, including AntConc (p. 28–29). Krieger (2003) also acknowledged the potential for student corpus research but argued that corpus research may be most useful for materials development, as teachers can "harness a corpus by filtering the data for students" ("Exploiting a Corpus," para. 1) to focus students' attention exclusively on understanding patterns of language use, as opposed to the process of actually locating relevant patterns.

Our study exhibits how a concordance program can prepare faculty—disciplinary outsiders or insiders—to develop instruction and materials by analyzing carefully chosen corpora to identify highly frequent disciplinary genre and discourse conventions, vocabulary, and phraseology (Hunston, 2002; Hyland & Tse, 2007; Stoller et al., 2005). Indeed, corpus research allows one to see patterns even members of the disciplinary community may not intuit (Liu, 2003; Stoller et al., 2005). Thus, with preparation through corpus research, those recruited to teach from outside a discipline may be in a uniquely useful position to guide graduate students working to develop more insider perspectives on their discipline.

Sociocultural Theory and Disciplinary Discourse Teaching and Learning

Literacy and writing studies faculty in disciplinary outsider positions can use corpus research to prepare situated literacy instruction that facilitates students' social acculturation toward more insider status. As disciplinary discourse is a complex, evolving social construction, sociocultural theory (SCT) helps us understand how students, regardless of language background (Curry, 2016), learn and internalize the discourse of an academic discipline and subsequently affect it, too. In SCT, meaning is located in the dialogue between human beings engaged in goal-directed behavior, not only in the signs or language itself (Lantolf & Thorne, 2006). For this reason, teaching highly frequent subtechnical phrases within a specific discipline should be based on a corpus of texts that reflects current and situated goal-directed behaviors so that findings are relevant to students studying a particular body of research, and relevant to their entrance and acclimation to the discipline or field.

Following Pál Heltai (1996) and Baker (1988), we characterize subtechnical language as abstract, low-imagery vocabulary and phraseology that is frequently used across academic discourses. Subtechnical language—*take effect* and *with respect to*, for example—may prove particularly difficult to understand and employ with precision because it is difficult to visualize and even define in some cases (Heltai, 1996). And though subtechnical language can be found across disciplines, which increases the chances students have encountered it, it may also function in unique ways depending on the disciplinary context (Casanave, 2008; Hyland & Tse, 2007).

The focus of discourse instruction, then, should be on patterns of meaning and "meaning potential" of phrases (Lantolf & Thorne, 2006, p. 9) within a corpus of relevant texts, not on a single definition divorced from the meaning-making context. Ken Hyland and Polly Tse's (2007) recent corpus research findings support teaching subtechnical language. From various widely used genres across disciplines, their analysis revealed that highly frequent items "are not used in the same way and do not mean exactly the same thing in different disciplinary contexts" (p. 249), thus challenging the notion that a general academic vocabulary exists across disciplinary environments and can or should be taught as such. For example, the word *expression* often characterizes emotional and/or verbal behavior, but in the phrase *gene expression*, the word characterizes a physical manifestation (Baker, 1988). Further, Casanave (2008) makes the noteworthy point that first language speakers may struggle more with "common words used in specialized ways" than second language speakers, "given the persistent connections [they make] of individual common words with their everyday connotations" (p. 20).

Highly Frequent Subtechnical Phrases as Scientific Concept

Unlike other theories concerned with the social context of learning, SCT is concerned with the psychological changes individuals undergo in the process of learning and *internalizing* what are known as *scientific* or *non-spontaneous concepts* through culturally constructed *mediating tools and artifacts* or "symbolic, communicative, and material resources" (Lantolf & Thorne, 2006, p. 233). Lev Vygotsky (1934/1986) made a key distinction between *spontaneous concepts* and *scientific concepts*. The former concepts are the product of the individual's everyday experiences; their development "know[s] no systematicity and goes from the phenomena upward toward generalizations" (p. 148). In other words, this is conceptual knowledge we develop—often unconsciously—by virtue of our life experiences or participation in a community of people who share certain goals. By contrast, scientific concepts are propositional, codified, documented knowledge that is "publicly accepted as a principled way of understanding phenomena within a particular discourse community" (Johnson, 2009, p. 15). We generally acquire scientific concepts through more explicit or purposeful instruction.

Corpus-derived, highly frequent subtechnical phrases can be characterized as scientific concepts if they have not been acquired unconsciously or through ongoing experiences. Such phrases in a particular discourse community can be understood as a conceptual group, as types of lexical units that students can be aware of as they build knowledge of the research in their field. Highly frequent subtechnical phrases that are introduced as the focus of instruction—and understood by students to be relevant to their own goals—are "conscious (and consciously applied)" (Swain, Kinnear & Steinman, 2011, p. 52). They are "systematic" and "not bound to context" (p. 52) in that they are used in closely related ways throughout a corpus of disciplinary texts. These uses are accepted by the discourse community as demonstrated through their patterned deployment. They are contextualized within the disciplinary knowledge and thus carry meaning for the discipline. We agree with Hyland and Tse (2007): "we need to identify students' target language needs as well as we can" and address them by "introducing, making salient, and practicing the specialized vocabulary of their fields or disciplines" (p. 249). Thus, highly frequent phrases like those identified in our corpus of PH research articles must be taught if not already known, and they must be understood by participants in this discourse community (Swales, 1990) if meaningful knowledge construction is the shared goal of students and faculty.

Understanding the meaning and sense—including the disciplinary function—of highly frequent disciplinary collocations provides learners with more conceptual understanding so they can "function appropriately in the range of settings in which they may find themselves" (Johnson, 2009, p. 14). As students develop deeper conceptual understanding of the highly frequent subtechnical language that allows researchers and scholars in their field to express relationships between and among complex ideas and factors, they "reframe the way they describe and interpret" (Johnson, 2009, p. 15) their experiences and knowledge: learners can apply a greater understanding of these patterned features of discourse in their field to engaging in more efficient and/or systematic approaches to reading and producing disciplinary work. Instruction can support learners as they begin to apply new concepts to concrete activity, thereby merging their conceptual and everyday knowledge (Johnson, 2009). As they internalize new concepts, they develop tools for building knowledge of research in their field. Concepts can be accessed consciously, metacognitively, until understanding becomes fully internalized.

Internalization Through Mediation

Internalization, defined from an SCT perspective, is "the internal reconstruction of an external operation" (Vygotsky, 1978, p. 56). That is, what is first learned through social interaction and is thus interpsychological next appears intrapsychologically (Vygotsky, 1978). Using internalized concepts, individuals engage in a continual process of reexternalizing internalized concepts such that those individuals have not only been psychologically constructed by culture but also contribute to its construction. As Karen Johnson (2009) describes, internalization occurs through activity that is "initially mediated by other people or cultural artifacts but later comes to be controlled by [the individual] as he or she appropriates and reconstructs resources to regulate his or her own activities" (p. 18).[3]

It is useful, then, to consider the concepts one aims to teach, as well as materials and methods, in terms of *mediating* tools required to facilitate internalization.

---

3   In SCT, a concept which is initially taught and internalized by way of mediating artifacts ultimately becomes a mediating artifact itself.

To teach corpus-derived, highly frequent subtechnical phrases, one can use mediating tools like corpus research results, concordance lines, and problem-posing activities to facilitate learning and internalization, where the latter is understood not as simple appropriation of concepts or knowledge, but as a dialogic process whereby individuals engage in activity that leads to "transformation of self *and* activity" (Johnson, 2009, p. 18). The agentive individual influences his or her internalization process and how it contributes to further growth and action (Johnson, 2009). Thus, internalization is understood as a dynamic, bi-directional process which is not about simply appropriating a copy of the external concept learned. Rather, internalization is about "making something one's own" (Lantolf & Thorne, 2006, p. 162), which can then be reexternalized to contribute to further cultural meaning-making. As students develop understanding of new concepts, their existing conceptual knowledge should serve to mediate their development. In learning highly frequent subtechnical phrases from a discipline-specific corpus, students can and should connect new concepts to existing knowledge.

SCT guides both the rationale for using corpus research to inform our teaching of disciplinary discourse and the subsequent development of corpus-based pedagogical applications. Next, we describe the methods and results of the corpus study we engaged in to inform instruction in a graduate reading and writing course for MPH students at Lehman College.

Context for a Public Health Corpus Study

For several years, including when this study was conducted,[4] Lehman College's Masters in Public Health (MPH) program offered a two-credit elective course in which students focused exclusively on developing their reading proficiency with disciplinary texts and their writing of discipline-situated summary, paraphrase, and analysis. Students in this program presented a range of literacy strengths and needs in terms of their experience with the language of their discipline, language characteristic of American academic English, and English for general communicative purposes. The goals and tight focus of the course meant that students benefited from our reading and writing discussions and exercises, regardless of their language backgrounds, a factor that might have been more significant in another context.

Many students in Lehman's program held field positions and had returned to school to improve their chances for career advancement; their strengths often lay in the practical knowledge they brought to their studies rather than in their command of more formal academic literacies. They were professional insiders, knowledgeable

---

4   Lehman College's MPH program has since merged with other CUNY public health programs and is now housed at another site.

from work experiences about key public health (PH) issues like diabetes, and generally able to use ubiquitous terminology like "*socioeconomic risk factors*" with ease. But back in school, they often struggled to interpret and command phrases comprising the connective tissue of their discipline's texts, what we address in our study as subtechnical language. For example, students recognized phrases including words like "*incidence*" and "*probability*" but often struggled to fully comprehend these phrases in context and struggled to use them confidently and precisely in discussion and writing.

While the majority of students in this MPH program did not go on to pursue careers in academic research, as graduate students, they were expected to engage with the field's research and scholarship on an advanced level. Outside of school, they would benefit from being able to more effectively read and draw on the research that could more fully inform their daily work. Regardless of professional goals, students pursuing advanced disciplinary study need precise understanding of the fundamental language their field most frequently uses to express relationships among key terms and concepts. For these reasons, the highly frequent subtechnical language became a particularly important aspect of PH texts to investigate, and it became clear that corpus research could help answer a question relevant to teaching students to own more of the fundamental language of their discipline: What are the most high-frequency subtechnical phrases that appear in a corpus of PH research articles, and what do they mean?

From hundreds of three- to five-word phrases ranked by frequency, several of the most frequently occurring phrases became the focus of inquiry for classroom application: *more likely to*, *was associated with*, and *the effect of*. These are three of a number of phrases we might have chosen to focus on; they are not the only three from our corpus worthy of consideration for classroom teaching. At first glance, phrases like *more likely to* may seem trivial; however, from usage patterns, it becomes evident that such phrases are subtle but important carriers of the discipline's ways of thinking and knowing. According to Hyland and Tse (2007), "all academic representations shape and manipulate language for disciplinary purposes, often refashioning everyday terms so that words take on more specific meanings" (p. 247). It is difficult to know whether highly frequent language in a given discipline is or is not used in unique ways without investigating it and comparing it to others. So, while *more likely to* may express the same type of relationship in PH as it does in sociology, its highly frequent use in PH is significant in and of itself because it exemplifies the complexity of phenomena being studied in PH. Since there are always numerous factors influencing any given phenomena of interest in PH, causation is virtually impossible to establish among the range of issues PH researchers address.

Results of corpus studies like the one described here can inform what key language and rhetorical moves we guide students to pay attention to in the texts they engage with as students and emerging professionals in their fields, both as critical readers and producers of text. This study contributed to the development of more disciplinarily situated instruction for students in the MPH program at Lehman College, including exercises that engaged students in interactive inquiry into disciplinary practices.

Methods and Results

Here, we describe the methodology and results of our small PH corpus study, followed by a discussion of socioculturally situated pedagogical applications of our corpus findings for students in the program that sparked the inquiry. The methodology provides a set of guidelines for outsiders or insiders engaged in corpus research for the development of disciplinary discourse knowledge and materials. The results of this study may also be relevant to others teaching PH students since the subtechnical language we focus on is derived from *The American Journal of Public Health*, a prominent publication in the field of public health.

Using AntConc (Anthony, 2011), free digital concordance software, our first research question can be answered with ease: What are the most high-frequency subtechnical phrases that appear in a corpus of public health texts? By carefully analyzing concordance lines in which the phrases appear, we can answer our second question: What do these phrases mean? Below, we outline our methods for developing the corpus, setting search parameters, choosing subtechnical phrases to focus on, and determining the meaning of those phrases. We combine the methods and results here because our methods for choosing and determining meaning of the subtechnical phrases are best understood alongside the results of our searches.

Corpus

Our selection of corpus texts was entirely pragmatic and specific to the goal of supporting students in a particular MPH reading and writing course at Lehman College. For several reasons, *The American Journal of Public Health* was an appropriate source from which to draw corpus texts: faculty in this graduate program drew on it frequently; the journal includes articles on a wide range of PH topics, as opposed to focusing on a particular area (e.g., *Journal of Health Politics, Policy, and Law*); and the journal includes traditional empirical research articles which faculty in this MPH program identified as very challenging for many students.[5]

---

5   Other sections of *The American Journal of Public Health* include PH scholarship; a study of these articles may yield different results in terms of most frequent phraseology.

From the "Research and Practice" section of *The American Journal of Public Health*, we selected a total of 36 issues and 108 articles.[6] Charts, tables, and bibliographic entries were not included in our corpus. Three separate files were created in order to run separate analyses on each year of the corpus, but we were able to run the analysis on all three files at once to see the most frequent phrases across the whole corpus and still see clearly the frequency and location of phrases by year of publication.

Concordance Lines

To determine which phrases appeared most frequently in our corpus, we used the AntConc Clusters tool and set the "n-gram" parameters for frequently occurring phrases at a minimum of three words and a maximum of four words (see Figure 13.1); it is simple and useful to play with these parameters in the context of materials development.

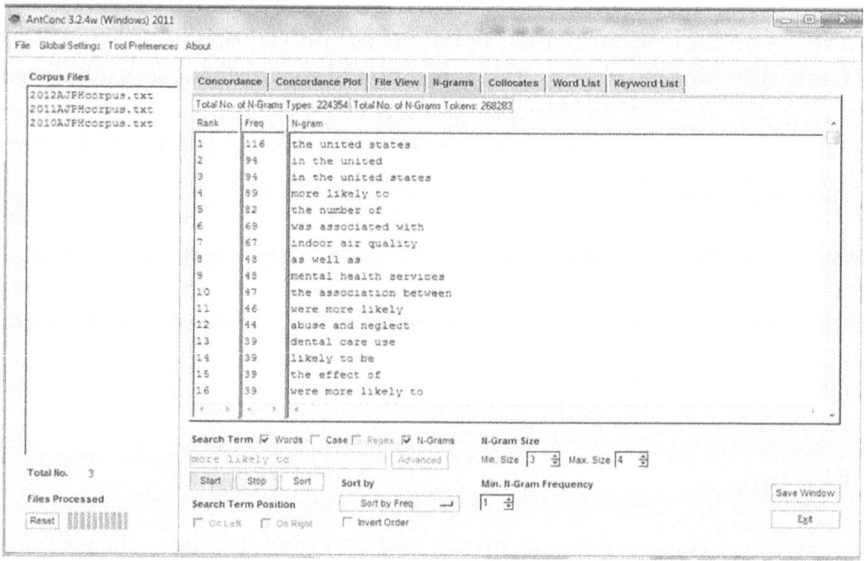

Figure 13.1. N-gram data.

After reviewing results of the query for most frequently occurring three- to four-word phrases, we discussed whether each expressed content or functioned as subtechnical language (see Table 13.1 for a list of the first 15 phrases) and reviewed concordance plots to verify that subtechnical phrases appeared throughout and content phrases appeared in concentrated parts of the corpus (see Figure 13.2). For example, the phrase *more likely to* functions as subtechnical language. It provides a means to express probability, which is of primary concern in issues of PH, and it appeared with

---

6   This study was conducted in 2013.

great frequency throughout the corpus, regardless of the focus of a given article. The concrete phrase *mental health services* expresses content, and AntConc's concordance plot tool confirmed that the phrase indeed appeared with great frequency in only one part of the corpus, the focus of one of the 108 articles (see Figure 13.2).

Table 13.1. Fifteen most frequent three- and four-word phrases;

Three- to Four-Word Phrases	Frequency	Content or Subtechnical Language Classification
the united states	116	Content
in the united	91	Content
in the united states	91	Content
more likely to	89	Subtechnical
the number of	74	Subtechnical
was associated with	69	Subtechnical
indoor air quality	67	Content
as well as	48	Subtechnical
mental health services	48	Content
the association between	47	Subtechnical
were more likely	46	Subtechnical
abuse and neglect	44	Content
dental care use	39	Content
likely to be	39	Subtechnical
the effect of	39	Subtechnical

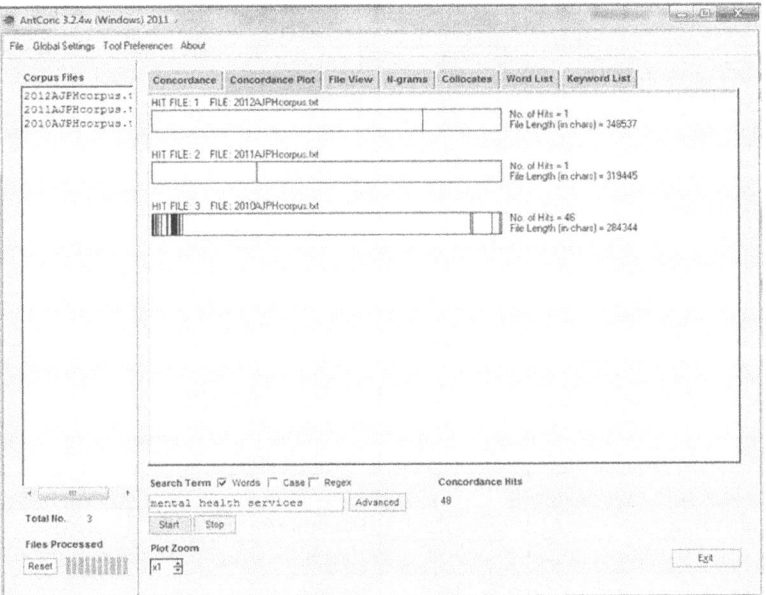

Figure 13.2. Concordance plot for mental health services.

After determining through our discussions whether the top 75 most frequently occurring three- to four-word phrases expressed content or functioned as subtechnical language, we isolated the subtechnical phrases for further consideration (see Table 13.2), since only phrases classified as subtechnical were relevant to our study. Initially, we determined the meaning of these phrases intuitively; then we studied the concordance lines for each phrase (see Figure 13.3 for a view of *more likely to* concordance lines). For example, while our classification of *more likely to* as an expression of probability did not change after studying the concordance lines, our classification of *on the basis of* did change; we initially guessed that *on the basis of* signals the use of empirical evidence to make a claim, but learned from the concordance lines that the phrase is used more generally to indicate any condition(s) underlying a claim, theory, decision, or action.

Table 13.2. Twenty-five most frequent subtechnical phrases

Three- to Four-Word Phrases	Frequency	Meaning
more likely to	89	Probability
the number of	82	Quantification
was associated with	69	Relationship between and among factors and outcomes
as well as	48	Expresses concurrence, modification
the association between	47	Relationship between a possible contributing factor and outcome
were more likely	46	Probability
likely to be	39	Probability
the effect of	39	Causality
were more likely to	39	Probability
included in the	38	Containment of something as part of a whole
in the past	35	Temporal
less likely to	35	Probability
we found that	34	Research process
the basis of/on the basis/on the basis of	31	Indicates an underlying condition
more likely to be	27	Probability
significantly associated with	27	Relationship between a possible contributing factor and outcome(s)
the odds of	27	Probability
we did not	27	Research process
with respect to	27	Referential
because of the	25	Causality
we controlled for	25	Research process
data from the	24	Referential
the prevalence of	24	Quantification

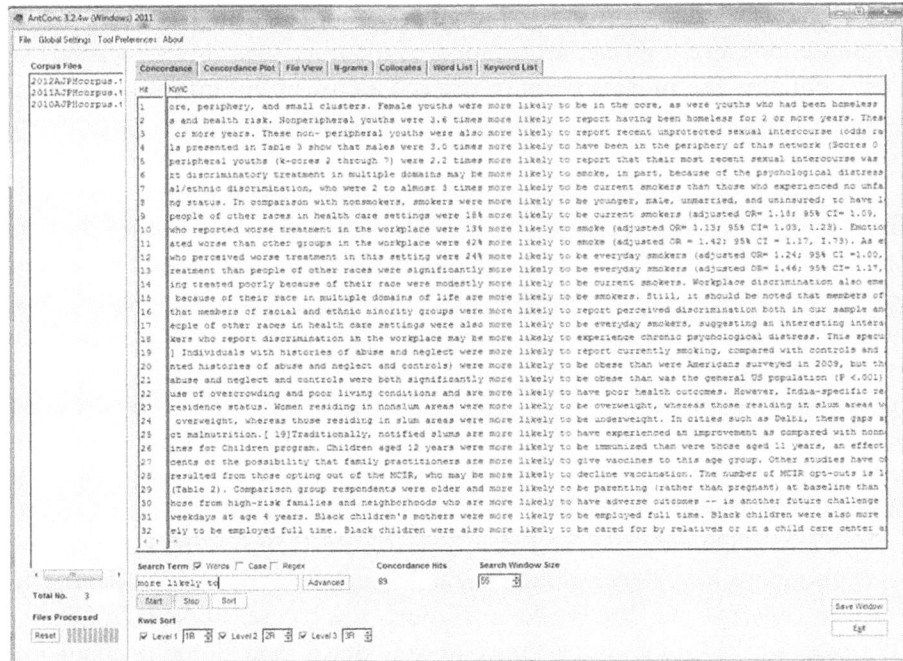

Figure 13.3. Concordances for more likely to.

Finally, we determined which subtechnical phrases were most interesting to us for the purposes of our development of course materials and instruction. Of the phrases qualifying as subtechnical, we chose to investigate three phrases appearing more than 30 times in the corpus: *more likely to, was associated with*, and *the effect of.*

Discussion

We chose to focus our development of pedagogical applications on frequently appearing abstract phrases expressing probability, causality, and relationships between factors and outcomes because these phrases are difficult to explain and understand outside of authentic contexts, and they carry important meaning in the field of public health. Students need to gain facility reading and using these phrases to succeed in their PH coursework, as well as in many PH professional environments. First, phrases including the word *likely* were of interest to us as they express probability and appeared with great frequency and in various collocations in this corpus: *more likely to, were more likely, likely to be, were more likely to, less likely to,* and *more likely to be.* The phrases *was associated with* and *the association between* were of interest as these phrases express relationships between and among factors and outcomes that are important to PH researchers. We chose to investigate *the effect of* because we wondered whether concordance lines would reveal that this phrase indicated a greater articulation of certainty than the "associated" and "likely" phrases. The phrases we have selected are by no means the only phrases worthy of close attention. The applications we describe are simply three illustrations of what is possible.

Throughout this corpus of disciplinary texts, the phrases we selected are used in a finite number of closely related ways. Lehman's MPH students needed to understand and gain facility with subtechnical phrases such as these, as well as the more specialized terminology of PH research, in order to contribute to meaningful knowledge construction in this discourse community. Throughout their coursework, they were explicitly introduced to and required to use the language of their field, which they did with varying degrees of success. Oftentimes, those who struggled to produce clear and accurate writing did so because they misused subtechnical language used to express clear and logical relationships between concepts and data. In the reading and writing course we have been discussing, students frequently expressed shock at how differently they and their peers could interpret the same sentence written to express fact. They realized on a new level how difficult, but essential, it is to explain concepts and data precisely. Through this course, students in Lehman's MPH program had a rare opportunity to slow down their thinking about reading and writing, and they were eager to practice carefully interpreting and using more effectively the language that surrounds all of the specialized vocabulary and content they had learned. Corpus research can usefully inform instruction in this environment.

The exercises we discuss next do not represent formulas for the authors, nor are they intended as prescriptions for readers. Rather, each exercise demonstrates how a single phrase or family of phrases could be the basis for explicit teaching in an actual class session. In the primary author's experience, exercises and discussion around phrases of interest were embedded organically throughout course meetings.

Pedagogical Application: *more likely to*

Public health research is focused on identifying and understanding trends in health issues, as well as proposing and studying the effects of preventive programming and interventions, and the phrase *more likely to* (as well as *were more likely, likely to be, less likely to*, etc.) provides a useful and discourse-familiar expression of probability. It is typically used to discuss trends and outcomes alongside numerical data in Results sections and without numerical data in Discussion sections.

A number of questions about precision and discourse conventions could be posed in a class setting such that students develop greater understanding of the meaning and sense of the highly frequent phrase *more likely to*: What does it mean that someone or something is more likely to be or do something in PH research? Does it mean 51 percent more likely to? Eighty-nine percent? How often is the phrase qualified by numerical values? Do usage patterns differ depending on the section of the article (Results or Discussion)? That is, might the phrase appear more frequently without qualifying numerical data in the Introduction or Discussion sections and more frequently with qualifying numerical data in Results sections?

The questions posed above can provide the basis for a useful interactive exercise. In a class setting, the instructor might present to students various tools to mediate instruction: their finding from the corpus analysis—the highly frequent phrase—as well as concordance lines in which the phrase appears (refer again to Figure 13.3), one or more articles from the corpus to show the phrase in larger context, and guiding questions. The instructor might begin by asking students, "What does this phrase mean to you? Do you notice it often?" And could then establish the relevance of this corpus-based lesson by asking, "What could we figure out by looking more closely at the phrase in the context of research articles from a prominent journal in PH?" With the questions that arise in the corpus analysis process and the full text of one or more articles included in the corpus, the students could then discuss or work collaboratively to observe usage patterns in the texts and report back to the group. Guiding questions could include:

- How often is the phrase qualified by numerical values?
- Are there sections of the article where the phrase is more or less likely to be qualified by numerical values?
- What other patterns are noticeable? What could be significant about them?
- What do your findings suggest about the use of data in your field?
- What does this help us understand about reading and writing research in public health?
- Do your findings cause you to think in new ways about how you read research articles in your field?

This exercise and the subsequent discussion engage students in abstract, critical, and analytical thinking about the nature of their field through the context of a specific lexical unit they will encounter often and must use carefully. Students may be interested to see the utility of a phrase like *more likely to*; from its frequency and usage patterns, it is clear that the phrase is indicative of the discipline's use of large data sets as a way of thinking and knowing about—and describing—important health phenomena. It may be difficult to ask students, novices to a discipline or profession, to consider the nature of their field. This exercise engages them in such an inquiry for pragmatic purposes while also supporting increasing awareness and fluency with a frequently used phrase. Indeed, Lehman MPH students were highly engaged in conversation around patterns of language use in their field, including group translation sessions around statements of research findings and group editing sessions around the students' own attempts to use probabilistic language to paraphrase others' research findings.

Sociocultural theory's notion of language as communicative activity positions "language learning as an emergent process [which] focuses more on doing, knowing, and becoming, rather than on the attainment of a steady state understood as a well-defined set of rules, principles, and parameters, etc." (Lantolf & Thorne, 2006, p. 138). As illustrated above in terms of classroom learning, the process of developing disciplinary discourse knowledge should be seen in terms of doing, knowing, and becoming since discourse is an ever-evolving set of socially constructed conventions and patterns created and used to carry out ever-evolving needs and interests of a given research and professional community. Students must come to understand the dialogic nature of this process, as well, and classroom instruction around disciplinary discourse patterns and conventions should engage them on an active, conceptual level if it is meant to facilitate participation and meaning-making from novices.

Pedagogical Application: *was associated with*

With 69 occurrences in the corpus, *was associated with* can frequently be seen conveying important evidence of relationships among factors and outcomes. The phrase is used to express degrees of association, a key objective of PH research, and is frequently followed by adjective-noun combinations communicating statistical possibility—"*increased odds*" or "*reduced probability*"—as well as actual occurrences—"*increased times*" or "*lower numbers.*"

While the phrase carries significant information, students in the MPH course we have been discussing struggled to accurately explain or paraphrase the findings expressed with those phrases, and perhaps more significant, did not realize that they frequently misrepresented findings. One of the course objectives is for students to discuss and write more clearly and accurately about source material. In class discussions, they often attempted to paraphrase information from a research article, and it was not uncommon for others to then disagree and offer counter representations. In these instances, it became clear that many were struggling to understand and/or re-present information from the text.

In some cases, students were unclear of a phrase's meaning; in others, they simply did not yet have access to alternatives that would show they could re-present it in equivalent terms. For students who could benefit from greater understanding of, or exposure to, the phrase *was associated with*, it would be useful to point out its patterns of use and observe them in context. For example, students might be presented with the following list of phrases that follow *was associated with* in the corpus:

was associated with	INCREASED	odds
		times
		probability
		uptake
		use
		risk
	REDUCED	numbers
		risk
		blood pressure
		odds
	BETTER	risk factor profile
	LOWER	odds
		mean BMI
		probability
		activity

One could ask students, then, "What patterns do you see?" And point out, if needed, "There are terms expressing statistical possibility and terms expressing actual occurrences." The differences between the two can be clarified, and then students can look at some of these phrases in context. (See Figure 13.4 for a view of *was associated with* concordance lines.) They can try to explain the statements to one another and determine together—with guidance from the instructor where needed—where they are clear or unclear about the findings expressed. Students in Lehman's MPH program often had work and research experiences they were eager to draw on as they contextualized new concepts; promoting such sharing is particularly useful to encourage as students without these experiences benefit from hearing about those of their peers. If, in this discovery process, students are surprised by their varying interpretations of the same phrase in context, this is in itself a useful realization for them; information of this kind can be communicated back to disciplinary faculty who may consider additional ways to address challenging statistical concepts in their teaching.

Subsequent exercises might engage students in processes of consciously attempting to employ phrases like those discussed here in their own writing, thereby "imitating" (Lantolf & Thorne, 2006, p. 151)—or intentionally modeling—the discipline's use of important phrases in their own written production of meaning. To usefully facilitate students' awareness of and integration into discourse communities, teachers must facilitate carefully mediated inquiry that allows students to draw on their experiences and knowledge as they develop and internalize new linguistic and conceptual knowledge relevant to their professional development.

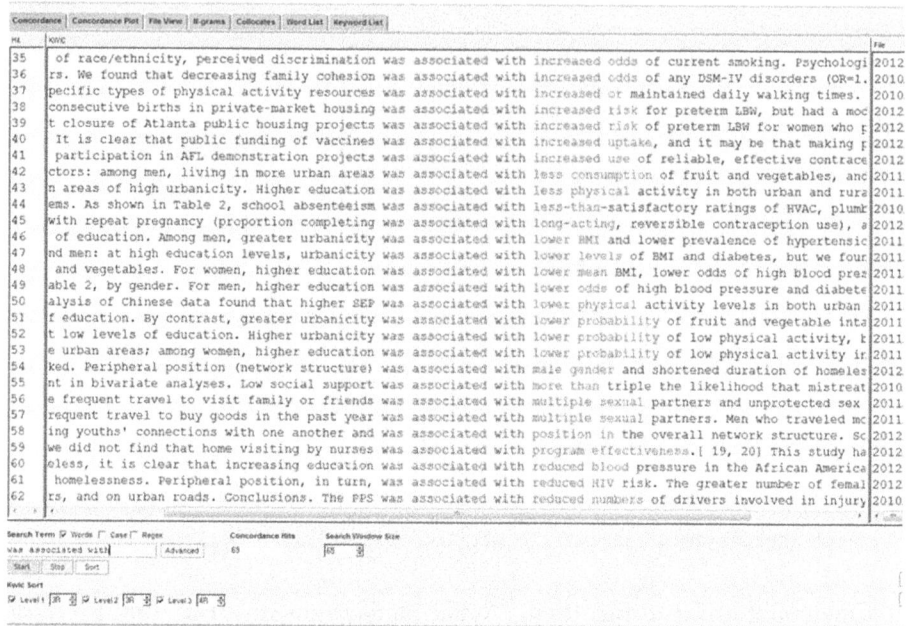

Figure 13.4. Concordances for was associated with.

Pedagogical Application: *the effect of*

While *the effect of* is among the most frequently used phrases throughout this corpus of research articles (39 times), it seemed interesting that this phrase expressing causality appeared less frequently than phrases that more generally express relationships—phrases including the word "*association.*" A closer look at the concordance lines and full text of the articles revealed that *the effect of* was typically used in the Results and Discussion sections to indicate the impact of one or more factors on a phenomenon of interest. In Results sections, the phrase was used along with indications of statistical significance; in Discussion sections, the phrase was used more generally to refer back to more precise data-based statements found in Results sections.

With this phrase, it would be useful to have students observe the difference in its uses in the Results and Discussion sections; one article in our corpus provides a particularly clear example of the two different uses, as it employs the phrase numerous times in both sections. Students could be given this article and asked to highlight occurrences of the phrase in the two sections and determine how it is used differently. In fact, this pattern held true for all three phrases we investigated. And because students in the MPH program we have been describing explicitly stated that the differences between Results and Discussion sections are not entirely clear to them, an exercise in which they can see clearly how a single phrase functions differently in these two sections may be a helpful step toward clarifying the distinction in concrete terms.

Conclusion

Graduate students benefit from a range of opportunities to orient to the discourse communities they seek to enter, and they often find such opportunities through field experiences and apprenticeships. Complementing these experiences, corpus-informed systematic and explicit disciplinary discourse instruction can help speed up discourse acquisition already in progress (Russell, 1995).

From a sociocultural perspective, the focus of discourse instruction should arise from the needs and interests of students. Our study investigated highly frequent subtechnical language in a corpus of disciplinary texts relevant to Masters in Public Health students at Lehman College. We focused on subtechnical language because students in the program demonstrated a lack of fluency with it, and this lack of fluency impeded their ability to understand and articulate new concepts and to contribute new knowledge. For Lehman MPH students, studying the language, structure, and rhetorical moves conventional in PH research articles in their field provided opportunities to look closely at a genre in ways they had not experienced before. Students benefited from collaboratively considering the meaning of patterns from the rich perspectives of their varied backgrounds as undergraduates—in chemistry, social work, and nursing, to name a few—and as working professionals—in research laboratories, community health, and non-profit advocacy. Through reading and guided discussion, they gained awareness of some of their field's underlying principles and goals, but also its evolving and flexible dimensions (Thaiss & Zawacki, 2006), especially as they compared and raised questions about language, structure, and rhetorical moves in research articles from various journals. A useful follow-up to our study of discourse features and applications for materials development would be a study of ways in which students' reading, writing, and discussion changed as a result of corpus-informed instruction.

Corpus research can be employed on large and small scales to inform literacy instruction that meets immediate interests and needs of students. It can provide background knowledge for composition, WAC/WID, or writing center faculty recruited to teach or support consultants and fellows outside of their disciplines and inform the development of materials to mediate instruction. For example, developing a corpus and conducting a small-scale corpus study like the one we have described could allow a writing center director, writing fellow, and faculty member from another discipline to prepare for classroom collaboration; from working together to build a relevant corpus, to sharing observations and questions regarding results of analyses, all collaborators would have opportunities to gain knowledge, awareness, and ideas for instruction. Corpus research is accessible and can be used to respond to varying agendas for discourse instruction, allowing outsiders and insiders to develop situated literacy instruction sensitive to the dynamic nature of disciplinary discourse.

References

Anthony, L. (2011). AntConc (Version 3.2.4) [Software]. Waseda University. http://www.antlab.sci.waseda.ac.jp/.

Aull, L. (2015). Linguistic attention in rhetorical genre studies and first-year writing. *Composition Forum, 31.* https://compositionforum.com/issue/31/linguistic-attention.php.

Baker, M. (1988). Sub-technical vocabulary and the ESP teacher: An analysis of some rhetorical items in medical journal articles. *Reading in a Foreign Language, 4*(2), 91–105. http://www.nflrc.hawaii.edu/rfl/PastIssues/rfl42baker.pdf.

Caplan, N. A. (2020). Genres and conflicts in MBA writing assignments. In M. Brooks-Gillies, E. G. Garcia, S. H. Kim, K. Manthey & T. G. Smith (Eds.), *Graduate writing across the disciplines: Identifying, teaching, and supporting.* The WAC Clearinghouse; University Press of Colorado. https://wac.colostate.edu/books/atd/graduate.

Casanave, C. P. (2008). Learning participatory practices in graduate school: Some perspective-taking by a mainstream educator. In C. P. Casanave & X. Li (Eds.), *Learning the literacy practices of graduate school* (pp. 14–31). University of Michigan Press.

Curry, M. J. (2016). More than language: Graduate student writing as "disciplinary becoming." In S. Simpson, N. A. Caplan, M. Cox & T. Phillips (Eds.), *Supporting graduate student writers: Research, curriculum, and program design* (pp. 78–96). University of Michigan Press.

Davies, M. (2012). *Corpus of contemporary American English.* http://corpus.byu.edu/coca/.

Heltai, P. (1996). Teaching abstract subtechnical vocabulary. *Cuadernos de Filología Inglesa, 5*(2), 71–82.

Hunston, S. (2002). *Corpora in applied linguistics.* Cambridge University Press.

Hyland, K. & Tse, P. (2007). Is there an "academic vocabulary?" *TESOL Quarterly, 41*(2), 235–253.

Johnson, K. (2009). *Second language teacher education: A sociocultural perspective.* Routledge.

Krieger, D. (2003). Corpus linguistics: What it is and how it can be applied to teaching. *The Internet TESL Journal, 9*(3). iteslj.org/Articles/Krieger-Corpus.html.

LaFrance, M. & Corbett, S. J. (2020). Discourse community fail! Negotiating choices in success/failure and graduate-level writing development. In M. Brooks-Gillies, E. G.

Garcia, S. H. Kim, K. Manthey & T. G. Smith (Eds.), *Graduate writing across the disciplines: Identifying, teaching, and supporting*. The WAC Clearinghouse; University Press of Colorado. https://wac.colostate.edu/books/atd/graduate.

Lantolf, J. P. & Thorne, S. L. (2006). *Sociocultural theory and the genesis of second language development*. Oxford University Press.

Liu, D. (2003). The most frequently used spoken American English idioms: A corpus analysis and its implications. *TESOL Quarterly, 37*(4), 671–700.

Russell, D. R. (1995). Activity theory and its implications for writing instruction. In J. Petraglia (Ed.), *Reconceiving writing, rethinking writing instruction* (pp. 51–77). Lawrence Erlbaum Associates.

Russell, D. R. (2002). *Writing in the academic disciplines, 1870–1990: A curricular history* (2nd ed.). Southern Illinois University Press.

Samraj, B. (2002). Introductions in research articles: Variations across disciplines. *English for Specific Purposes, 21*(1), 1–17.

Stoller, F. L., Jones, J. K., Costanza-Robinson, M. S. & Robinson, M. S. (2005). Demystifying disciplinary writing: A case study in the writing of chemistry. *Across the Disciplines, 2*. https://wac.colostate.edu/docs/atd/lds/stoller.pdf.

Swain, M., Kinnear, P. & Steinman, L. (2011). *Sociocultural theory in language education: An introduction through narratives*. Multilingual Matters.

Swales, J. (1990). *Genre analysis: English in academic and research settings*. Cambridge University Press.

Swales, J. & Feak, C. (2012). *Academic writing for graduate students: Essential tasks and skills* (3rd ed.). University of Michigan Press.

Thaiss, C. & Zawacki, T. M. (2006). *Engaged writers and dynamic disciplines: Research on the academic writing life*. Boynton/Cook.

Tribble, C. & Wingate, U. (2013). From text to corpus—a genre-based approach to academic literacy instruction. *System, 41*, 307–321.

Vygotsky, L. (1978). *Mind in society: The development of higher psychological processes*. M. Cole, V. John-Steiner, S. Scribner & E. Souberman (Eds.). Harvard University Press.

Vygotsky, L. (1986). *Thought and language*. (A Kozulin, Trans.). MIT Press. (Original work published 1934)

Genres and Conflicts in MBA Writing Assignments

Nigel A. Caplan
UNIVERSITY OF DELAWARE

> **Abstract**: Although Master of Business Administration (MBA) degrees are popular for international students and complex in terms of their linguistic demands, research and pedagogy offer little advice for non-native speakers of English preparing for the written and oral genres of this professional degree. This chapter describes a needs analysis conducted by one pre-matriculation program that teaches international MBA students speaking English as a Second Language (ESL). In addition to online surveys and focus groups, a verbal protocol analysis was conducted with four MBA professors to better understand one key written genre that emerged from the analysis as both important for and challenging to ESL students: the case study write-up. A structure for the genre is presented along with the faculty's evaluative criteria. The study is discussed through a framework of four overlapping theories: genre studies, cognitive strategy instruction, activity theory, and cultural capital. Implications and strategies for preparing MBA students are suggested.
>
> **Keywords**: MBA, English as a Second Language, Second Language Writing, Genre Studies, Strategy Instruction, Needs Analysis, Cultural-Historical Activity Theory, Cultural Capital, Systemic Functional Linguistics, English for Academic Purposes

Demand for Master of Business Administration (MBA) and related graduate business degrees has historically been strong, with almost a quarter of a million prospective students worldwide taking the Graduate Management Admissions Test (GMAT) at the time the study reported in this chapter was conducted in 2012. The United States has been the most popular destination for international business students, followed by other Anglophone countries (Graduate Management Admission Council, 2016). In the UK, for example, international students, many of whom are non-native speakers of English, constitute as many as one third of enrollees in business-related graduate degrees (Nathan, 2013). Success in business school requires writing in complex genres, which are often unfamiliar and especially challenging for students writing in their second language (L2). Furthermore, the nature of the MBA degree is contested: at once professional preparation and academic master's (Freedman, Adam & Smart, 1994). Like many professional graduate degrees, therefore, the MBA forces faculty and students to negotiate between these sometimes "conflicting demands," which are especially evident in writing assignments (Flower, 1994). Is the intended reader the CEO of a company or the professor? Is the text's purpose to offer strategic advice or display knowledge of course content? Will the text be evaluated by its real-world impact or graded on a professor's rubric? These are questions which often go unasked but which affect the writing process and the written product.

Despite the popularity of the MBA and the complexity of its written genres, little scholarship has directly addressed this topic, and even less so L2 writers' graduate business writing (e.g., Nathan, 2013). Business English as a Second Language (ESL) textbooks tend to focus on the needs of working professionals rather than MBA students, and they are generally published in the UK, written in British English, and aimed at the European context (e.g., Dubicka, O'Keefe, Falvey, Kent & Cotton, 2011).[1] Even the most established writing textbook for (L2) graduate students offers little specific advice for students entering business school since it is mostly focused on research rather than professional degrees (Swales & Feak, 2012). However, business schools have genres that are unique to their discipline, such as the case study and its associated network of oral and written genres (Forman & Rymer, 1999a, 1999b; Freedman et al., 1994). For students who lack the linguistic and cultural "capital" (Bourdieu, 1986) to recognize, analyze, and reproduce these genres, the MBA may prove to be an especially frustrating experience.

The study reported in this chapter was motivated by these frustrations, although they originated from business school faculty rather than students. The university where I teach offers conditional admission to international students, which means they have to meet departments' English proficiency requirements through intensive pre-matriculation English courses before starting graduate classes, rather than on standardized language tests. Many of the full-time MBA students at the university are graduates of our program, and it is not unusual to see business classes in which up to half of the students are international. Since students must demonstrate a very high level of linguistic proficiency and submit a satisfactory GMAT score to matriculate, we were surprised and disturbed to hear in 2011 that some of them were not subsequently flourishing in the MBA. Therefore, in order to better identify and address the source of these difficulties in our classes, we conducted a needs analysis. Although we solicited feedback from both international students and faculty, we focused on the MBA faculty, who had initially raised concerns with us regarding the growth of international student enrollment in their program. As Johns (2011)

---

1   In the first two units of this popular textbook, *Market Leader Advanced Coursebook* (Dubicka et al., 2011), dates are written in the British format (17 November not November 17), British spelling and idioms are presented ("could you do me a favour and pass the water?"), British business correspondence style is taught ("Dear Sir/Madam"), the CEO of a German company operating in the UK is interviewed, and European education systems are discussed. The first American reference is a Cleveland-based company, but this case study focuses on its UK and Ireland sales team.

has suggested, in order to improve students' "genre awareness," it is first necessary to investigate disciplinary faculty's expectations. A similar approach has been taken in other needs analyses at both the graduate and undergraduate levels, (e.g., Caplan & Stevens, 2017; Cooper & Bikowski, 2007; Evans, Anderson & Eggington, 2015; Ferris & Tagg, 1996; Horowitz, 1986; Nesi & Gardner, 2012; Trice, 2003).

Methods and Frameworks

The needs analysis of language skills required for L2 students in the MBA program involved three stages: online surveys of international students and faculty, focus groups and interviews with MBA faculty, and a verbal protocol analysis in which four MBA professors "thought aloud" as they evaluated student writing. The surveys and focus groups are briefly summarized below since they led to the creation of the final stage, which is the focus of this chapter. As the analysis evolved, so too did the theoretical frameworks which governed it, and these are also introduced as they provide the lenses through which the results are interpreted. The chapter concludes with specific pedagogical recommendations for cognitive strategies (MacArthur, 2011) that turn genre awareness into cultural and linguistic capital, particularly for L2 writers (Bourdieu, 1986).

Online Surveys

In order to learn more about the discipline-specific language needs and areas of difficulty faced by international MBA students, an online questionnaire (https://nigelteacher.files.wordpress.com/2012/06/actual-faculty-survey.pdf) was distributed via the chair of the Department of Business Administration to all faculty who teach graduate students in the College of Business and Economics. Twenty-eight responses were received between October 2011 and March 2012. Since it was not possible to determine the exact size of the sample frame, a response rate cannot be accurately calculated. However, the department website lists 41 members of the faculty, which would indicate a response as high as 69 percent. Almost all the respondents (22) were teaching or had taught ESL MBA students.

The core of the survey asked respondents to rate the importance of 23 tasks and activities on a scale of 1 (not at all important) to 5 (very important). The list of tasks was derived from previous research (Cooper & Bikowski, 2007; Hale et al., 1996; Zhu, 2004) as well as prior conversations with MBA faculty.

The survey was motivated by genre theories, and in particular those aligned with the so-called "Sydney School" of Systemic Functional Linguistics, or SFL (Rose & Martin, 2012). Scholars in the SFL tradition have explored how genres constitute and are constituted by the "context of culture" in which they emerge, such that by analyzing relations between genres, it is possible to "map" the culture, in this case the culture of the MBA program at this university (Martin & Rose, 2008; Nesi & Gardner, 2012). Educators working with SFL aim to foster both "mastery of" and "critical control over" high-stakes genres (Martin, 2009; Rothery, 1996), which aligns well with the goals of the needs analysis. Tasks on the survey were phrased as much as possible in language that suggested specific genres and practices (e.g., "reading journal articles" and "participating in class discussions") rather than broad language skills (reading, writing, listening, speaking) or rhetorical modes (e.g., persuasion, comparison, process). Respondents were then asked to rate their overall perception of their international students' performance on each skill on a scale of 1 (very unsuccessful) to 5 (very successful).[2] A similar survey was also sent to matriculated international students in the MBA program. However, the response rate was not high enough to permit analysis of these data.

An additional theoretical lens used here was English for Academic Purposes, or EAP (Swales, 1990), which focuses on the communicative purposes of academic genres. EAP research has always been concerned with raising awareness of and providing exposure to discipline-specific tasks (Swales & Feak, 2012). Therefore, EAP needs analysis often starts with syllabi and assignments or surveys such as the one in this study (e.g., Cooper & Bikowski, 2007).[3] Thus, in order to build a picture of the linguistic terrain which MBA students need to navigate, MBA syllabi were also collected.

Focus Groups and Interviews

As a follow-up to the survey, focus groups and interviews were conducted with seven faculty and administrators. Preliminary analysis of these discussions as well as the survey revealed two findings which prompted further research. First, the case study method, a pedagogy developed at the founding of the Harvard Business School in the early twentieth century for its nascent MBA (Forman & Rymer, 1999b), was widespread, although its implementation varied somewhat by class and professor. In the Harvard method, students read a published study of a business dilemma in order to participate in a class discussion, the crux of the teaching and learning in this pedagogy. During the discussion, the skillful instructor guides stu-

---

2   While not all international students in the MBA are non-native speakers of English, the vast majority are Chinese, and we did not presume that MBA faculty would be familiar with acronyms such as ESL or L2. Therefore, "international students" was used as a shorthand for "international students for whom English is not their first language."

3   SFL scholars, on the other hand, would usually start with student texts. However, there is some overlap: Nathan (2013) applied an EAP lens to his study of the case write-up, but his careful analysis of the use of linguistic resources such as modality, verb tense, and hedging are reminiscent of SFL genre descriptions.

dents through "practical problem solving in real situations" that provide "engaged interaction between students and instructor" (Forman & Rymer, 1999b, p. 379). According to Forman and Rymer, the associated written genre, the case write-up or analysis, is merely a "warm-up act" (p. 382), assigned largely for preparation and to ensure students have read the case in advance.

However, for members of the focus groups, case analyses at our institution are far more than a "secondary genre" (Forman & Rymer, 1999b, p. 382). They vary from a single paragraph to a capstone project but could also be formal papers and examination tasks; only one professor interviewed follows the canonical Harvard procedure. Therefore, it was clear that further investigation was needed to better understand the case study genre sequence at the local level.

Secondly, it emerged that many international students were struggling to understand the purpose and expectations of both key written genres (such as the research paper and case write-up) and communicative practices (class discussions and group work). For instance, one professor felt the international students saw case discussions as just "chatting" and not instructional time, whereas from his perspective, the discussions themselves, including "relevant tangents," were the nexus of teaching and learning in her course. Since participation is graded in some classes, two teachers were concerned that international students spoke just for the sake of speaking rather than to contribute to the construction of knowledge through the case discussion. Another professor observed that some international students were unable to apply theoretical frameworks from the textbook to their written case analyses. Several faculty noted problems with research papers, although their expectations for research papers varied widely from an integrative literature review to a consultant's report. Common problems for international students included selecting the wrong sources (e.g., an over-reliance on *BusinessWeek*) and writing a "serial summary" without synthesizing multiple perspectives. All these comments might be explained by students' lack of genre awareness, both of key genres in American business courses and of the ways that assignments may vary even when they are ostensibly in the same genre (cf. Samraj, 2004).

In order to apply these insights to pedagogy, a think-aloud study (http://nigelteacher.files.wordpress.com/2012/06/think-aloud-protocol.docx) was conducted. The purpose of this additional stage of the needs analysis was to explore one key genre, the case write-up, more deeply in order to help international students improve their awareness of and success in an important and common assignment.

Think-Aloud or Verbal Protocol Analysis

Verbal protocol analysis, sometimes known as a think-aloud study, was developed by cognitive psychologists in order to study the processes which experts use to solve problems. Hayes and Flower (1980) first applied this methodology to the study of writing and in doing so founded a thread of literacy research that has attempted to deduce the cognitive process in which expert writers engage and thus to develop strategies that novice and struggling writers can consciously apply (e.g., Graham & Perin, 2007; MacArthur, 2011).

The present study was concerned with readers rather than writers and, in particular, their evaluative criteria for grading case analyses because previous research with different populations suggests that raising students' awareness about evaluative criteria can improve their subsequent writing (Moore & MacArthur, 2011). The case analysis was selected as the sole target genre for three reasons: it was ranked as important by a large number of professors in the survey, it appears to be a relatively stable genre, and it is a written genre that has a closely related oral genre (the case discussion) with which international students also often struggle, according to our needs analysis. It would be logistically more difficult to conduct a verbal protocol for a class discussion, so the written form was used for this study in the hope that it would also reveal some of the expectations for case discussions.

The think-aloud protocol was conducted with four full-time faculty members who had indicated willingness to follow up in person on the online survey: Bob, the department chair and a professor of organizational behavior; Samantha, a Harvard-educated assistant professor of management; William, an instructor of management with extensive experience in industry; and Adam, an associate professor of marketing.[4] Before the interview, each professor was asked to choose two student case write-ups: one strong, one weak. After explaining the assignment to the interviewer, I asked each participant to analyze the stronger paper with this prompt: "Please walk me through the paper, telling me what makes it a strong case-study analysis. Since I don't know the assignment or the paper, please tell me everything you notice as you look at it again in terms of evaluating it." A similar question was asked for the weaker paper. The professors were reminded to speak specifically about the papers they had selected and not about the assignment or writing in general. This was supposed to ensure that their comments would reflect students' actual writing and not idealized models.

Each interview lasted around an hour, although they did not all closely follow the planned structure. Bob does not assign case write-ups in his class but participated because he was eager to support the project. Instead, he borrowed and discussed two of Samantha's papers, which I then discussed with Samantha herself. Adam produced a pile of case reports rather than the requested two and proceeded to talk through five of them, identifying their strengths and weaknesses. However, each interview did identify evaluative criteria and differences between strong

---

4 Permission to conduct this research was granted by the relevant Institutional Review Board. All names are pseudonyms. Samantha did not say whether she had taken the survey but was recommended for this portion of the study by Bob.

and weak student papers. Participants were not asked specifically to choose papers written by native or non-native speakers of English (they were nearly all papers by domestic students in the end) because the purpose was to identify the features and evaluative criteria of the genre rather than analyze specific students' use of language. The interviews were recorded for analysis.

The theoretical lens for this final stage of the needs analysis was cultural-historical activity theory, CHAT (Engeström, 1987), a rich and complex heuristic for analyzing human behavior in and through context. CHAT proposes six factors which interact in an activity system and provides a useful means to incorporate a sociocultural analysis of genre with the more cognitive verbal protocol analysis. In a CHAT analysis, genres are the *tools*, the "conscious goal-directed actions" that "mediate between activities directed toward societal motives, and nonconscious operations conditioned by the context" (Roth, 2007, p. 45). As conscious actions, they involve cognitive processes, meaning that the choice and understanding of genre are problem-solving tasks amenable to strategy instruction (MacArthur, 2011). The *outcomes* in an activity system are the products of *subjects* (i.e., the students and faculty) who have *motives* which may be multiple and conflicting. The activity is further mediated by the *norms* of the community within which it occurs (such as the expectations for grading and the standards of citation and source use) and the *division of labor* that ascribes roles and responsibilities to the various participants.

Activity theory is a valuable lens in this research because it can identify tensions and contradictions not only within each component of the triangle, such as the dual academic and professional outcomes of the MBA, but along the vertices between them and between intersecting activity systems, such as different courses in the degree program (Roth, Lee & Hsu, 2009; Russell & Yañez, 2003). Since international students in particular—but not exclusively—may not share the cultural capital which is often assumed in U.S. academic settings, the think-aloud study aimed to make visible professors' sometimes unspoken expectations, motives, norms, and desired outcomes. These explicit and implicit evaluative criteria would then be available to inform us as we help international students prepare for their graduate programs.

Results

Surveys, Focus Groups, and Interviews

Based on the 25 collected syllabi, the faculty survey, and the focus groups, a tentative genre system for the MBA at our university is presented in Figure 14.1. The genres are organized as a system, or network of genres in the SFL tradition (Christie & Derewianka, 2008; Martin & Rose, 2008). That is, they have been subdivided into groups with similar characteristics. The genres are categorized along the interpersonal dimension (i.e., by considering the relationship between the writer and the reader), which is also consistent with an EAP approach to genre; audience is at the top of Swales and Feak's (2012) considerations for graduate writers. Tasks range from highly personal (e.g., reflections) to highly public and even authentic professional products, such as reports prepared for local businesses. However, there is an important caveat to this representation: at some level, all the assignments have as their actual audience the professor. Therefore, while a genre like the case analysis appears to have a professional purpose (recommending a solution to a company's dilemma), it does not exist beyond the classroom (Forman & Rymer, 1999b), the reader is not really the CEO of the company, and the motive for the assignment is not to give business advice, but to demonstrate certain types of knowledge and dispositions, as is seen in Figure 14.1 and Table 14.1.

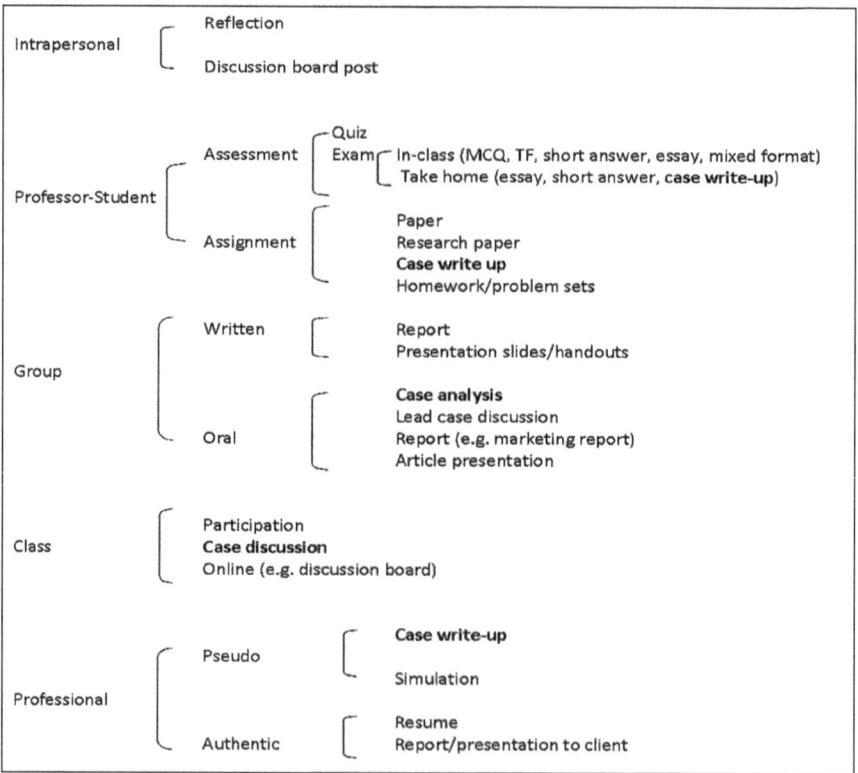

Figure 14.1. Tentative genre system for the MBA. Note: MCQ = Multiple-Choice Questions. Genres in bold are discussed in detail in this chapter.

The survey data give some clue as to the overall value of some of these genres in the MBA. Case reports (oral or written), exams, quizzes, and group work are important across the program, but many genres are very important in some classes and not at all in others (see Table 14.1). For example, research papers were reported as important or very important by nine faculty, suggesting that they are major assignments in those professors' courses, but are not assigned at all by the other respondents. From a practical perspective, this means that students should expect to encounter a wide range of tasks, genres, and practices, which concords with studies in other universities and countries (Caplan & Stevens, 2017; Cooper & Bikowski, 2007; Northcott, 2001; Zhu, 2004).

Table 14.1. Importance and difficulty of skills and genres according to MBA faculty

Task / Activity	Importance[a]		Success[b]	
	Mean	SD	Mean	SD
Understanding lectures	4.96	0.2	3.26	0.69
Critical thinking	4.79	0.41	3.17	0.82
Participating in class discussions	4.64	0.49	2.43	0.99
Participating in group discussions/activities	4.58	0.5	3.04	0.82
Speaking clearly	4.46	0.66	2.38	0.77
Reading textbooks	4.38	1.13	3.57	1.03
Reading and discussing case studies	4.33	0.92	2.86	0.89
Using sources (paraphrasing, avoiding plagiarism)	4.33	0.96	2.78	0.94
Asking questions in/after class	4.32	0.63	2.7	0.97
Writing case study reports	4.21	1.14	2.9	0.91
Taking notes	4.2	0.65	3.5	0.65
Giving group presentations	4.09	1.28	2.89	0.66
Writing papers or reports as a group	3.83	1.4	3.17	0.86
Reading journal articles	3.79	1.06	3.41	0.71
Taking essay exams	3.75	1.48	2.94	0.83
Writing short answers on tests	3.71	1.43	3.06	0.8
Writing essays individually out of class	3.63	1.35	3	0.87
Adapting to U.S./university culture	3.63	1.28	2.94	0.64
Leading discussions	3.46	0.88	2.21	0.85
Giving individual presentations	3.42	1.5	3	0.65
Taking multiple-choice tests	3.13	1.51	3.21	0.7
Writing research papers	3	1.59	3	1
Social interactions (receptions, etc.)	2.71	1.4	2.77	0.6

Notes. n = 28. [a] *How important are the following tasks and activities in your classes? 1 = not at all important; 2 = not important; 3 = neither important nor unimportant; 4 = important; 5 = very important.* [b] *How well do your international/ESL students perform on these tasks and activities? 1 = very unsuccessfully; 2 = unsuccessfully; 3 = adequately; 4 = successfully; 5 = very successfully*

The case write-up genre chosen for the think-aloud study scored an average of 4.21 out of a possible 5 in importance, although the large variance (standard deviation of 1.14) indicates that case study is either very important or not used at all in class. Nonetheless, the case write-up was the highest ranked writing assignment overall in terms of importance. International students' performance was rated on average slightly below satisfactory on this task (mean score 2.9).

Verbal Protocol Analysis

While there were variations between the professors' expectations of student case write-ups, a relatively stable genre emerged from the think-aloud interviews (Table 14.2), which is reminiscent of, but not identical to, a problem/solution text (Swales & Feak, 2012). Samantha provided the clearest explanation of the case analysis genre. She had both studied and taught under the case method at Harvard, although her use of the written assignment as an assessment tool still differs considerably from the traditional pedagogy (Forman & Rymer, 1999a). Hers was the only assignment that explicitly included a reflection stage, although this has been reported elsewhere and so is included as an optional stage (Nathan, 2013).[5] The stages of the genre are explained in Table 14.2 and were crucial to all the professors' evaluations of students' writing. The stages corresponded to different subheadings in some professors' assignments. For instance, William's typically included an industry analysis (setup), external and internal analyses (diagnosis), selection analysis, and implementation (recommendations). It is helpful, however, for students to see beyond the headings to the rhetorical function of each part of the analysis.

Table 14.2. Stages in the case write-up genre

Stage	Description & Function
Setup	Identify and introduce the key players, the dilemma, and opportunities (but not a summary of the case)
Diagnosis	Analysis (not description) of the problem or opportunity in terms of "root causes"
Recommendation	Alternative solutions plus the writer's chosen solution with justification, sometimes accompanied by a specific action plan
Reflection (required in some assignments only)	What did you learn from the case? How does it connect to the theories in the course?

---

5   Nathan (2013) found a similar genre structure in his EAP-oriented analysis of MBA case analyses at one UK university, published after these data were collected. Nathan's analysis is somewhat more complex and includes some stages that were not identified in this study, for instance "discussion of methodology." However, the three stages that he identified as obligatory concur with my think-aloud results: orientation (setup), analysis (diagnosis), and advice (recommendation).

By comparing stronger and weaker essays, the verbal protocols revealed expectations about each stage of the genre, only some of which are made explicit to students in some courses. For instance, the setup should not summarize the case (because it is already known to the reader); keywords, facts, characters, and statistics from the case should be referenced; and format and style conventions must be observed, such as a title page, an executive summary in some assignments, and font and margin sizes. Professors' expectations may be idiosyncratic, and students should expect variation in the criteria for content, organization, grammar, and presentation. Adam, for instance, claimed that his assignments were "unstructured," which might mislead students into disregarding organization; in fact, he still expected the same stages as the other faculty, but he felt that presenting a "formula" to follow in the write-up would trivialize the task. This seems to put students at a disadvantage if they fail to recognize the unspoken expectations. Similarly, students without strong genre awareness might not realize that for some professors, the focus is on the case itself and the quality of the solution, while for others, the case is incidental, and it is the business principles behind the dilemma which should be emphasized.

Two of the interviewees shared their grading schemes, which again showed the range in evaluative practices. Samantha provides her students with an analytical rubric that clearly sets out her expectations for each stage of the analysis. For example: "Does the diagnosis highlight the important facts about the people and situation of the case then help us to understand the dilemma? Do you describe why these facts are important to understanding the dilemma?" William, on the other hand, uses a grading scheme in which two points are available in each of these broad categories: presentation, writing, grammar, analysis, and comprehensiveness. Overall, though, these data suggest that a student who has mastered the criteria for one professor would have little difficulty adapting to the expectations of another. The key is to raise awareness about the genre and the ways it is received.

All the respondents discussed language or grammar as an issue for ESL writers, even when we were not specifically discussing international students' papers at the time. William, for instance, began by arguing that language proficiency alone was the difficulty for international students. However, in the course of the interview, it became clear that language was rarely the major weakness of unsuccessful papers, even in William's classes. All four professors explicitly grade grammar, sometimes subsuming it under the heading of "presentation." Two of them started out by highlighting the importance of accuracy of written language, but this concern soon gave way to other considerations which turned out to be more important in their evaluation of the students' writing. This is not to say that linguistic proficiency is unimportant. On the contrary, papers perceived to have weak grammar are heavily penalized, but correctness in itself is, unsurprisingly, insufficient.

There was broad agreement that good writers display some quality that goes beyond facility with language and comprehension of the case. This factor was given many names throughout the interviews, for instance, *insight, creativity, intuition,* and *perceptiveness*. It was described as a "way of thought" and a "mindset" and contrasted to writing that is "canned." Faculty praised papers that displayed "depth of analysis." Overall, faculty are looking for written evidence of "critical thinking," a notoriously slippery term, which often elided into the student's "capacity for thinking and intelligence" (Bob). As Adam concluded, "You can get a really good grade if you have one really good idea that's not intuitively obvious."

This reminder that the assignment is graded is important on two levels. First, the underlying, sometimes implicit, motive of the case assignment is typically to test students' mastery of concepts in the course and their ability to apply them to a real-world situation. For this reason, strong papers include references to the textbook, course concepts, and other cases. In Samantha and Tom's course (they teach the same class, which is typically taken early in the MBA program), all the sources are introduced in class, and the textbook is the typical reference. Second, students are also expected to see beyond the particular instance of the case and recognize the broader principles at stake. Adam wants above all to see connections with other cases. William gives no guidance on external sources but accepts references to the business press, industry newsletters, annual reports, and interviews. For him, the ability to select the correct sources and "pick what's important" is the mark of learning. His course is the capstone in both the undergraduate and graduate business programs, which may partially explain his high expectations.

These results provide clues to the types of thinking and writing that MBA faculty value. As can be seen, sourcing is one such expectation. Additional research into these writing assignments might be able to further unpack the assumptions hidden in words like *perceptiveness* and *insight*. For instance, historians have been found—through think-aloud studies of professional writing—to value sourcing, contextualization, and corroboration (Wineburg, 2001), and literacy scholars have turned these into discipline-specific cognitive strategies that can teach "historical understanding" even to students with learning disabilities (Ferretti, MacArthur & Okolo, 2005). Tentatively, the present think-aloud data point to such strategies in MBA case analyses: *sourcing*, *justification* (supporting recommendations with numerical data, connected cases, and management theories), and *tolerating ambiguity* (considering alternative hypotheses; accepting "imperfect answers," in Adam's words). These are far more amenable to instruction than contested and culturally-loaded terms such as "critical thinking" (Atkinson, 1997).

One of the most interesting aspects of the case write-up, which partly explains the variations among professors' expectations, is its dual nature (Freedman & Adam, 1996). Some faculty explicitly ask students to write in the imagined role of "a consultant to the top echelon of the company" (William). For Samantha, the writer is similarly "a coach, advisor, or mentor." However, the last section of her assignment is a reflection on learning, which breaks from the consultant mode and must be written in the student's voice; indeed, she expects the use of the first-person pronoun in this section (one paper avoided the first person, which she found "distant" and "not personal"). Bob was less interested in the consultant persona, praising a student who used a concept from the textbook: "professors like that . . . The writer understands that assignments are given in context." Likewise, Adam focused on the "teaching principles" of the case rather than the content of the case itself. He noted that students usually "buy in" to the method because they see the utility of case study both for understanding the concepts (an academic goal) and for professional preparation. His assignments look more like business reports (they start with an executive summary, for example), but he requires references to the textbook, which would clearly not be found in professional writing.

Discussion

This needs analysis surveyed MBA faculty at one university to identify important and challenging genres, skills, and practices for ESL students in one graduate business degree. Subsequently, verbal protocols were conducted to explore one of these genres—the case write-up—in more depth. Although the results of this study should not be generalized beyond the local context, in many ways, the case analysis is emblematic of MBA writing assignments generally, perhaps even the entire degree. Professional master's programs differ from doctoral degrees—the focus of much research into graduate-level writing (e.g., Casanave & Li, 2008; McAlpine & Amundsen, 2011; for exceptions, see Fredrick et al., this collection; Henderson & Cook, this collection; Tierney, 2016)—in one critical way: the *outcome*, to use the term from activity theory, is always dual. On the one hand, the MBA is a business degree which typically leads to management positions or is taken part-time by working professionals. The program announces that the MBA "gives students the skills and confidence to navigate today's ever-changing business world" ("Master of Business Administration," n.d.). This goal was reflected in several professors' comments. For example, Adam complained that many students in their early case write-ups have "unrealistic expectations about what happens out there" in the business world. He expects students to "think of everything from the company's perspective." William commented at the end of his interview that the task gives students experience with types of writing that will be useful in the future to "impress superiors."

However, as Freedman et al. (1994) observed in their analysis of case reports in a Canadian university, "the university context clearly shaped the social relations between reader and writer, the rhetorical and social goals of the writing, and the nature of the reading and writing practices in ways that had profound implications for the writing" (p. 202). For instance, in Freedman et al.'s study and mine, students were expected to cite sources, an academic and not a business practice. This "doubleness," to use Freedman et al.'s term, is indicative of the Janus-like tension at the heart of the MBA, which is at once a professional preparation and a *Master* of Business Administration, with all that the academic credential entails. These conflicting outcomes (earning grades versus becoming a better manager; evaluating and grading versus supervising and mentoring) feed back through the activity system.

Consequently, students might have conflicting *motives*, which affects their identity as *subjects*, the *tools* (genres) they should choose, the *division of labor* between reader and writer, and the *norms* of the discourse community: are they supposed to write as consultants and propose the best solution for the company (as John and William seem to want) or write as students to please the professor, as Bob suggested? This can be especially problematic for ESL students, who may have undertaken preparation programs geared at a broadly painted general academic competency rather than building discipline-specific cultural and linguistic capital. As a consequence, they may be struggling to adopt any kind of academic or professional persona in English, and having to switch between them could be very problematic. This has been explored in other graduate fields (e.g., Casanave & Li, 2008), but further research is needed into ESL students' writing for such MBA assignments, especially given the dramatic growth in enrollment in master's degrees, particularly among international and traditionally underrepresented demographic groups (Caplan & Cox, 2016).

If activity theory's *motive* can be equated to the communicative purpose of the genre (in an EAP analysis) or its social function (from an SFL perspective), then the case write-up presents a special type of "mutt genre" (Wardle, 2009). Wardle's mutts are first-year compositions that are crossed with disciplinary writing, for example, a sociology research paper written for a first-year writing class. These texts risk devolving into mindless mimicry, genres whose purpose is just "to write the genre." The resulting mutt genres are empty because they have been divorced of their social function: to create and transmit knowledge between members of a disciplinary community. In the context of the MBA, the case write-up is more complex because its purpose is not, as in Wardle's situation, simply to learn a form of writing: students are supposed to be learning principles of management so that they will be able to make similar decisions for themselves in the future. At the same time, professors believe that students are learning a style of writing that will carry over into the workplace and "impress" their supervisors. As such, the assignment is designed for transfer, even though the genre itself is entirely a pedagogical invention (Forman & Rymer, 1999b).

Freedman et al. (1994) cast doubt on the extent to which such transfer can occur: "Only through ... exposure to relevant professional contexts, with the situated learning entailed, will writers acquire the genres appropriate to these milieus" (p. 222). However, an activity systems perspective combined with an EAP or SFL theory of genre is more hopeful. Learning to write a case analysis means adding a new tool to the toolbox, a new genre to the student's linguistic repertoire. Arguably, it is through experiencing conflicts in the activity that learning occurs: the purpose of identifying tensions in an activity system is not to expose weaknesses but to find loci of transformation (Smith, 2010). As one of my participants noted at the end of his interview, students do improve at the task after many iterations. Furthermore, activity systems are interlinked (Russell & Yañez, 2003): the outcome of a first-semester MBA class is access to a higher-level class; all the courses have the degree and ultimately the workplace as additional outcomes. All participants (faculty or students) carry with them their previous experiences into the next activity: the tools are not created entirely anew each time. New genres are not only acquired *in situ*; their structure can be deduced by writers with sufficiently developed genre awareness (Johns, 2011). Furthermore, it must be remembered that in SFL, the goal is not just to learn the genre; it is to access the epistemologies of a discipline (Martin, 2009). Thus, several faculty commented on the importance of using the correct vocabulary, a gatekeeper into the language of this highly specialized form of schooling and the profession to which it leads.[6]

In addition to these benefits, mastery of the case write-up increases cultural capital, both the unembodied form (genre knowledge) and its embodiment (Alfred Lerner College of Business and Economics MBA diploma and future career opportunities). However, for this to happen with non-mainstream learners such as ESL students, the pedagogy needs to be made visible, and faculty need a metalanguage to describe the strengths and weaknesses of students' writing in ways that learners can use. The proliferation of generic advice to think critically, be creative, find non-intuitive solutions, and "flesh out" paragraphs may be unclear, especially to non-native speakers of (academic) English. Without such instruction, education at any level can only serve the function that Bourdieu and Passeron (1977) identified, of reproducing social structures "by proving to the privileged that they deserve their success and to the excluded that they deserve their exclusion" (p. 210). And since academic English "has never been anyone's mother tongue" (Bourdieu & Passeron, 1977, p. 115), this discussion pertains to other non-traditional groups of MBA students besides international students.

Implications

This study supports an approach to preparing and teaching international MBA students that combines genre and cognitive strategies. The case analysis was repeatedly described as a problem-solving task in essence. This has two implications: First, from a genre perspective, the case analysis to some extent follows the structure and

---

6 Other authors in this collection have reminded me that corpus studies might be helpful to establish a base of genre-specific vocabulary for pre-teaching (cf. Blazer and DeCapua, this collection). I am grateful for feedback on earlier drafts of this chapter from them, the editors, and Dr. Charles MacArthur.

functions of a problem-solution text (Swales & Feak, 2012, Chapter 3). Second, as for all such problems, cognitive strategies exist that can be described, taught, learned, and employed to reach a solution (MacArthur, 2011).

The evaluative criteria discerned in this study can be turned into self-regulated strategies. For example, as a result of this research, we added a case analysis to the curriculum of our pre-matriculation class for international MBA students, the criteria for which are presented with the assignment in the form of a rubric or checklist. Students can be taught to apply the rubric to sample papers, use it to write papers collaboratively, and finally apply the criteria as part of peer review and in both the planning and revision of their independent writing. This strategy has been found to significantly improve the persuasive writing of community college students in basic writing classes (MacArthur & Philippakos, 2013). The benefit of this form of instruction is that it raises students' awareness about genre-specific writing expectations. This is especially helpful for ESL students who may have had very limited exposure to variation among genres. If this is done consistently, students develop the metacognitive skill of analyzing an assignment effectively. At the very least, understanding that genres vary systematically and that assignments have particular requirements may make it less likely that students will produce the wrong genre, such as the common mistake of treating the exercise as a narrative not an analysis.

Another strategy that has been validated with younger ESL writers is color coding (Olson & Land, 2007). Students learn to mark up their texts with different colored highlighters or pencils: for Olson and Land's seventh-grade English-language learners' writing literary analysis, the categories were plot summary (yellow), commentary (blue), and supporting detail (green). The goal is to reduce the yellow, increase the blue, and ensure there is enough green to support the commentary. Olson and Land call this a "making-visible revision strategy" (p. 285), and they found positive and sustained effects on ESL students' writing by teaching this and other cognitive strategies. The color-coding strategy could easily be adapted to the case write-up: yellow for narrative of the case, blue for analysis of the problems and solutions, and green for supporting evidence, statistics, and citations. While this strategy by itself may not produce papers that display creativity and intuition, it should help students learn to focus on analysis and effective use of sources, thus developing the ability to write like an MBA student.

Strategies such as these can readily be incorporated into a genre-based pedagogy such as SFL's teaching/learning cycle (Martin, 2009; Rothery, 1996), which was designed to scaffold mastery of high-stakes genres for low-achieving students, especially those without a background in standard written English. The teachers guide students in an analysis of examples of the genre in order to highlight its structure and important linguistic resources. It is at this stage that grammar and vocabulary instruction can take place for ESL students who need it. Next, students work in groups or as a class to write a new text in the genre collaboratively. Here, explicit strategy instruction (such as applying evaluative criteria) can be usefully employed. Finally, once they are ready to succeed, students produce an assignment independently, using strategies for planning, drafting, and revising (such as the color-coding strategy). Although this is not a pedagogy that is likely to take root in the MBA classroom itself, students who learn to analyze, write, and revise critical genres effectively in pre-matriculation intensive English programs will be well placed to tackle future writing assignments.

Equipping international MBA students with the genres and strategies they will need has the intentional side-effect of increasing their cultural capital (see also Field, Stevens, Cherian & Asenavage, 2016, for a co-curriculum program of engagement and integration resulting in part from this needs analysis). This must be accompanied with other aspects of cultural capital, such as knowledge of American business practices, which is especially important for students coming from countries that do not espouse free-market economics. Case studies are ideal for this. By engaging in practices that approximate those of the MBA classroom (reading, discussing, and writing about case studies), preparatory programs can help students develop their linguistic resources and cultural schema in parallel. At the same time, students are learning to think in ways that U.S. business faculty value by discussing and applying the standards that their professors will use to judge their perceptiveness, insights, and critical thinking abilities (Ferretti et al., 2005).

Finally, it is important that both faculty and students recognize the conflicts and tensions in the MBA activity system. This should enable professors to give clear directions that incorporate the motives for each assignment (professional, academic, or a combination of the two), the role they expect students to play (e.g., as consultants), and the tools available to them (the genres they should write and the sources they should cite). As Starke-Meyerring (2011) has shown, graduate faculty are often unaware of the criteria by which they evaluate students' writing since disciplinary—and, by extension, professional—writing is "transparent" to them but often highly opaque to students, particularly L2 writers. Think-aloud research thus has the potential to make expectations for writing visible to everyone, which can improve pre-matriculation programs, reduce disciplinary faculty's frustration, and shine a light for students on the writing practices in which they are engaged. Ultimately, awareness of the dual and contested nature of the MBA can help students navigate their assignments, choose the most effective linguistic resources, and negotiate the multiple motives and outcomes.

References

Alfred Lerner College of Business and Economics (n.d.). Master of Business Administration. Retrieved January 21, 2020 https://business.online.udel.edu/mba.

Atkinson, D. (1997). A critical approach to critical thinking in TESOL. *TESOL Quarterly, 31*, 71–94. http://doi.org/10.2307/3587975

Blazer, S. & DeCapua, S. E. (2020). Disciplinary corpus research for situated literacy instruction. In M. Brooks-Gillies, E. G. Garcia, S. H. Kim, K. Manthey & T. G. Smith (Eds.), *Graduate writing across the disciplines: Identifying, teaching, and supporting*. The WAC Clearinghouse; University Press of Colorado. https://wac.colo state.edu/books/atd/graduate.

Bourdieu, P. (1986). The forms of capital. (R. Rice, Trans.). In J. G. Richardson (Ed.), *Handbook of theory and research for the sociology of education* (pp. 241–258). Greenwood Press.

Bourdieu, P. & Passeron, J. C. (1977). *Reproduction in education, society and culture* (R. Nice, Trans.). Sage.

Caplan, N. A. & Cox, M. (2016). The state of graduate communication support: Results of an international survey. In S. Simpson, N. A. Caplan, M. Cox & T. Phillips (Eds.), *Supporting graduate student writers: Research, curriculum, and program design* (pp. 22–51). University of Michigan Press.

Caplan, N. A. & Stevens, S. G. (2017). "Step out of the cycle": Needs, challenges, and successes of international undergraduates at a U.S. university. *English for Specific Purposes, 46*, 15–28. https://doi.org/10.1016/j.esp.2016.11.003.

Casanave, C. P. & Li, X. M. (2008). *Learning the literacy practices of graduate school: Insiders' reflections on academic enculturation*. University of Michigan Press.

Christie, F. & Derewianka, B. (2008). *School discourse: Learning to write across the years of schooling*. Continuum.

Cooper, A. & Bikowski, D. (2007). Writing at the graduate level: What tasks do professors actually require? *Journal of English for Academic Purposes, 6*(3), 206–221. https://doi.org/10.1016/j.jeap.2007.09.008.

Dubicka, I., O'Keefe, M., Falvey, D., Kent, S. & Cotton, D. (2011). *Market leader advanced coursebook* (3rd ed.). Pearson Longman.

Engeström, Y. (1987). *Learning by expanding: An activity theoretical approach to developmental research*. Orienta-Konsultit Oy. http://lchc.ucsd.edu/MCA/Paper /Engestrom/expanding/toc.htm.

Evans, N., Anderson, N. & Eggington, W. (2015). *ESL readers and writers in higher education: Understanding challenges, providing support*. Routledge.

Ferretti, R. P., MacArthur, C. D. & Okolo, C. M. (2005). Misconceptions about history: Reflections on teaching for historical understanding in an inclusive fifth-grade classroom. In T. E. Scruggs & M. A. Mastropieri (Eds.), *Advances in learning and behavioral disabilities* (Vol. 18, pp. 261–299). Emerald.

Ferris, D. & Tagg, T. (1996). Academic oral communication needs of EAP learners: What subject-matter instructors actually require. *TESOL Quarterly, 30*(1), 31–58.

Field, M., Stevens, S. G., Cherian, S. & Asenavage, K. (2016). A model of integration and engagement for international students in professional programs: The University of Delaware Graduate Cohort Program. In S. Simpson, N. A. Caplan, M. Cox & T. Phillips (Eds.), *Supporting graduate student writers: Research, curriculum, and program design* (pp. 207–221). University of Michigan Press.

Flower, L. (1994). *The construction of negotiated meaning: A social cognitive theory of writing*. Southern Illinois University Press.

Forman, J. & Rymer, J. (1999a). Defining the genre of the "case write-up." *International Journal of Business Communication, 36*(2), 103–133. https://doi.org/10.1177/002194369903600201.

Forman, J. & Rymer, J. (1999b). The genre system of the Harvard case method. *Journal of Business and Technical Communication, 13*(4), 373–400. https://doi.org/10.1177/105065199901300401.

Fredrick, T., Stravalli, K., May, S. & Brookman-Smith, J. (2020). The space between: MA students enculturate to graduate reading and writing. In M. Brooks-Gillies, E. G. Garcia, S. H. Kim, K. Manthey & T. G. Smith (Eds.), *Graduate writing across the disciplines: Identifying, teaching, and supporting*. The WAC Clearinghouse; University Press of Colorado. https://wac.colostate.edu/books/atd/graduate.

Freedman, A. & Adam, C. (1996). Learning to write professionally. *Journal of Business and Technical Communication, 10*(4), 395–427.

Freedman, A., Adam, C. & Smart, G. (1994). Wearing suits to class: Simulating genres and simulations as genre. *Written Communication, 11*(2), 193–226. https://doi.org/10.1177/0741088394011002002.

Graduate Management Admission Council. (2016). *2016 mba.com prospective students survey* [Survey report]. Reston, VA: Graduate Management Admission Council. http://www.gmac.com.

Graham, S. & Perin, D. (2007). A meta-analysis of writing instruction for adolescent students. *Journal of Educational Psychology, 99*(3), 445–476.

Hale, G. A., Taylor, C., Bridgeman, B., Carson, J., Kroll, B. & Kantor, R. (1996). *A study of writing tasks assigned in academic degree programs* (Report No. TOEFL-RR–54). Educational Testing Service.

Hayes, J. R. & Flower, L. (1980). Identifying the organization of writing processes. In L. W. Gregg & E. R. Steinberg (Eds.), *Cognitive processes in writing: An interdisciplinary approach* (pp. 1–30). Lawrence Erlbaum.

Henderson, B. R. & Cook, P. G. (2020). Voicing graduate student writing experiences: A study of cross-level courses at two master's-level, regional institutions. In M. Brooks-Gillies, E. G. Garcia, S. H. Kim, K. Manthey & T. G. Smith (Eds.), *Graduate writing across the disciplines: Identifying, teaching, and supporting*. The WAC Clearinghouse; University Press of Colorado. https://wac.colostate.edu/books/atd/graduate.

Horowitz, D. (1986). What professors really require: Academic tasks for the ESL classroom. *TESOL Quarterly, 20*, 445–462.

Johns, A. M. (2011). The future of genre in L2 writing: Fundamental, but contested, instructional decisions. *Journal of Second Language Writing, 20*(1), 56–68.

MacArthur, C. A. (2011). Strategies instruction. In K. R. Harris, S. Graham & T. Urdan (Eds.), *APA educational psychology handbook* (Vol. 3) (pp. 379–401). American Psychological Society. https://doi.org/10.1037/13275-015.

MacArthur, C. A. & Philippakos, Z. A. (2013). Self-regulated strategy instruction in developmental writing: A design research project. *Community College Review, 41*(2), 176–195. https://doi.org/10.1177/0091552113484580.

Martin, J. R. (2009). Genre and language learning: A social semiotic perspective. *Linguistics and Education, 20*(1), 10–21.

Martin, J. R. & Rose, D. (2008). *Genre relations: Mapping culture*. Equinox.

McAlpine, L. & Amundsen, C. (Eds.). (2011). *Doctoral education: Research-based strategies for doctoral students, supervisors and administrators*. Springer.

Moore, N. S. & MacArthur, C. A. (2011). The effects of being a reader and of observing readers on fifth-grade students' argumentative writing and revising. *Reading and Writing, 25*(6), 1449–1478. https://doi.org/10.1007/s11145-011-9327-6.

Nathan, P. (2013). Academic writing in the business school: The genre of the business case report. *Journal of English for Academic Purposes, 12*(1), 57–68. https://doi.org/10.1016/j.jeap.2012.11.003.

Nesi, H. & Gardner, S. (2012). *Genres across the disciplines: Student writing in higher education*. Cambridge University Press.

Northcott, J. (2001). Towards an ethnography of the MBA classroom: A consideration of the role of interactive lecturing styles within the context of one MBA programme. *English for Specific Purposes, 20*(1), 15–37.

Olson, C. B. & Land, R. (2007). A cognitive strategies approach to reading and writing instruction for English language learners in secondary school. *Research in the Teaching of English, 41*(3), 269–303.

Rose, D. & Martin, J. R. (2012). *Learning to write, reading to learn: Genre, knowledge and pedagogy in the Sydney School*. Equinox.

Roth, W. (2007). Emotion at work: A contribution to third-generation cultural-historical Activity Theory. *Mind, Culture, and Activity, 14*(1–2), 40–63.

Roth, W.-M., Lee, Y.-J. & Hsu, P.-L. (2009). A tool for changing the world: Possibilities of cultural-historical activity theory to reinvigorate science education. *Studies in Science Education, 45*(2), 131–167.

Rothery, J. (1996). Making changes: Developing an educational linguistics. In R. Hasan & G. Williams (Eds.), *Literacy in society* (pp. 86–123). Longman.

Russell, D. R. & Yañez, A. (2003). Big picture people rarely become historians: Genre systems and the contradictions of general education. In C. Bazerman & D. R. Russell (Eds.), *Writing selves/writing societies: Research from activity perspectives* (pp. 331–362). Fort Collins, Colorado: The WAC Clearinghouse; Mind, Culture, and Activity. https://wac.colostate.edu/books/perspectives/selves-societies/.

Samraj, B. (2004). Discourse features of the student-produced academic research paper: Variations across disciplinary courses. *Journal of English for Academic Purposes, 3*(1), 5–22.

Simpson, S., Caplan, N. A., Cox, M. & Phillips, T. (Eds.). (2016). *Supporting graduate student writers: Research, curriculum, and program design*. University of Michigan Press.

Smith, S. U. (2010). *Doctoral students' perceptions of learning in a blended research methods course: Three telling cases* [Doctoral dissertation, University at Albany, State University of New York]. ProQuest Dissertations & Theses Global (3432542).

Starke-Meyerring, D. (2011). The paradox of writing in doctoral education: Student experiences. In L. McAlpine & C. Amundsen (Eds.), *Doctoral education: Research-based strategies for doctoral students, supervisors and administrators* (pp. 75–95). Springer.

Swales, J. M. (1990). *Genre analysis: English in academic and research settings*. Cambridge University Press.
Swales, J. M. & Feak, C. B. (2012). *Academic writing for graduate students: Essential tasks and skills* (3rd ed.). University of Michigan Press.
Tierney, J. (2016). Supporting graduate and professional communications: Yale English Language Programs. In S. Simpson, N. A. Caplan, M. Cox & T. Phillips (Eds.), *Supporting graduate student writers: Research, curriculum, and program design* (pp. 272–285). University of Michigan Press.
Trice, A. G. (2003). Faculty perceptions of graduate international students: The benefits and challenges. *Journal of Studies in International Education, 7*, 379–403.
Wardle, E. (2009). "Mutt genres" and the goal of FYC: Can we help students write the genres of the university? *College Composition and Communication, 60*(4), 765–789.
Wineburg, S. S. (2001). *Historical thinking and other unnatural acts: Charting the future of teaching the past*. Temple University Press.
Zhu, W. (2004). Writing in business courses: An analysis of assignment types, their characteristics, and required skills. *English for Specific Purposes, 23*(2), 111–135.

Contributors

Laural L. Adams is a graduate from Bowling Green State University's doctoral program in Rhetoric and Writing, where she taught writing for social change and meaningful work. She currently teaches organizational communication at Virginia Commonwealth University's School of Business. Her most recent publications concern leadership communication, and in 2018, she published a tutorial-style digital textbook for project-based curricula called *Essentials of Business Communication for Emerging Professionals* with Kendall Hunt.

Megan Adams is Assistant Professor of Communication at the University of Findlay. Her current research interests meet at the intersections of digital storytelling, community literacies, and feminist rhetorical practices. Prior to pursuing higher education, Megan worked as a journalist in both print and broadcast mediums. She continues to hone her skills in videography and photography by taking advantage of opportunities to collaborate with others within and outside of the academy.

Pauline Baird is Professor of EFL at Kanazawa Technical College in Japan. Baird's research interests include ESL/EFL composition, English for STEM, and communities. She has drawn on cultural rhetorics research and interdisciplinary training to publish scholarly articles, essays, peer reviews, ESL/EFL writing, and Caribbean village historiographies. Her work appears in publications in journals including *The Micronesian Educator*, *Callaloo*, and *JALT*.

Estee Beck is Assistant Professor of Professional and Technical Writing/Digital Humanities in the Department of English at The University of Texas at Arlington. She earned a Ph.D. in English, with a specialization in rhetoric and writing, from Bowling Green State University in 2015. Her research and teaching engagements span computers & writing, digital rhetoric, rhetoric of digital surveillance and privacy, rhetorical examinations of computer algorithms, and makerspaces.

Kristine L. Blair is Professor of English and Dean of the McAnulty College and Graduate School of Liberal Arts at Duquesne University. Throughout her career, she has taught courses in digital composing, research methods, scholarly publication, and media and cultural studies. In addition to her publications in the areas of gender and technology, online learning, and graduate student mentoring, Blair currently serves as editor of *Computers and Composition* print and online. She is a recipient of the CCCC Technology Innovator Award, the Computers and Composition Charles Moran Award for Distinguished Contributions to the Field, and the Lisa Ede Mentoring Award from the Coalition of Feminist Scholars in the History of Rhetoric and Composition.

Sarah Blazer is Assistant Professor and Associate Director in the Writing Studio at Fashion Institute of Technology, The State University of New York. Her research and practice focus on writing center staff education towards linguistic and epistemic inclusivity and justice. Her work has appeared in *The Writing Center Journal*, *College English*, and *The TESOL Encyclopedia of English Language Teaching*.

Jami Brookman-Smith is a graduate of the MA program at Eastern Illinois University. She is currently living in Charleston, IL with her daughter and is employed as a home-based Feasibility Analyst for a top ten global clinical research organization. She enjoys visiting her alma mater to speak with students about the value of a humanities education in a science and business industry.

Marilee Brooks-Gillies is Assistant Professor of English and the Director of the University Writing Center at Indiana University–Purdue University Indianapolis. Her scholarship is situated within cultural rhetorics and writing center studies with an emphasis on place-making in communities of practice. Her work has been published in *The Peer Review*, *Across the Disciplines*, *Harlot*, and *enculturation*. Her current projects focus on power dynamics, emotional labor, assessment practices, and professional development in writing centers. When she's not writing, mentoring, teaching, or trying to sleep, she enjoys hiking with her family and crafting with yarn.

Gretchen Busl earned her Ph.D. from the University of Notre Dame, where she also served as the Associate Program Director of Grants and Fellowships in the Graduate School. She is currently Assistant Professor in the English, Speech, and Foreign Languages Department at Texas Woman's University and Director of the First-Year Composition Program. She co-organizes regular dissertation and thesis boot camps and "Just Write" sessions for faculty and staff.

Matthew Capdevielle is Director of the Writing Center and Associate Professor of the Practice in the University Writing Program at the University of Notre Dame. He teaches writing and writing pedagogy and coordinates writing support for undergraduates, graduate students, and faculty at the University.

Nigel A. Caplan is Associate Professor at the University of Delaware English Language Institute in the United States. His research interests include graduate-level writing, collaborative writing, and genre-based writing pedagogy.

Rebecca Clemens, formerly part of the Mechanical Engineering Department, is now Director of the Office of Student Learning at New Mexico Tech, where she oversees campus tutoring, first-year student advising, and Living Learning Communities.

April Conway is a lecturer in the Sweetland Center for Writing at the University of Michigan. April holds a Ph.D. in English with a specialization in rhetoric and writing from Bowling Green State University. Her research interests include literacy studies, writing research methods and methodologies, multimodal composing, feminist praxis, and place-based studies.

Paul G. Cook is Associate Professor of English and Director of Writing at Indiana University Kokomo, where he teaches courses in writing, editing, and new media theory. Paul's current research interests circulate around tracking the spread of misinformation via social networks and developing pedagogical solutions for enhancing digital information literacy in a complex, hyper-fast media environment. He lives in Indianapolis with his dog, Joni, and two annoying cats.

Steven J. Corbett is Director of the University Writing Center and Associate Professor of English at Texas A&M University, Kingsville. He is the author of *Beyond Dichotomy: Synergizing Writing Center and Classroom Pedagogies* (2015), and co-editor (with Michelle LaFrance and Teagan E. Decker) of *Peer Pressure, Peer Power: Theory and Practice in Peer Review and Response for the Writing Classroom* (2014), (with Michelle LaFrance) *Student Peer Review and Response: A Critical Sourcebook* (2018), and (with Jennifer Lin LeMesurier, Teagan E. Decker, and Betsy Cooper) *Writing in and about the Performing and Visual Arts: Creating, Performing, and Teaching* (2019). His articles on writing and rhetoric pedagogy have appeared in a variety of journals, periodicals, and collections.

Sarah E. DeCapua earned her Ph.D. in Composition & TESOL at Indiana University of Pennsylvania in 2016. She is Assistant Professor in Residence in Second Language Writing in the First-Year Writing (FYW) Program at the University of Connecticut (Storrs). Her research interests include teaching writing to international students, student response to written teacher feedback in FYW, and corpus analysis.

Kara Lee Donnelly is an English teacher at Old Saybrook High School. She has a Ph.D. in English with a focus on contemporary literature and literary institutions. She works to build bridges between the study of English at the high school and college level.

Jennifer Douglas received her Ph.D. in English from the University of Rochester. She is currently Dean of Graduate Studies and Research at American Military University | American Public University in West Virginia. Her research interests include the scholarship of teaching and learning, composition for non-native English speakers, and contemporary Irish drama.

Julie Dyke Ford is Professor of Technical Communication (housed in the Mechanical Engineering Department) at New Mexico Tech, where she coordinates and teaches in the capstone design clinic as well as teaches graduate-level engineering communication courses. She is currently working on an NSF-funded grant focused on investigating engineering students' transfer of skills from the capstone design course to the workplace. She has published and presented widely, including work in the *Journal of Engineering Education*, the *Journal of STEM Education: Innovations and Research*, *IEEE Transactions on Professional Communication*, the *Journal of Technical Writing and Communication*, *Technical Communication*, and *Technical Communication Quarterly*.

Terri Fredrick is Professor of English at Eastern Illinois University, where she coordinates the Professional Writing Program and teaches composition. Among other areas, her research focuses on strategies for effectively evaluating the writing of high school and college students across disciplines.

Elena G. Garcia is Associate Professor in the Department of Literacies & Composition and the Faculty Director of the Writing Center at Utah Valley University. Her research and institutional work focuses on writing support for graduate students and faculty, working-class and workplace writing, and fostering inclusive institutional and research relationships.

Brian R. Henderson is Associate Professor of English at Southern Illinois University Edwardsville, where he serves as the Graduate Advisor for the Teaching of Writing Program and teaches a variety of undergraduate writing courses as well as graduate courses in composition pedagogy and rhetoric. His scholarly interests tend to involve questions of place, power, and pedagogy. His current work explores how new materialist conceptions of subjectivity might offer a productive way to rethink rhetorical agency in pedagogical contexts.

Drea Rae Killingsworth, formerly part of the Earth and Environmental Sciences Department, is now pursuing a Master's in Education at Western New Mexico University and is a teacher in Silver City, New Mexico.

Soo Hyon Kim is Assistant Professor of English at the University of New Hampshire in the United States. She earned a Ph.D. in Second Language Studies at Michigan State University, and a master's degree in TESOL at the University of Illinois at Urbana-Champaign. Her main research interests include second language writing, second language acquisition (SLA), English for Academic Purposes, and mixed methods research methodology.

Michelle LaFrance is Associate Professor of English and formerly directed the Writing Across the Curriculum Program at George Mason University. Michelle has published on peer review, preparing students to write across the curriculum, e-portfolios, e-research, and Institutional Ethnography. She is an avid home brewer, community gardener, and concert-goer.

Amy Lannin, Associate Professor in English Education, directs the Campus Writing Program at the University of Missouri and is the director of the Missouri Writing Project. Lannin teaches courses on reading and writing across the curriculum and the teaching of writing. Lannin's research focuses on writing and literacy across the curriculum. Lannin currently serves on the lead editorial board for *Literacy Research: Theory, Method, and Practice*, a publication of the Literacy Research Association.

Katie Manthey is Assistant Professor of English and Director of the Writing Center at Salem College, a small women's college in Winston Salem, NC. Her research and teaching are focused around professional writing, cultural rhetorics, dress studies, and fat studies. She is a body positive activist and moderates the website Dress Profesh, which highlights the ways that dress codes are racist, cissexist, ageist, classist, etc. Her work has appeared in *Jezebel* and *Oppression and the*

Body: Roots, Resistance, and Resolutions, and is currently working on a manuscript titled *Writing the Body: Fat Fashion, Body Positivity, and Ethical Reading*, which is under contract with the University of Nebraska Press.

Scott May received his Master's in Composition and Rhetoric from Eastern Illinois University. His pedagogical interests, related to his contribution here, remain with the evaluation of student writing and its effects on student motivation.

Lee Nickoson is Professor and Chair of the Department of English at Bowling Green State University and a member of the Rhetoric & Writing doctoral program. She regularly teaches courses on research methods, writing assessment, and composition pedagogy. Her research interests include feminist research methods and pedagogy and community-based studies of literate practices.

Laurie A. Pinkert is Assistant Professor of Writing and Rhetoric at the University of Central Florida where she has coordinated undergraduate major, minor, and certificate programs and co-developed a cross-disciplinary writing initiative to support graduate school preparation for students who are typically underrepresented in higher education. Her research examines the intersections between writing practices, pedagogies, and programs with an emphasis on developing infrastructures that are responsive to emerging needs in the educational landscape.

Jesse Priest is Assistant Professor of English at New Mexico Tech, where he teaches FYW courses and undergraduate and graduate courses in technical communication. He now directs the Writing and Oral Presentation Center. He is currently working on a project involving Tech Writing pedagogy in STEM, and is collecting data from the Writing Center as he works with tutors to expand the WC's role in the campus community.

Martha Schaffer is Associate Director of Composition at Case Western Reserve University. Her teaching and research focus on development of writers' potential, self-assessment practices, and cultural theory. She oversees first-year writing placement and the Foundational Writing Program, and teaches courses in advanced grammar and linguistics.

Elliot Shapiro is Senior Lecturer and Knight Foundation Director of Writing in the Majors in Cornell University's John S. Knight Institute for Writing in the Disciplines. He also directs the Faculty Seminar in Writing Instruction. Publications include articles on American literature and film as well as the teaching of writing.

Steve Simpson is Associate Professor of Communication at New Mexico Tech and teaches courses in scientific and technical communication for graduate and undergraduate students. Formerly the Writing and Oral Presentation Center Director at the time this chapter was written, he is now the chair of the Department of Communication, Liberal Arts, and Social Sciences, as well as the co-chair of the Consortium on Graduate Communication.

Trixie G. Smith is Director of The Writing Center and the Red Cedar Writing Project at Michigan State University, where she is Associate Professor in the

Department of Writing, Rhetoric, and American Cultures and Assistant Director of the graduate program. Her teaching and research are infused with issues of gender and activism even as they revolve around writing center theory and practice, writing across the curriculum, and teacher training. Likewise, these areas often intersect with her interests in pop culture, community engagement, and the idea that we're just humans learning with/from other humans (you know, with bodies, feelings, lives outside the academy).

Kaylin Stravalli is a former graduate student in literature and creative writing. She currently lives and works in St. Louis, MO and continues to build her career as a freelance writer and author.

Martha A. (Marty) Townsend directed the University of Missouri's Campus Writing Program from 1991 to 2006. She is Professor Emerita in the Department of English, having taught graduate and undergraduate courses in rhetoric and composition. She earned her Ph.D. from Arizona State University in 1991, and is a Fellow of the Bryn Mawr HERS Summer Institute for Women in Higher Education Administration. Townsend's specialization is Writing Across the Curriculum. Her research and consulting have taken her to over 90 colleges and universities in the U.S. and numerous international destinations.

Shari Wolke completed her Master of Arts in Writing and Rhetoric-Critical Studies in Literacy and Pedagogy in 2012 at Michigan State University (MSU). During her tenure at MSU, she worked as a Writing Instructor, Writing Center Consultant, and Graduate Writing Group Facilitator, and focused her research on multilingual writers and the linguicism these writers often experience (see Zuidema, 2005). After some time spent working as an adjunct instructor, she is now teaching English at the secondary level, at Novi High School in Novi, Michigan.

www.ingramcontent.com/pod-product-compliance
Ingram Content Group UK Ltd.
Pitfield, Milton Keynes, MK11 3LW, UK
UKHW021945200326
4879IPUK00005B/102